MEDIEVAL LITERATURE
A BASIC ANTHOLOGY

Medieval Literature
A Basic Anthology

DOVER THRIFT EDITIONS

DOVER PUBLICATIONS, INC.
MINEOLA, NEW YORK

DOVER THRIFT EDITIONS

GENERAL EDITOR: SUSAN L. RATTINER
EDITOR OF THIS VOLUME: GREGORY KOUTROUBY

Copyright

Bibliographical Note

Medieval Literature: A Basic Anthology is a new work, first published by Dover Publications, Inc., in 2017. John Grafton has selected the works in the anthology and has provided the introductory notes. Source material is from standard texts.

International Standard Book Number

ISBN-13: 978-0-486-81342-4
ISBN-10: 0-486-81342-8

Manufactured in the United States by LSC Communications
81342803   2020
www.doverpublications.com

Contents

Note

It isn't possible to encapsulate or summarize the literature of the Middle Ages in a volume of this length. The idea behind this volume was something different: It was to select a few basic works, works which have been widely read over the centuries since they were written, and which are still widely read today, and to use them to provide a very brief, and very basic but still reasonable introduction to this vast literature. In a few cases we were able to provide the complete text of a given work, but in most cases, for reasons of length, we had to rely on excerpts to give an idea of the nature of the work it represents. It is certainly hoped that many readers will find at least a few of the works represented here by excerpts interesting enough to seek out their complete texts.

Even in a brief anthology such as this, it has been possible to represent in some degree the amazing variety which characterizes the literature of the Middle Ages. In this volume we have religious works written in the 4th (St. Augustine), 6th (Boethius), and 15th (Thomas à Kempis) centuries, a historical work from the 8th century (Bede), a heroic poem from perhaps the 9th or 10th century (*Beowulf*), a philosophical autobiography from the 12th century (Abélard), and a wealth of stories told in various ways from the 12th and later centuries (Marie de France, the anonymous authors of *The Mabinogion*, Boccaccio, Chaucer). We end with a play from the 15th century (*Everyman*).

The human desire to tell a story—sometimes one's own story, sometimes some other kind of story—is much older than the Middle Ages. But these centuries do certainly provide many curious and entertaining manifestations of this desire. Some of them are captured in this anthology.

THE CONFESSIONS OF ST. AUGUSTINE

St. Augustine

The Confessions of St. Augustine, *one of the most influential books in the Christian tradition and a masterpiece of Western literature, recounts crucial episodes in the author's life, including his relationship with his devoutly Christian mother; his origins in rural Algeria in the mid-fourth century* A.D.; *his experiences at the imperial court in Milan; his struggle with sexual desires; his eventual renunciation of secular ambitions and marriage; and the final recovery of his Catholic faith. Though an intensely personal record, Augustine's* Confessions *has always been essential reading for anyone interested in the history of Christianity and Western culture. Included here are Books Three, Five, and Eight, which respectively depict Augustine's student days in Carthage, his life in Milan, and his final conversion to Christ.*

BOOK THREE

The story of his student days in Carthage, his discovery of Cicero's Hortensius, *the enkindling of his philosophical interest, his infatuation with the Manichean heresy, and his mother's dream which foretold his eventual return to the true faith and to God.*

CHAPTER I

1. I came to Carthage, where a caldron of unholy loves was seething and bubbling all around me. I was not in love as yet, but I was in love with love; and, from a hidden hunger, I hated myself for not feeling more intensely a sense of hunger. I was looking for something to love, for I was in love with loving, and I hated security and a smooth way, free from snares. Within me I had a dearth of that inner

1

food which is thyself, my God—although that dearth caused me no hunger. And I remained without any appetite for incorruptible food—not because I was already filled with it, but because the emptier I became the more I loathed it. Because of this my soul was unhealthy; and, full of sores, it exuded itself forth, itching to be scratched by scraping on the things of the senses.[1] Yet, had these things no soul, they would certainly not inspire our love.

To love and to be loved was sweet to me, and all the more when I gained the enjoyment of the body of the person I loved. Thus I polluted the spring of friendship with the filth of concupiscence and I dimmed its luster with the slime of lust. Yet, foul and unclean as I was, I still craved, in excessive vanity, to be thought elegant and urbane. And I did fall precipitately into the love I was longing for. My God, my mercy, with how much bitterness didst thou, out of thy infinite goodness, flavor that sweetness for me! For I was not only beloved but also I secretly reached the climax of enjoyment; and yet I was joyfully bound with troublesome ties, so that I could be scourged with the burning iron rods of jealousy, suspicion, fear, anger, and strife.

CHAPTER II

2. Stage plays also captivated me, with their sights full of the images of my own miseries: fuel for my own fire. Now, why does a man like to be made sad by viewing doleful and tragic scenes, which he himself could not by any means endure? Yet, as a spectator, he wishes to experience from them a sense of grief, and in this very sense of grief his pleasure consists. What is this but wretched madness? For a man is more affected by these actions the more he is spuriously involved in these affections. Now, if he should suffer them in his own person, it is the custom to call this "misery." But when he suffers with another, then it is called "compassion." But what kind of compassion is it that arises from viewing fictitious and unreal sufferings? The spectator is not expected to aid the sufferer but merely to grieve for him. And the more he grieves the more he applauds the actor of these fictions. If the misfortunes of the characters—whether historical or entirely imaginary—are represented so as not to touch

---

[1] Cf. Job 2:7, 8.

the feelings of the spectator, he goes away disgusted and complaining. But if his feelings are deeply touched, he sits it out attentively, and sheds tears of joy.

3. Tears and sorrow, then, are loved. Surely every man desires to be joyful. And, though no one is willingly miserable, one may, nevertheless, be pleased to be merciful so that we love their sorrows because without them we should have nothing to pity. This also springs from that same vein of friendship. But whither does it go? Whither does it flow? Why does it run into that torrent of pitch which seethes forth those huge tides of loathsome lusts in which it is changed and altered past recognition, being diverted and corrupted from its celestial purity by its own will? Shall, then, compassion be repudiated? By no means! Let us, however, love the sorrows of others. But let us beware of uncleanness, O my soul, under the protection of my God, the God of our fathers, who is to be praised and exalted—let us beware of uncleanness. I have not yet ceased to have compassion. But in those days in the theaters I sympathized with lovers when they sinfully enjoyed one another, although this was done fictitiously in the play. And when they lost one another, I grieved with them, as if pitying them, and yet had delight in both grief and pity. Nowadays I feel much more pity for one who delights in his wickedness than for one who counts himself unfortunate because he fails to obtain some harmful pleasure or suffers the loss of some miserable felicity. This, surely, is the truer compassion, but the sorrow I feel in it has no delight for me. For although he that grieves with the unhappy should be commended for his work of love, yet he who has the power of real compassion would still prefer that there be nothing for him to grieve about. For if good will were to be ill will—which it cannot be—only then could he who is truly and sincerely compassionate wish that there were some unhappy people so that he might commiserate them. Some grief may then be justified, but none of it loved. Thus it is that thou dost act, O Lord God, for thou lovest souls far more purely than we do and art more incorruptibly compassionate, although thou art never wounded by any sorrow. Now "who is sufficient for these things?"[2]

4. But at that time, in my wretchedness, I loved to grieve; and I sought for things to grieve about. In another man's misery, even though it was feigned and impersonated on the stage, that performance

---

[2] II Cor. 2:16.

of the actor pleased me best and attracted me most powerfully which moved me to tears. What marvel then was it that an unhappy sheep, straying from thy flock and impatient of thy care, I became infected with a foul disease? This is the reason for my love of griefs: that they would not probe into me too deeply (for I did not love to suffer in myself such things as I loved to look at), and they were the sort of grief which came from hearing those fictions, which affected only the surface of my emotion. Still, just as if they had been poisoned fingernails, their scratching was followed by inflammation, swelling, putrefaction, and corruption. Such was my life! But was it life, O my God?

CHAPTER III

5. And still thy faithful mercy hovered over me from afar. In what unseemly iniquities did I wear myself out, following a sacrilegious curiosity, which, having deserted thee, then began to drag me down into the treacherous abyss, into the beguiling obedience of devils, to whom I made offerings of my wicked deeds. And still in all this thou didst not fail to scourge me. I dared, even while thy solemn rites were being celebrated inside the walls of thy church, to desire and to plan a project which merited death as its fruit. For this thou didst chastise me with grievous punishments, but nothing in comparison with my fault, O thou my greatest mercy, my God, my refuge from those terrible dangers in which I wandered with stiff neck, receding farther from thee, loving my own ways and not thine—loving a vagrant liberty!

6. Those studies I was then pursuing, generally accounted as respectable, were aimed at distinction in the courts of law—to excel in which, the more crafty I was, the more I should be praised. Such is the blindness of men that they even glory in their blindness. And by this time I had become a master in the School of Rhetoric, and I rejoiced proudly in this honor and became inflated with arrogance. Still I was relatively sedate, O Lord, as thou knowest, and had no share in the wreckings of "The Wreckers"[3] (for this stupid and diabolical name was regarded as the very badge of gallantry) among whom I lived with

---

[3] *Eversores*, "overturners," from *evertere*, to overthrow or ruin. This was the nickname of a gang of young hoodlums in Carthage, made up largely, it seems, of students in the schools.

a sort of ashamed embarrassment that I was not even as they were. But I lived with them, and at times I was delighted with their friendship, even when I abhorred their acts (that is, their "wrecking") in which they insolently attacked the modesty of strangers, tormenting them by uncalled-for jeers, gratifying their mischievous mirth. Nothing could more nearly resemble the actions of devils than these fellows. By what name, therefore, could they be more aptly called than "wreckers"?—being themselves wrecked first, and altogether turned upside down. They were secretly mocked at and seduced by the deceiving spirits, in the very acts by which they amused themselves in jeering and horseplay at the expense of others.

CHAPTER IV

7. Among such as these, in that unstable period of my life, I studied the books of eloquence, for it was in eloquence that I was eager to be eminent, though from a reprehensible and vainglorious motive, and a delight in human vanity. In the ordinary course of study I came upon a certain book of Cicero's, whose language almost all admire, though not his heart. This particular book of his contains an exhortation to philosophy and was called *Hortensius*.[4] Now it was this book which quite definitely changed my whole attitude and turned my prayers toward thee, O Lord, and gave me new hope and new desires. Suddenly every vain hope became worthless to me, and with an incredible warmth of heart I yearned for an immortality of wisdom and began now to arise that I might return to thee. It was not to sharpen my tongue further that I made use of that book. I was now nineteen; my father had been dead two years,[5] and my mother was providing the money for my study of rhetoric. What won me in it [i.e., the *Hortensius*] was not its style but its substance.

8. How ardent was I then, my God, how ardent to fly from earthly things to thee! Nor did I know how thou wast even then dealing with me. For with thee is wisdom. In Greek the love of wisdom is

---

[4] A minor essay now lost. We know of its existence from other writers, but the only fragments that remain are in Augustine's works: *Contra Academicos,* III, 14:31; *De beata vita,* X; *Soliloquia,* I, 17; *De civitate Dei,* III, 15; *Contra Julianum,* IV, 15:78; *De Trinitate,* XIII, 4:7, 5:8; XIV, 9:12, 19:26; *Epist.* CXXX, 10.

[5] Note this merely parenthetical reference to his father's death and contrast it with the account of his mother's death in Bk. IX, Chs. X-XII.

called "philosophy," and it was with this love that that book inflamed me. There are some who seduce through philosophy, under a great, alluring, and honorable name, using it to color and adorn their own errors. And almost all who did this, in Cicero's own time and earlier, are censored and pointed out in his book. In it there is also manifest that most salutary admonition of thy Spirit, spoken by thy good and pious servant: "Beware lest any man spoil you through philosophy and vain deceit, after the tradition of men, after the rudiments of the world, and not after Christ: for in him all the fullness of the Godhead dwells bodily."[6] Since at that time, as thou knowest, O Light of my heart, the words of the apostle were unknown to me, I was delighted with Cicero's exhortation, at least enough so that I was stimulated by it, and enkindled and inflamed to love, to seek, to obtain, to hold, and to embrace, not this or that sect, but wisdom itself, wherever it might be. Only this checked my ardor: that the name of Christ was not in it. For this name, by thy mercy, O Lord, this name of my Saviour thy Son, my tender heart had piously drunk in, deeply treasured even with my mother's milk. And whatsoever was lacking that name, no matter how erudite, polished, and truthful, did not quite take complete hold of me.

CHAPTER V

9. I resolved, therefore, to direct my mind to the Holy Scriptures, that I might see what they were. And behold, I saw something not comprehended by the proud, not disclosed to children, something lowly in the hearing, but sublime in the doing, and veiled in mysteries. Yet I was not of the number of those who could enter into it or bend my neck to follow its steps. For then it was quite different from what I now feel. When I then turned toward the Scriptures, they appeared to me to be quite unworthy to be compared with the dignity of Tully.[7] For my inflated pride was repelled by their style, nor could the sharpness of my wit penetrate their inner meaning. Truly they were of a sort to aid the growth of little ones, but I scorned to be a little one and, swollen with pride, I looked upon myself as fully grown.

---

[6] Col. 2:8, 9.
[7] I.e., Marcus Tullius Cicero.

CHAPTER VI

10. Thus I fell among men, delirious in their pride, carnal and voluble, whose mouths were the snares of the devil—a trap made out of a mixture of the syllables of thy name and the names of our Lord Jesus Christ and of the Paraclete.[8] These names were never out of their mouths, but only as sound and the clatter of tongues, for their heart was empty of truth. Still they cried, "Truth, Truth," and were forever speaking the word to me. But the thing itself was not in them. Indeed, they spoke falsely not only of thee—who truly art the Truth—but also about the basic elements of this world, thy creation. And, indeed, I should have passed by the philosophers themselves even when they were speaking truth concerning thy creatures, for the sake of thy love, O Highest Good, and my Father, O Beauty of all things beautiful.

O Truth, Truth, how inwardly even then did the marrow of my soul sigh for thee when, frequently and in manifold ways, in numerous and vast books, [the Manicheans] sounded out thy name though it was only a sound! And in these dishes—while I starved for thee—they served up to me, in thy stead, the sun and moon thy beauteous works—but still only thy works and not thyself; indeed, not even thy first work. For thy spiritual works came before these material creations, celestial and shining though they are. But I was hungering and thirsting, not even after those first works of thine, but after thyself the Truth, "with whom is no variableness, neither shadow of turning."[9] Yet they still served me glowing fantasies in those dishes. And, truly, it would have been better to have loved this very sun—which at least is true to our sight—than those illusions of theirs which deceive the mind through the eye. And yet because I supposed the

---

[8] These were the Manicheans, a pseudo-Christian sect founded by a Persian religious teacher, Mani (c. A.D. 216–277). They professed a highly eclectic religious system chiefly distinguished by its radical dualism and its elaborate cosmogony in which good was co-ordinated with light and evil with darkness. In the sect, there was an esoteric minority called *perfecti,* who were supposed to obey the strict rules of an ascetic ethic; the rest were *auditores,* who followed, at a distance, the doctrines of the *perfecti* but not their rules. The chief attraction of Manicheism lay in the fact that it appeared to offer a straightforward, apparently profound and rational solution to the problem of evil, both in nature and in human experience. Cf. H. C. Puech, *Le Manichéisme, son fondateur—sa doctrine* (Paris, 1949); F. C. Burkitt, *The Religion of the Manichees* (Cambridge, 1925); and Steven Runciman, *The Medieval Manichee* (Cambridge, 1947).

[9] James 1:17.

illusions to be from thee I fed on them—not with avidity, for thou
didst not taste in my mouth as thou art, and thou wast not these
empty fictions. Neither was I nourished by them, but was instead
exhausted. Food in dreams appears like our food awake; yet the
sleepers are not nourished by it, for they are asleep. But the fantasies
of the Manicheans were not in any way like thee as thou hast spoken
to me now. They were simply fantastic and false. In comparison to
them the actual bodies which we see with our fleshly sight, both
celestial and terrestrial, are far more certain. These true bodies even
the beasts and birds perceive as well as we do and they are more
certain than the images we form about them. And again, we do with
more certainty form our conceptions about them than, from them,
we go on by means of them to imagine of other greater and infinite
bodies which have no existence. With such empty husks was I then
fed, and yet was not fed.

But thou, my Love, for whom I longed in order that I might be
strong, neither art those bodies that we see in heaven nor art thou
those which we do not see there, for thou hast created them all and
yet thou reckonest them not among thy greatest works. How far,
then, art thou from those fantasies of mine, fantasies of bodies which
have no real being at all! The images of those bodies which actually
exist are far more certain than these fantasies. The bodies themselves
are more certain than the images, yet even these thou art not. Thou
art not even the soul, which is the life of bodies; and, clearly, the life
of the body is better than the body itself. But thou art the life of
souls, life of lives, having life in thyself, and never changing, O Life
of my soul.[10]

11. Where, then, wast thou and how far from me? Far, indeed,
was I wandering away from thee, being barred even from the husks
of those swine whom I fed with husks.[11] For how much better were
the fables of the grammarians and poets than these snares [of the
Manicheans]! For verses and poems and "the flying Medea"[12] are
still more profitable truly than these men's "five elements," with
their various colors, answering to "the five caves of darkness"[13] (none
of which exist and yet in which they slay the one who believes in
them). For verses and poems I can turn into food for the mind, for

---

[10] Cf. Plotinus, *Enneads,* V, 3:14.
[11] Cf. Luke 15:16.
[12] Cf. Ovid, *Metamorphoses,* VII, 219–224.
[13] For the details of the Manichean cosmogony, see Burkitt, *op. cit.,* ch. 4.

though I sang about "the flying Medea" I never believed it, but those other things [the fantasies of the Manicheans] I did believe. Woe, woe, by what steps I was dragged down to "the depths of hell"[14]—toiling and fuming because of my lack of the truth, even when I was seeking after thee, my God! To thee I now confess it, for thou didst have mercy on me when I had not yet confessed it. I sought after thee, but not according to the understanding of the mind, by means of which thou hast willed that I should excel the beasts, but only after the guidance of my physical senses. Thou wast more inward to me than the most inward part of me; and higher than my highest reach. I came upon that brazen woman, devoid of prudence, who, in Solomon's obscure parable, sits at the door of the house on a seat and says, "Stolen waters are sweet, and bread eaten in secret is pleasant."[15] This woman seduced me, because she found my soul outside its own door, dwelling on the sensations of my flesh and ruminating on such food as I had swallowed through these physical senses.

CHAPTER VII

12. For I was ignorant of that other reality, true Being. And so it was that I was subtly persuaded to agree with these foolish deceivers when they put their questions to me: "Whence comes evil?" and, "Is God limited by a bodily shape, and has he hairs and nails?" and, "Are those patriarchs to be esteemed righteous who had many wives at one time, and who killed men and who sacrificed living creatures?" In my ignorance I was much disturbed over these things and, though I was retreating from the truth, I appeared to myself to be going toward it, because I did not yet know that evil was nothing but a privation of good (that, indeed, it has no being)[16]; and how should I have seen this when the sight of my eyes went no farther than physical objects, and the sight of my mind reached no farther than to fantasms? And I did not know that God is a spirit who has no parts extended in length and breadth, whose being has no mass—for every mass is less in a part than in a whole—and if it be an infinite mass it must be less in such parts as are limited by a certain space than in its

---

[14] Prov. 9:18.
[15] Cf. Prov. 9:17; see also Prov. 9:13 (Vulgate text).
[16] Cf. *Enchiridion*, IV.

infinity. It cannot therefore be wholly everywhere as Spirit is, as God is. And I was entirely ignorant as to what is that principle within us by which we are like God, and which is rightly said in Scripture to be made "after God's image."

13. Nor did I know that true inner righteousness—which does not judge according to custom but by the measure of the most perfect law of God Almighty—by which the mores of various places and times were adapted to those places and times (though the law itself is the same always and everywhere, not one thing in one place and another in another). By this inner righteousness Abraham and Isaac, and Jacob and Moses and David, and all those commended by the mouth of God were righteous and were judged unrighteous only by foolish men who were judging by human judgment and gauging their judgment of the mores of the whole human race by the narrow norms of their own mores. It is as if a man in an armory, not knowing what piece goes on what part of the body, should put a greave on his head and a helmet on his shin and then complain because they did not fit. Or as if, on some holiday when afternoon business was forbidden, one were to grumble at not being allowed to go on selling as it had been lawful for him to do in the forenoon. Or, again, as if, in a house, he sees a servant handle something that the butler is not permitted to touch, or when something is done behind a stable that would be prohibited in a dining room, and then a person should be indignant that in one house and one family the same things are not allowed to every member of the household. Such is the case with those who cannot endure to hear that something was lawful for righteous men in former times that is not so now; or that God, for certain temporal reasons, commanded then one thing to them and another now to these: yet both would be serving the same righteous will. These people should see that in one man, one day, and one house, different things are fit for different members; and a thing that was formerly lawful may become, after a time, unlawful—and something allowed or commanded in one place that is justly prohibited and punished in another. Is justice, then, variable and changeable? No, but the times over which she presides are not all alike because they are different times. But men, whose days upon the earth are few, cannot by their own perception harmonize the causes of former ages and other nations, of which they had no experience, and compare them with these of which they do have experience; although in one and the same body, or day, or family, they can readily see that

what is suitable for each member, season, part, and person may differ. To the one they take exception; to the other they submit.

14. These things I did not know then, nor had I observed their import. They met my eyes on every side, and I did not see. I composed poems, in which I was not free to place each foot just anywhere, but in one meter one way, and in another meter another way, nor even in any one verse was the same foot allowed in all places. Yet the art by which I composed did not have different principles for each of these different cases, but the same law throughout. Still I did not see how, by that righteousness to which good and holy men submitted, all those things that God had commanded were gathered, in a far more excellent and sublime way, into one moral order; and it did not vary in any essential respect, though it did not in varying times prescribe all things at once but, rather, distributed and prescribed what was proper for each. And, being blind, I blamed those pious fathers, not only for making use of present things as God had commanded and inspired them to do, but also for foreshadowing things to come, as God revealed it to them.

CHAPTER VIII

15. Can it ever, at any time or place, be unrighteous for a man to love God with all his heart, with all his soul, and with all his mind; and his neighbor as himself?[17] Similarly, offenses against nature are everywhere and at all times to be held in detestation and should be punished. Such offenses, for example, were those of the Sodomites; and, even if all nations should commit them, they would all be judged guilty of the same crime by the divine law, which has not made men so that they should ever abuse one another in that way. For the fellowship that should be between God and us is violated whenever that nature of which he is the author is polluted by perverted lust. But these offenses against customary morality are to be avoided according to the variety of such customs. Thus, what is agreed upon by convention, and confirmed by custom or the law of any city or nation, may not be violated at the lawless pleasure of any, whether citizen or stranger. For any part that is not consistent with its whole

---

[17] Cf. Matt. 22:37–39.

is unseemly. Nevertheless, when God commands anything contrary to the customs or compacts of any nation, even though it were never done by them before, it is to be done; and if it has been interrupted, it is to be restored; and if it has never been established, it is to be established. For it is lawful for a king, in the state over which he reigns, to command that which neither he himself nor anyone before him had commanded. And if it cannot be held to be inimical to the public interest to obey him—and, in truth, it would be inimical if he were not obeyed, since obedience to princes is a general compact of human society—how much more, then, ought we unhesitatingly to obey God, the Governor of all his creatures! For, just as among the authorities in human society, the greater authority is obeyed before the lesser, so also must God be above all.

16. This applies as well to deeds of violence where there is a real desire to harm another, either by humiliating treatment or by injury. Either of these may be done for reasons of revenge, as one enemy against another, or in order to obtain some advantage over another, as in the case of the highwayman and the traveler; else they may be done in order to avoid some other evil, as in the case of one who fears another; or through envy as, for example, an unfortunate man harming a happy one just because he is happy; or they may be done by a prosperous man against someone whom he fears will become equal to himself or whose equality he resents. They may even be done for the mere pleasure in another man's pain, as the spectators of gladiatorial shows or the people who deride and mock at others. These are the major forms of iniquity that spring out of the lust of the flesh, and of the eye, and of power.[18] Sometimes there is just one; sometimes two together; sometimes all of them at once. Thus we live, offending against the Three and the Seven, that harp of ten strings, thy Decalogue, O God most high and most sweet.[19] But now how can offenses of vileness harm thee who canst not be defiled; or how can deeds of violence harm thee who canst not be harmed? Still thou dost punish these sins which men commit against themselves because, even when they sin against thee, they are also committing impiety against their own souls. Iniquity gives itself the lie, either by corrupting or by perverting that nature which thou hast made and

---

[18] Cf. I John 2:16. And see also Bk. X, Chs. XXX–XLI, for an elaborate analysis of them.

[19] Cf. Ex. 20:3–8; Ps. 144:9. In Augustine's *Sermon* IX, he points out that in the Decalogue *three* commandments pertain to God and *seven* to men.

ordained. And they do this by an immoderate use of lawful things; or by lustful desire for things forbidden, as "against nature"; or when they are guilty of sin by raging with heart and voice against thee, rebelling against thee, "kicking against the pricks"[20]; or when they cast aside respect for human society and take audacious delight in conspiracies and feuds according to their private likes and dislikes.

This is what happens whenever thou art forsaken, O Fountain of Life, who art the one and true Creator and Ruler of the universe. This is what happens when through self-willed pride a part is loved under the false assumption that it is the whole. Therefore, we must return to thee in humble piety and let thee purge us from our evil ways, and be merciful to those who confess their sins to thee, and hear the groanings of the prisoners and loosen us from those fetters which we have forged for ourselves. This thou wilt do, provided we do not raise up against thee the arrogance of a false freedom—for thus we lose all through craving more, by loving our own good more than thee, the common good of all.

CHAPTER IX

17. But among all these vices and crimes and manifold iniquities, there are also the sins that are committed by men who are, on the whole, making progress toward the good. When these are judged rightly and after the rule of perfection, the sins are censored but the men are to be commended because they show the hope of bearing fruit, like the green shoot of the growing corn. And there are some deeds that resemble vice and crime and yet are not sin because they offend neither thee, our Lord God, nor social custom. For example, when suitable reserves for hard times are provided, we cannot judge that this is done merely from a hoarding impulse. Or, again, when acts are punished by constituted authority for the sake of correction, we cannot judge that they are done merely out of a desire to inflict pain. Thus, many a deed which is disapproved in man's sight may be approved by thy testimony. And many a man who is praised by men is condemned—as thou art witness—because frequently the deed itself, the mind of the doer, and the hidden exigency of the situation all vary among themselves. But when, contrary to human

---

[20] Acts 9:5.

expectation, thou commandest something unusual or unthought of—indeed, something thou mayest formerly have forbidden, about which thou mayest conceal the reason for thy command at that particular time; and even though it may be contrary to the ordinance of some society of men[21]—who doubts but that it should be done because only that society of men is righteous which obeys thee? But blessed are they who know what thou dost command. For all things done by those who obey thee either exhibit something necessary at that particular time or they foreshow things to come.

CHAPTER X

18. But I was ignorant of all this, and so I mocked those holy servants and prophets of thine. Yet what did I gain by mocking them save to be mocked in turn by thee? Insensibly and little by little, I was led on to such follies as to believe that a fig tree wept when it was plucked and that the sap of the mother tree was tears. Notwithstanding this, if a fig was plucked, by not his own but another man's wickedness, some Manichean saint might eat it, digest it in his stomach, and breathe it out again in the form of angels. Indeed, in his prayers he would assuredly groan and sigh forth particles of God, although these particles of the most high and true God would have remained bound in that fig unless they had been set free by the teeth and belly of some "elect saint"[22]! And, wretch that I was, I believed that more mercy was to be shown to the fruits of the earth than unto men, for whom these fruits were created. For, if a hungry man—who was not a Manichean—should beg for any food, the morsel that we gave to him would seem condemned, as it were, to capital punishment.

CHAPTER XI

19. And now thou didst "stretch forth thy hand from above"[23] and didst draw up my soul out of that profound darkness [of Manicheism] because my mother, thy faithful one, wept to thee on

---

[21] An example of this which Augustine doubtless had in mind is God's command to Abraham to offer up his son Isaac as a human sacrifice. Cf. Gen. 22:1, 2.

[22] *Electi sancti.* Another Manichean term for the *perfecti,* the elite and "perfect" among them.

[23] Ps. 144:7.

my behalf more than mothers are accustomed to weep for the bodily deaths of their children. For by the light of the faith and spirit which she received from thee, she saw that I was dead. And thou didst hear her, O Lord, thou didst hear her and despised not her tears when, pouring down, they watered the earth under her eyes in every place where she prayed. Thou didst truly hear her.

For what other source was there for that dream by which thou didst console her, so that she permitted me to live with her, to have my meals in the same house at the table which she had begun to avoid, even while she hated and detested the blasphemies of my error? In her dream she saw herself standing on a sort of wooden rule, and saw a bright youth approaching her, joyous and smiling at her, while she was grieving and bowed down with sorrow. But when he inquired of her the cause of her sorrow and daily weeping (not to learn from her, but to teach her, as is customary in visions), and when she answered that it was my soul's doom she was lamenting, he bade her rest content and told her to look and see that where she was there I was also. And when she looked she saw me standing near her on the same rule.

Whence came this vision unless it was that thy ears were inclined toward her heart? O thou Omnipotent Good, thou carest for every one of us as if thou didst care for him only, and so for all as if they were but one!

20. And what was the reason for this also, that, when she told me of this vision, and I tried to put this construction on it: "that she should not despair of being someday what I was," she replied immediately, without hesitation, "No; for it was not told me that 'where he is, there you shall be' but 'where you are, there he will be' "? I confess my remembrance of this to thee, O Lord, as far as I can recall it—and I have often mentioned it. Thy answer, given through my watchful mother, in the fact that she was not disturbed by the plausibility of my false interpretation but saw immediately what should have been seen—and which I certainly had not seen until she spoke—this answer moved me more deeply than the dream itself. Still, by that dream, the joy that was to come to that pious woman so long after was predicted long before, as a consolation for her present anguish.

Nearly nine years passed in which I wallowed in the mud of that deep pit and in the darkness of falsehood, striving often to rise, but being all the more heavily dashed down. But all that time this chaste, pious, and sober widow—such as thou dost love—was now more buoyed up with hope, though no less zealous in her weeping and mourning; and she did not cease to bewail my case before thee, in all the hours of her supplication. Her prayers entered thy presence, and yet thou didst allow me still to tumble and toss around in that darkness.

CHAPTER XII

21. Meanwhile, thou gavest her yet another answer, as I remember—for I pass over many things, hastening on to those things which more strongly impel me to confess to thee—and many things I have simply forgotten. But thou gavest her then another answer, by a priest of thine, a certain bishop reared in thy Church and well versed in thy books. When that woman had begged him to agree to have some discussion with me, to refute my errors, to help me to unlearn evil and to learn the good[24]—for it was his habit to do this when he found people ready to receive it—he refused, very prudently, as I afterward realized. For he answered that I was still unteachable, being inflated with the novelty of that heresy, and that I had already perplexed divers inexperienced persons with vexatious questions, as she herself had told him. "But let him alone for a time," he said, "only pray God for him. He will of his own accord, by reading, come to discover what an error it is and how great its impiety is." He went on to tell her at the same time how he himself, as a boy, had been given over to the Manicheans by his misguided mother and not only had read but had even copied out almost all their books. Yet he had come to see, without external argument or proof from anyone else, how much that sect was to be shunned—and had shunned it. When he had said this she was not satisfied, but repeated more earnestly her entreaties, and shed copious tears, still beseeching him to see and talk with me. Finally the bishop, a little vexed at her importunity, exclaimed, "Go your way; as you live, it cannot be that the son of these tears should perish." As she often told me afterward, she accepted this answer as though it were a voice from heaven.

---

[24] *Dedocere me mala ac docere bona*; a typical Augustinian wordplay.

BOOK FIVE

A year of decision. Faustus comes to Carthage and Augustine is disenchanted in his hope for solid demonstration of the truth of Manichean doctrine. He decides to flee from his known troubles at Carthage to troubles yet unknown at Rome. His experiences at Rome prove disappointing and he applies for a teaching post at Milan. Here he meets Ambrose, who confronts him as an impressive witness for Catholic Christianity and opens out the possibilities of the allegorical interpretation of Scripture. Augustine decides to become a Christian catechumen.

CHAPTER I

1. Accept this sacrifice of my confessions from the hand of my tongue. Thou didst form it and hast prompted it to praise thy name. Heal all my bones and let them say, "O Lord, who is like unto thee?"[25] It is not that one who confesses to thee instructs thee as to what goes on within him. For the closed heart does not bar thy sight into it, nor does the hardness of our heart hold back thy hands, for thou canst soften it at will, either by mercy or in vengeance, "and there is no one who can hide himself from thy heat."[26] But let my soul praise thee, that it may love thee, and let it confess thy mercies to thee, that it may praise thee. Thy whole creation praises thee without ceasing: the spirit of man, by his own lips, by his own voice, lifted up to thee; animals and lifeless matter by the mouths of those who meditate upon them. Thus our souls may climb out of their weariness toward thee and lean on those things which thou hast created and pass through them to thee, who didst create them in a marvelous way. With thee, there is refreshment and true strength.

CHAPTER II

2. Let the restless and the unrighteous depart, and flee away from thee. Even so, thou seest them and thy eye pierces through the shadows in which they run. For lo, they live in a world of beauty and yet are themselves most foul. And how have they harmed thee?

---

[25] Ps. 35:10.
[26] Cf. Ps. 19:6.

Or in what way have they discredited thy power, which is just and perfect in its rule even to the last item in creation? Indeed, where would they fly when they fled from thy presence? Wouldst thou be unable to find them? But they fled that they might not see thee, who sawest them; that they might be blinded and stumble into thee. But thou forsakest nothing that thou hast made. The unrighteous stumble against thee that they may be justly plagued, fleeing from thy gentleness and colliding with thy justice, and falling on their own rough paths. For in truth they do not know that thou art everywhere; that no place contains thee, and that only thou art near even to those who go farthest from thee. Let them, therefore, turn back and seek thee, because even if they have abandoned thee, their Creator, thou hast not abandoned thy creatures. Let them turn back and seek thee—and lo, thou art there in their hearts, there in the hearts of those who confess to thee. Let them cast themselves upon thee, and weep on thy bosom, after all their weary wanderings; and thou wilt gently wipe away their tears.[27] And they weep the more and rejoice in their weeping, since thou, O Lord, art not a man of flesh and blood. Thou art the Lord, who canst remake what thou didst make and canst comfort them. And where was I when I was seeking thee? There thou wast, before me; but I had gone away, even from myself, and I could not find myself, much less thee.

CHAPTER III

3. Let me now lay bare in the sight of God the twenty-ninth year of my age. There had just come to Carthage a certain bishop of the Manicheans, Faustus by name, a great snare of the devil; and many were entangled by him through the charm of his eloquence. Now, even though I found this eloquence admirable, I was beginning to distinguish the charm of words from the truth of things, which I was eager to learn. Nor did I consider the dish as much as I did the kind of meat that their famous Faustus served up to me in it. His fame had run before him, as one very skilled in an honorable learning and preeminently skilled in the liberal arts.

And as I had already read and stored up in memory many of the injunctions of the philosophers, I began to compare some of their

---

[27] Cf. Rev. 21:4.

doctrines with the tedious fables of the Manicheans; and it struck me that the probability was on the side of the philosophers, whose power reached far enough to enable them to form a fair judgment of the world, even though they had not discovered the sovereign Lord of it all. For thou art great, O Lord, and thou hast respect unto the lowly, but the proud thou knowest afar off.[28] Thou drawest near to none but the contrite in heart, and canst not be found by the proud, even if in their inquisitive skill they may number the stars and the sands, and map out the constellations, and trace the courses of the planets.

4. For it is by the mind and the intelligence which thou gavest them that they investigate these things. They have discovered much; and have foretold, many years in advance, the day, the hour, and the extent of the eclipses of those luminaries, the sun and the moon. Their calculations did not fail, and it came to pass as they predicted. And they wrote down the rules they had discovered, so that to this day they may be read and from them may be calculated in what year and month and day and hour of the day, and at what quarter of its light, either the moon or the sun will be eclipsed, and it will come to pass just as predicted. And men who are ignorant in these matters marvel and are amazed; and those who understand them exult and are exalted. Both, by an impious pride, withdraw from thee and forsake thy light. They foretell an eclipse of the sun before it happens, but they do not see their own eclipse which is even now occurring. For they do not ask, as religious men should, what is the source of the intelligence by which they investigate these matters. Moreover, when they discover that thou didst make them, they do not give themselves up to thee that thou mightest preserve what thou hast made. Nor do they offer, as sacrifice to thee, what they have made of themselves. For they do not slaughter their own pride—as they do the sacrificial fowls—nor their own curiosities by which, like the fishes of the sea, they wander through the unknown paths of the deep. Nor do they curb their own extravagances as they do those of "the beasts of the field,"[29] so that thou, O Lord, "a consuming fire,"[30] mayest burn up their mortal cares and renew them unto immortality.

5. They do not know the way which is thy word, by which thou didst create all the things that are and also the men who measure

---

[28] Cf. Ps. 138:6.
[29] Ps. 8:7.
[30] Heb. 12:29.

them, and the senses by which they perceive what they measure, and the intelligence whereby they discern the patterns of measure. Thus they know not that thy wisdom is not a matter of measure.[31] But the Only Begotten hath been "made unto us wisdom, and righteousness, and sanctification"[32] and hath been numbered among us and paid tribute to Caesar.[33] And they do not know this "Way" by which they could descend from themselves to him in order to ascend through him to him. They did not know this "Way," and so they fancied themselves exalted to the stars and the shining heavens. And lo, they fell upon the earth, and "their foolish heart was darkened."[34] They saw many true things about the creature but they do not seek with true piety for the Truth, the Architect of Creation, and hence they do not find him. Or, if they do find him, and know that he is God, they do not glorify him as God; neither are they thankful but become vain in their imagination, and say that they themselves are wise, and attribute to themselves what is thine. At the same time, with the most perverse blindness, they wish to attribute to thee their own quality—so that they load their lies on thee who art the Truth, "changing the glory of the incorruptible God for an image of corruptible man, and birds, and four-footed beasts, and creeping things."[35] "They exchanged thy truth for a lie, and worshiped and served the creature rather than the Creator."[36]

6. Yet I remembered many a true saying of the philosophers about the creation, and I saw the confirmation of their calculations in the orderly sequence of seasons and in the visible evidence of the stars. And I compared this with the doctrines of Mani, who in his voluminous folly wrote many books on these subjects. But I could not discover there any account, of either the solstices or the equinoxes, or the eclipses of the sun and moon, or anything of the sort that I had learned in the books of secular philosophy. But still I was ordered to believe, even where the ideas did not correspond with—even when they contradicted—the rational theories established by mathematics and my own eyes, but were very different.

---

[31] An echo of the opening sentence, Bk. I, Ch. I, 1.
[32] Cf. I Cor. 1:30.
[33] Cf. Matt. 22:21.
[34] Cf. Rom. 1:21 ff.
[35] Cf. Rom. 1:23.
[36] Cf. Rom. 1:25.

CHAPTER IV

7. Yet, O Lord God of Truth, is any man pleasing to thee because he knows these things? No, for surely that man is unhappy who knows these things and does not know thee. And that man is happy who knows thee, even though he does not know these things. He who knows both thee and these things is not the more blessed for his learning, for thou only art his blessing, if knowing thee as God he glorifies thee and gives thanks and does not become vain in his thoughts.

For just as that man who knows how to possess a tree, and give thanks to thee for the use of it—although he may not know how many feet high it is or how wide it spreads—is better than the man who can measure it and count all its branches, but neither owns it nor knows or loves its Creator: just so is a faithful man who possesses the world's wealth as though he had nothing, and possesses all things through his union through thee, whom all things serve, even though he does not know the circlings of the Great Bear. Just so it is foolish to doubt that this faithful man may truly be better than the one who can measure the heavens and number the stars and weigh the elements, but who is forgetful of thee "who hast set in order all things in number, weight, and measure."[37]

CHAPTER V

8. And who ordered this Mani to write about these things, knowledge of which is not necessary to piety? For thou hast said to man, "Behold, godliness is wisdom"[38]—and of this he might have been ignorant, however perfectly he may have known these other things. Yet, since he did not know even these other things, and most impudently dared to teach them, it is clear that he had no knowledge of piety. For, even when we have a knowledge of this worldly lore, it is folly to make a *profession* of it, when piety comes from *confession* to thee. From piety, therefore, Mani had gone astray, and all his show of learning only enabled the truly learned to perceive, from his ignorance of what they knew, how little he was to be trusted to make

---

[37] Wis. 11:20.
[38] Cf. Job 28:28.

plain these more really difficult matters. For he did not aim to be lightly esteemed, but went around trying to persuade men that the Holy Spirit, the Comforter and Enricher of thy faithful ones, was personally resident in him with full authority. And, therefore, when he was detected in manifest errors about the sky, the stars, the movements of the sun and moon, even though these things do not relate to religious doctrine, the impious presumption of the man became clearly evident; for he not only taught things about which he was ignorant but also perverted them, and this with pride so foolish and mad that he sought to claim that his own utterances were as if they had been those of a divine person.

9. When I hear of a Christian brother, ignorant of these things, or in error concerning them, I can tolerate his uninformed opinion; and I do not see that any lack of knowledge as to the form or nature of this material creation can do him much harm, as long as he does not hold a belief in anything which is unworthy of thee, O Lord, the Creator of all. But if he thinks that his secular knowledge pertains to the essence of the doctrine of piety, or ventures to assert dogmatic opinions in matters in which he is ignorant—there lies the injury. And yet even a weakness such as this, in the infancy of our faith, is tolerated by our Mother Charity until the new man can grow up "unto a perfect man," and not be "carried away with every wind of doctrine."[39]

But Mani had presumed to be at once the teacher, author, guide, and leader of all whom he could persuade to believe this, so that all who followed him believed that they were following not an ordinary man but thy Holy Spirit. And who would not judge that such great madness, when it once stood convicted of false teaching, should then be abhorred and utterly rejected? But I had not yet clearly decided whether the alternation of day and night, and of longer and shorter days and nights, and the eclipses of sun and moon, and whatever else I read about in other books could be explained consistently with his theories. If they could have been so explained, there would still have remained a doubt in my mind whether the theories were right or wrong. Yet I was prepared, on the strength of his reputed godliness, to rest my faith on his authority.

---

[39] Eph. 4:13, 14.

CHAPTER VI

10. For almost the whole of the nine years that I listened with unsettled mind to the Manichean teaching I had been looking forward with unbounded eagerness to the arrival of this Faustus. For all the other members of the sect that I happened to meet, when they were unable to answer the questions I raised, always referred me to his coming. They promised that, in discussion with him, these and even greater difficulties, if I had them, would be quite easily and amply cleared away. When at last he did come, I found him to be a man of pleasant speech, who spoke of the very same things they themselves did, although more fluently and in a more agreeable style. But what profit was there to me in the elegance of my cupbearer, since he could not offer me the more precious draught for which I thirsted? My ears had already had their fill of such stuff, and now it did not seem any better because it was better expressed nor more true because it was dressed up in rhetoric; nor could I think the man's soul necessarily wise because his face was comely and his language eloquent. But they who extolled him to me were not competent judges. They thought him able and wise because his eloquence delighted them. At the same time I realized that there is another kind of man who is suspicious even of truth itself, if it is expressed in smooth and flowing language. But thou, O my God, hadst already taught me in wonderful and marvelous ways, and therefore I believed—because it is true—that thou didst teach me and that beside thee there is no other teacher of truth, wherever truth shines forth. Already I had learned from thee that because a thing is eloquently expressed it should not be taken to be as necessarily true; nor because it is uttered with stammering lips should it be supposed false. Nor, again, is it necessarily true because rudely uttered, nor untrue because the language is brilliant. Wisdom and folly both are like meats that are wholesome and unwholesome, and courtly or simple words are like town-made or rustic vessels—both kinds of food may be served in either kind of dish.

11. That eagerness, therefore, with which I had so long awaited this man, was in truth delighted with his action and feeling in a disputation, and with the fluent and apt words with which he clothed his ideas. I was delighted, therefore, and I joined with others—and even exceeded them—in exalting and praising him. Yet it was a source of annoyance to me that, in his lecture room, I was not allowed

to introduce and raise any of those questions that troubled me, in a familiar exchange of discussion with him. As soon as I found an opportunity for this, and gained his ear at a time when it was not inconvenient for him to enter into a discussion with me and my friends, I laid before him some of my doubts. I discovered at once that he knew nothing of the liberal arts except grammar, and that only in an ordinary way. He had, however, read some of Tully's orations, a very few books of Seneca, and some of the poets, and such few books of his own sect as were written in good Latin. With this meager learning and his daily practice in speaking, he had acquired a sort of eloquence which proved the more delightful and enticing because it was under the direction of a ready wit and a sort of native grace. Was this not even as I now recall it, O Lord my God, Judge of my conscience? My heart and my memory are laid open before thee, who wast even then guiding me by the secret impulse of thy providence and wast setting my shameful errors before my face so that I might see and hate them.

CHAPTER VII

12. For as soon as it became plain to me that Faustus was ignorant in those arts in which I had believed him eminent, I began to despair of his being able to clarify and explain all these perplexities that troubled me—though I realized that such ignorance need not have affected the authenticity of his piety, if he had not been a Manichean. For their books are full of long fables about the sky and the stars, the sun and the moon; and I had ceased to believe him able to show me in any satisfactory fashion what I so ardently desired: whether the explanations contained in the Manichean books were better or at least as good as the mathematical explanations I had read elsewhere. But when I proposed that these subjects should be considered and discussed, he quite modestly did not dare to undertake the task, for he was aware that he had no knowledge of these things and was not ashamed to confess it. For he was not one of those talkative people— from whom I had endured so much—who undertook to teach me what I wanted to know, and then said nothing. Faustus had a heart which, if not right toward thee, was at least not altogether false toward himself; for he was not ignorant of his own ignorance, and he did not choose to be entangled in a controversy from which he could not draw back or retire gracefully. For this I liked him all the more.

For the modesty of an ingenious mind is a finer thing than the acquisition of that knowledge I desired; and this I found to be his attitude toward all abstruse and difficult questions.

13. Thus the zeal with which I had plunged into the Manichean system was checked, and I despaired even more of their other teachers, because Faustus who was so famous among them had turned out so poorly in the various matters that puzzled me. And so I began to occupy myself with him in the study of his own favorite pursuit, that of literature, in which I was already teaching a class as a professor of rhetoric among the young Carthaginian students. With Faustus then I read whatever he himself wished to read, or what I judged suitable to his bent of mind. But all my endeavors to make further progress in Manicheism came completely to an end through my acquaintance with that man. I did not wholly separate myself from them, but as one who had not yet found anything better I decided to content myself, for the time being, with what I had stumbled upon one way or another, until by chance something more desirable should present itself. Thus that Faustus who had entrapped so many to their death—though neither willing nor witting it—now began to loosen the snare in which I had been caught. For thy hands, O my God, in the hidden design of thy providence did not desert my soul; and out of the blood of my mother's heart, through the tears that she poured out by day and by night, there was a sacrifice offered to thee for me, and by marvelous ways thou didst deal with me. For it was thou, O my God, who didst it: for "the steps of a man are ordered by the Lord, and he shall choose his way."[40] How shall we attain salvation without thy hand remaking what it had already made?

CHAPTER VIII

14. Thou didst so deal with me, therefore, that I was persuaded to go to Rome and teach there what I had been teaching at Carthage. And how I was persuaded to do this I will not omit to confess to thee, for in this also the profoundest workings of thy wisdom and thy constant mercy toward us must be pondered and acknowledged. I did not wish to go to Rome because of the richer fees and the higher dignity which my friends promised me there—though these

---

[40] Ps. 36:23 (Vulgate).

considerations did affect my decision. My principal and almost sole motive was that I had been informed that the students there studied more quietly and were better kept under the control of stern discipline, so that they did not capriciously and impudently rush into the classroom of a teacher not their own—indeed, they were not admitted at all without the permission of the teacher. At Carthage, on the contrary, there was a shameful and intemperate license among the students. They burst in rudely and, with furious gestures, would disrupt the discipline which the teacher had established for the good of his pupils. Many outrages they perpetrated with astounding effrontery, things that would be punishable by law if they were not sustained by custom. Thus custom makes plain that such behavior is all the more worthless because it allows men to do what thy eternal law never will allow. They think that they act thus with impunity, though the very blindness with which they act is their punishment, and they suffer far greater harm than they inflict.

The manners that I would not adopt as a student I was compelled as a teacher to endure in others. And so I was glad to go where all who knew the situation assured me that such conduct was not allowed. But thou, "O my refuge and my portion in the land of the living,"[41] didst goad me thus at Carthage so that I might thereby be pulled away from it and change my worldly habitation for the preservation of my soul. At the same time, thou didst offer me at Rome an enticement, through the agency of men enchanted with this death-in-life—by their insane conduct in the one place and their empty promises in the other. To correct my wandering footsteps, thou didst secretly employ their perversity and my own. For those who disturbed my tranquillity were blinded by shameful madness and also those who allured me elsewhere had nothing better than the earth's cunning. And I who hated actual misery in the one place sought fictitious happiness in the other.

15. Thou knewest the cause of my going from one country to the other, O God, but thou didst not disclose it either to me or to my mother, who grieved deeply over my departure and followed me down to the sea. She clasped me tight in her embrace, willing either to keep me back or to go with me, but I deceived her, pretending that I had a friend whom I could not leave until he had a favorable wind to set sail. Thus I lied to my mother—and such a mother!—and

---

[41] Ps. 142:5.

escaped. For this too thou didst mercifully pardon me—fool that I was—and didst preserve me from the waters of the sea for the water of thy grace; so that, when I was purified by that, the fountain of my mother's eyes, from which she had daily watered the ground for me as she prayed to thee, should be dried. And, since she refused to return without me, I persuaded her, with some difficulty, to remain that night in a place quite close to our ship, where there was a shrine in memory of the blessed Cyprian. That night I slipped away secretly, and she remained to pray and weep. And what was it, O Lord, that she was asking of thee in such a flood of tears but that thou wouldst not allow me to sail? But thou, taking thy own secret counsel and noting the real point to her desire, didst not grant what she was then asking in order to grant to her the thing that she had always been asking.

The wind blew and filled our sails, and the shore dropped out of sight. Wild with grief, she was there the next morning and filled thy ears with complaints and groans which thou didst disregard, although, at the very same time, thou wast using my longings as a means and wast hastening me on to the fulfillment of all longing. Thus the earthly part of her love to me was justly purged by the scourge of sorrow. Still, like all mothers—though even more than others—she loved to have me with her, and did not know what joy thou wast preparing for her through my going away. Not knowing this secret end, she wept and mourned and saw in her agony the inheritance of Eve—seeking in sorrow what she had brought forth in sorrow. And yet, after accusing me of perfidy and cruelty, she still continued her intercessions for me to thee. She returned to her own home, and I went on to Rome.

CHAPTER IX

16. And lo, I was received in Rome by the scourge of bodily sickness; and I was very near to falling into hell, burdened with all the many and grievous sins I had committed against thee, myself, and others—all over and above that fetter of original sin whereby we all die in Adam. For thou hadst forgiven me none of these things in Christ, neither had he abolished by his cross the enmity[42] that I

---

[42] Cf. Eph. 2:15.

had incurred from thee through my sins. For how could he do so by the crucifixion of a phantom, which was all I supposed him to be? The death of my soul was as real then as the death of his flesh appeared to me unreal. And the life of my soul was as false, because it was as unreal as the death of his flesh was real, though I believed it not.

My fever increased, and I was on the verge of passing away and perishing; for, if I had passed away then, where should I have gone but into the fiery torment which my misdeeds deserved, measured by the truth of thy rule? My mother knew nothing of this; yet, far away, she went on praying for me. And thou, present everywhere, didst hear her where she was and had pity on me where I was, so that I regained my bodily health, although I was still disordered in my sacrilegious heart. For that peril of death did not make me wish to be baptized. I was even better when, as a lad, I entreated baptism of my mother's devotion, as I have already related and confessed.[43] But now I had since increased in dishonor, and I madly scoffed at all the purposes of thy medicine which would not have allowed me, though a sinner such as I was, to die a double death. Had my mother's heart been pierced with this wound, it never could have been cured, for I cannot adequately tell of the love she had for me, or how she still travailed for me in the spirit with a far keener anguish than when she bore me in the flesh.

17. I cannot conceive, therefore, how she could have been healed if my death (still in my sins) had pierced her inmost love. Where, then, would have been all her earnest, frequent, and ceaseless prayers to thee? Nowhere but with thee. But couldst thou, O most merciful God, despise the "contrite and humble heart"[44] of that pure and prudent widow, who was so constant in her alms, so gracious and attentive to thy saints, never missing a visit to church twice a day, morning and evening—and this not for vain gossiping, nor old wives' fables, but in order that she might listen to thee in thy sermons, and thou to her in her prayers? Couldst thou, by whose gifts she was so inspired, despise and disregard the tears of such a one without coming to her aid—those tears by which she entreated thee, not for gold or silver, and not for any changing or fleeting good, but for the salvation of the soul of her son? By no means, O Lord. It is certain that thou wast near and wast hearing and wast carrying out the plan

---

[43] Bk. I, Ch. XI, 17.
[44] Cf. Ps. 51:17.

by which thou hadst predetermined it should be done. Far be it from thee that thou shouldst have deluded her in those visions and the answers she had received from thee—some of which I have mentioned, and others not—which she kept in her faithful heart, and, forever beseeching, urged them on thee as if they had thy own signature. For thou, "because thy mercy endureth forever,"[45] hast so condescended to those whose debts thou hast pardoned that thou likewise dost become a debtor by thy promises.

CHAPTER X

18. Thou didst restore me then from that illness, and didst heal the son of thy handmaid in his body, that he might live for thee and that thou mightest endow him with a better and more certain health. After this, at Rome, I again joined those deluding and deluded "saints"; and not their "hearers" only, such as the man was in whose house I had fallen sick, but also with those whom they called "the elect." For it still seemed to me "that it is not we who sin, but some other nature sinned in us." And it gratified my pride to be beyond blame, and when I did anything wrong not to have to confess that *I* had done wrong—"that thou mightest heal my soul because it had sinned against thee"[46]—and I loved to excuse my soul and to accuse something else inside me (I knew not what) but which was not I. But, assuredly, it was I, and it was my impiety that had divided me against myself. That sin then was all the more incurable because I did not deem myself a sinner. It was an execrable iniquity, O God Omnipotent, that I would have preferred to have thee defeated in me, to my destruction, than to be defeated by thee to my salvation. Not yet, therefore, hadst thou set a watch upon my mouth and a door around my lips that my heart might not incline to evil speech, to make excuse for sin with men that work iniquity.[47] And, therefore, I continued still in the company of their "elect."

19. But now, hopeless of gaining any profit from that false doctrine, I began to hold more loosely and negligently even to those points which I had decided to rest content with, if I could find nothing better. I was now half inclined to believe that those philosophers

---

[45] A constant theme in The Psalms and elsewhere; cf. Ps. 136.

[46] Cf. Ps. 41:4.

[47] Cf. Ps. 141:3f.

whom they call "The Academics"[48] were wiser than the rest in holding that we ought to doubt everything, and in maintaining that man does not have the power of comprehending any certain truth, for, although I had not yet understood their meaning, I was fully persuaded that they thought just as they are commonly reputed to do. And I did not fail openly to dissuade my host from his confidence which I observed that he had in those fictions of which the works of Mani are full. For all this, I was still on terms of more intimate friendship with these people than with others who were not of their heresy. I did not indeed defend it with my former ardor; but my familiarity with that group—and there were many of them concealed in Rome at that time[49]—made me slower to seek any other way. This was particularly easy since I had no hope of finding in thy Church the truth from which they had turned me aside, O Lord of heaven and earth, Creator of all things visible and invisible. And it still seemed to me most unseemly to believe that thou couldst have the form of human flesh and be bounded by the bodily shape of our limbs. And when I desired to meditate on my God, I did not know what to think of but a huge extended body—for what did not have bodily extension did not seem to me to exist—and this was the greatest and almost the sole cause of my unavoidable errors.

20. And thus I also believed that evil was a similar kind of substance, and that it had its own hideous and deformed extended body—either in a dense form which they called the earth or in a thin and subtle form as, for example, the substance of the air, which they imagined as some malignant spirit penetrating that earth. And because my piety—such as it was—still compelled me to believe that the good God never created any evil substance, I formed the idea of two masses, one opposed to the other, both infinite but with the evil more contracted and the good more expansive. And from this diseased beginning, the other sacrileges followed after.

For when my mind tried to turn back to the Catholic faith, I was cast down, since the Catholic faith was not what I judged it to be.

---

[48] Followers of the skeptical tradition established in the Platonic Academy by Arcesilaus and Carneades in the third century B.C. They taught the necessity of ἐποχή, suspended judgment, in all questions of truth, and would allow nothing more than the consent of probability. This tradition was known in Augustine's time chiefly through the writings of Cicero; cf. his *Academica*. This kind of skepticism shook Augustine's complacency severely, and he wrote one of his first dialogues, *Contra Academicos,* in an effort to clear up the problem posed thereby.

[49] The Manicheans were under an official ban in Rome.

And it seemed to me a greater piety to regard thee, my God—to whom I make confession of thy mercies—as infinite in all respects save that one: where the extended mass of evil stood opposed to thee, where I was compelled to confess that thou art finite—than if I should think that thou couldst be confined by the form of a human body on every side. And it seemed better to me to believe that no evil had been created by thee—for in my ignorance evil appeared not only to be some kind of substance but a corporeal one at that. This was because I had, thus far, no conception of mind, except as a subtle body diffused throughout local spaces. This seemed better than to believe that anything could emanate from thee which had the character that I considered evil to be in its nature. And I believed that our Saviour himself also—thy Only Begotten—had been brought forth, as it were, for our salvation out of the mass of thy bright shining substance. So that I could believe nothing about him except what I was able to harmonize with these vain imaginations. I thought, therefore, that such a nature could not be born of the Virgin Mary without being mingled with the flesh, and I could not see how the divine substance, as I had conceived it, could be mingled thus without being contaminated. I was afraid, therefore, to believe that he had been born in the flesh, lest I should also be compelled to believe that he had been contaminated by the flesh. Now will thy spiritual ones smile blandly and lovingly at me if they read these confessions. Yet such was I.

CHAPTER XI

21. Furthermore, the things they censured in thy Scriptures I thought impossible to be defended. And yet, occasionally, I desired to confer on various matters with someone well learned in those books, to test what he thought of them. For already the words of one Elpidius, who spoke and disputed face to face against these same Manicheans, had begun to impress me, even when I was at Carthage; because he brought forth things out of the Scriptures that were not easily withstood, to which their answers appeared to me feeble. One of their answers they did not give forth publicly, but only to us in private—when they said that the writings of the New Testament had been tampered with by unknown persons who desired to ingraft the Jewish law into the Christian faith. But they themselves never brought forward any uncorrupted copies. Still thinking in corporeal

categories and very much ensnared and to some extent stifled, I was borne down by those conceptions of bodily substance. I panted under this load for the air of thy truth, but I was not able to breathe it pure and undefiled.

CHAPTER XII

22. I set about diligently to practice what I came to Rome to do—the teaching of rhetoric. The first task was to bring together in my home a few people to whom and through whom I had begun to be known. And lo, I then began to learn that other offenses were committed in Rome which I had not had to bear in Africa. Just as I had been told, those riotous disruptions by young blackguards were not practiced here. Yet, now, my friends told me, many of the Roman students—breakers of faith, who, for the love of money, set a small value on justice—would conspire together and suddenly transfer to another teacher, to evade paying their master's fees. My heart hated such people, though not with a "perfect hatred"[50]; for doubtless I hated them more because I was to suffer from them than on account of their own illicit acts. Still, such people are base indeed; they fornicate against thee, for they love the transitory mockeries of temporal things and the filthy gain which begrimes the hand that grabs it; they embrace the fleeting world and scorn thee, who abidest and invitest us to return to thee and who pardonest the prostituted human soul when it does return to thee. Now I hate such crooked and perverse men, although I love them if they will be corrected and come to prefer the learning they obtain to money and, above all, to prefer thee to such learning, O God, the truth and fullness of our positive good, and our most pure peace. But then the wish was stronger in me for my own sake not to suffer evil from them than was my desire that they should become good for thy sake.

CHAPTER XIII

23. When, therefore, the officials of Milan sent to Rome, to the prefect of the city, to ask that he provide them with a teacher of

---

[50] Ps. 139:22.

rhetoric for their city and to send him at the public expense, I applied for the job through those same persons, drunk with the Manichean vanities, to be freed from whom I was going away—though neither they nor I were aware of it at the time. They recommended that Symmachus, who was then prefect, after he had proved me by audition, should appoint me.

And to Milan I came, to Ambrose the bishop, famed through the whole world as one of the best of men, thy devoted servant. His eloquent discourse in those times abundantly provided thy people with the flour of thy wheat, the gladness of thy oil, and the sober intoxication of thy wine.[51] To him I was led by thee without my knowledge, that by him I might be led to thee in full knowledge. That man of God received me as a father would, and welcomed my coming as a good bishop should. And I began to love him, of course, not at the first as a teacher of the truth, for I had entirely despaired of finding that in thy Church—but as a friendly man. And I studiously listened to him—though not with the right motive—as he preached to the people. I was trying to discover whether his eloquence came up to his reputation, and whether it flowed fuller or thinner than others said it did. And thus I hung on his words intently, but, as to his subject matter, I was only a careless and contemptuous listener. I was delighted with the charm of his speech, which was more erudite, though less cheerful and soothing, than Faustus' style. As for subject matter, however, there could be no comparison, for the latter was wandering around in Manichean deceptions, while the former was teaching salvation most soundly. But "salvation is far from the wicked,"[52] such as I was then when I stood before him. Yet I was drawing nearer, gradually and unconsciously.

CHAPTER XIV

24. For, although I took no trouble to learn what he said, but only to hear how he said it—for this empty concern remained foremost

---

[51] A mixed figure here, put together from Ps. 4:7; 45:7; 104:15; the phrase *sobriam vini ebrietatem* is almost certainly an echo of a stanza of one of Ambrose's own hymns, *Splendor paternae gloriae,* which Augustine had doubtless learned in Milan: "*Bibamus sobriam ebrietatem spiritus.*" Cf. W. I. Merrill, *Latin Hymns* (Boston, 1904), pp. 4, 5.

[52] Ps. 119:155.

with me as long as I despaired of finding a clear path from man to thee—yet, along with the eloquence I prized, there also came into my mind the ideas which I ignored; for I could not separate them. And, while I opened my heart to acknowledge how skillfully he spoke, there also came an awareness of how *truly* he spoke—but only gradually. First of all, his ideas had already begun to appear to me defensible; and the Catholic faith, for which I supposed that nothing could be said against the onslaught of the Manicheans, I now realized could be maintained without presumption. This was especially clear after I had heard one or two parts of the Old Testament explained allegorically—whereas before this, when I had interpreted them literally, they had "killed" me spiritually.[53] However, when many of these passages in those books were expounded to me thus, I came to blame my own despair for having believed that no reply could be given to those who hated and scoffed at the Law and the Prophets. Yet I did not see that this was reason enough to follow the Catholic way, just because it had learned advocates who could answer objections adequately and without absurdity. Nor could I see that what I had held to heretofore should now be condemned, because both sides were equally defensible. For that way did not appear to me yet vanquished; but neither did it seem yet victorious.

25. But now I earnestly bent my mind to inquire if there was possible any way to prove the Manicheans guilty of falsehood. If I could have conceived of a spiritual substance, all their strongholds would have collapsed and been cast out of my mind. But I could not. Still, concerning the body of this world, nature as a whole—now that I was able to consider and compare such things more and more— I now decided that the majority of the philosophers held the more probable views. So, in what I thought was the method of the Academics—doubting everything and fluctuating between all the options—I came to the conclusion that the Manicheans were to be abandoned. For I judged, even in that period of doubt, that I could not remain in a sect to which I preferred some of the philosophers. But I refused to commit the cure of my fainting soul to the philosophers, because they were without the saving name of Christ. I resolved, therefore, to become a catechumen in the Catholic Church—which

---

[53] Cf. II Cor. 3:6. The discovery of the allegorical method of interpretation opened new horizons for Augustine in Biblical interpretation and he adopted it as a settled principle in his sermons and commentaries; cf. M. Pontet, *L'Exégèse de Saint Augustin prédicateur* (Lyons, 1946).

my parents had so much urged upon me—until something certain shone forth by which I might guide my course.

BOOK EIGHT

Conversion to Christ. Augustine is deeply impressed by Simplicianus' story of the conversion to Christ of the famous orator and philosopher, Marius Victorinus. He is stirred to emulate him, but finds himself still enchained by his incontinence and preoccupation with worldly affairs. He is then visited by a court official, Ponticianus, who tells him and Alypius the stories of the conversion of Anthony and also of two imperial "secret service agents." These stories throw him into a violent turmoil, in which his divided will struggles against himself. He almost succeeds in making the decision for continence, but is still held back. Finally, a child's song, overheard by chance, sends him to the Bible; a text from Paul resolves the crisis; the conversion is a fact. Alypius also makes his decision, and the two inform the rejoicing Monica.

CHAPTER I

1. O my God, let me remember with gratitude and confess to thee thy mercies toward me. Let my bones be bathed in thy love, and let them say: "Lord, who is like unto thee?[54] Thou hast broken my bonds in sunder, I will offer unto thee the sacrifice of thanksgiving."[55] And how thou didst break them I will declare, and all who worship thee shall say, when they hear these things: "Blessed be the Lord in heaven and earth, great and wonderful is his name."[56]

Thy words had stuck fast in my breast, and I was hedged round about by thee on every side. Of thy eternal life I was now certain, although I had seen it "through a glass darkly."[57] And I had been relieved of all doubt that there is an incorruptible substance and that it is the source of every other substance. Nor did I any longer crave greater certainty about thee, but rather greater steadfastness in thee.

---

[54] Ps. 35:10.
[55] Cf. Ps. 116:16, 17.
[56] Cf. Ps. 8:1.
[57] I Cor. 13:12.

But as for my temporal life, everything was uncertain, and my heart had to be purged of the old leaven. "The Way"—the Saviour himself—pleased me well, but as yet I was reluctant to pass through the strait gate.

And thou didst put it into my mind, and it seemed good in my own sight, to go to Simplicianus, who appeared to me a faithful servant of thine, and thy grace shone forth in him. I had also been told that from his youth up he had lived in entire devotion to thee. He was already an old man, and because of his great age, which he had passed in such a zealous discipleship in thy way, he appeared to me likely to have gained much wisdom—and, indeed, he had. From all his experience, I desired him to tell me—setting before him all my agitations—which would be the most fitting way for one who felt as I did to walk in thy way.

2. For I saw the Church full; and one man was going this way and another that. Still, I could not be satisfied with the life I was living in the world. Now, indeed, my passions had ceased to excite me as of old with hopes of honor and wealth, and it was a grievous burden to go on in such servitude. For, compared with thy sweetness and the beauty of thy house—which I loved—those things delighted me no longer. But I was still tightly bound by the love of women; nor did the apostle forbid me to marry, although he exhorted me to something better, wishing earnestly that all men were as he himself was.

But I was weak and chose the easier way, and for this single reason my whole life was one of inner turbulence and listless indecision, because from so many influences I was compelled—even though unwilling—to agree to a married life which bound me hand and foot. I had heard from the mouth of Truth that "there are eunuchs who have made themselves eunuchs for the Kingdom of Heaven's sake"[58] but, said he, "He that is able to receive it, let him receive it." Of a certainty, all men are vain who do not have the knowledge of God, or have not been able, from the good things that are seen, to find him who is good. But I was no longer fettered in that vanity. I had surmounted it, and from the united testimony of thy whole creation had found thee, our Creator, and thy Word—God with thee, and together with thee and the Holy Spirit, one God—by whom thou hast created all things. There is still another sort of wicked

---

[58] Matt. 19:12.

men, who "when they knew God, they glorified him not as God, neither were thankful."[59] Into this also I had fallen, but thy right hand held me up and bore me away, and thou didst place me where I might recover. For thou hast said to men, "Behold the fear of the Lord, this is wisdom,"[60] and, "Be not wise in your own eyes,"[61] because "they that profess themselves to be wise become fools."[62] But I had now found the goodly pearl; and I ought to have sold all that I had and bought it—yet I hesitated.

CHAPTER II

3. I went, therefore, to Simplicianus, the spiritual father of Ambrose (then a bishop), whom Ambrose truly loved as a father. I recounted to him all the mazes of my wanderings, but when I mentioned to him that I had read certain books of the Platonists which Victorinus—formerly professor of rhetoric at Rome, who died a Christian, as I had been told—had translated into Latin, Simplicianus congratulated me that I had not fallen upon the writings of other philosophers, which were full of fallacies and deceit, "after the beggarly elements of this world,"[63] whereas in the Platonists, at every turn, the pathway led to belief in God and his Word.

Then, to encourage me to copy the humility of Christ, which is hidden from the wise and revealed to babes, he told me about Victorinus himself, whom he had known intimately at Rome. And I cannot refrain from repeating what he told me about him. For it contains a glorious proof of thy grace, which ought to be confessed to thee: how that old man, most learned, most skilled in all the liberal arts; who had read, criticized, and explained so many of the writings of the philosophers; the teacher of so many noble senators; one who, as a mark of his distinguished service in office had both merited and obtained a statue in the Roman Forum—which men of this world esteem a great honor—this man who, up to an advanced age, had been a worshiper of idols, a communicant in the sacrilegious

---

[59] Rom. 1:21.
[60] Job 28:28.
[61] Prov. 3:7.
[62] Rom. 1:22.
[63] Col. 2:8.

rites to which almost all the nobility of Rome were wedded; and who had inspired the people with the love of Osiris and

> "The dog Anubis, and a medley crew
> Of monster gods who 'gainst Neptune stand in arms
> 'Gainst Venus and Minerva, steel-clad Mars,"[64]

whom Rome once conquered, and now worshiped; all of which old Victorinus had with thundering eloquence defended for so many years—despite all this, he did not blush to become a child of thy Christ, a babe at thy font, bowing his neck to the yoke of humility and submitting his forehead to the ignominy of the cross.

4. O Lord, Lord, "who didst bow the heavens and didst descend, who didst touch the mountains and they smoked,"[65] by what means didst thou find thy way into that breast? He used to read the Holy Scriptures, as Simplicianus said, and thought out and studied all the Christian writings most studiously. He said to Simplicianus—not openly but secretly as a friend—"You must know that I am a Christian." To which Simplicianus replied, "I shall not believe it, nor shall I count you among the Christians, until I see you in the Church of Christ." Victorinus then asked, with mild mockery, "Is it then the walls that make Christians?" Thus he often would affirm that he was already a Christian, and as often Simplicianus made the same answer; and just as often his jest about the walls was repeated. He was fearful of offending his friends, proud demon worshipers, from the height of whose Babylonian dignity, as from the tops of the cedars of Lebanon which the Lord had not yet broken down, he feared that a storm of enmity would descend upon him.

But he steadily gained strength from reading and inquiry, and came to fear lest he should be denied by Christ before the holy angels if he now was afraid to confess him before men. Thus he came to appear to himself guilty of a great fault, in being ashamed of the sacraments of the humility of thy Word, when he was not ashamed of the sacrilegious rites of those proud demons, whose pride he had imitated and whose rites he had shared. From this he became bold-faced against vanity and shamefaced toward the truth. Thus, suddenly and unexpectedly, he said to Simplicianus—as he himself told me— "Let us go to the church; I wish to become a Christian." Simplicianus went with him, scarcely able to contain himself for joy. He was

---

[64] Virgil, *Aeneid*, VIII, 698.
[65] Ps. 144:5.

admitted to the first sacraments of instruction, and not long afterward gave in his name that he might receive the baptism of regeneration. At this Rome marveled and the Church rejoiced. The proud saw and were enraged; they gnashed their teeth and melted away! But the Lord God was thy servant's hope and he paid no attention to their vanity and lying madness.

5. Finally, when the hour arrived for him to make a public profession of his faith—which at Rome those who are about to enter into thy grace make from a platform in the full sight of the faithful people, in a set form of words learned by heart—the presbyters offered Victorinus the chance to make his profession more privately, for this was the custom for some who were likely to be afraid through bashfulness. But Victorinus chose rather to profess his salvation in the presence of the holy congregation. For there was no salvation in the rhetoric which he taught: yet he had professed that openly. Why, then, should he shrink from naming thy Word before the sheep of thy flock, when he had not shrunk from uttering his own words before the mad multitude?

So, then, when he ascended the platform to make his profession, everyone, as they recognized him, whispered his name one to the other, in tones of jubilation. Who was there among them that did not know him? And a low murmur ran through the mouths of all the rejoicing multitude: "Victorinus! Victorinus!" There was a sudden burst of exaltation at the sight of him, and suddenly they were hushed that they might hear him. He pronounced the true faith with an excellent boldness, and all desired to take him to their very heart— indeed, by their love and joy they did take him to their heart. And they received him with loving and joyful hands.

CHAPTER III

6. O good God, what happens in a man to make him rejoice more at the salvation of a soul that has been despaired of and then delivered from greater danger than over one who has never lost hope, or never been in such imminent danger? For thou also, O most merciful Father, "dost rejoice more over one that repents than over ninety and nine just persons that need no repentance."[66] And we listen with much delight whenever we hear how the lost sheep is brought home

---

[66] Luke 15:4.

again on the shepherd's shoulders while the angels rejoice; or when the piece of money is restored to its place in the treasury and the neighbors rejoice with the woman who found it.[67] And the joy of the solemn festival of thy house constrains us to tears when it is read in thy house: about the younger son who "was dead and is alive again, was lost and is found." For it is thou who rejoicest both in us and in thy angels, who are holy through holy love. For thou art ever the same because thou knowest unchangeably all things which remain neither the same nor forever.

7. What, then, happens in the soul when it takes more delight at finding or having restored to it the things it loves than if it had always possessed them? Indeed, many other things bear witness that this is so—all things are full of witnesses, crying out, "So it is." The commander triumphs in victory; yet he could not have conquered if he had not fought; and the greater the peril of the battle, the more the joy of the triumph. The storm tosses the voyagers, threatens shipwreck, and everyone turns pale in the presence of death. Then the sky and sea grow calm, and they rejoice as much as they had feared. A loved one is sick and his pulse indicates danger; all who desire his safety are themselves sick at heart; he recovers, though not able as yet to walk with his former strength; and there is more joy now than there was before when he walked sound and strong. Indeed, the very pleasures of human life—not only those which rush upon us unexpectedly and involuntarily, but also those which are voluntary and planned—men obtain by difficulties. There is no pleasure in eating and drinking unless the pains of hunger and thirst have preceded. Drunkards even eat certain salt meats in order to create a painful thirst—and when the drink allays this, it causes pleasure. It is also the custom that the affianced bride should not be immediately given in marriage so that the husband may not esteem her any less, whom as his betrothed he longed for.

8. This can be seen in the case of base and dishonorable pleasure. But it is also apparent in pleasures that are permitted and lawful: in the sincerity of honest friendship; and in him who was dead and lived again, who had been lost and was found. The greater joy is everywhere preceded by the greater pain. What does this mean, O Lord my God, when thou art an everlasting joy to thyself, and some creatures about thee are ever rejoicing in thee? What does it mean

---

[67] Cf. Luke, ch. 15.

that this portion of creation thus ebbs and flows, alternately in want and satiety? Is this their mode of being and is this all thou hast allotted to them: that, from the highest heaven to the lowest earth, from the beginning of the world to the end, from the angels to the worm, from the first movement to the last, thou wast assigning to all their proper places and their proper seasons—to all the kinds of good things and to all thy just works? Alas, how high thou art in the highest and how deep in the deepest! Thou never departest from us, and yet only with difficulty do we return to thee.

CHAPTER IV

9. Go on, O Lord, and act: stir us up and call us back; inflame us and draw us to thee; stir us up and grow sweet to us; let us now love thee, let us run to thee. Are there not many men who, out of a deeper pit of darkness than that of Victorinus, return to thee—who draw near to thee and are illuminated by that light which gives those who receive it power from thee to become thy sons? But if they are less well-known, even those who know them rejoice less for them. For when many rejoice together the joy of each one is fuller, in that they warm one another, catch fire from each other; moreover, those who are well-known influence many toward salvation and take the lead with many to follow them. Therefore, even those who took the way before them rejoice over them greatly, because they do not rejoice over them alone. But it ought never to be that in thy tabernacle the persons of the rich should be welcome before the poor, or the nobly born before the rest—since "thou hast rather chosen the weak things of the world to confound the strong; and hast chosen the base things of the world and things that are despised, and the things that are not, in order to bring to nought the things that are."[68] It was even "the least of the apostles" by whose tongue thou didst sound forth these words. And when Paulus the proconsul had his pride overcome by the onslaught of the apostle and he was made to pass under the easy yoke of thy Christ and became an officer of the great King, he also desired to be called Paul instead of Saul, his former name, in testimony to such a great victory.[69] For the enemy is more overcome in one

---

[68] 1 Cor. 1:27.
[69] A garbled reference to the story of the conversion of Sergius Paulus, proconsul of Cyprus, in Acts 13:4–12.

on whom he has a greater hold, and whom he has hold of more completely. But the proud he controls more readily through their concern about their rank and, through them, he controls more by means of their influence. The more, therefore, the world prized the heart of Victorinus (which the devil had held in an impregnable stronghold) and the tongue of Victorinus (that sharp, strong weapon with which the devil had slain so many), all the more exultingly should Thy sons rejoice because our King hath bound the strong man, and they saw his vessels taken from him and cleansed, and made fit for thy honor and "profitable to the Lord for every good work."[70]

CHAPTER V

10. Now when this man of thine, Simplicianus, told me the story of Victorinus, I was eager to imitate him. Indeed, this was Simplicianus' purpose in telling it to me. But when he went on to tell how, in the reign of the Emperor Julian, there was a law passed by which Christians were forbidden to teach literature and rhetoric; and how Victorinus, in ready obedience to the law, chose to abandon his "school of words" rather than thy Word, by which thou makest eloquent the tongues of the dumb—he appeared to me not so much brave as happy, because he had found a reason for giving his time wholly to thee. For this was what I was longing to do; but as yet I was bound by the iron chain of my own will. The enemy held fast my will, and had made of it a chain, and had bound me tight with it. For out of the perverse will came lust, and the service of lust ended in habit, and habit, not resisted, became necessity. By these links, as it were, forged together— which is why I called it "a chain"—a hard bondage held me in slavery. But that new will which had begun to spring up in me freely to worship thee and to enjoy thee, O my God, the only certain Joy, was not able as yet to overcome my former willfulness, made strong by long indulgence. Thus my two wills—the old and the new, the carnal and the spiritual—were in conflict within me; and by their discord they tore my soul apart.

11. Thus I came to understand from my own experience what I had read, how "the flesh lusts against the Spirit, and the Spirit against the flesh."[71] I truly lusted both ways, yet more in that which

---

[70] II Tim. 2:21.
[71] Gal. 5:17.

I approved in myself than in that which I disapproved in myself. For in the latter it was not now really I that was involved, because here I was rather an unwilling sufferer than a willing actor. And yet it was through me that habit had become an armed enemy against me, because I had willingly come to be what I unwillingly found myself to be.

Who, then, can with any justice speak against it, when just punishment follows the sinner? I had now no longer my accustomed excuse that, as yet, I hesitated to forsake the world and serve thee because my perception of the truth was uncertain. For now it was certain. But, still bound to the earth, I refused to be thy soldier; and was as much afraid of being freed from all entanglements as we ought to fear to be entangled.

12. Thus with the baggage of the world I was sweetly burdened, as one in slumber, and my musings on thee were like the efforts of those who desire to awake, but who are still overpowered with drowsiness and fall back into deep slumber. And as no one wishes to sleep forever (for all men rightly count waking better)—yet a man will usually defer shaking off his drowsiness when there is a heavy lethargy in his limbs; and he is glad to sleep on even when his reason disapproves, and the hour for rising has struck—so was I assured that it was much better for me to give myself up to thy love than to go on yielding myself to my own lust. Thy love satisfied and vanquished me; my lust pleased and fettered me.[72] I had no answer to thy calling to me, "Awake, you who sleep, and arise from the dead, and Christ shall give you light."[73] On all sides, thou didst show me that thy words are true, and I, convicted by the truth, had nothing at all to reply but the drawling and drowsy words: "Presently; see, presently. Leave me alone a little while." But "presently, presently," had no present; and my "leave me alone a little while" went on for a long while. In vain did I "delight in thy law in the inner man" while "another law in my members warred against the law of my mind and brought me into captivity to the law of sin which is in my members." For the law of sin is the tyranny of habit, by which the mind is drawn and held, even against its will. Yet it deserves to be so held because it so willingly falls into the habit. "O wretched man that I am! Who

---

[72] The text here is a typical example of Augustine's love of wordplay and assonance, as a conscious literary device: *tuae caritati me* dedere *quam meae cupiditati* cedere; *sed illud* placebat *et* vincebat, *hoc* libebat *et* vinciebat.

[73] Eph. 5:14.

shall deliver me from the body of this death" but thy grace alone, through Jesus Christ our Lord?[74]

CHAPTER VI

13. And now I will tell and confess unto thy name, O Lord, my helper and my redeemer, how thou didst deliver me from the chain of sexual desire by which I was so tightly held, and from the slavery of worldly business.[75] With increasing anxiety I was going about my usual affairs, and daily sighing to thee. I attended thy church as frequently as my business, under the burden of which I groaned, left me free to do so. Alypius was with me, disengaged at last from his legal post, after a third term as assessor, and now waiting for private clients to whom he might sell his legal advice as I sold the power of speaking (as if it could be supplied by teaching). But Nebridius had consented, for the sake of our friendship, to teach under Verecundus—a citizen of Milan and professor of grammar, and a very intimate friend of us all—who ardently desired, and by right of friendship demanded from us, the faithful aid he greatly needed. Nebridius was not drawn to this by any desire of gain—for he could have made much more out of his learning had he been so inclined—but as he was a most sweet and kindly friend, he was unwilling, out of respect for the duties of friendship, to slight our request. But in this he acted very discreetly, taking care not to become known to those persons who had great reputations in the world. Thus he avoided all distractions of mind, and reserved as many hours as possible to pursue or read or listen to discussions about wisdom.

14. On a certain day, then, when Nebridius was away—for some reason I cannot remember—there came to visit Alypius and me at our house one Ponticianus, a fellow countryman of ours from Africa, who held high office in the emperor's court. What he wanted with us I do not know; but we sat down to talk together, and it chanced that he noticed a book on a game table before us. He took it up, opened it, and, contrary to his expectation, found it to be the

---

[74] Rom. 7:22–25.

[75] The last obstacles that remained. His intellectual difficulties had been cleared away and the intention to become a Christian had become strong. But incontinence and immersion in his career were too firmly fixed in habit to be overcome by an act of conscious resolution.

apostle Paul, for he imagined that it was one of my wearisome rhetoric textbooks. At this, he looked up at me with a smile and expressed his delight and wonder that he had so unexpectedly found this book and only this one, lying before my eyes; for he was indeed a Christian and a faithful one at that, and often he prostrated himself before thee, our God, in the church in constant daily prayer. When I had told him that I had given much attention to these writings, a conversation followed in which he spoke of Anthony, the Egyptian monk, whose name was in high repute among thy servants, although up to that time not familiar to me. When he learned this, he lingered on the topic, giving us an account of this eminent man, and marveling at our ignorance. We in turn were amazed to hear of thy wonderful works so fully manifested in recent times—almost in our own—occurring in the true faith and the Catholic Church. We all wondered—we, that these things were so great, and he, that we had never heard of them.

15. From this, his conversation turned to the multitudes in the monasteries and their manners so fragrant to thee, and to the teeming solitudes of the wilderness, of which we knew nothing at all. There was even a monastery at Milan, outside the city's walls, full of good brothers under the fostering care of Ambrose—and we were ignorant of it. He went on with his story, and we listened intently and in silence. He then told us how, on a certain afternoon, at Trier,[76] when the emperor was occupied watching the gladiatorial games, he and three comrades went out for a walk in the gardens close to the city walls. There, as they chanced to walk two by two, one strolled away with him, while the other two went on by themselves. As they rambled, these first two came upon a certain cottage where lived some of thy servants, some of the "poor in spirit" ("of such is the Kingdom of Heaven"), where they found the book in which was written the life of Anthony! One of them began to read it, to marvel and to be inflamed by it. While reading, he meditated on embracing just such a life, giving up his worldly employment to seek thee alone. These two belonged to the group of officials called "secret service agents."[77] Then, suddenly being overwhelmed with a holy love and

---

[76] Trèves, an important imperial town on the Moselle; the emperor referred to here was probably Gratian. Cf. E. A. Freeman, "Augusta Trevororum," in the *British Quarterly Review* (1875), 62, pp. 1–45.

[77] *Agentes in rebus*, government agents whose duties ranged from postal inspection and tax collection to espionage and secret police work. They were ubiquitous

a sober shame and as if in anger with himself, he fixed his eyes on his friend, exclaiming: "Tell me, I beg you, what goal are we seeking in all these toils of ours? What is it that we desire? What is our motive in public service? Can our hopes in the court rise higher than to be 'friends of the emperor'[78]? But how frail, how beset with peril, is that pride! Through what dangers must we climb to a greater danger? And when shall we succeed? But if I chose to become a friend of God, see, I can become one now." Thus he spoke, and in the pangs of the travail of the new life he turned his eyes again onto the page and continued reading; he was inwardly changed, as thou didst see, and the world dropped away from his mind, as soon became plain to others. For as he read with a heart like a stormy sea, more than once he groaned. Finally he saw the better course, and resolved on it. Then, having become thy servant, he said to his friend: "Now I have broken loose from those hopes we had, and I am determined to serve God; and I enter into that service from this hour in this place. If you are reluctant to imitate me, do not oppose me." The other replied that he would continue bound in his friendship, to share in so great a service for so great a prize. So both became thine, and began to "build a tower," counting the cost—namely, of forsaking all that they had and following thee.[79] Shortly after, Ponticianus and his companion, who had walked with him in the other part of the garden, came in search of them to the same place, and having found them reminded them to return, as the day was declining. But the first two, making known to Ponticianus their resolution and purpose, and how a resolve had sprung up and become confirmed in them, entreated them not to take it ill if they refused to join themselves with them. But Ponticianus and his friend, although not changed from their former course, did nevertheless (as he told us) bewail themselves and congratulated their friends on their godliness, recommending themselves to their prayers. And with hearts inclining again toward earthly things, they returned to the palace. But the other two, setting their affections on heavenly things, remained in the cottage. Both of them had affianced brides who, when they heard of this, likewise dedicated their virginity to thee.

---

and generally dreaded by the populace; cf. J. S. Reid, "Reorganization of the Empire," in *Cambridge Medieval History*, Vol. I, pp. 36–38.

[78] The inner circle of imperial advisers; usually rather informally appointed and usually with precarious tenure.

[79] Cf. Luke 14:28–33.

CHAPTER VII

16. Such was the story Ponticianus told. But while he was speaking, thou, O Lord, turned me toward myself, taking me from behind my back, where I had put myself while unwilling to exercise self-scrutiny. And now thou didst set me face to face with myself, that I might see how ugly I was, and how crooked and sordid, bespotted and ulcerous. And I looked and I loathed myself; but whither to fly from myself I could not discover. And if I sought to turn my gaze away from myself, he would continue his narrative, and thou wouldst oppose me to myself and thrust me before my own eyes that I might discover my iniquity and hate it. I had known it, but acted as though I knew it not—I winked at it and forgot it.

17. But now, the more ardently I loved those whose wholesome affections I heard reported—that they had given themselves up wholly to thee to be cured—the more did I abhor myself when compared with them. For many of my years— perhaps twelve—had passed away since my nineteenth, when, upon the reading of Cicero's *Hortensius*, I was roused to a desire for wisdom. And here I was, still postponing the abandonment of this world's happiness to devote myself to the search. For not just the finding alone, but also the bare search for it, ought to have been preferred above the treasures and kingdoms of this world; better than all bodily pleasures, though they were to be had for the taking. But, wretched youth that I was— supremely wretched even in the very outset of my youth—I had entreated chastity of thee and had prayed, "Grant me chastity and continence, but not yet." For I was afraid lest thou shouldst hear me too soon, and too soon cure me of my disease of lust which I desired to have satisfied rather than extinguished. And I had wandered through perverse ways of godless superstition—not really sure of it, either, but preferring it to the other, which I did not seek in piety, but opposed in malice.

18. And I had thought that I delayed from day to day in rejecting those worldly hopes and following thee alone because there did not appear anything certain by which I could direct my course. And now the day had arrived in which I was laid bare to myself and my conscience was to chide me: "Where are you, O my tongue? You said indeed that you were not willing to cast off the baggage of vanity for uncertain truth. But behold now it is certain, and still that burden oppresses you. At the same time those who have not worn themselves out with searching for it as you have, nor spent ten years and more

in thinking about it, have had their shoulders unburdened and have received wings to fly away." Thus was I inwardly confused, and mightily confounded with a horrible shame, while Ponticianus went ahead speaking such things. And when he had finished his story and the business he came for, he went his way. And then what did I not say to myself, within myself? With what scourges of rebuke did I not lash my soul to make it follow me, as I was struggling to go after thee? Yet it drew back. It refused. It would not make an effort. All its arguments were exhausted and confuted. Yet it resisted in sullen disquiet, fearing the cutting off of that habit by which it was being wasted to death, as if that were death itself.

CHAPTER VIII

19. Then, as this vehement quarrel, which I waged with my soul in the chamber of my heart, was raging inside my inner dwelling, agitated both in mind and countenance, I seized upon Alypius and exclaimed: "What is the matter with us? What is this? What did you hear? The uninstructed start up and take heaven, and we—with all our learning but so little heart—see where we wallow in flesh and blood! Because others have gone before us, are we ashamed to follow, and not rather ashamed at our not following?" I scarcely knew what I said, and in my excitement I flung away from him, while he gazed at me in silent astonishment. For I did not sound like myself: my face, eyes, color, tone expressed my meaning more clearly than my words.

There was a little garden belonging to our lodging, of which we had the use—as of the whole house—for the master, our landlord, did not live there. The tempest in my breast hurried me out into this garden, where no one might interrupt the fiery struggle in which I was engaged with myself, until it came to the outcome that thou knewest though I did not. But I was mad for health, and dying for life; knowing what evil thing I was, but not knowing what good thing I was so shortly to become.

I fled into the garden, with Alypius following step by step; for I had no secret in which he did not share, and how could he leave me in such distress? We sat down, as far from the house as possible. I was greatly disturbed in spirit, angry at myself with a turbulent indignation because I had not entered thy will and covenant, O my God, while all my bones cried out to me to enter, extolling it to the skies.

The way therein is not by ships or chariots or feet—indeed it was not as far as I had come from the house to the place where we were seated. For to go along that road and indeed to reach the goal is nothing else but the will to go. But it must be a strong and single will, not staggering and swaying about this way and that—a changeable, twisting, fluctuating will, wrestling with itself while one part falls as another rises.

20. Finally, in the very fever of my indecision, I made many motions with my body; like men do when they will to act but cannot, either because they do not have the limbs or because their limbs are bound or weakened by disease, or incapacitated in some other way. Thus if I tore my hair, struck my forehead, or, entwining my fingers, clasped my knee, these I did because I willed it. But I might have willed it and still not have done it, if the nerves had not obeyed my will. Many things then I did, in which the will and power to do were not the same. Yet I did not do that one thing which seemed to me infinitely more desirable, which before long I should have power to will because shortly when I willed, I would will with a single will. For in this, the power of willing is the power of doing; and as yet I could not do it. Thus my body more readily obeyed the slightest wish of the soul in moving its limbs at the order of my mind than my soul obeyed itself to accomplish in the will alone its great resolve.

CHAPTER IX

21. How can there be such a strange anomaly? And why is it? Let thy mercy shine on me, that I may inquire and find an answer, amid the dark labyrinth of human punishment and in the darkest contritions of the sons of Adam. Whence such an anomaly? And why should it be? The mind commands the body, and the body obeys. The mind commands itself and is resisted. The mind commands the hand to be moved and there is such readiness that the command is scarcely distinguished from the obedience in act. Yet the mind is mind, and the hand is body. The mind commands the mind to will, and yet though it be itself it does not obey itself. Whence this strange anomaly and why should it be? I repeat: The will commands itself to will, and could not give the command unless it wills; yet what is commanded is not done. But actually the will does not will entirely; therefore it does not command entirely. For as far as it wills, it

commands. And as far as it does not will, the thing commanded is not done. For the will commands that there be an act of will—not another, but itself. But it does not command entirely. Therefore, what is commanded does not happen; for if the will were whole and entire, it would not even command it to be, because it would already be. It is, therefore, no strange anomaly partly to will and partly to be unwilling. This is actually an infirmity of mind, which cannot wholly rise, while pressed down by habit, even though it is supported by the truth. And so there are two wills, because one of them is not whole, and what is present in this one is lacking in the other.

CHAPTER X

22. Let them perish from thy presence, O God, as vain talkers and deceivers of the soul perish, who, when they observe that there are two wills in the act of deliberation, go on to affirm that there are two kinds of minds in us: one good, the other evil. They are indeed themselves evil when they hold these evil opinions—and they shall become good only when they come to hold the truth and consent to the truth that thy apostle may say to them: "You were formerly in darkness, but now are you in the light in the Lord."[80] But they desired to be light, not "in the Lord," but in themselves. They conceived the nature of the soul to be the same as what God is, and thus have become a thicker darkness than they were; for in their dread arrogance they have gone farther away from thee, from thee "the true Light, that lights every man that comes into the world." Mark what you say and blush for shame; draw near to him and be enlightened, and your faces shall not be ashamed.[81]

While I was deliberating whether I would serve the Lord my God now, as I had long purposed to do, it was I who willed and it was also I who was unwilling. In either case, it was I. I neither willed with my whole will nor was I wholly unwilling. And so I was at war with myself and torn apart by myself. And this strife was against my will; yet it did not show the presence of another mind, but the punishment of my own. Thus it was no more I who did it, but the sin that dwelt in me—the punishment of a sin freely committed by Adam, and I was a son of Adam.

---

[80] Eph. 5:8.
[81] Cf. Ps. 34:5.

23. For if there are as many opposing natures as there are opposing wills, there will not be two but many more. If any man is trying to decide whether he should go to their conventicle or to the
theater, the Manicheans at once cry out, "See, here are two natures—
one good, drawing this way, another bad, drawing back that way;
for how else can you explain this indecision between conflicting
wills?" But I reply that both impulses are bad—that which draws
to them and that which draws back to the theater. But they do not
believe that the will which draws to them can be anything but
good. Suppose, then, that one of us should try to decide, and
through the conflict of his two wills should waver whether he
should go to the theater or to our church. Would not those also
waver about the answer here? For either they must confess, which
they are unwilling to do, that the will that leads to our church is
as good as that which carries their own adherents and those captivated by their mysteries; or else they must imagine that there are
two evil natures and two evil minds in one man, both at war with
each other, and then it will not be true what they say, that there is
one good and another bad. Else they must be converted to the
truth, and no longer deny that when anyone deliberates there is
one soul fluctuating between conflicting wills.

24. Let them no longer maintain that when they perceive two
wills to be contending with each other in the same man the contest
is between two opposing minds, of two opposing substances, from
two opposing principles, the one good and the other bad. Thus, O
true God, thou dost reprove and confute and convict them. For
both wills may be bad: as when a man tries to decide whether he
should kill a man by poison or by the sword; whether he should
take possession of this field or that one belonging to someone else,
when he cannot get both; whether he should squander his money
to buy pleasure or hold onto his money through the motive of
covetousness; whether he should go to the circus or to the theater,
if both are open on the same day; or, whether he should take a third
course, open at the same time, and rob another man's house; or, a
fourth option, whether he should commit adultery, if he has the
opportunity—all these things concurring in the same space of time
and all being equally longed for, although impossible to do at one
time. For the mind is pulled four ways by four antagonistic wills—
or even more, in view of the vast range of human desires—but even
the Manicheans do not affirm that there are these many different
substances. The same principle applies as in the action of good wills.

For I ask them, "Is it a good thing to have delight in reading the apostle, or is it a good thing to delight in a sober psalm, or is it a good thing to discourse on the gospel?" To each of these, they will answer, "It is good." But what, then, if all delight us equally and all at the same time? Do not different wills distract the mind when a man is trying to decide what he should choose? Yet they are all good, and are at variance with each other until one is chosen. When this is done the whole united will may go forward on a single track instead of remaining as it was before, divided in many ways. So also, when eternity attracts us from above, and the pleasure of earthly delight pulls us down from below, the soul does not will either the one or the other with all its force, but still it is the same soul that does not will this or that with a united will, and is therefore pulled apart with grievous perplexities, because for truth's sake it prefers this, but for custom's sake it does not lay that aside.

CHAPTER XI

25. Thus I was sick and tormented, reproaching myself more bitterly than ever, rolling and writhing in my chain till it should be utterly broken. By now I was held but slightly, but still was held. And thou, O Lord, didst press upon me in my inmost heart with a severe mercy, redoubling the lashes of fear and shame; lest I should again give way and that same slender remaining tie not be broken off, but recover strength and enchain me yet more securely.

I kept saying to myself, "See, let it be done now; let it be done now." And as I said this I all but came to a firm decision. I all but did it—yet I did not quite. Still I did not fall back to my old condition, but stood aside for a moment and drew breath. And I tried again, and lacked only a very little of reaching the resolve—and then somewhat less, and then all but touched and grasped it. Yet I still did not quite reach or touch or grasp the goal, because I hesitated to die to death and to live to life. And the worse way, to which I was habituated, was stronger in me than the better, which I had not tried. And up to the very moment in which I was to become another man, the nearer the moment approached, the greater horror did it strike in me. But it did not strike me back, nor turn me aside, but held me in suspense.

26. It was, in fact, my old mistresses, trifles of trifles and vanities of vanities, who still enthralled me. They tugged at my fleshly garments

and softly whispered: "Are you going to part with us? And from that moment will we never be with you any more? And from that moment will not this and that be forbidden you forever?" What were they suggesting to me in those words "this or that"? What is it they suggested, O my God? Let thy mercy guard the soul of thy servant from the vileness and the shame they did suggest! And now I scarcely heard them, for they were not openly showing themselves and opposing me face to face; but muttering, as it were, behind my back; and furtively plucking at me as I was leaving, trying to make me look back at them. Still they delayed me, so that I hesitated to break loose and shake myself free of them and leap over to the place to which I was being called—for unruly habit kept saying to me, "Do you think you can live without them?"

27. But now it said this very faintly; for in the direction I had set my face, and yet toward which I still trembled to go, the chaste dignity of continence appeared to me—cheerful but not wanton, modestly alluring me to come and doubt nothing, extending her holy hands, full of a multitude of good examples—to receive and embrace me. There were there so many young men and maidens, a multitude of youth and every age, grave widows and ancient virgins; and continence herself in their midst: not barren, but a fruitful mother of children—her joys—by thee, O Lord, her husband. And she smiled on me with a challenging smile as if to say: "Can you not do what these young men and maidens can? Or can any of them do it of themselves, and not rather in the Lord their God? The Lord their God gave me to them. Why do you stand in your own strength, and so stand not? Cast yourself on him; fear not. He will not flinch and you will not fall. Cast yourself on him without fear, for he will receive and heal you." And I blushed violently, for I still heard the muttering of those "trifles" and hung suspended. Again she seemed to speak: "Stop your ears against those unclean members of yours, that they may be mortified. They tell you of delights, but not according to the law of the Lord thy God." This struggle raging in my heart was nothing but the contest of self against self. And Alypius kept close beside me, and awaited in silence the outcome of my extraordinary agitation.

CHAPTER XII

28. Now when deep reflection had drawn up out of the secret depths of my soul all my misery and had heaped it up before the sight of my heart, there arose a mighty storm, accompanied by a mighty rain of tears. That I might give way fully to my tears and lamentations, I stole away from Alypius, for it seemed to me that solitude was more appropriate for the business of weeping. I went far enough away that I could feel that even his presence was no restraint upon me. This was the way I felt at the time, and he realized it. I suppose I had said something before I started up and he noticed that the sound of my voice was choked with weeping. And so he stayed alone, where we had been sitting together, greatly astonished. I flung myself down under a fig tree—how I know not—and gave free course to my tears. The streams of my eyes gushed out an acceptable sacrifice to thee. And, not indeed in these words, but to this effect, I cried to thee: "And thou, O Lord, how long? How long, O Lord? Wilt thou be angry forever? Oh, remember not against us our former iniquities."[82] For I felt that I was still enthralled by them. I sent up these sorrowful cries: "How long, how long? Tomorrow and tomorrow? Why not now? Why not this very hour make an end to my uncleanness?"

29. I was saying these things and weeping in the most bitter contrition of my heart, when suddenly I heard the voice of a boy or a girl—I know not which—coming from the neighboring house, chanting over and over again, "Pick it up, read it; pick it up, read it."[83] Immediately I ceased weeping and began most earnestly to think whether it was usual for children in some kind of game to sing such a song, but I could not remember ever having heard the like. So, damming the torrent of my tears, I got to my feet, for I could not but think that this was a divine command to open the Bible and read the first passage I should light upon. For I had heard[84] how Anthony, accidentally coming into church while the gospel was being read, received the admonition as if what was read had been addressed to him: "Go and sell what you have and give it to the poor, and you shall have treasure in heaven; and come and follow me."[85] By such an oracle he was forthwith converted to thee.

---

[82] Cf. Ps. 6:3; 79:8.
[83] This is the famous *Tolle, lege; tolle, lege.*
[84] Doubtless from Ponticianus, in their earlier conversation.
[85] Matt. 19:21.

So I quickly returned to the bench where Alypius was sitting, for there I had put down the apostle's book when I had left there. I snatched it up, opened it, and in silence read the paragraph on which my eyes first fell: "Not in rioting and drunkenness, not in chambering and wantonness, not in strife and envying, but put on the Lord Jesus Christ, and make no provision for the flesh to fulfill the lusts thereof."[86] I wanted to read no further, nor did I need to. For instantly, as the sentence ended, there was infused in my heart something like the light of full certainty and all the gloom of doubt vanished away.[87]

30. Closing the book, then, and putting my finger or something else for a mark I began—now with a tranquil countenance—to tell it all to Alypius. And he in turn disclosed to me what had been going on in himself, of which I knew nothing. He asked to see what I had read. I showed him, and he looked on even further than I had read. I had not known what followed. But indeed it was this, "Him that is weak in the faith, receive."[88] This he applied to himself, and told me so. By these words of warning he was strengthened, and by exercising his good resolution and purpose—all very much in keeping with his character, in which, in these respects, he was always far different from and better than I—he joined me in full commitment without any restless hesitation.

Then we went in to my mother, and told her what happened, to her great joy. We explained to her how it had occurred—and she leaped for joy triumphant; and she blessed thee, who art "able to do exceedingly abundantly above all that we ask or think."[89] For she saw that thou hadst granted her far more than she had ever asked for in all her pitiful and doleful lamentations. For thou didst so convert me to thee that I sought neither a wife nor any other of this world's hopes, but set my feet on that rule of faith which so many years before thou hadst showed her in her dream about me. And so thou didst turn her grief into gladness more plentiful than she had ventured to desire, and dearer and purer than the desire she used to cherish of having grandchildren of my flesh.

---

[86] Rom. 13:13.

[87] Note the parallels here to the conversion of Anthony and the *agentes in rebus*.

[88] Rom. 14:1.

[89] Eph. 3:20.

THE CONSOLATION OF PHILOSOPHY

Anicius Manlius Severinus Boethius

A tremendously influential book written in the sixth century A.D. that bridged the classical philosophy of the ancient world and the religious piety of the Middle Ages, The Consolation of Philosophy *was written in a prison cell by Anicius Manlius Severinus Boethius (c. 480–524), Roman scholar, theologian, philosopher, and statesman. Boethius was imprisoned by the Ostrogothic king Theodoric, probably on false charges of treason, and was eventually tried and executed.*

While awaiting his fate, Boethius wrote this dialogue in alternating prose and poetry between himself and his spiritual guardian. Its subject is the possibility of achieving happiness considering the suffering and disappointments that characterize human existence. As Richard H. Green, the translator, notes in his introduction,[1] "For the reader of the Christian Middle Ages, The Consolation of Philosophy *celebrated the life of the mind, or reason, and the possibility of its ultimate victory over the misfortunes and frustrations which attend fallen man's pursuit of transitory substitutes for the Supreme Good which alone can satisfy human desires." Reprinted here is Book One of* The Consolation of Philosophy *with the sections originally in poetry presented in a literal prose translation for the purpose of clarity.*

BOOK I

POEM 1

I who once wrote songs with keen delight am now by sorrow driven to take up melancholy measures. Wounded Muses tell me

---

[1] Richard H. Green, *Boethius, The Consolation of Philosophy*, translated with an Introduction and Notes (Indianapolis: Bobbs-Merrill Company, 1962).

what I must write, and elegiac verses bathe my face with real tears. Not even terror could drive from me these faithful companions of my long journey Poetry, which was once the glory of my happy and flourishing youth, is still my comfort in this misery of my old age.

Old age has come too soon with its evils, and sorrow has commanded me to enter the age which is hers. My hair is prematurely gray, and slack skin shakes on my exhausted body. Death, happy to men when she does not intrude in the sweet years, but comes when often called in sorrow, turns a deaf ear to the wretched and cruelly refuses to close weeping eyes.

The sad hour that has nearly drowned me came just at the time that faithless Fortune favored me with her worthless gifts. Now that she has clouded her deceitful face, my accursed life seems to go on endlessly. My friends, why did you so often think me happy? Any man who has fallen never stood securely.

PROSE 1

Lady Philosophy appears to him and drives away the Muses of poetry.

While I silently pondered these things, and decided to write down my wretched complaint, there appeared standing above me a woman of majestic countenance whose flashing eyes seemed wise beyond the ordinary wisdom of men. Her color was bright, suggesting boundless vigor, and yet she seemed so old that she could not be thought of as belonging to our age. Her height seemed to vary: sometimes she seemed of ordinary human stature, then again her head seemed to touch the top of the heavens. And when she raised herself to her full height she penetrated heaven itself, beyond the vision of human eyes. Her clothing was made of the most delicate threads, and by the most exquisite workmanship; it had—as she afterwards told me—been woven by her own hands into an everlasting fabric. Her clothes had been darkened in color somewhat by neglect and the passage of time, as happens to pictures exposed to smoke. At the lower edge of her robe was woven a Greek Π, at the top the letter Θ, and between them were seen clearly marked stages, like stairs, ascending from the lowest level to the highest.[2] This robe had been torn, however, by

---

[2] Π and Θ are the first letters of the Greek words for the two divisions of philosophy, theoretical and practical. Boethius wrote (*In Porph. Dial* I. 3): ". . . for

the hands of violent men, who had ripped away what they could. In her right hand, the woman held certain books; in her left hand, a scepter.

When she saw the Muses of poetry standing beside my bed and consoling me with their words, she was momentarily upset and glared at them with burning eyes.[3] "Who let these whores from the theater come to the bedside of this sick man?" she said. "They cannot offer medicine for his sorrows; they will nourish him only with their sweet poison. They kill the fruitful harvest of reason with the sterile thorns of the passions; they do not liberate the minds of men from disease, but merely accustom them to it. I would find it easier to bear if your flattery had, as it usually does, seduced some ordinary dull-witted man; in that case, it would have been no concern of mine. But this man has been educated in the philosophical schools of the Eleatics and the Academy.[4] Get out, you Sirens; your sweetness leads to death. Leave him to be cured and made strong by my Muses."

And so the defeated Muses, shamefaced and with downcast eyes, went sadly away. My sight was so dimmed by tears that I could not tell who this woman of imperious authority might be, and I lay there astonished, my eyes staring at the earth, silently waiting to see what she would do. She came nearer and sat at the foot of my bed. When she noticed my grief-stricken, downcast face, she reproved my anxiety with this song.

---

philosophy is a genus of which there are two species, one of which is called theoretical, the other practical, that is, speculative and active."

[3] Boethius' condemnation of the Muses provided the enemies of poetry in the later Middle Ages with a powerful, if specious, argument. In his authoritative and influential *Genealogy of the Gods,* Boccaccio argues that Boethius is here condemning only a certain kind of obscene theatrical poetry; he cites Boethius' extensive use of ancient poetry and myth as evidence of a high regard for poetry. See *Boccaccio on Poetry,* tr. C. G. Osgood, "Library of Liberal Arts," No. 82 (New York, 1956), pp. 94–96.

[4] The Eleatics represent a school of Greek philosophy at Elea in Italy. Zeno, one of its members in the fifth century B.C., was thought to be the inventor of dialectic, the art of reasoning about matters of opinion. The Academy is the traditional name for Plato's school of philosophy.

POEM 2

"Alas! how this mind is dulled, drowned in the overwhelming depths. It wanders in outer darkness, deprived of its natural light. Sick anxiety, inflated by worldly winds, swells his thoughts to bursting.

"Once this man was free beneath the ocean heaven, and he used to run along heavenly paths. He saw the splendor of the red sun, the heaven of the cold moon. And any star that pursued its vagrant paths, returning through various spheres, this master understood by his computations.

"Beyond all this, he sought the causes of things: why the sighing winds vex the seawaves; what spirit turns the stable world; and why the sun rises out of the red east to fall beneath the western ocean. He sought to know what tempers the gentle hours of spring and makes them adorn the earth with rosy flowers; what causes fertile autumn to flow with bursting grapes in a good year.

"This man used to explore and reveal Nature's secret causes. Now he lies here, bound down by heavy chains, the light of his mind gone out; his head is bowed down and he is forced to stare at the dull earth.

PROSE 2

Seeing his desperate condition, Philosophy speaks more gently and promises to cure him.

"But," she said, "it is time for medicine rather than complaint," Fixing me with her eyes, she said: "Are you not he who once was nourished by my milk and brought up on my food; who emerged from weakness to the strength of a virile soul? I gave you weapons that would have protected you with invincible power, if you had not thrown them away. Don't you recognize me? Why don't you speak? Is it shame or astonishment that makes you silent? I'd rather it were shame, but I see that you are overcome by shock." When she saw that I was not only silent but struck dumb, she gently laid her hand on my breast and said: "There is no danger. You are suffering merely from lethargy, the common illness of deceived minds. You have forgotten yourself a little, but you will quickly be yourself again when you recognize me. To bring you to your senses, I shall quickly wipe the dark cloud of mortal things from your eyes." Then, she dried my tear-filled eyes with a fold of her robe.

POEM 3

Then, when the night was over, darkness left me and my eyes regained their former strength; just as when the stars are covered by swift Corus, and the sky is darkened by storm clouds, the sun hides and the stars do not shine; night comes down to envelop the earth. But if Boreas, blowing from his Thracian cave, beats and lays open the hiding day, then Phoebus shines forth, glittering with sudden light, and strikes our astonished eyes with his rays.[5]

PROSE 3

Boethius recognizes Lady Philosophy. She promises to help him as she has always helped those who love and serve her.

In a similar way, I too was able to see the heavens again when the clouds of my sorrow were swept away; I recovered my judgment and recognized the face of my physician. When I looked at her closely, I saw that she was Philosophy, my nurse, in whose house I had lived from my youth. "Mistress of all virtues," I said, "why have you come, leaving the arc of heaven, to this lonely desert of our exile? Are you a prisoner, too, charged as I am with false accusations?"

She answered, "How could I desert my child, and not share with you the burden of sorrow you carry, a burden caused by hatred of my name? Philosophy has never thought it right to leave the innocent man alone on his journey. Should I fear to face my accusers, as though their enmity were something new? Do you suppose that this is the first time wisdom has been attacked and endangered by wicked men? We fought against such rashness and folly long ago, even before the time of our disciple Plato. And in Plato's own time, his master Socrates, with my help, merited the victory of an unjust death.[6] Afterwards, the inept schools of Epicureans, Stoics, and others, each seeking its own interests, tried to steal the inheritance of Socrates and to possess

---

[5] Corus, the north-west wind; Boreas, the north wind. Thrace, part of modern Turkey, was regarded by the ancients as an extreme northern place. Phoebus is the sun.

[6] Socrates was accused of corrupting youth and ridiculing the gods. In 399 B.C., the Athenian state condemned him to death (by drinking poison). For a description of the death scene of Socrates, see Plato, *Phaedo* 115a–118.

me (in spite of my protests and struggles), as though I were the spoils of their quarreling. They tore this robe which I had woven with my own hands and, having ripped off some little pieces of it, went away supposing that they possessed me wholly.[7] Then, when traces of my garments were seen on some of them, they were rashly thought to be my friends, and they were therefore condemned by the error of the profane mob.

"Perhaps you have not heard of the banishment of Anaxagoras, the poisoning of Socrates, the torments of Zeno,[8] for these men were strange to you. But you probably know about Canius, Seneca, and Soranus,[9] for their fame is recent and widely known. They were disgraced only because they had been trained in my studies and therefore seemed obnoxious to wicked men. You should not be surprised, then, if we are blown about by stormy winds in the voyage of this life, since our main duty is to oppose the wicked. But, even though our enemies are numerous, we should spurn them because they are without leadership and are driven frantically this way and that by error. And if they sometimes attack us with extraordinary force, our leader withdraws her followers into a fortress, leaving our enemies to waste their energies on worthless spoils. While they fight over things of no value, we laugh at them from above, safe from their fury and defended by a strength against which their aggressive folly cannot prevail.

---

[7] Boethius, and most other medieval thinkers until the late thirteenth century, regarded Plato as the greatest of the ancient philosophers. Philosophy's robe is the figure of the unity of true philosophy; this unity was, in Boethius' opinion, shattered by such limited philosophies as Epicureanism, based on the principle of pleasure, and Stoicism, based on the principle that whatever happens must be accepted without grief or joy. Epicurus founded his school in Greece late in the fourth century B.C. The Stoic school was founded by Zeno of Athens at about the same time.

[8] Anaxagoras, a Greek astronomer and philosopher, was banished from Athens when his theory of the heavens led to his being accused of impiety. He was exiled about 450 B.C. Zeno of Elea was tortured by Nearchus from whose tyranny he had sought to deliver his country. Boethus is comparing his own predicament to those of earlier philosophers who were punished for honoring their principles.

[9] Julius Canius was executed about A.D. 40 for reproaching the Roman Emperor Caligula. Seneca, the great Roman poet and philosopher of the first century, and a high public official under Nero, was accused of conspiracy by the emperor and forced to commit suicide. Soranus was also a victim of Nero's tyranny; he was condemned to death in A.D. 66.

POEM 4

"The serene man who has ordered his life stands above menacing fate and unflinchingly faces good and bad fortune. This virtuous man can hold up his head unconquered. The threatening and raging ocean storms which churn the waves cannot shake him; nor can the bursting furnace of Vesuvius, aimlessly throwing out its smoky fire; nor the fiery bolts of lightning which can topple the highest towers. Why then are we wretched, frightened by fierce tyrants who rage without the power to harm us? He who hopes for nothing and fears nothing can disarm the fury of these impotent men; but he who is burdened by fears and desires is not master of himself. He throws away his shield and retreats; he fastens the chain by which he will be drawn.

PROSE 4

Boethius gives an account of his public career and especially of the causes of his present misery.[10]

"Do you understand what I have told you," Philosophy asked; "have my words impressed you at all, or are you 'like the ass which cannot hear the lyre'?[11] Why are you crying? Speak out, don't hide what troubles you. If you want a doctor's help, you must uncover your wound."[12]

I pulled myself together and answered: "Do I have to explain; isn't the misery of my misfortune evident enough? I should think this place alone would make you pity me. Compare this prison with my library at home which you chose as your own and in which you often discussed with me the knowledge of human and divine things. Did I look like this? Was I dressed this way when I studied nature's mysteries with you, when you mapped the courses of the stars for me with your geometer's rod, when you formed my moral standards and my whole view of life according to the norm of the heavenly

---

[10] Refer to introductory note on page 56 above regarding the historical circumstances of Boethius' imprisonment and death.

[11] Boethius here cites the Greek proverb: ὄνος λύρας.

[12] Cf. Homer, *Iliad* I. 363.

order?[13] Are these miseries the rewards your servants should expect? You yourself proposed the course I have followed when you made Plato say that civil governments would be good if wise men were appointed rulers, or if those appointed to rule would study wisdom.[14] Further, you decreed in the words of the same philosopher that government of the commonwealth ought to be in the hands of wise men; that if it should be left to unscrupulous and wicked men, they would bring about the ruin of the good.[15]

"On this authority, I decided to apply to public administration the principles I had learned privately from you. You, and God who gave you to the minds of wise men, know that I became a magistrate only because of the unanimous wish of all good men. For these reasons I have become involved in grave and hopeless trouble with dishonest men; and, as always happens to the administrator of independent conscience, I have had to be willing to make powerful enemies in the interest of safeguarding justice.

"I have often opposed the greed of Conigastus in his swindling of the poor. I have condemned the crimes of Triguilla, Provost of the King's house, both in their beginnings and after they had been committed. At grave risk to my position I have protected the weak from the lies and avarice of cruel men in power. No man ever corrupted my administration of justice. I was as depressed as those who suffered the losses when I saw the wealth of our citizens dissipated either by private fraud or oppressive taxation. At the time of the severe famine, when prices were set so exorbitantly high that the province of Campania seemed about to starve, I carried on the people's fight against the Praetorian Prefect himself and, with the King's approval, I won—the fixed prices were not enforced.

"I saved Paulinus, the former Consul, from the howling dogs of the court who hoped to devour his wealth. In order to save Albinus, another former Consul, from unjust punishment, I risked the hatred of his accuser, Cyprian. One would think I had stirred up enough opposition. But I ought to have been defended by others, especially since, through devotion to justice, I had given up the favor of the courtiers who might have saved me. But who were the accusers who overthrew me? One of them was Basil who had earlier been expelled from the King's service and was now forced by his debts to testify

---

[13] Cf. Plato, *Republic* 592b.
[14] Cf. Plato, *Republic* 473d, 487e.
[15] Cf. Plato, *Epistle X* 350b; *Republic* 347c.

against me. My other accusers were Opilio and Gaudentius, also men banished by royal decree for their many corrupt practices. They tried to avoid exile by taking sanctuary, but when the King heard of it he decreed that, if they did not leave Ravenna by a certain day, they should be branded on the forehead and forcibly expelled. How could the King's judgment have been more severe? And yet on that very day their testimony against me was accepted. Why should this have happened? Did I deserve it? Did their criminal records make them just accusers? Fortune ought to have been shamed, if not by the innocence of the accused, then at least by the villainy of the accusers.

"Finally, what am I accused of? They say I desired the safety of the Senate. But how? I am convicted of having hindered their accuser from giving evidence that the Senate is guilty of treason. What is your judgment, my teacher? Shall I deny the charge in order to avoid shaming you? But I did desire to protect the Senate, and I always will. And how can I confess, since I have already stopped hindering their accuser? Shall I consider it a crime to have supported the integrity of the Senate? It is true that the Senate itself, by its decrees against me, has made my position a crime. But folly, driven by self-deception, cannot change the merits of the case; nor, following the rule of Socrates, can I think it right either to hide the truth or concede a lie.[16] I leave it to you, and to the judgment of the wise, whether my course of action is right. I have put this in writing so that posterity may know the truth and have a record of these events.

"Why should I even mention the spurious letters in which I am charged with having hoped for Roman liberty? That fraud would have been exposed had I been permitted to use the confession of my accusers, the strongest evidence in any case. But there is now no hope for freedom of any kind—I only wish there were. I should have answered in the words of Canius when Gaius Caesar, son of Germanicus,[17] accused Canius of having known of a conspiracy against him: 'If I had known of it,' Canius said, 'you would never have known.' But I am not so discouraged by what has happened to me that I complain now of the attacks of wicked men against virtue; the reason for my surprise is that they have accomplished what they set out to do. The desire to do evil may be due to human weakness; but for the wicked to overcome the innocent in the sight of God— that is monstrous. I cannot blame that friend of yours who said, 'If

---

[16] Plato, *Theaetetus* 151d and *Republic* 485c.
[17] Gaius Caesar is the Emperor Caligula. (See above, note 8.)

there is a God, why is there evil? And if there is no God, how can there be good?'[18] It is not surprising that evil men, who want to destroy all just men, and the Senate too, should try to overthrow one who stood up for justice and the Senate. But surely I did not deserve the same treatment from the Senators themselves.

"You remember well that you always directed me in everything I said and everything I tried to do or say. You recall, for example, the time at Verona when the King wanted to overturn the government and tried to involve the whole Senate in the treason of which Albinus was accused; then, at great risk to my personal safety I defended the innocence of the whole Senate. You know that this is true, and that I have never acted out of a desire for praise; for integrity of conscience is somehow spoiled when a man advertises what he has done and receives the reward of public recognition. But you see where my innocence has brought me; instead of being rewarded for true virtue, I am falsely punished as a criminal. Even the full confession of a crime does not usually make all the judges in the case equally severe; some, at least, temper their severity by recognizing the errors of human judgment and the uncertain conditions of fortune to which all mortals are subject. If I had been accused of plotting the burning of churches, the murder of priests, even the murder of all good men, even then I would have been sentenced only after I had confessed and been convicted, and when I was present before the court. But now, five hundred miles away, mute and defenseless, I am condemned to proscription and death because of my concern for the safety of the Senate. The Senate deserves that no one should ever again be convicted for such a 'crime'!

"Even my accusers understood the honor implicit in the charges they brought against me, and, in order to confuse the issue by the appearance of some crime, they falsely alleged that I had corrupted my conscience with sacrilege out of a desire for advancement. But your spirit, alive within me, had driven from my soul all sordid desire for earthly success, and those whom you protect do not commit sacrilege. You have daily reminded me of Pythagoras' saying: 'Follow God.'[19] It is not likely that I would have sought the protection of evil spirits at a time when you were forming in me that

---

[18] The friend is Epicurus; the quotation is from Lactantius, *De ira Dei* 13. 21.

[19] Boethius gives the Greek ἔπου θεῷ This saying of Pythagoras is quoted frequently in classical literature, e.g., Iamblichus, *Vita Pyth.* 18 (86), and Seneca, *De vita beata* 15. 5.

excellence which makes man like God. Moreover, the innocence of my family, the honesty of my closest friends, the goodness of my father-in-law,[20] who is as worthy of honor as yourself—all these ought to have shielded me from any suspicion of this crime. But the worst is that my enemies readily believe that wisdom itself is capable of the crime of ambition, and so they associate me with such misconduct because I am imbued with your knowledge and endowed with your virtues. So, my reverence for you is no help; their hatred of me leads them to dishonor you.

"Finally, and this is the last straw, the judgment of most people is based not on the merits of a case but on the fortune of its outcome; they think that only things which turn out happily are good. As a result, the first thing an unfortunate man loses is his good reputation. I cannot bear to think of the rumors and various opinions that are now going around; I can only say that the final misery of adverse fortune is that when some poor man is accused of a crime, it is thought that he deserves whatever punishment he has to suffer. Well, here am I, stripped of my possessions and honors, my reputation ruined, punished because I tried to do good.

"It seems to me that I can see wicked men everywhere celebrating my fall with great pleasure, and all the criminally depraved concocting new false charges. I see good men terrorized into helplessness by my danger, and evil men encouraged to risk any crime with impunity and able to get away with it by bribery. The innocent are deprived not only of their safety, but even of any defense. Now hear my appeal.

POEM 5

Boethius concludes with a prayer.

"Creator of the star-filled universe, seated upon your eternal throne You move the heavens in their swift orbits. You hold the stars in their assigned paths, so that sometimes the shining moon is full in the light of her brother sun and hides the lesser stars; sometimes, nearer the sun she wanes and loses her glory. You ordain that Hesperus, after rising at nightfall to drive the cold stars before him, should change his role and, as Lucifer, grow pale before the rising sun.[21]

---

[20] Symmachus, also executed by Theodoric.

[21] Evening Star (Hesperus) and Morning Star (Lucifer) both signify the planet Venus. Literally the poet says that Hesperus changes his customary reins (i.e., his

"When the cold of winter makes the trees bare, You shorten the day to a briefer span; but when warm summer comes, You make the night hours go swiftly. Your power governs the changing year: in spring, Zephyrus renews the delicate leaves[22] that Boreas, the wind of winter, had destroyed; and Sirius burns the high corn in autumn that Arcturus had seen in seed.[23]

"Nothing escapes Your ancient law; nothing can avoid the work of its proper station. You govern all things, each according to its destined purpose. Human acts alone, O Ruler of All, You refuse to restrain within just bounds. Why should uncertain Fortune control our lives?

"Harsh punishment, deserved by the criminal, afflicts the innocent. Immoral scoundrels now occupy positions of power and unjustly trample the rights of good men. Virtue, which ought to shine forth, is covered up and hides in darkness, while good men must suffer for the crimes of the wicked. Perjury and deceit are not held blameworthy as long as they are covered by the color of lies. When these scoundrels choose to use their power they can intimidate even powerful kings, because the masses fear them.

"O God, whoever you are who joins all things in perfect harmony, look down upon this miserable earth! We men are no small part of Your great work, yet we wallow here in the stormy sea of fortune. Ruler of all things, calm the roiling waves and, as You rule the immense heavens, rule also the earth in stable concord."

PROSE 5

Philosophy suggests that the source of the prisoner's trouble is within himself and begins to reassure him.

While I poured out my long sad story, Philosophy looked on amiably, quite undismayed by my complaints. Then she said: "When I first saw you downcast and crying, I knew you were in misery and exile. But without your story I would not have known how desperate your exile is. You have not been driven out of your homeland; you have willfully wandered away. Or, if you prefer to think that

---

chariot) to become Lucifer.

[22] Zephyrus, the west wind, was said to produce fruits and flowers by his breath.

[23] Sirius, the dog-star, supposedly supplied great heat to cause crops to ripen. Arcturus was the brightest star in the constellation Boötes.

you have been driven into exile, you yourself have done the driving, since no one else could do it. For if you can remember your true country you know that it is not, as Athens once was, ruled by many persons; rather 'it has one ruler and one king,'[24] who rejoices in the presence of citizens, not in their expulsion. To be governed by his power and subject to his laws is the greatest liberty. Surely you know the oldest law of your true city, that the citizen who has chosen to establish his home there has a sacred right not to be driven away.[25] The man who lives within the walls of that city need not fear banishment; but if he loses his desire to live there, he loses also the assurance of safety. And so, I am not so much disturbed by this prison as by your attitude. I do not need your library with its glass walls and ivory decoration, but I do need my place in your mind. For there I have placed not books but that which gives value to books, the ideas which are found in my writings.

"What you have said about your merits in the commonwealth is true; your many services deserve even more than you claim. And what you have said about the truth or falsity of the accusations against you is well known to everyone. You were right to speak sparingly of the crimes and deceit of your enemies; such things are better talked about by the man in the street who hears about them. You have sharply protested the injustice done you by the Senate; and you have expressed sorrow for the accusations against me and the weakening of my place in the public esteem. Finally, you protested against Fortune in sorrow and anger, and complained that rewards are not distributed equally on the grounds of merit. At the end of your bitter poem, you expressed the hope that the same peace which rules the heavens might also rule the earth. But because you are so upset by sorrow and anger, and so blown about by the tumult of your feelings, you are not now in the right frame of mind to take strong medicine. For the time being, then, I shall use more gentle treatment, so that your hardened and excited condition may be softened by gentle handling and thus prepared for more potent remedies.

---

[24] Homer, *Iliad* II. 204.

[25] Boethius compares the inner security of the philosopher with the civil rights provided by Roman law.

POEM 6

"The fool who plants his seed in the hard ground when summer burns with the sun's heat[26] must feed on acorns in the fall, because his hope of harvest is in vain. Do not look for violets in purple meadows when fields are blasted by winter winds. And do not cut your vine branches in the spring if you want to enjoy the grapes, for Bacchus brings his fruit in autumn.[27]

"God assigns to every season its proper office; and He does not permit the condition He has set to be altered. Every violent effort to upset His established order will fail in the end.

PROSE 6

Philosophy begins to remind Boethius of certain basic truths which will place his misfortunes in proper perspective.

"First," Philosophy said, "will you let me test your present attitude with a few questions, so that I can decide on a way to cure you?"

"Ask whatever you like," I replied, "and I will try to answer."

"Do you think," she began, "that this world is subject to random chance, or do you believe that it is governed by some rational principle?"

"I cannot suppose that its regular operation can be the result of mere chance; indeed, I know that God the Creator governs his work, and the day will never come when I can be shaken from the truth of this judgment."

"That is true," Philosophy answered, "and you said as much in your poem a while ago when you deplored the fact that only men were outside Gods care. You did not doubt that all other things were ruled by reason. Strange, isn't it, that one who has so healthy an attitude should be so sick with despair. We must search further, because obviously something is missing. Tell me, since you have no doubt that the world is ruled by God, do you know *how* it is governed?"

"I don't quite get the point of your question, so I am unable to answer."

---

[26] Literally, "when the sign of Cancer, heavy with the rays of Apollo, burns down."

[27] Bacchus, god of wine.

"You see, I was right in thinking that you had some weakness, like a breach in the wall of a fort, through which the sickness of anxiety found its way into your soul.

"But tell me, do you remember what the end, or goal, of all things is—the goal toward which all nature is directed?"

"I heard it once," I answered, "but grief has dulled my memory."

"Well, do you know where all things come from?"

I answered that I knew all things came from God.

"How then," she went on, "is it possible that you can know the origin of all things and still be ignorant of their purpose? But this is the usual result of anxiety; it can change a man, but it cannot break him and cannot destroy him.

I want you to answer this, too: do you remember that you are a man?"

"How could I forget that," I answered.

"Well then, what is a man? Can you give me a definition?"

"Do you mean that I am a rational animal, and mortal? I know that, and I admit that I am such a creature."

"Do you know nothing else about what you are?"

"No, nothing."

"Now, I know another cause of your sickness, and the most important: you have forgotten what you are. And so I am fully aware of the reason for your sickness and the remedy for it too. You are confused because you have forgotten what you are, and, therefore, you are upset because you are in exile and stripped of all your possessions. Because you are ignorant of the purpose of things, you think that stupid and evil men are powerful and happy. And, because you have forgotten how the world is governed, you suppose that these changes of your fortune came about without purpose. Such notions are enough to cause not only sickness but death. But be grateful to the Giver of health that nature has not entirely forsaken you. For you have the best medicine for your health in your grasp of the truth about the way the world is governed. You believe that the world is not subject to the accidents of chance, but to divine reason. Therefore, you have nothing to fear. From this tiny spark, the living fire can be rekindled. But the time has not yet come for stronger remedies. It is the nature of men's minds that when they throw away the truth they embrace false ideas, and from these comes the cloud of anxiety which obscures their vision of truth. I shall try to dispel this cloud by gentle treatment, so that when the darkness of deceptive feeling is removed you may recognize the splendor of true light.

POEM 7

"Stars hidden by black clouds send down no light. If the wild south wind[28] churns up the sea, the waves which once were clear as glass, as clear as the bright days, seem muddy and filthy to the beholder. The flowing stream, tumbling down from the high mountain, is often blocked by the stone broken off from the rocky cliff.

"So it is with you. If you want to see the truth in clear light, and follow the right road, you must cast off all joy and fear. Fly from hope and sorrow. When these things rule, the mind is clouded and bound to the earth."

---

[28] In the text the south wind is called Auster.

THE ECCLESIASTICAL HISTORY OF THE ENGLISH PEOPLE

The Venerable Bede

The first account of English history, The Ecclesiastical History of the English People, *was written in 731 A.D. by The Venerable Bede, a Northumbrian Monk. The manuscript chronicled the growth of Christianity in Anglo-Saxon England, starting with the Roman invasion of Britain led by Julius Caesar in 55–54 B.C. and ending with its author's death in the eighth century. Invaluable as a primary source from a period that did not produce a great deal of written documentation, it tells the tales and stories of the kings, bishops, monks, and nuns involved in the very early development of Britain's religious and political institutions. The three brief excerpts reprinted here give a good idea of the flavor of the work:*

1. Book III, Chapter VI: "Of King Oswald's wonderful piety and religion. (635–642 A.D.)"
2. Book III, Chapter XV: "How Bishop Aidan foretold to certain seamen that a storm would arise, and gave them some holy oil to calm it. (Between 642 and 645 A.D.)"
3. Book IV, Chapter XXI: "How Bishop Theodore made peace between the Kings Egfried and Ethelred. (679 A.D.)"

BOOK III

CHAPTER VI

Of King Oswald's wonderful piety and religion. [635–642 A.D.]

King Oswald, with the English nation which he governed, being instructed by the teaching of this bishop, not only learned to hope for a heavenly kingdom unknown to his fathers, but also obtained of the one God, Who made heaven and earth, a greater earthly kingdom than any of his ancestors. In brief, he brought under his dominion all the nations and provinces of Britain, which are divided into four languages, to wit, those of the Britons, the Picts, the Scots, and the English. Though raised to that height of regal power, wonderful to relate, he was always humble, kind, and generous to the poor and to strangers.

To give one instance, it is told, that when he was once sitting at dinner, on the holy day of Easter, with the aforesaid bishop, and a silver dish full of royal dainties was set before him, and they were just about to put forth their hands to bless the bread, the servant, whom he had appointed to relieve the needy, came in on a sudden, and told the king, that a great multitude of poor folk from all parts was sitting in the streets begging alms of the king; he immediately ordered the meat set before him to be carried to the poor, and the dish to be broken in pieces and divided among them. At which sight, the bishop who sat by him, greatly rejoicing at such an act of piety, clasped his right hand and said, "May this hand never decay." This fell out according to his prayer, for his hands with the arms being cut off from his body, when he was slain in battle, remain uncorrupted to this day, and are kept in a silver shrine, as revered relics, in St. Peter's church in the royal city,[1] which has taken its name from Bebba, one of its former queens. Through this king's exertions the provinces of the Deiri and the Bernicians, which till then had been at variance, were peacefully united and moulded into one people. He was nephew to King Edwin through his sister Acha; and it was fit that so great a predecessor should have in his own family such an one to succeed him in his religion and sovereignty.

---

[1] Bamborough (Bebbanburh, Bebburgh, Babbanburch, etc. There are many forms of the name). It is uncertain who the queen was. Nennius says she was the wife of Ethelfrid. His wife, Oswald's mother, was Acha (*v. infra*), but he may have been married twice. It was Ida, the first king of Bernicia, who founded Bamborough (Sax. Chron.).

BOOK III

CHAPTER XV

*How Bishop Aidan foretold to certain seamen that a storm would arise,
and gave them some holy oil to calm it.* [Between 642 and 645 A.D.]

How great the merits of Aidan were, was made manifest by the
Judge of the heart, with the testimony of miracles, whereof it will
suffice to mention three, that they may not be forgotten. A certain
priest, whose name was Utta, a man of great weight and sincerity,
and on that account honoured by all men, even the princes of the
world, was sent to Kent, to bring thence, as wife for King Oswy,
Eanfled, the daughter of King Edwin, who had been carried thither
when her father was killed. Intending to go thither by land, but to
return with the maiden by sea, he went to Bishop Aidan, and entreated
him to offer up his prayers to the Lord for him and his company,
who were then to set out on so long a journey. He, blessing them,
and commending them to the Lord, at the same time gave them
some holy oil, saying, "I know that when you go on board ship, you
will meet with a storm and contrary wind; but be mindful to cast
this oil I give you into the sea, and the wind will cease immediately;
you will have pleasant calm weather to attend you and send you
home by the way that you desire."

All these things fell out in order, even as the bishop had foretold.
For first, the waves of the sea raged, and the sailors endeavoured to
ride it out at anchor, but all to no purpose; for the sea sweeping over
the ship on all sides and beginning to fill it with water, they all perceived that death was at hand and about to overtake them. The priest
at last, remembering the bishop's words, laid hold of the phial and
cast some of the oil into the sea, which at once, as had been foretold,
ceased from its uproar. Thus it came to pass that the man of God,
by the spirit of prophecy, foretold the storm that was to come to
pass, and by virtue of the same spirit, though absent in the body,
calmed it when it had arisen. The story of this miracle was not told
me by a person of little credit, but by Cynimund, a most faithful
priest of our church,[2] who declared that it was related to him by
Utta, the priest, in whose case and through whom the same was
wrought.

---

[2] The monastery of Wearmouth and Jarrow.

BOOK IV

CHAPTER XXI

How Bishop Theodore made peace between the kings Egfrid and Ethelred.
[679 A.D.]

In the ninth year of the reign of King Egfrid, a great battle[3] was fought between him and Ethelred, king of the Mercians, near the river Trent, and Aelfwine, brother to King Egfrid, was slain, a youth about eighteen years of age, and much beloved by both provinces; for King Ethelred had married his sister Osthryth. There was now reason to expect a more bloody war, and more lasting enmity between those kings and their fierce nations; but Theodore, the bishop, beloved of God, relying on the Divine aid, by his wholesome admonitions wholly extinguished the dangerous fire that was breaking out; so that the kings and their people on both sides were appeased, and no man was put to death, but only the due mulct[4] paid to the king who was the avenger for the death of his brother; and this peace continued long after between those kings and between their kingdoms.

---

[3] The Battle of the Trent in 679. It was on the anniversary of Wilfrid's expulsion; he is said to have foretold a calamity. The place may, perhaps, be identified with Elford-on-Trent, in Staffordshire; it is supposed that the name may be a reminiscence of Aelfwine. By this battle Mercia regained Lindsey, which never again became Northumbrian.

[4] The "Wergild," i.e., pecuniary value set upon every man's life according to his status (*v.* Stubbs, "Constitutional History").

BEOWULF

Anonymous

One of the most universally studied of the English classics, Beowulf *is considered the finest heroic poem in Old English. Written ten centuries ago by an anonymous Anglo-Saxon poet, it celebrates the character and exploits of Beowulf, a young nobleman of the Geats, a people of southern Sweden. The exact date of the composition of* Beowulf *is a matter of debate among scholars; it has been established that the oldest surviving manuscript was produced between 975 and 1025 A.D. The text includes echoes of actual historical events from several centuries before those dates.*

Beowulf rescues the royal house of Denmark from marauding monsters, then returns to rule his people for fifty years, ultimately losing his life in a battle to defend the Geats from a dragon's rampage. After his death, his body is cremated and a tower is erected in his memory. The poem combines mythical elements, Christian and pagan sensibilities, and actual historical figures and events in a narrative that ranges from vivid descriptions of fierce fighting and detailed portrayals of court life to earnest considerations of social and moral dilemmas. Originally written in Old English verse, the complete text is presented here in an authoritative prose translation by R. K. Gordon.

GENEALOGIES

DANISH ROYAL FAMILY

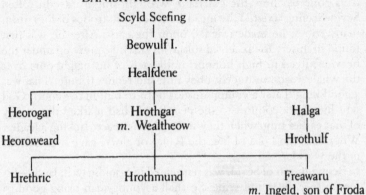

Scyld Scefing

Beowulf I.

Healfdene

Heorogar — Hrothgar *m.* Wealtheow — Halga

Heoroweard — Hrothulf

Hrethric — Hrothmund — Freawaru *m.* Ingeld, son of Froda

GEAT ROYAL FAMILY

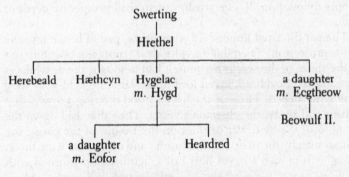

Swerting

Hrethel

Herebeald — Hæthcyn — Hygelac *m.* Hygd — a daughter *m.* Ecgtheow

Beowulf II.

a daughter *m.* Eofor — Heardred

SWEDISH ROYAL FAMILY

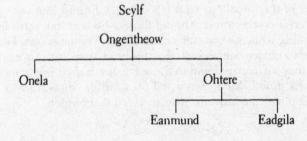

Scylf

Ongentheow

Onela — Ohtere

Eanmund — Eadgila

I

Lo! we have heard the glory of the kings of the Spear-Danes in days gone by, how the chieftains wrought mighty deeds. Often Scyld-Scefing wrested the mead-benches from troops of foes, from many tribes; he made fear fall upon the earls. After he was first found in misery (he received solace for that), he grew up under the heavens, lived in high honour, until each of his neighbours over the whale-road must needs obey him and render tribute. That was a good king! Later a young son was born to him in the court, God sent him for a comfort to the people; He had marked the misery of that earlier time when they suffered long space, lacking a leader. Wherefore the Lord of life, the Ruler of glory, gave him honour in the world.

Beowulf, son of Scyld, was renowned in Scandinavian lands—his repute spread far and wide. So shall a young man bring good to pass with splendid gifts in his father's possession, so that when war comes willing comrades shall stand by him again in his old age, the people follow him. In every tribe a man shall prosper by deeds of love.

Then at the fated hour Scyld, very brave, passed hence into the Lords protection. Then did they, his dear comrades, bear him out to the shore of the sea, as he himself had besought them, whilst as friend of the Scyldings, loved lord of the land, he held sway long time with speech. There at the haven stood the ring-prowed ship radiant and ready, the chieftain's vessel. Then they laid down the loved lord, the bestower of rings on the bosom of the barge, the famous man by the mast. Many treasures and ornaments were there, brought from afar. I never heard of a sightlier ship adorned with weapons of war and garments of battle, swords and corslets. Many treasures lay on his bosom that were to pass far with him into the power of the flood. No whit less did they furnish him with gifts, with great costly stores, than did those who sent him forth in the beginning while he was still a child alone over the waves. Further they set a golden banner high over his head; they let the ocean bear him; they surrendered him to the sea. Sad was their mind, mournful their mood. Men cannot tell for a truth, counsellors in hall, heroes under the heavens, who received that burden.

II

Then Beowulf of the Scyldings, beloved king of the people, was famed among warriors long time in the strongholds—his father had passed hence, the prince from his home—until noble Healfdene was born to him; aged and fierce in fight, he ruled the Scyldings graciously while he lived. Four children sprang from him in succession, Heorogar, prince of troops, and Hrothgar, and Halga the good; I heard that Sigeneow was Onela's queen, consort of the war-Scylfing. Then good fortune in war was granted to Hrothgar, glory in battle, so that his kinsmen gladly obeyed him, until the younger warriors grew to be a mighty band.

It came into his mind that he would order men to make a hall-building, a mighty mead-dwelling, greater than ever the children of men had heard of; and therein that he should part among young and old all which God gave unto him except the nation and the lives of men. Then I heard far and wide of work laid upon many a tribe throughout this world, the task of adorning the place of assembly. Quickly it came to pass among men that it was perfect; the greatest of hall-dwellings; he whose word had wide sway gave it the name of Heorot. He broke not his pledge, he bestowed bracelets and treasure at the banquet. The hall towered up, lofty and wide-gabled; it endured the surges of battle, of hostile fire. The time was not yet come when the feud between son-in-law and father-in-law was fated to flare out after deadly hostility.

Then the mighty spirit who dwelt in darkness angrily endured the torment of hearing each day high revel in the hall. There was the sound of the harp, the clear song of the minstrel. He who could tell of men's beginning from olden times spoke of how the Almighty wrought the world, the earth bright in its beauty which the water encompasses; the Victorious One established the brightness of sun and moon for a light to dwellers in the land, and adorned the face of the earth with branches and leaves; He also created life of all kinds which move and live. Thus the noble warriors lived in pleasure and plenty, until a fiend in hell began to contrive malice. The grim spirit was called Grendel, a famous march-stepper, who held the moors, the fen and the fastness. The hapless creature sojourned for a space in the sea-monsters' home after the Creator had condemned him. The eternal Lord avenged the murder on the race of Cain, because he slew Abel. He did not rejoice in that feud. He, the Lord, drove him far from mankind for that crime. Thence sprang all evil spawn, ogres and elves and sea-monsters, giants too, who struggled long time against God. He paid them requital for that.

III

He went then when night fell to visit the high house, to see how the Ring-Danes had disposed themselves in it after the beer-banquet. Then he found therein the band of chieftains slumbering after the feast; they knew not sorrow, the misery of men, aught of misfortune. Straightway he was ready, grim and ravenous, savage and raging; and seized thirty thanes on their couches. Thence he departed homewards again, exulting in booty, to find out his dwelling with his fill of slaughter.

Then at dawn with the breaking of day the war-might of Grendel was made manifest to men; then after the feasting arose lamentation, a loud cry in the morning. The renowned ruler, the prince long famous, sat empty of joy; strong in might, he suffered, sorrowed for his men when they saw the track of the hateful monster, the evil spirit. That struggle was too hard, too hateful, and lasting. After no longer lapse than one night again he wrought still more murders, violence and malice, and mourned not for it; he was too bent on that. Then that man was easy to find who sought elsewhere for himself a more remote resting-place, a bed after the banquet, when the hate of the hall-visitant was shown to him, truly declared by a plain token; after that he kept himself further off, and more securely. He escaped the fiend.

Thus one against all prevailed and pitted himself against right until the peerless house stood unpeopled. That was a weary while. For the space of twelve winters the friend of the Scyldings bitterly suffered every woe, deep sorrows; wherefore it came to be known to people, to the children of men, sadly in songs, that Grendel waged long war with Hrothgar; many years he bore bitter hatred, violence and malice, an unflagging feud; peace he would not have with any man of Danish race, nor lay aside murderous death, nor consent to be bought off. Nor did any of the councillors make bold to expect fairer conditions from the hands of the slayer; but the monster, the deadly creature, was hostile to warriors young and old; he plotted and planned. Many nights he held the misty moors. Men do not know whither the demons go in their wanderings.

Thus the foe of men, the dread lone visitant, oftentimes wrought many works of malice, sore injuries; in the dark nights he dwelt in

Heorot, the treasure-decked hall. He might not approach the throne, the precious thing, for fear of the Lord, nor did he know his purpose.

That was heavy sorrow, misery of mind for the friend of the Scyldings. Many a mighty one sat often in council; they held debate what was best for bold-minded men to do against sudden terrors. Sometimes in their temples they vowed sacrifices, they petitioned with prayers that the slayer of souls should succour them for the people's distress. Such was their wont, the hope of the heathen. Their thoughts turned to hell; they knew not the Lord, the Judge of deeds; they wist not the Lord God; nor in truth could they praise the Protector of the heavens, the Ruler of glory. Woe is it for him who must needs send forth his soul in unholiness and fear into the embrace of the fire, hope for no solace, suffer no change! Well is it for him who may after the day of death seek the Lord, and crave shelter in the Father's embrace!

IV

Thus the son of Healfdene was ever troubled with care; nor could the sage hero sweep aside his sorrows. That struggle was too hard, too hateful and lasting, which fell on the people—fierce hostile oppression, greatest of night-woes.

Hygelac's thane, a valiant man among the Geats, heard of that at home, of the deeds of Grendel. He was the greatest in might among men at that time, noble and powerful. He bade a good ship to be built for him; he said that he was set on seeking the warlike king, the famous prince over the swan-road, since he had need of men. No whit did wise men blame him for the venture, though he was dear to them; they urged on the staunch-minded man, they watched the omens. The valiant man had chosen warriors of the men of the Geats, the boldest he could find; with fourteen others he sought the ship. A man cunning in knowledge of the sea led them to the shore.

Time passed on; the ship was on the waves, the boat beneath the cliff. The warriors eagerly embarked. The currents turned the sea against the sand. Men bore bright ornaments, splendid war-trappings, to the bosom of the ship. The men, the heroes on their willing venture, shoved out the well-timbered ship. The foamy-necked floater like a bird went then over the wave-filled sea, sped by the wind, till after due time on the next day the boat with twisted prow had gone so far that the voyagers saw land, the sea-cliffs shining, the steep headlands, the broad sea-capes. Then the sea was traversed, the journey at an end. The men of the Weders mounted thence quickly to the land; they made fast the ship. The armour rattled, the garments of battle. They thanked God that the sea voyage had been easy for them.

Then the watchman of the Scyldings whose duty it was to guard the sea-cliffs saw from the height bright shields and battle-equipment ready for use borne over the gangway. A desire to know who the men were pressed on his thoughts. The thane of Hrothgar went to the shore riding his steed; mightily he brandished his spear in his hands, spoke forth a question: "What warriors are ye, clad in corslets, who have come thus bringing the high ship over the way of waters, hither over the floods? Lo! for a time I have been guardian of our coasts, I have kept watch by the sea lest any enemies should make ravage with their sea-raiders on the land of the Danes. No shield-bearing warriors have ventured here more openly; nor do ye know at all that ye have the permission of warriors, the consent of kinsmen. I never saw in the world a greater earl than one of your band is, a hero in his harness. He is no mere retainer decked out with weapons, unless his face belies him, his excellent front. Now I must know your race rather than ye should go further hence and be thought spies in the land of the Danes. Now, ye far-dwellers, travellers of the sea, hearken to my frank thought. It is best to tell forth quickly whence ye are come."

V

The eldest answered him; the leader of the troop unlocked his word-hoard: "We are men of the race of the Geats and hearth-companions of Hygelac. My father was famed among the peoples, a noble high prince called Ecgtheow; he sojourned many winters ere he passed away, the old man from his dwelling. Far and wide through-out the earth every wise man remembers him well. We have come with gracious intent to seek out thy lord, the son of Healfdene, the protector of his people. Be kindly to us in counsel. We have a great errand to the famous prince of the Danes. Nor shall anything be hidden there, I hope. Thou knowest if the truth is, as indeed we heard tell, that some sort of foe, a secret pursuer, works on the dark nights evil hatred, injury and slaughter, spreading terror. I can give Hrothgar counsel from a generous mind, how he may overcome the enemy wisely and well, if for him the torment of ills should ever cease, relief come again, and the surges of care grow cooler; or if he shall ever after suffer a time of misery and pain while the best of houses stands there in its lofty station."

The watchman spoke, the fearless servant, where he sat his steed—a bold shield-warrior who ponders well shall pass judgment on both words and deeds: "I hear that this is a troop friendly to the prince of the Scyldings. Go forth and bear weapons and trappings; I will guide you. Likewise I will bid my henchmen honourably guard your vessel against all enemies, your newly-tarred ship on the sand, until once more the boat with twisted prow shall bear the beloved man to the coast of the Weders; to such a valiant one it shall be vouchsafed to escape unscathed from the rush of battle."

They went on their way then. The ship remained at rest; the broad-bosomed vessel was bound by a rope, fast at anchor. The boar-images shone over the cheek armour, decked with gold; gay with colour and hardened by fire they gave protection to the brave men. The warriors hastened, went up together, until they could see the well-built hall, splendid and gold-adorned. That was foremost of buildings under the heavens for men of the earth, in which the mighty one dwelt; the light shone over many lands.

The man bold in battle pointed out to them the abode of brave men, as it gleamed, so that they could go thither. One of the warriors turned his horse, then spoke a word: "It is time for me to go. The almighty Father guard you by his grace safe in your venture. I will to the sea to keep watch for a hostile horde."

VI

The street was paved with stones of various colours, the road kept the warriors together. The war-corslet shone, firmly hand-locked, the gleaming iron rings sang in the armour as they came on their way in their trappings of war even to the hall. Weary from the sea, they set down their broad shields, their stout targes against the wall of the building; they sat down on the bench then. The corslets rang out, the warriors' armour. The spears, the weapons of seamen, of ash wood grey at the tip, stood all together. The armed band was adorned with war-gear. Then a haughty hero asked the men of battle as to their lineage: "Whence bear ye plated shields, grey corslets and masking helmets, this pile of spears? I am Hrothgar's messenger and herald. I have not seen so many men of strange race more brave in bearing. I suppose ye have sought Hrothgar from pride, by no means as exiles but with high minds."

The bold man, proud prince of the Weders, answered him, spoke a word in reply, stern under his helmet: "We are Hygelac's table-companions; Beowulf is my name. I wish to tell my errand to the son of Healfdene, the famous prince, thy lord, if he will grant that we may greet him who is so gracious." Wulfgar spoke—he was a man of the Wendels; his courage, his bravery and his wisdom had been made known to many: "I will ask the friend of the Danes, the prince of the Scyldings, the giver of rings, the renowned ruler, about thy venture as thou desirest, and speedily make known to thee the answer which the gracious one thinks fit to give me." He turned quickly then to where Hrothgar sat, aged and grey-haired, amid the band of earls; the bold man went till he stood before the shoulders of the Danish prince; he knew courtly custom. Wulfgar spoke to his gracious master: "Men of the Geats, come from afar, have been brought here over the stretch of the ocean. The warriors call the eldest one Beowulf. They request, my lord, that they may exchange words with thee. Refuse them not thy answer, gracious Hrothgar. They seem in their war-gear worthy of respect from the noble-born. Of a truth the leader is valiant who guided the heroes hither."

VII

Hrothgar spoke, the protector of the Scyldings: "I knew him when he was a youth. His aged father was called Ecgtheow; to him Hrethel of the Geats gave his only daughter in marriage. His son has now come here boldly, has sought a gracious friend. Then seafaring men, who brought precious gifts of the Geats hither as a present, said that he, mighty in battle, had the strength of thirty men in the grip of his hand. May Holy God in his graciousness send him to us, to the West-Danes, as I hope, against the terror of Grendel. I shall offer treasures to the valiant one for his courage. Do thou hasten, bid them enter to see the friendly band all together; tell them also with words that they are welcome to the people of the Danes." Then Wulfgar went toward the door of the hall, spoke a word in the doorway: "My victorious lord, prince of the East-Danes, bade me tell you that he knows your lineage, and that ye, bold in mind, are welcome hither over the sea-surges. Now ye may go in your war-gear under battle-helmets to see Hrothgar; let your battle-shields, spears, deadly shafts, await here the issue of the speaking."

The mighty one rose then, around him many a warrior, excellent troop of thanes. Some waited there, kept watch over their trappings, as the bold man bade them. They hastened together, as the warrior guided, under the roof of Heorot; the man, resolute in mind, stern under his helmet, went till he stood within the hall. Beowulf spoke— on him his corslet shone, the shirt of mail sewn by the art of the smith: "Hail to thee, Hrothgar; I am Hygelac's kinsman and thane. I have in my youth undertaken many heroic deeds. The ravages of Grendel were made known to me in my native land. Seafarers say that this hall, the noblest building, stands unpeopled and profitless to all warriors, after the light of evening is hidden under cover of heaven. Then my people counselled me, the best of men in their wisdom, that I should seek thee, Prince Hrothgar, because they knew the power of my strength, they saw it themselves, when I came out of battles, blood-stained from my foes, where I bound five, ruined the race of the monsters and slew by night the sea-beasts mid the waves, suffered sore need, avenged the wrong of the Weders, killed the foes—they embarked on an unlucky venture. And now alone I shall achieve the exploit against Grendel, the monster, the giant. I wish now at this time to ask thee one boon, prince of the Bright-Danes, protector of the Scyldings: that thou, defence of warriors, friendly prince of the people, wilt not refuse me, now I have come thus far, that I and my band of earls', this bold troop, may cleanse Heorot unaided. I have also heard that the monster in his madness cares naught for weapons; wherefore I scorn to bear sword or broad shield, yellow targe to the battle, so may Hygelac my lord be gracious in mind to me; but with my grip I shall seize the fiend and strive for his life, foe against foe. There he whom death takes must needs trust to the judging of the Lord. I think that he is minded, if he can bring it to pass, to devour fearlessly in the battle-hall the people of the Geats, the flower of men, as he often has done. Not at all dost thou need to protect my head, but if death takes me he will have me drenched in blood; he will carry off the bloody corpse, will think to hide it; the lone-goer will feed without mourning, he will stain the moor-refuges. No longer needst thou care about the sustenance of my body. Send to Hygelac, if battle takes me off, the best of battle-garments that arms my breast, the finest of corslets. That is a heritage from Hrethel, the work of Weland. Fate ever goes as it must."

VIII

Hrothgar spoke, the protector of the Scyldings: "Thou hast sought us, my friend Beowulf, for battle and from graciousness. Thy father achieved the greatest of feuds; he became the slayer of Heatholaf among the Wulfings; then the race of the Weders would not receive him because of threatening war. Thence he sought the people of the South-Danes, the honourable Scyldings, over the surging of the waves. Then I had just begun to rule the Danish people and in youth held a wide-stretched kingdom, a stronghold of heroes. Then Heregar was dead, my elder kinsman, the son of Healfdene had ceased to live; he was better than I. Afterwards I ended the feud with money; I sent old treasures to the Wulfings over the back of the water; he swore oaths to me. It is sorrow for me in my mind to tell any man what malice and sudden onslaughts Grendel has wrought on Heorot with his hostile thoughts. Thinned is my troop in hall, my war-band. Fate has swept them away to the dread Grendel. God may easily part the bold enemy from his deeds.

"Full often did warriors drunken with beer boast over the ale-cup that they would await Grendel's attack with dread blades in the beer-hall. Then in the morning, when day dawned, this mead-hall, the troop-hall, was stained with blood; all the ale-benches drenched with gore, the hall with blood shed in battle. I had so many the less trusty men, dear veterans, since death had carried off these. Sit down now at the banquet, and speak thy mind, tell the men of victorious fame, as thy mind prompts."

Then a bench was cleared in the beer-hall for the men of the Geats together; there the bold-minded ones went and sat down, exceeding proud. A thane who bore in his hands the decked ale-cup performed the office, poured out the gleaming beer. At times the minstrel sang clearly in Heorot; there was joy of heroes, a great band of warriors, Danes and Weders.

IX

Unferth spoke, son of Ecglaf, who sat at the feet of the prince of the Scyldings. He began dispute—the journey of Beowulf, the brave seafarer, was a great bitterness to him, because he did not grant that any other man in the world accomplished greater exploits under heaven than he himself: "Art thou that Beowulf who strove with

Breca, contended on the wide sea for the prize in swimming, where ye two tried the floods in your pride, and risked your lives in the deep water from presumption? Nor could any man, friend or foe, prevent the sorrowful journey; then ye two swam on the sea, where ye plied the ocean-streams with your arms, measured the sea-paths, threw aside the sea with your hands, glided over the surge; the deep raged with its waves, with its wintry flood. Seven nights ye toiled in the power of the water; he outstripped thee in swimming, had greater strength. Then in the morning the sea bore him to the land of the Heathoremes. Thence, dear to his people, he sought his loved country, the land of the Brondings, the fair stronghold, where he ruled over people, castle and rings. The son of Beanstan in truth fulfilled all his pledge to thee. Wherefore I expect a worse fate for thee, though everywhere thou hast withstood battle-rushes, grim war, if thou durst await Grendel throughout the night near at hand."

Beowulf spoke, son of Ecgtheow: "Lo! thou hast spoken a great deal, friend Unferth, about Breca, drunken as thou art with beer; thou hast told of his journey. I count it as truth that I had greater might in the sea, hardships mid the waves, than any other man.

"We arranged that and made bold, while we were youths—we were both then still in our boyhood—that we two should risk our lives out on the sea; and thus we accomplished that. We held naked swords boldly in our hands when we swam in the ocean; we thought to protect ourselves against the whales. In no wise could he swim far from me on the waves of the flood, more quickly on the sea; I would not consent to leave him. Then we were together on the sea for the space of five nights till the flood forced us apart, the surging sea, coldest of storms, darkening night, and a wind from the north, battle-grim, came against us. Wild were the waves; the temper of the sea-monsters was stirred. There did my shirt of mail hard-locked by hand stand me in good stead against foes; the woven battle-garment, adorned with gold, lay on my breast. A spotted deadly foe drew me to the depths, had me firmly and fiercely in his grip; yet it was granted to me that I pierced the monster with my point, my battle-spear. The rush of battle carried off the mighty sea-monster by my hand.

X

"Thus oftentimes malicious foes pressed me hard. I served them with my good sword, as was fitting. They had not joy of their feasting, the evildoers, from devouring me, from sitting round the banquet near the bottom of the sea; but in the morning they lay cast up on the shore, wounded with swords, laid low by blades, so that no longer they hindered seafarers on their voyage over the high flood. Light came from the east, bright beacon of God. The surges sank down, so that I could behold the sea-capes, the windy headlands. Fate often succours the undoomed warrior when his valour is strong.

"Yet it was my fortune to slay with the sword nine sea-monsters. I have not heard under the arching sky of heaven of harder fighting by night, nor of a more hapless man in the streams of ocean. Yet I escaped with my life from the grasp of foes, weary of travel. Then the sea, the flood, the raging surges bore me to the shore in the land of the Finns.

"I have not heard such exploits told of thee, dread deeds, terror of swords; never yet did Breca or either of you two in the play of battle perform so bold a deed with gleaming blades—I do not boast of the struggle—though thou earnest to be the murderer of thy brother, thy near kinsman. For that thou must needs suffer damnation in hell, though thy wit is strong. Forsooth, I tell thee, son of Ecglaf, that Grendel, the fearful monster, had never achieved so many dread deeds against thy prince, malice on Heorot, if thy thoughts and mind had been as daring as thou thyself sayest. But he has found out that he need not sorely dread the feud, the terrible sword-battle of your people, the victorious Scyldings; he takes pledges by force, he spares none of the Danish people, but he lives in pleasure, sleeps and feasts; he looks for no fight from the Spear-Danes. But soon now I shall show him battle, the might and courage of the Geats. He who may will go afterwards, brave to the mead, when the morning light of another day, the sun clothed with sky-like brightness, shines from the south over the children of men."

Then glad was the giver of treasure, grey-haired and famed in battle; the prince of the Bright-Danes trusted in aid; the protector of the people heard in Beowulf a resolute purpose. There was laughter of heroes; talk was heard; words were winsome.

Wealtheow went forth, Hrothgar's queen, mindful of what was fitting; gold-adorned, she greeted the warriors in hall; and the free-born woman first offered the goblet to the guardian of the East-Danes; bade him be of good cheer at the beer-banquet, be dear to his people. He gladly took part in the banquet and received the hall-goblet, the king mighty in victory. Then the woman of the Helmings went about everywhere among old and young warriors, proffered the precious cup, till the time came that she, the ring-decked queen, excellent in mind, bore the mead-flagon to Beowulf. She greeted the prince of the Geats, thanked God with words of sober wisdom that her wish had been fulfilled, that she might trust to some earl as a comfort in trouble. He, the warrior fierce in fight, took that goblet from Wealtheow, and then, ready for battle, uttered speech.

Beowulf spoke, son of Ecgtheow: "That was my purpose when I launched on the ocean, embarked on the sea-boat with the band of my warriors, that I should work the will of your people to the full, or fall a corpse fast in the foe's grip. I shall accomplish deeds of heroic might, or endure my last day in the mead-hall."

Those words, the boasting speech of the Geat, pleased the woman well. Decked with gold, the free-born queen of the people went to sit by her prince. Then again as before there was excellent converse in hall, the warriors in happiness, the sound of victorious people, till all at once Healfdene's son was minded to seek his evening's rest. He knew that war was destined to the high hall by the monster after they could no longer see the light of the sun, and when, night growing dark over all, the shadowy creatures came stalking, black beneath the clouds. The troop all rose.

Then one warrior greeted the other, Hrothgar Beowulf, and wished him success, power over the wine-hall, and spoke these words: "Never before did I trust to any man, since I was able to lift hand and shield, the excellent hall of the Danes, except to thee now. Have now and hold the best of houses. Be mindful of fame, show a mighty courage, watch against foes. Nor shalt thou lack what thou desirest, if with thy life thou comest out from that heroic task."

XI

Then Hrothgar went his way with his band of heroes, the protector of Scyldings out of the hall; the warlike king was minded to seek Wealtheow the queen for his bedfellow. The glorious king had, as men learned, set a hall-guardian against Grendel; he performed a special service for the prince of the Danes, kept watch against monsters. Truly the prince of the Geats relied firmly on his fearless might, and the grace of the Lord. Then he laid aside his iron corslet, the helmet from his head, gave his ornamented sword, best of blades, to his servant and bade him keep his war-gear.

Then the valiant one, Beowulf of the Geats, spoke some words of boasting ere he lay down on his bed: "I do not count myself less in war-strength, in battle-deeds, than Grendel does himself; wherefore I will not slay him, spoil him of life by sword, although I might. He knows not the use of weapons so as to strike at me, hew my shield, though he may be mighty in works of malice; but we two shall do without swords in the night, if he dare to seek war without weapons, and afterwards the wise God, the holy Lord, shall award fame to whatever side seems good to Him." The bold warrior lay down, the earl's face touched the bolster; and round him many a mighty sea-hero bent to his couch in the hall. None of them thought that he should go thence and seek again the loved land, the people or stronghold where he was fostered; but they had heard that murderous death had ere now carried off far too many of Danish people in the wine-hall. But the Lord gave them success in war, support and succour to the men of the Weders, so that through the strength of one, his own might, they all overcame their foe. The truth has been made known, that mighty God has ever ruled over mankind.

The shadowy visitant came stalking in the dark night. The warriors slept, who were to keep the antlered building, all save one. That was known to men that the ghostly enemy might not sweep them off among the shadows, for the Lord willed it not; but he, watching in anger against foes, awaited in wrathful mood the issue of the battle.

XII

Then from the moor under the misty cliffs came Grendel, he bore God's anger. The foul foe purposed to trap with cunning one of the men in the high hall; he went under the clouds till he might see most clearly the wine-building, the gold-hall of warriors, gleaming with plates of gold. That was not the first time he had sought Hrothgar's home; never in his life-days before or since did he find bolder heroes and hall-thanes. The creature came, bereft of joys, making his way to the building. Straightway the door, firm clasped by fire-hardened fetters, opened, when he touched it with his hands; then, pondering evil, he tore open the entry of the hall when he was enraged. Quickly after that the fiend trod the gleaming floor, moved angry in mood. A baleful light like flame flared from his eyes. He saw in the building many heroes, the troop of kinsmen sleeping together, the band of young warriors. Then his mind exulted. The dread monster purposed ere day came to part the life of each one from the body, for the hope of a great feasting filled him. No longer did fate will that after that night he might seize more of mankind. The kinsman of Hygelac, exceeding strong, beheld how the foul foe was minded to act with his sudden grips.

Nor did the monster think to delay, but first he quickly seized a sleeping warrior; suddenly tore him asunder, devoured his body, drank the blood from his veins, swallowed him with large bites. Straightway he had consumed all the body, even the feet and hands. He stepped forward nearer, laid hold with his hands of the resolute warrior on his couch; the fiend stretched his hand towards him. Beowulf met the attack quickly and propped himself on his arm. Forthwith the upholder of crime found that he had not met in the world, on the face of the earth among other men, a mightier hand-grip. Fear grew in his mind and heart; yet in spite of that he could not make off. He sought to move out; he was minded to flee to his refuge, to seek the troop of devils. His task there was not such as he had found in former days.

Then the brave kinsman of Hygelac remembered his speech in the evening; he stood upright and seized him firmly. The fingers burst, the monster was moving out; the earl stepped forward. The famous one purposed to flee further, if only he might, and win away thence to the fen-strongholds; he knew the might of his fingers was in the grip of his foe. That was an ill journey when the ravager came to Heorot. The warriors' hall resounded. Terror fell on all the Danes, on the castle-dwellers, on each of the bold men, on the earls. Wroth were they both, angry contestants for the house. The building rang aloud.

Then was it great wonder that the wine-hall withstood the bold fighters; that it fell not to the ground, the fair earth-dwelling; but it was too firmly braced within and without with iron bands of skilled workmanship. There many a mead-bench decked with gold bent away from the post, as I have heard, where the foemen fought. The wise men of the Scyldings looked not for that before, that any man could ever shatter it, rend it with malice in any way, excellent and bone-adorned as it was, unless the embrace of fire could swallow it in smoke. A sound arose, passing strange. Dread fear came upon each of the North-Danes who heard the cry from the wall, the lament of God's foe rise, the song of defeat; the hell-bound creature, crying out in his pain. He who was strongest in might among men at that time held him too closely.

XIII

The protector of earls was minded in no wise to release the deadly visitant alive, nor did he count his life as useful to any man.

There most eagerly this one and that of Beowulf's men brandished old swords, wished to save their leader's life, the famous prince, if only they could. They did not know, when they were in the midst of the struggle, the stern warriors, and wished to strike on all sides, how to seek Grendel's life. No choicest of swords on the earth, no war-spear, would pierce the evil monster; but Beowulf had given up victorious weapons, all swords. His parting from life at that time was doomed to be wretched, and the alien spirit was to travel far into the power of the fiends.

Then he who before in the joy of his heart had wrought much malice on mankind—he was hostile to God—found that his body would not follow him, for the brave kinsman of Hygelac held him by the hand. Each was hateful to the other while he lived. The foul monster suffered pain in his body. A great wound was seen in his shoulder, the sinews sprang apart, the body burst open. Fame in war was granted to Beowulf. Grendel must needs flee thence under the fen-cliffs mortally wounded, seek out his joyless dwelling. He knew but too well the end of his life was come, the full count of his days. The desire of all the Danes was fulfilled after the storm of battle.

Then he who erstwhile came from afar, shrewd and staunch, had cleansed the hall of Hrothgar, freed it from battle. He rejoiced in the night-work, in heroic deeds. The prince of the Geat warriors had fulfilled his boast to the East-Danes; likewise he cured all their sorrows, sufferings from malicious foes, which they endured before and were forced to bear in distress, no slight wrong. That was a clear token when the bold warrior laid down the hand, the arm and shoulder under the wide roof—it was all there together—the claw of Grendel.

XIV

Then in the morning, as I have heard, around the gift-hall was many a warrior; leaders came from far and near throughout the wide ways to behold the wonder, the tracks of the monster. His going from life did not seem grievous to any man who saw the course of the inglorious one, how, weary in mind, beaten in battle, fated and fugitive, he left behind him on his way thence to the mere of the monsters marks of his life-blood. Then the water was surging with blood, the foul welter of waves all mingled with hot gore; it boiled with the blood of battle. The death-doomed one dived in, then bereft of joy in his fen-refuge he laid down his life, his heathen soul, when hell received him. Thence again old comrades went, also many a young man, in merry companionship, the brave men riding on horses from the mere, warriors on bay steeds. There Beowulf's fame was proclaimed. Oftentimes many a one said that neither south nor north between the seas, over the wide earth, under the vault of the sky, was there any better among warriors, more worthy of a kingdom. Nor in truth did they blame their friendly lord, gracious Hrothgar, for that was a good king.

At times the men doughty in battle let their sorrel horses run, race against one another, where the land-ways seemed fair to them, known for their good qualities; at times the king's thane, a man with many tales of exploits, mindful of measures, he who remembered a great number of the old legends, made a new story of things that were true. The man began again wisely to frame Beowulf's exploit and skilfully to make deft measures, to deal in words. He spoke all that he had heard told of Sigemund's mighty deeds, much that was unknown, the warfare of the son of Wæls, the far journeys, the hostility and malice of which the children of men knew not at all, except Fitela who was with him when he was minded to say somewhat of such things, the uncle to his nephew; for they were always in every struggle bound together by kinship. They had felled with their swords very many of the race of giants. There sprang up for Sigemund after his death no little fame when the man bold in battle killed the dragon, the guardian of the treasure. Under the grey stone he ventured alone, the son of a chieftain, on the daring deed; Fitela was not with him. Yet it was granted to him that that sword pierced the monstrous dragon, so that it stood in the wall, the noble blade. The dragon died violently. The hero had brought it to pass by his valour that he could use the ring-hoard as he chose. The son of Wæls loaded the sea-boat, bore to the ship's bosom the bright ornaments. The dragon melted in heat.

He was by far the most famous of adventurers among men, protector of warriors by mighty deeds; he prospered by that earlier, when the boldness, the strength and the courage of Heremod lessened. He was betrayed among the Eotens into the power of his enemies, quickly driven out. Surges of sorrow pressed him too long; he became a deadly grief to his people, to all his chieftains. So also many a wise man who trusted to him as a remedy for evils lamented in former times the valiant one's journey, that the prince's son was destined to prosper, inherit his father's rank, rule over the people, the treasure and the prince's fortress, the kingdom of heroes, the land of the Scyldings. There did he, the kinsman of Hygelac, become dearer to all men and to his friends than he. Treachery came upon him.

At times in rivalry they measured the yellow streets with their horses. Then the light of morning had quickly mounted up. Many a retainer went bold-minded to the high hall to behold the rare wonder; the king himself also, the keeper of ring-treasures, came glorious from his wife's chamber, famed for his virtues, with a great troop, and his queen with him measured the path to the mead-hall with a band of maidens.

XV

Hrothgar spoke—he went to the hall, stood on the doorstep, looked on the lofty gold-plated roof and Grendel's hand—"For this sight thanks be straightway rendered to the Almighty. I suffered much that was hateful, sorrows at the hands of Grendel; ever may God, the glorious Protector, perform wonder after wonder.

"That was not long since when I looked not ever to find solace for any of my woes, when the best of houses stood blood-stained, gory from battle; woe wide-spread among all councillors who had no hope of ever protecting the fortress of warriors against foes, against demons and evil spirits. Now the warrior has performed the deed through the Lords might which formerly all of us could not contrive with our cunning. Lo! a woman who has borne such a son among the peoples, if she yet lives, may say that the ancient Lord was gracious to her in the birth of her son. Now I will love thee in my heart as my son, Beowulf, best of men; keep well the new kinship. Thou shalt lack none of the things thou desirest in the world, which I can command. Full often have I for less cause bestowed reward on a slighter warrior, a weaker in combat, to honour him with treasures. Thou hast brought it to pass for thyself by deeds that thy glory shall live forever. The All-Ruler reward thee with good things as He has done till now."

Beowulf spoke, son of Ecgtheow: "We accomplished that heroic deed, that battle, through great favour. We risked ourselves boldly against the might of the monster. I had rather that thou couldst have seen him, the fiend in his trappings, weary unto death. I thought to bind him speedily with strong clasps on his death-bed, so that he must needs lie in his death-agony by my hand-grip, unless his body should slip away. I could not, since the Lord willed it not, prevent his passing out. I did not hold him closely enough, the deadly enemy; the foe was too mighty in going. Nevertheless he left his hand, arm and shoulder, to serve as a token of his flight. Yet the wretched creature won no solace there; no longer lives the malicious foe pressed by sins, but pain has embraced him closely with hostile grasp, with ruinous bonds. There the creature stained with sin must needs await the great doom, what judgment the bright Lord will award him."

Then the son of Ecglaf was a more silent man in boasting of war-deeds, when the chieftains beheld by the strength of the earl the hand, the fingers of the monster, stretching up to the high roof; each at its tip, each place where the nails were, was like steel, the heathen's claw, the monstrous spike of the fighter. Everyone said that no well-tried sword of brave men would wound him, would shorten the monster's bloody battle-fist.

XVI

Then it was quickly commanded that Heorot should be decked within with hands. There were many there, men and women, who made ready the wine-building, the guest-hall. Woven hangings gleamed, gold-adorned, on the walls, many wondrous sights for all men who look on such things. That bright building was all sorely shattered, though firm within with its iron clasps; its door-hinges burst. The roof alone survived all scatheless, when the monster stained with evil deeds turned in flight, despairing of life. That is not easy to avoid—let him do it who will—but he must needs seek the place forced on him by necessity, prepared for all who bear souls, for the children of men, for the dwellers on earth, where his body sleeps after the banquet fast in its narrow bed.

Then was the time convenient and fitting that Healfdene's son should go to the hall; the king himself wished to join in the banquet. I have not heard of a people who showed a nobler bearing with a greater troop about their giver of treasure. The famous ones then sat down on the bench, rejoiced in the feast; in seemly fashion they took many a mead-goblet; brave-minded kinsmen were in the high hall,

Hrothgar and Hrothulf. Heorot within was filled with friends. Not yet at this time had the Scyldings practised treachery.

The son of Healfdene gave then to Beowulf a golden ensign as a reward for victory, an ornamented banner with a handle, a helmet and corslet, a famous precious sword. Many saw them borne before the warrior. Beowulf took the goblet in hall; he needed not to be ashamed in front of the warriors of the bestowing of gifts.

I have not heard of many men giving to others on the ale-bench in more friendly fashion four treasures decked with gold. Around the top of the helmet a jutting ridge twisted with wires held guard over the head, so that many an old sword, proved hard in battle, could not injure the bold man, when the shield-bearing warrior was destined to go against foes. Then the protector of earls commanded eight horses with gold-plated bridles to be led into the hall, into the house; on one of them lay a saddle artfully adorned with gold, decked with costly ornament. That was the war-seat of the noble king, when the son of Healfdene was minded to practise sword-play. Never did the bravery of the far-famed man fail in the van when corpses were falling. Then the protector of the friends of Ing gave power over both to Beowulf, over horses and weapons; he bade him use them well. Thus manfully did the famous prince, the treasure-keeper of heroes, reward the rushes of battle with steeds and rich stores, so that he who wishes to speak truth in seemly fashion will never scoff at them.

XVII

Further the lord of earls bestowed treasure on the mead-bench, ancient blades, to each of those who travelled the ocean path with Beowulf; and he bade recompense to be made with gold for the one whom Grendel before murderously killed. So he was minded to do with more of them, if wise God and the man's courage had not turned aside such a fate from them. The Lord ruled over all mankind as He still does. Wherefore understanding, forethought of soul, is everywhere best. He who sojourns long in the world in these days of sorrow must needs suffer much of weal and woe.

There was song and music mingled before Healfdene's chieftain; the harp was touched; a measure often recited at such times as it fell to Hrothgar's minstrel to proclaim joy in hall along the mead-bench. Hnæf of the Scyldings, a hero of the Half-Danes, was fated to fall in the Frisian battle-field when the sudden onslaught came upon them, the sons of Finn. "Nor in truth had Hildeburh cause to praise the faith of the Eotens; sinless, she was spoiled of her dear ones at the shield-play, a son and a brother; wounded with the spear, they fell in succession. She was a sorrowing woman. Not without cause did the daughter of Hoc lament her fate, when morning came when she might see the slaughter of kinsmen under the sky. Where erstwhile he had had greatest joy in the world, war carried off all the thanes of Finn except a very few, so that in no wise could he offer fight to Hengest in the battle-field, nor protect by war the sad survivors from the prince's thane; but they offered them conditions, that they would give up to them entirely another building, the hall and high seat; that they might have power over half of it with the men of the Eotens, and that the son of Folcwalda would honour the Danes each day with gifts at the bestowal of presents, would pay respect to Hengest's troop with rings, just as much as he would encourage the race of the Frisians in the beer-hall with ornaments of plated gold. Then on both sides they had faith in firm-knit peace. Finn swore to Hengest deeply, inviolably with oaths, that he would treat the sad survivors honourably according to the judgment of the councillors, that no man there should break the bond by word or deed, nor should they ever mention it in malice, although they had followed the slayer of their giver of rings after they had lost their leader, since the necessity was laid upon them; if then any one of the Frisians should recall to mind by dangerous speech the deadly hostility, then it must needs recall also the edge of the sword.

"The oath was sworn and rich gold taken from the treasure. The best of the heroes of the warlike Scyldings was ready on the funeral fire. On that pyre the blood-stained shirt of mail was plain to see, the swine-image all gold, the boar hard as iron, many a chieftain slain with wounds. Many had fallen in the fight. Then Hildeburh bade her own son to be given over to the flames at Hnæf's pyre, his body to be burned and placed on the funeral fire. The woman wept, sorrowing by his side; she lamented in measures. The warrior mounted up. The greatest of funeral fires wound up to the clouds, it roared in front of the mound. Heads melted, wounds burst open, while blood gushed forth from the gashes in the bodies. The fire, greediest of spirits, consumed all those of both peoples whom war carried off there. Their mightiest men had departed.

XVIII

"The warriors went then, bereft of friends, to visit the dwellings, to see the land of the Frisians, the homes and the stronghold. Then Hengest dwelt yet in peace with Finn for a winter stained with the blood of the slain; he thought of his land though he could not drive the ring-prowed ship on the sea (the ocean surged with storm, rose up against the wind; winter bound the waves with fetters of ice), till another year came into the dwellings; as those still do now who ever await an opportunity, the bright clear weather. Then winter was past; the bosom of the earth was fair; the exile purposed to depart, the guest out of the castle; he thought rather of vengeance for sorrow than of the sea journey, if he could bring the battle to pass in which he thought to take vengeance on the children of the Eotens. So he let things take their course when Hunlafing laid in his bosom the gleaming sword, best of blades. Its edges were famed among the Eotens. Even so did deadly death by the sword come upon brave Finn in his own home, when Guthlaf and Oslaf after their sea journey sorrowfully lamented the grim attack; they were wroth at their manifold woes; their restless spirit could not be ruled in their breast. Then was the hall reddened with corpses of foes, Finn slain likewise, the king mid his troop, and the queen taken. The warriors of the Scyldings bore to the ships all the house-treasure of the king of the land, whatever they could find at Finn's home of ornaments and jewels. They bore away on the sea voyage the noble woman to the Danes, led her to her people."

The song was sung, the glee-man's measure. Joy rose again, bench-music rang out clear, servants gave out wine from wondrous goblets. Then Wealtheow, under her golden circlet, came forth where the two valiant ones were sitting, uncle and nephew. At that time there was peace yet between them, each true to the other. Likewise Unferth sat there as a squire at the feet of the prince of the Scyldings. Each of them trusted his heart, that he had a noble mind, though he had not been faithful to his kinsmen at the play of swords. Then spoke the queen of the Scyldings: "Receive this goblet, my prince, giver of treasure. Rejoice, gold-friend of warriors, and speak to the Geats with kindly words, as it is fitting to do. Be gracious to the Geats, mindful of gifts; far and near now thou hast peace. They said that thou wast minded to take the warrior for son. Heorot is cleansed, the bright ring-hall; be generous with many rewards while thou mayst, and leave to thy kinsmen subjects and kingdom, when thou must needs go forth to face thy destiny. I know my gracious Hrothulf, that he will treat the young men honourably, if thou, friend of the Scyldings, pass from the world before him. I think that he will richly reward our children, if he forgets not all the favours we formerly showed him for his pleasure and honour, while he was still a child."

She turned then towards the bench where her sons were, Hrethric and Hrothmund, and the sons of heroes, the young men together; there the valiant one, Beowulf of the Geats, sat by the two brothers.

XIX

To him was the flagon borne and a friendly invitation offered with words and the twisted gold vessel graciously presented; two bracelets, a corslet and rings, greatest of necklaces, of those which I have heard of on earth.

I have not heard of a better treasure-hoard of heroes under the sky since Hama carried off to the gleaming castle the necklace of the Brosings, the trinket and treasure; he fled the malicious hostility of Eormenric; he chose everlasting gain. Hygelac of the Geats, grandson of Swerting, had the ring on his last expedition, when beneath his banner he defended the treasure, guarded the booty of battle. Fate took him off, when in his pride he suffered misfortune in fight against the Frisians; the mighty prince bore the ornament, the precious stones over the sea; he fell under his shield. Then the king's body passed into the power of the Franks, his breast-garments and the ring also; less noble warriors stripped the bodies of the men of the Geats after the carnage of war; their bodies covered the battle-field. The hall rang with shouts of approval.

Wealtheow spoke, she uttered words before the troop: "Enjoy this ring happily, dear young Beowulf; and use this corslet, the great treasures, and prosper exceedingly; make thyself known mightily, and be to these youths kindly in counsel. I will not forget thy reward for that. Thou hast brought it about that far and near men ever praise thee, even as far as the sea hems in the home of the winds, the head-lands. Blessed be thou while thou livest, nobly-born man. I will grant thee many treasures. Be thou gracious in deeds to my son, thou who art now in happiness. Here each earl is true to the other, gentle in mind, loyal to the lord. The thanes are willing, the people all ready, noble warriors after drinking. Do as I bid."

She went then to the seat. There was the choicest of banquets; the men drank wine; they knew not fate, dread destiny, as it had been dealt out to many of the earls. Afterwards came evening, and Hrothgar went to his chamber, the mighty one to his couch. A great band of earls occupied the hall, as they often did before; they cleared away bench-boards; it was spread over with beds and bolsters. One of the revellers, ready and fated, sank to his couch in the hall. At their heads they placed the war-shields, the bright bucklers. There on the bench was plainly seen above the chieftains the helmet rising high in battle, the ringed corslet, the mighty spear. It was their custom that often both at home and in the field they should be ready for war, and equally in both positions at all such times as distress came upon their lord. Those people were good.

XX

They sank then to sleep. One sorely paid for his evening rest, as had full often come to pass for them, when Grendel held the gold-hall, and did wickedness until the end came, death after sins. That was seen, widely known among men, that an avenger, Grendel's mother, a she-monster, yet survived the hateful one, a long while after the misery of war. She who was doomed to dwell in the dread water, the cold streams, after Cain killed his only brother, his father's son, forgot not her misery. He departed then fated, marked with murder, to flee from the joys of men; he dwelt in the wilderness. Thence sprang many fated spirits; Grendel was one of them, a hateful fierce monster; he found at Heorot a man keeping watch, waiting for war. There the monster came to grips with him; yet he remembered the power of his strength, the precious gift which God gave him, and he trusted for support, for succour and help, to Him who rules over all. By that he overcame the fiend, laid low the spirit of hell. Then he departed, the foe of mankind, in misery, reft of joy, to seek his death-dwelling. And his mother then still purposed to go on the sorrowful journey, greedy and darkly-minded, to avenge her son's death.

She came then to Heorot where the Ring-Danes slept throughout that hall. Then straightway the old fear fell on the earls, when Grendel's mother forced her way in. The dread was less by just so much as the strength of women, the war-terror of a woman, is less than a man, when the bound sword shaped by the hammer, the blood-stained blade strong in its edges, cuts off the boar-image on the foeman's helmet. Then in the hall was the strong blade drawn, the sword over the seats; many a broad buckler raised firmly in hand. He thought not of helmet nor of broad corslet, when the terror seized him.

She was in haste, was minded to go thence and save her life when she was discovered. Quickly she had seized one of the chieftains with firm grip; then she went to the fen. That was the dearest of heroes to Hrothgar among his followers between the seas, a mighty shield-warrior, whom she slew on his couch, a noble man of great fame. Beowulf was not there, but another lodging had been set apart for him earlier, after the giving of treasure to the famous Geat. There was clamour in Heorot. She had carried off the famous blood-stained hand. Care was created anew, brought to pass in the dwellings. That was no good bargain which they had to pay for in double measure with lives of friends. Then the wise king, the grey battle-warrior, was troubled in heart, when he knew that the noble thane was life-less, that the dearest one was dead.

Beowulf was quickly brought to the castle, the victorious warrior. At dawn that earl, the noble hero himself with his comrades, went to where the wise man was waiting to see whether the All-Ruler would ever bring to pass a change after the time of woe. Then the man famous in fight went with his nearest followers along the floor— (the hall-wood resounded)—till he greeted the wise one with words, the prince of the friends of Ing; he asked if, as he hoped, he had had a peaceful night.

XXI

Hrothgar spoke, protector of the Scyldings: "Ask thou not after happiness. Sorrow is made anew for the Danish people. Æschere is dead, Yrmenlaf's elder brother, my counsellor and my adviser, trusted friend, in such times as we fended our heads in war, when the foot-warriors crashed together and hewed the helms. Such should an earl be, a trusty chieftain, as Æschere was.

"That unjust slaughterous spirit slew him with her hands in Heorot. I know not whither the monster, made known by her feasting, journeyed back exulting in the corpse. She avenged the fight in which last night thou didst violently kill Grendel with hard grips because too long he lessened and slew my people. He fell in combat, guilty of murder, and now another mighty evil foe has come; she was minded to make requital for her son, and she has overmuch avenged the hostile deed, as it may seem to many a thane who grieves in mind for the giver of treasure with heavy heart-sorrow. Now low lies the hand which was ready for all your desires.

"I heard dwellers in the land, my people, counsellors in hall, say that they saw two such great march-steppers, alien spirits, hold the moors. One of them was, as far as they could certainly know, the likeness of a woman; the other wretched creature trod the paths of exile in man's shape, except that he was greater than any other man. Him in days past the dwellers in the land named Grendel; his father they know not; nor whether there were born to him earlier any dark spirits.

"They possess unknown land, wolf-cliffs, windy crags, a dangerous fen-path, where the mountain stream falls down under the darkness of the rocks, a flood under the earth. That is not a mile hence where the mere stands; over it hang rime-covered groves; the wood firm-rooted overshadows the water. There each night a baleful wonder may be seen, a fire on the flood. There is none so wise of the children of men who knows those depths. Though the heath-stepper hard pressed by the hounds, the hart strong in antlers, should seek the forest after a long chase, rather does he yield up his life, his spirit on the shore, than hide his head there. That is an eerie place. Thence the surge of waves mounts up dark to the clouds, when the wind stirs up hostile storms till the air darkens, the skies weep.

"Now once more help must come from thee alone. Thou dost not yet know the lair, the dangerous place, where thou mayest find the sinful creature; seek if thou darest. If thou comest away alive, I will reward thee for that onslaught, as erstwhile I did, with treasures, old precious things, twisted gold."

XXII

Beowulf spoke, son of Ecgtheow: "Sorrow not, wise warrior. It is better for each to avenge his friend than greatly to mourn. Each of us must needs await the end of life in the world; let him who can achieve fame ere death. That is best for a noble warrior when life is over. Rise up, guardian of the realm; let us go quickly hence to behold the track of Grendel's kinswoman. I promise thee she shall not escape under covering darkness, nor in the earth's embrace, nor in the mountain forest, nor in the water's depths—go where she will. Have thou, as I expect from thee, patience for all thy woes this day."

The aged one leaped up then; thanked God, the mighty Lord, for what the man spoke. Then Hrothgar's horse was bitted, the steed with twisted mane. The wise prince went forth in splendour; the foot-troop of shield-bearing warriors stepped forward. The tracks were widely seen along the forest paths, the course over the fields. Away over the dark moor she went; she bore the best of thanes, reft of life, who with Hrothgar ruled the land. Then the son of princes strode over the high rocky cliffs, the narrow paths, the straitened tracks, the unknown road, the steep crags, many a monster's abode. He with a few other wise men went ahead to spy out the land, until suddenly he found the mountain trees hanging above the grey rock. The water beneath lay blood-stained and troubled. All the Danes, the friends of the Scyldings, were mournful in mood; many a thane had to suffer; there was sorrow for many of the earls, when they found Æschere's head on the cliff by the mere.

The flood surged with blood, with hot gore; the people beheld it. At times the horn sang its eager war-song. The troop all sat down; then they saw along the water many of the dragon kind, strange sea-dragons moving over the mere, also monsters lying on the rocky headlands; then at midday the dragons and wild beasts often go on a sorrowful journey on the sail-road. They fell away bitter and angered; they heard the clang, the war-horn sounding. The prince of the Geats with his bow parted one of them from life, from the struggle of the waves, so that the stout war-shaft stood in his heart. He was the more sluggish at swimming in the water, because death carried him off. Speedily the wondrous wave-dweller was hard pressed in the waves with boar-spears of deadly barbs, beset by hostile attacks and drawn out on the headland. The men beheld the dread creature.

Beowulf clad himself in warrior's armour; he lamented not his life. The war-corslet, hand-woven, broad, cunningly adorned, must needs try the water; it knew how to guard his body so that the grip of war might not wound his heart, the malicious clutch of an angry foe his life. And the gleaming helmet, which was to mingle with the depths of the mere, to seek the welter of the waves, decked with treasure, circled with diadems, as the smith of weapons wrought it in days long past, wondrously adorned it, set it round with boar-images, guarded his head so that no sword or battle-blades could pierce it. That was not the least then of mighty helps that Hrothgar's squire lent him in his need. That hilted sword was called Hrunting; it was an excellent old treasure; the brand was iron, marked with poisonous twigs, hardened in the blood of battle. It never failed any men in war who seized it with their hands, who ventured to go on dire journeys, to the meeting-place of foes. That was not the first time that it was to accomplish a mighty deed.

In truth the son of Ecglaf mighty in strength did not remember what erstwhile he spoke when drunken with wine, when he lent the weapon to a better sword-warrior. He himself durst not risk his life beneath the tossing of the waves, accomplish heroic deeds. There he forfeited fame, repute for might. Not so was it with the other when he had clad himself for war.

XXIII

Beowulf spoke, son of Ecgtheow: "Consider now, famous son of Healfdene, wise prince, gold-friend of warriors, now I am ready for the venture, what we spoke of a while since; if I should depart from life in thy cause, that thou shouldst ever be in the place of a father when I am gone. Be thou a guardian to my followers, my comrades, if war takes me. Likewise, dear Hrothgar, do thou send the treasures thou hast given me to Hygelac. The lord of the Geats may perceive by that gold, the son of Hrethel may see when he looks upon that treasure, that I found an excellent good giver of rings, that I took joy while I could. And do thou let Unferth have the ancient blade, the far-famed man have the precious sword with wavy pattern and sharp edge; I shall achieve fame for myself with Hrunting, or death will carry me off."

After those words the prince of the Weder-Geats hastened exceedingly; he would in no wise wait for an answer. The surge of waters received the war-hero. Then there was a spell of time ere he might behold the bottom of the mere.

She who had held for fifty years the domain of the floods, eager for battle, grim and greedy, discovered straightway that a man was seeking from above the dwelling of monsters. She reached out against him then, seized the warrior with dread claws; nevertheless she injured not the sound body; the ring-mail guarded it round about so that she could not pierce the corslet, the locked mail-shirt, with hostile fingers. When she came to the bottom, the sea-wolf bore the prince of rings to her lair, so that he could not (yet was he brave) use weapons; and too many monsters set upon him in the water, many a sea-beast rent his war-corslet with battle-tusks; they pursued the hero. Then the earl noticed he was in some kind of hostile hall, where no water in any way touched him, nor could the sudden clutch of the flood come near him because of the roofed hall; he saw the light of fire, a gleaming radiance shining brightly.

Then the valiant one perceived the she-wolf of the depths, the mighty mere-woman; he repaid the mighty rush with the battle-sword; the hand drew not back from the stroke, so that the sword, adorned with rings, sang a greedy war-chant on her head. Then the stranger found that the sword would not bite or injure life, but the edge failed the prince in his need. It had endured in times past many battles, often had cut through the helmet, the mail of a doomed man. That was the first time for the costly treasure that its repute failed.

Once again the kinsman of Hygelac was resolute, mindful of heroic deeds, no whit lax in courage. Then the angry warrior cast down the sword with its twisted ornaments, set round with decorations, so that it lay on the ground, strong and steel-edged. He trusted in his strength, his mighty hand-grip. Thus a man must needs do when he is minded to gain lasting praise in war, nor cares for his life.

Then the prince of the War-Geats seized Grendel's mother by the hair; he feared not the fight. Then stern in strife he swung the monster in his wrath so that she bent to the ground. She quickly gave him requital again with savage grips, and grasped out towards him. Weary in mood then she overthrew the strongest of fighters, the foot-warrior, so that he fell down. Then she sat on the visitor to her hall, and drew her knife, broad and bright-edged; she was minded to avenge her child, her only son. The woven breast-net lay on his shoulder; that guarded his life; it opposed the entrance of point and edge. Then the son of Ecgtheow, the hero of the Geats, would have found death under the wide waters if the war-corslet, the stout battle-net, had not afforded him help, and if holy God, the wise Lord, had not achieved victory in war; the Ruler of the heavens brought about a right issue, when once more he stood up with ease.

XXIV

He saw then among weapons a victorious blade, an old sword of giants, strong in its edges, the glory of warriors. That was the choicest of weapons; save only it was greater than any other man could bear to the battle-play, trusty and splendid, the work of giants. The hero of the Scyldings, angered and grim in battle, seized the belted hilt, wheeled the ring-marked sword, despairing of life; he struck furiously, so that it gripped her hard against the neck. It broke the bone-rings; the blade went straight through the doomed body. She fell on the floor. The brand was bloody; the man rejoiced in his work.

The gleam was bright, the light stood within, just as the candle of the sky shines serenely from heaven. He went along the dwelling; then he turned to the wall; Hygelac's thane, raging and resolute, raised the weapon firmly by its hilts. The sword was not useless to the warrior, but he was minded quickly to requite Grendel for the many onslaughts which far more than once he made on the West-Danes, when he slew Hrothgar's hearth-companions in their sleep, devoured fifteen men of the Danish people while they slumbered, and bore away as many more, a hateful sacrifice. He, the furious hero, avenged that upon him there where he saw Grendel lying, weary of war, reft of life, as erstwhile the battle at Heorot despatched him. The body gaped wide, when after death it suffered a stroke, a hard battle-blow: and then he hewed off its head.

Straightway the wise men who gazed on the mere with Hrothgar saw that the surge of waves was all troubled, the water stained with blood. Grey-haired old men spoke together of the valiant man, that they did not expect to see the chieftain again, or that he should come as a conqueror to seek the famous prince. Then it seemed to many that the sea-wolf had slain him. Then came the ninth hour of the day. The bold Scyldings forsook the headland; thence the gold-friend of men departed homewards. The strangers sat sick at heart, and stared at the mere; they felt desire and despair of seeing their friendly lord himself.

Then that sword, the battle-brand, began to vanish in drops of gore after the blood shed in fight. That was a great wonder, that it all melted like ice when the Father loosens the bond of the frost, unbinds the fetters of the floods; He has power over times and seasons. That is the true Lord.

The prince of the Weder-Geats took no more of the precious hoardings in those haunts, though he saw many there, save the head and with it the treasure-decked hilts. The sword had melted before, the inlaid brand had burned away, so hot was that blood and so poisonous the alien spirit who died in it. Straightway he fell to swimming; he, who before in the struggle endured the fall of foes, dived up through the water. The wave-surges were all cleansed, the great haunts where the alien spirit gave up his life and this fleeting state.

Then the protector of sea-men, brave-minded, came swimming to land; he took pleasure in the sea-booty, in the mighty burden which he bore with him. They went to meet him, the excellent troop of thanes; they thanked God; they rejoiced in the prince, that they could behold him safe and sound. Then helm and corslet were loosed with speed from off the brave man; the lake lay still, the water under the clouds, stained with the blood of battle.

They set out thence on the foot-tracks, joyous at heart; they paced the path, the well-known street. Men nobly bold bore the head from the cliff with toil for each of the very brave ones. Four men with difficulty had to carry Grendel's head to the gold-hall on the battle-spear, until of a sudden the fourteen brave warlike Geats came to the hall; their lord trod the fields about the mead-hall with them, fearless among his followers.

Then the prince of thanes, the man bold in deeds, made glorious with fame, the hero terrible in battle, came in to greet Hrothgar. Then Grendel's head was borne by the hair into the hall where the men were drinking—a dread object for the earls and the queen with them; the men looked at the wondrous sight.

XXV

Beowulf spoke, son of Ecgtheow: "Lo! son of Healfdene, prince of the Scyldings, we have brought thee with pleasure, as a token of glory, these sea-trophies which thou beholdest here. Scarcely did I survive that with my life, the struggle beneath the water, barely did I accomplish the task, the fight was all but ended, if God had not protected me.

"I could do naught with Hrunting in the fight, though that weapon is worthy, but the Ruler of men vouchsafed that I should see a huge old sword hang gleaming on the wall—most often He has guided those bereft of friends—so that I swung the weapon. Then in the struggle I slew the guardians of the house when the chance was given me. Then that battle-brand, the inlaid sword, burned away as soon as the blood spurted out, hottest battle-gore. Thence from the foes I carried off that hilt; I avenged, as was fitting, the deeds of malice, the massacre of the Danes.

"So I promise thee that thou mayest sleep in Heorot, free from sorrow with the band of thy warriors and all the thanes among thy people, the youths and veterans; that thou, prince of the Scyldings, dost not need to dread death for the earls from the quarter thou didst formerly."

Then the gold hilt, the ancient work of giants, was given into the hands of the old warrior, the grey-haired leader. It came into the possession of the prince of the Danes, the work of cunning smiths, after the death of the monsters, and after the creature of hostile heart, God's foe, guilty of murder, and his mother also had left this world. It came into the power of the best of mighty kings between the seas who dealt out money in Scandinavia.

Hrothgar spoke; he beheld the hilt, the old heirloom. On it was written the beginning of a battle of long ago, when a flood, a rushing sea, slew the race of giants; they had lived boldly; that race was estranged from the eternal Lord. The Ruler gave them final requital for that in the surge of the water. Thus on the plates of bright gold it was clearly marked, set down and expressed in runic letters, for whom that sword, the best of blades, was first wrought with its twisted haft and snake images.

Then the wise man spoke, the son of Healfdene. All were silent. "Lo! he who achieves truth and right among the people may say that this earl was born excellent (the old ruler of the realm recalls all things from the past). Thy renown is raised up throughout the wide ways, my friend Beowulf, among all peoples. Thou preservest all steadfastly, thy might with wisdom of mind. I shall show thee my favour, as before we agreed. Thou shalt be granted for long years as a solace to thy people, as a help to heroes.

"Not so did Heremod prove to the sons of Ecgwela, the honourable Scyldings; his way was not as they wished, but to the slaughter and butchery of the people of the Danes. Savage in mood he killed his table-companions, his trusty counsellors, until he, the famous prince, departed alone from the joys of men, although mighty God had made him great by the joys of power and by strength, had raised him above all men. Yet there grew in his heart a bloodthirsty brood of thoughts. He gave out no rings to the Danes according to custom; joyless he dwelt, so that he reaped the reward of his hostility, the long evil to his people. Learn thou by this; lay hold on virtue. I have spoken this for thy good from the wisdom of many years.

"It is wonderful to tell how mighty God with his generous thought bestows on mankind wisdom, land and rank. He has dominion over all things. At times He allows man's thoughts to turn to love of famous lineage; He gives him in his land the joys of domain, the stronghold of men to keep. He puts the parts of the world, a wide kingdom, in such subjection to him that he cannot in his folly conceive an end to that. He lives in plenty; nothing afflicts him, neither sickness nor age; nor does sorrow darken his mind, nor does strife anywhere show forth sword-hatred, but all the world meets his desire.

XXVI

"He knows nothing worse till within him his pride grows and springs up. Then the guardian slumbers, the keeper of the soul—the sleep is too heavy—pressed round with troubles; the murderer very near who shoots maliciously from his bow. Then he is stricken in the breast under the helmet by a sharp shaft—he knows not how to guard himself—by the crafty evil commands of the ill spirit. That which he had long held seems to him too paltry, he covets fiercely, he bestows no golden rings in generous pride, and he forgets and neglects the destiny which God, the Ruler of glory, formerly gave him, his share of honours. At the end it comes to pass that the mortal body sinks into ruin, falls doomed; another comes to power who bestows treasures gladly, old wealth of the earl; he takes joy in it. Keep thyself from such passions, dear Beowulf, best of warriors, and choose for thyself that better part, lasting profit. Care not for pride, famous hero. Now the repute of thy might endures for a space; straightway again shall age, or edge of the sword, part thee from thy strength, or the embrace of fire, or the surge of the flood, or the grip of the blade, or the flight of the spear, or hateful old age, or the gleam of eyes shall pass away and be darkened; on a sudden it shall come to pass that death shall vanquish thee, noble warrior.

"Thus have I ruled over the Ring-Danes under the heavens for fifty years, and guarded them by my war-power from many tribes throughout this world, from spears and swords, so that I thought I had no foe under the stretch of the sky. Lo! a reverse came upon me in my land, sorrow after joy, when Grendel grew to be a foe of many years, my visitant. I suffered great sorrow of heart continually from that persecution. Thanks be to God, the eternal Lord, that I have survived with my life, that I behold with my eyes that blood-stained head after the old struggle. Go now to the seat, enjoy the banquet, thou who art made illustrious by war; very many treasures shall be parted between us when morning comes."

The Geat was glad in mind; straightway he went to seek out his seat as the wise man bade him. Then again as before the meal was fairly spread once more for men in hall famed for their courage. The covering night grew dark over the noble warriors. The veterans all rose up; the grey-haired aged Scylding was minded to seek his bed. It pleased the Geat, the mighty shield-warrior, exceeding well to rest. Forthwith a hall-thane, who ministered in fitting fashion to all the needs of a thane which the warlike seafarers should have that day, guided him forth, weary as he was from his journey, come from afar. The great-hearted man took his rest; the building towered up wide-gabled and gold-plated; the guest slumbered within till the black raven merrily proclaimed the joy of heaven.

Then came the bright light gliding after the shadow. The warriors hastened, the chieftains were ready to go again to their people, the stout-hearted sojourner was minded to seek the boat far thence. Then the brave man, the son of Ecglaf, bade him bear Hrunting, take his sword, his dear blade; he thanked him for the gift; said that he counted him a good friend in battle, mighty in war; in no wise did he belittle the sword's edge; that was a brave warrior. And the men of war then, ready in war-trappings, were about to depart; the chieftain, dear to the Danes, went to the throne where the other was, the hero dreaded in battle; he greeted Hrothgar.

XXVII

Beowulf spoke, son of Ecgtheow: "Now we seafarers, come from afar, wish to say that we purpose to seek Hygelac. We have been as kindly treated here as we could wish; thou hast been good unto us. If I can in any way on earth win a greater love from thee, lord of men, for warlike deeds than I have yet done, I am ready forthwith. If beyond the compass of the floods I hear that thy neighbours press upon thee with dread war, as at times foes have done to thee, I shall bring to thy help a thousand thanes and heroes. I know that Hygelac, the lord of the Geats, protector of the people, though he is young, will aid me in words and deeds to support thee well and bear a spear to thy aid, mighty succour, if thou hast need of men. If Hrethric, a prince's son, betake himself to the court of the Geats, he may find many friends there. For him who trusts his own merit it is better to visit distant lands."

Hrothgar spoke to him in answer: "The wise Lord has sent those speeches into thy mind. I have not heard a man of such young age discourse more wisely. Thou art strong in might and wise in mind, prudent in speeches. It is my expectation, if it comes to pass that the spear, grim war, sickness, or steel should carry off the son of Hrethel, thy prince, the protector of the people, and thou art still alive, that the Sea-Geats will have no better king to choose, treasure-guardian of heroes, if thou wilt rule the kingdom of thy kinsmen. Thy mind pleases me the better as time goes on, dear Beowulf. Thou hast brought it to pass that there shall be peace between the peoples, the men of the Geats and the Spear-Danes, and that strife shall cease, the treacherous hostility they formerly suffered; while I rule over the wide realm treasures shall be in common; many a man shall greet another with gifts across the gannet's bath; the ring-prowed ship shall bear offerings and love-tokens over the sea. I know the people from old tradition to be wholly blameless towards friend and foe when they are of one mind."

Then moreover the protector of earls, the son of Healfdene, gave in the house twelve treasures; he bade him seek his dear people in safety with those offerings, come again speedily. Then the king of noble race, the prince of the Scyldings, kissed the best of thanes, and fell upon his neck; tears fell from him, the grey-haired man. There was the chance of two things for him, the old man full of years, but more of one, that they should not see one another again, brave men in talk together. That man was so dear to him, that he could not stifle the trouble in his heart, but, fast bound in the thoughts of his heart, the secret longing for the loved man burned in his blood. Thence Beowulf strode over the grass meadow, the warrior proud of his gold, glorying in treasure. The sea-goer riding at anchor awaited its lord. Then Hrothgar's gift was often praised on the voyage. That was a king blameless in all ways, till old age, which has done hurt to many, robbed him of the joys of strength.

XXVIII

Then the troop of exceeding brave warriors came to the flood; they bore ring-woven corslets, locked shirts of mail. The watchman spied the return of the earls as erstwhile he did.

He did not salute the strangers from the edge of the cliff with insult, but rode towards them; he told the people of the Weders that the warriors with gleaming armour went welcome to the ship. Then the spacious ship laden with war garments was on the sand, the ring-prowed vessel with horses and treasures; the mast towered aloft above Hrothgar's precious hoardings.

He gave to the guardian of the ship a sword bound with gold, so that afterwards on the mead-bench he was the more esteemed for the treasure, the ancient sword. He embarked on the ship, to plough the deep water; left the land of the Danes. Then by the mast was a sea-cloth, a sail bound by a rope. The timbers creaked; the wind over the billows did not force the wave-floater from her course. The sea-goer went on her way, the foamy-necked one floated forth over the waves, the boat with bound prow over the ocean-streams, till they could see the cliffs of the Geats, the well-known headlands. The boat drove ashore; urged by the wind it rested on the land.

Quickly the haven-watchman, who for a long time had gazed out afar at the waters expecting the dear men, was ready by the sea. He bound the broad-bosomed ship to the sand firmly with anchor-bonds, lest the might of the waves should drive away the winsome vessel. Then he bade the treasure of chieftains, adornments and beaten gold, to be carried up. He had not far to go thence to seek the giver of treasure, Hygelac, son of Hrethel, where he dwells at home, himself with his comrades near the sea-wall.

The house was splendid, the ruler a mighty king in the high hall, Hygd very young, wise, high-minded, although she, the daughter of Haereth, had lived few years in the stronghold. Yet was she not petty, nor too grudging in gifts and treasures to the people of the Geats. She, the splendid queen of the people, had not the pride or the dread hostility of Thryth. No brave one of the dear comrades, except the mighty prince, durst venture to look upon her openly with his eyes; but he might count upon deadly bonds hand-woven made ready for him. Quickly after that the wrong-doer was destined to the sword, so that the inlaid brand might give judgment, might proclaim the deadly evil. Such is not queenly usage for a woman to practise, though she is splendid; that she who was meant to establish peace should seek the life of a dear subject because of fancied wrong. In truth the kinsmen of Hemming detested that.

Men at their ale-drinking told another tale, that she brought less evils on the people, crafty acts of malice, as soon as she was given, gold-adorned, to the young warrior, to the brave chieftain, when by her father's counsel she sought in her journey the hall of Offa over the yellow flood, where afterwards on the throne she well employed while she lived what was granted her in life, a good famous woman. She kept a noble love towards the prince of heroes, the best, as I have heard, of all mankind, of the race of men between the seas. For Offa was a skilled spearman, widely honoured for gifts and victories; he ruled his realm with wisdom. From him sprang Eomær for a help to heroes, kinsman of Hemming, grandson of Garmund, mighty in onslaught.

XXIX

Then the bold man went himself with his troop to tread the meadow by the sea, the wide shores. The world-candle shone, the sun bright from the south. They went on their way; quickly they marched till they heard that the protector of earls, the slayer of Ongentheow, the worthy young war-king, was bestowing rings in the court. Beowulf's arrival was quickly proclaimed to Hygelac, that the defender of warriors, the shield-comrade, was come alive to the palace there, to the court, unscathed from the battle-play.

With speed, as the mighty one ordered, a space was cleared within the hall for the new-comers. Then he who survived the combat sat down opposite him, kinsman opposite kinsman, when in solemn speech with chosen words he greeted his gracious lord. The daughter of Hæreth went about throughout that hall-building with mead-vessels; she loved the people, bore the flagon to the hands of the Heath-dwellers. Hygelac began graciously to question his companion in the high hall; desire to know the exploits of the Sea-Geats was strong upon him.

"How fared ye on the voyage, dear Beowulf, when on a sudden thou hadst desire to seek combat afar over the salt water, warfare at Heorot? Surely thou hast somewhat mended for Hrothgar, the famous prince, his wide-known sorrow? In my heart's grief for that I was troubled with surgings of sorrow; I put no trust in my loved man's venture; long while I besought thee that thou shouldst have naught to do with the murderous monster, let the South-Danes themselves fight out the struggle with Grendel. I utter thanks to God, that it is granted me to behold thee unscathed."

Beowulf spoke, son of Ecgtheow: "That is known, my lord Hygelac, to many men, the famous encounter; what struggle there was between Grendel and me in that place, where he brought very many sorrows upon the victorious Scyldings, lasting oppression. I avenged all that. Thus none of Grendel's kin upon earth has cause to boast of that uproar at dawn, not he who lives longest of the loathly race, snared in sin.

"Even there did I come to that ring-hall to greet Hrothgar. Straightway the famous son of Healfdene, when he knew my purpose, assigned me a seat beside his own son. His troop was making merry; I have never seen under the vault of heaven greater mead-joy of men sitting in hall. At times the famous queen, she who establishes peace among the peoples, moved throughout the hall, encouraged the young men; often she gave a ring to a warrior ere she went to her seat. At times Hrothgar's daughter bore the ale-flagon before the veterans, to the earls in the high places; then I heard men sitting in hall name Freawaru, where she bestowed the nail-studded vessel on the heroes; she, young, gold-adorned, is promised to the gracious son of Froda. The friend of the Scyldings, the ruler of the realm, has brought that about, and counts it a gain that he should settle with the woman a part of his deadly feuds and struggles. It is always a rare thing, when a little while after the fall of the prince the murderous spear sinks to rest, even though the bride is of worth.

XXX

"That may rankle with the prince of the Heathobards and each thane among the people, when he goes in hall with the bride, that a noble scion of the Danes should tend the warriors. On him gleams the armour of his forefathers, hard and ringmarked, the treasure of the Heathobards, whilst they were able to wield those weapons, until they led their dear comrades and themselves to ruin at the shield-play.

"Then an old spear-warrior who gazes on the treasure, who bears in mind all the slaughter of men, speaks at the beer-drinking—grim is his heart—he begins in mournful mood to test the thoughts of the young warrior by the musings of his mind, to stir up evil strife—and he utters these words:

"'Canst thou, my friend, recognise the sword, the precious blade, thy father bore to battle, where the Danes slew him when under his helmet for the last time; the bold Scyldings held the field when Withergyld lay low, after the fall of heroes. Now some youth or other of those murderers exulting in his adornments walks here in the hall; boasts of the slaughter and wears the treasure, which thou shouldst rightfully own.'

"Thus at all times he admonishes and stirs up memories with baneful words till the season comes when the bride's thane slumbers, stained with blood after the sword-stroke, his life forfeited because of her father's deeds. The other escapes with his life, he knows the country well. Then on both sides are broken the solemn oaths of earls. Afterwards deadly hatreds surge up against Ingeld, and his love for his wife grows cooler from his anguish of mind. Wherefore I look not for the good-will of the Heathobards, nor for much loyalty, void of malice, to the Danes, nor firm friendship.

"I shall speak on once again about Grendel, that thou, the giver of treasure, mayest know well what was later the issue of the hand-struggle of heroes.

"After the jewel of the sky glided over the fields, the monster came raging, the dread night-foe, to seek us out, where safe and sound we held the hall. There was war fatal to Hondscio, a violent death to the doomed man. He was the first to fall, the girded warrior. Grendel devoured him, the famous liege-man; he swallowed the whole body of the loved man. Nevertheless the bloody toothed slayer, his thought set on evil, was not minded to go out again from the gold-hall empty-handed; but, strong in his might, he pitted himself against me, laid hold with ready hand. A pouch hung wide and wondrous, made firm with artful clasps; it was all cunningly devised by the power of the devil and with dragon skins. He, the savage worker of deeds, purposed to put me into it, though guiltless, with many others; it could not come to pass thus when I stood upright in my wrath.

"It is too long to tell how I gave requital to the people's foe for every ill deed. There, my prince, did I bring honour on thy people by my deeds. He escaped forth; for a short space he enjoyed the pleasures of life; yet his right hand remained in Heorot for a token of him; and he, departing thence wretched, sank down, sad in mind, to the bottom of the mere.

"When morning came and we had sat down to the banquet, the friend of the Scyldings rewarded me richly for the deadly onslaught with beaten gold, with many treasures. There was singing and merriment. An aged Scylding of great experience told tales of long ago. At times one bold in battle drew sweetness from the harp, the joy-wood; at times wrought a measure true and sad; at times the large-hearted king told a wondrous story in fitting fashion. At times again an old warrior bowed down with age began to speak to the youths of prowess in fight; his heart swelled within him, when, old in years, he brought to mind many things.

"Thus we took our pleasure there the livelong day, till another night came to men. Then forthwith again Grendel's mother was ready to avenge her grief; sorrowful, she journeyed. Death, the hostility of the Weders, had carried off her son. The monstrous woman avenged her child, she slew a warrior in her might. There life went out from Æschere, a wise councillor through many years. Nor, when morning came, might they, the men of the Danes, consume with fire him who had been made powerless by death; nor lay the loved man on the pyre. She bore off that body in a fiend's embrace under the mountain stream. That was to Hrothgar the heaviest of the sorrows which for a long while had laid hold on the prince of the people. Then the prince, lamenting, entreated me by thy life, that, in the press of the floods, I should perform a deed of prowess, should hazard my life, should achieve an heroic exploit. He promised me reward. Then I found the grim, terrible guardian of the depths of the surging water, who is known far and wide. There for a space was hand-to-hand grappling; the water welled with blood, and in that hall in the depths I cut off the head of Grendel's mother with a gigantic sword; with violence I tore her life from her; I was not yet doomed to death, but the protector of earls, the son of Healfdene, gave me again many a treasure.

XXXI

"Thus did the king of the people live as was fitting; in no way did I lose the rewards, the guerdon of my strength; but he, the son of Healfdene, gave me treasures into my own keeping. Them I will bring and gladly proffer to thee, king of warriors. Once more all favours come from thee. I have few close kinsmen save thee, Hygelac."

Then he commanded to be brought in the boar-image, the banner, the helmet riding high in battle, the grey corslet, the splendid war-sword. Afterwards he spoke:

"Hrothgar, the wise prince, gave me this battle-garment; he expressly bade that I should first declare his good-will to thee. He said that king Heorogar, prince of the Scyldings, had it, the breast-armour, for a long space; that nevertheless he would not give it to his son, the bold Heoroweard, though he was loyal to him. Use all things well."

I heard that four horses, reddish yellow, every whit alike, came next in order; he gave him possession of steeds and stores; thus must a kinsman do, and not weave a cunning net for another, prepare death for a comrade with secret guile. To Hygelac, stout in fight, his nephew was very loyal, and each was mindful of the other's pleasure.

I heard that he presented to Hygd that neck-band, the precious, wondrous treasure, which Wealtheow, the prince's daughter, gave him, together with three steeds full of grace and furnished with gleaming saddles. When she had taken the ring her breast was made fair.

Thus the son of Ecgtheow, a man famous in battle, was bold in brave deeds; he lived honourably; never did he slay his hearth-companions in his drunkenness; his was not a savage mind, but, fearless in fight, he guarded the precious gift which God had given him with the greatest strength among men. Long was he despised, for the men of the Geats accounted him worthless; nor was the lord of troops minded to do him much honour on the mead-bench; they thought indeed that he was slothful, an unfit chieftain. A recompense came to the famous man for every slight.

Then the protector of earls, the king mighty in battle, bade them bring in the sword of Hrethel, decked with gold; there was not at that time with the Geats a better treasure among swords; he laid that in Beowulf's bosom, and gave him seven thousand measures of land, a house and princely rank. To them both in that country land, domain, ancestral claims, had come by natural right, but more to Hygelac, a wide realm, in that he was the more illustrious.

It came to pass in later days among the warriors, when Hygelac was laid low and battle-swords slew Heardred under cover of his shield, after the bold battle-heroes, the warlike Scylfings, sought him mid his victorious troop, pressed hard in fight the nephew of Hereric, that then the wide realm came under Beowulf's sway. He ruled well for fifty years—he was then an aged king, an old guardian of the land—till a dragon which guarded treasure in a burial mound, a steep rock, began to show his might on the dark nights. A pathway lay beneath, unknown to men; some man entered there, greedily seized the pagan hoard . . . tricked the keeper of the treasure with thievish cunning while he slept . . . so that he was enraged.

XXXII

He who did himself sore hurt did not violate the dragon's hoard eagerly of his own free will; but some thane of the sons of heroes was fleeing in great distress from hostile blows, and pressed down by his guilt, lacking a shelter, the man took hiding there. Straightway he looked in . . . dread of the monster lay upon him, yet in his misery . . . then the sudden attack seized him. . . .[1]

There were in the cave many such ancient treasures, which in days gone by some men carefully hid there, great relics of a noble race, precious store.

Death took them all off in past times, and still that one veteran of the people who tarried there longest, a watchman wearying for his friends, looked toward the like fate, that but for a short space he might have sway over the long-gathered treasures. The barrow stood all ready on open ground, hard by the waves, newly-raised near the headland, strong in artful barriers. Into it the guardian of the rings bore the precious heap of the treasures of earls, of beaten gold. Few words he spoke:

"Now, earth, do thou hold, now that heroes cannot, the wealth of earls! Lo! valiant men erstwhile took it from thee. Death in war, a sweeping slaughter, took off each of the men, each of my people, who gave up this life; they had seen joy in hall. I have no one who can wield the sword or polish the golden vessel, the precious flagon; the old warriors have departed. The stout helmet adorned with gold must be reft of its beaten plates. The polishers slumber who should make splendid the battle-masks; and the corslet likewise, which endured the stroke of swords in war mid the cracking of shields, follows the warrior to decay. The coat of mail cannot journey afar by the side of heroes after the passing of the warrior. There is no joy of the harp, delight of the timbrel, nor does the good hawk sweep through the hall, nor the swift steed stamp in the court. Violent death has caused to pass many generations of men."

Thus, sad in mind, the latest left of all lamented his sorrow; day and night he wept joyless, till the surge of death touched his heart. The old twilight-foe, the naked hostile dragon, who seeks out barrows, flaming as he goes, who flies by night compassed with fire, found the costly treasure. Him the dwellers in the land greatly fear. He must needs seek the hoard in the earth, where, old in years, he holds possession of the pagan gold; nor shall he profit one whit by that.

Thus did the people's foe guard that mighty treasure-house in the earth for three hundred years, till a man angered him in mind. He bore the plated goblet to his master, begged his lord for protection. Then the treasure was found, the hoard of rings was lessened; the

---

[1] Words are missing in the manuscript.

boon was granted to the unhappy man. For the first time the prince beheld the ancient work of men.

Then the dragon awoke, wrath was rekindled; he sprang along the rock; brave in heart, he came upon the enemy's foot-track; he had stepped with stealthy craft near the dragon's head. Thus may a man, not destined to fall, who relies on the Almighty's protection, easily survive sorrow and exile.

The treasure-guardian, sore and savage in mind, made eager search along the ground; was set on finding the man, him who had done him scathe while he slept; often he made a whole circuit of the mound outside. There was no man in that waste place. Yet he was keen for the conflict, the work of war; at times he turned to the barrow, sought the treasure. Forthwith he found that some man had ransacked the gold, the rich stores. With difficulty did the treasure-guardian delay till evening came; then wrathful was the warden of the barrow; the foul creature was determined to avenge with fire the precious flagon.

Then day had departed, as the dragon desired; no longer would he wait on the wall, but went forth with fire, furnished with flame. The first onslaught was terrifying to the people in the land, even as it was speedily ended with sorrow for their giver of treasure.

Then the monster began to belch forth flames, to burn the bright dwellings. The flare of the fire brought fear upon men. The loathly air-flier wished not to leave aught living there. The warring of the dragon was widely seen, the onslaught of the cruel foe far and near, how the enemy of the people of the Geats wrought despite and devastation. He hastened back to the hoard, to his hidden hall, ere it was day. He had compassed the dwellers in the land with fire, with flames and with burning; he trusted in the barrow, in bravery and the rampart. His hope deceived him.

XXXIII

Then quickly the terror was made known to Beowulf according to the truth, that his own abode, the best of buildings, the gift-throne of the Geats, was melting in the surges of flame. That was sorrow to the good man's soul, greatest of griefs to the heart. The wise man thought that, breaking established law, he had bitterly angered God, the Lord everlasting. His breast was troubled within by dark thoughts, as was not his wont.

The fire-dragon had destroyed with flames the stronghold of his subjects, the land by the sea from without, the countryside. The warlike king, the prince of the Weders, gave him requital for that. Then the protector of warriors, the lord of earls, bade an iron shield, a splendid war-targe, to be wrought for him. Full well he knew that wood could not help him; linden wood against fire. The chieftain long famous was fated to endure the end of fleeting days, of life in the world, and the dragon with him, though for long space he had held the treasure-store.

Then the prince of rings scorned to seek the far-flier with a troop of men, with a great host. He feared not the fight, nor did he account as aught the valour of the dragon, his power and prowess; because ere this, defying danger, he had come through many onslaughts, wild attacks, when he, the man of victory, purged Hrothgar's hall, and in war killed with his grip the kin of Grendel, the hateful race.

That was not the most paltry of hand-to-hand struggles, where they slew Hygelac, when the king of the Geats, the friendly prince of the peoples, the son of Hrethel, died in the rushes of battle in the land of the Frisians, his blood shed by the sword, beaten down by the brand. Beowulf came thence by his own strength; swam over the sea. Alone he held on his arm thirty suits of armour when he set out on the sea. The Hetware, who bore the linden shields forward against him, had no cause to boast of the battle on foot. Few escaped from that battle-hero to seek their home. The son of Ecgtheow swam over the stretch of the gulfs, the hapless solitary man back to his people, where Hygd tendered him treasure and kingdom, rings and the throne; she did not trust her son, that he could hold his fatherland against hostile hosts, now that Hygelac was dead.

Yet the unhappy men could in no way win the chieftain's consent that he would be lord over Heardred, or that he would elect to rule the realm. Nevertheless he upheld him among the people with friendly counsel, graciously with support, until Heardred grew older; he ruled the Weder-Geats. Exiles, the sons of Ohtere, sought him over the sea. They had risen against the protector of the Scylfings, the best of sea-kings who gave out treasure in Sweden, a famous prince. That ended his life. Deadly wounds from sword-slashes he, the son of Hygelac, gained there for his hospitality; and the son of Ongentheow departed again to seek his home when Heardred was laid low; he let Beowulf hold the throne, rule over the Geats. That was a good king.

XXXIV

In after days he forgot not requital for the prince's fall; he became a friend to the wretched Eadgils. He aided the son of Ohtere overseas with a troop, with warriors and weapons. He took vengeance afterwards with cold, sad marches; he deprived the king of life.

Thus he, the son of Ecgtheow, had survived every onslaught, dread battles, mighty ventures, until that day when he was to encounter the dragon. The lord of the Geats went then with eleven others, raging with anger, to behold the dragon. He had heard then whence the feud arose, the hostility of warriors; the famous costly vessel came into his possession through the hand of the finder.

He who brought about the beginning of that strife, fettered, sad in mind, was the thirteenth man in the troop; he was forced, though in misery, to show the way. He went against his will, till he could spy that cave, the barrow under the ground, hard by the surge of the waters, the struggle of the waves. Within, it was full of jewels and wire ornaments. The monstrous guardian, the ready fighter, grown old beneath the earth, held the treasures. That was no easy matter for any man to enter there.

The king, mighty in onslaught, sat down then on the headland, whilst he, the gold-friend of the Geats, wished good fortune to his hearth-companions. His mind was sad, restless, brooding on death; fate exceeding near which was destined to come on the old man, to seek the treasure of his soul, to part asunder life from the body. Not for long after that was the chieftain's spirit clothed in flesh.

Beowulf spoke, son of Ecgtheow: "In my youth I came through many rushes of war, times of combat. I remember all that. I was seven years old when the prince of treasures, the friendly ruler of the peoples, took me from my father; King Hrethel brought me up and fostered me, bestowed on me treasure and banqueting, bore in mind our kinship; in his life I was no less loved by him, a child in the court, than any of his children, Herebeald and Hæthcyn, or my Hygelac. For the eldest a bed of death was made ready by deeds not fit for a kinsman, when Hæthcyn smote him with curved bow, his friendly prince with an arrow; he missed his mark and shot his kinsman, one brother the other with bloody shaft. That was a violent deed not to be atoned for by gifts, cunningly wrought, weighing sore on the heart. Yet in spite of that the chieftain must needs pass from life unavenged.

"In like manner it is sad for an aged man to endure, that his son in his youth should swing from the gallows. Then he makes a measure, a song of sorrow, when his son hangs, a delight for the raven, and he, aged and full of years, can in no way bring him help. He is ever reminded each morning of his son's death; he cares not to await the birth of another son in his court after the one has made acquaintance with evil deeds by the agony of death. Sorrowful he gazes on his son's room, the deserted wine-hall, a resting-place for the winds, reft of noise. The horsemen slumber, the heroes in their graves; there is no music of the harp, joy in the palace, as there was of yore.

XXXV

"He goes then to his sleeping-place, sings a song of sorrow, one man for another; his lands and dwelling seemed all too spacious for him. Thus did the protector of the Weders bear surging sorrow in his heart for Herebeald; he could no whit avenge the murderous deed on the slayer. Nor could he work hurt to the warrior, though he was not dear to him. Then with that grief which came sorely upon him, he forsook joy of men, chose God's light; left to his sons, as a worthy man does, land and cities, when he departed from life.

"Then guilt and strife came to be the portion of Swedes and Geats over the wide water, a bitter hostility after Hrethel died, and Ongentheow's sons were brave and bold in fight. They did not wish to keep up friendship over the lakes, but often they cunningly contrived dread slaughter near Hreosnaburh. That did my friendly kinsmen avenge, the feud and the outrage, as was well known, though one of them paid for it at a dear price with his life. To Hæthcyn, lord of the Geats, war proved fatal. Then I heard that in the morning one brother avenged the other on the slayer with the sword-edge. There Ongentheow seeks out Eofor. The war-helmet was shattered, the aged Scylfing fell mortally stricken; the hand forgot not the feud; it drew not back from the deadly blow.

"With gleaming sword I repaid in war, as chance was given me, the treasures he bestowed on me. He gave me land, domain, an ancestral seat. There was no need for him to seek among the Gepidæ, or the Spear-Danes, or in the kingdom of the Swedes for less worthy warriors, to buy them with treasure. Ever I wished to be before him on foot, alone in the van, and so shall I do battle while my life lasts, while this sword endures that early and late has often followed me.

Afterwards I slew Dæghrefn, the champion of the Hugas, in the presence of the veterans. He was not able at all to bring adornments, breast-ornaments, to the king of the Frisians, but the keeper of the banner, the chieftain in his might, fell amid the warriors. The sword was not the slayer, but my battle-grip crushed the surges of his heart and his body. Now the edge of the sword, the hand and the keen blade, shall wage war for the treasure."

Beowulf spoke, he uttered pledges for the last time: "In my youth I passed through many battles; yet I, aged protector of the people, wish to seek the fight, to achieve the heroic deed, if the foul foe comes out of his cave to face me."

Then for the last time he greeted each of the men, brave bearers of helmets, dear comrades: "I would not bear a sword, a weapon against the dragon, if I knew how else I could make good my boast against the monster, as erstwhile I did against Grendel; but here I expect hot battle-flame, a blast of breath, and poison. Wherefore I bear shield and corslet. I will not give back the space of a foot before the keeper of the barrow, but the fight shall be between us at the wall, as Fate, the master of every man, shall decide for us. I am brave in mind, so that I can keep from boasting against the winged fighter. Do ye, clad in corslets, warriors in battle-array, bide on the barrow to see which of us two can better survive wounds after the deadly onslaught. This is not your venture, nor is it in any man's power, except mine alone, to strive with his strength against the monster, to perform heroic deeds. With my might I shall gain the gold; or war, a perilous violent death, shall carry off your prince."

Then by his shield the strong warrior arose, stern under his helmet; he bore the battle-corslet under the rocky cliffs; he trusted in the strength of a single man. Such is no coward's venture.

Then he, excellent in virtues, who had survived very many combats, wild attacks, when foot-warriors crashed together, saw a stone arch standing by the wall, a stream gushing out thence from the barrow. The surge of the spring was hot with battle-fires; by reason of the dragon's flame he could not endure for any time unburnt the recess near the treasure. The prince of the Weder-Geats, when he was angered, let a word go out from his breast; the strong-hearted man was wrathful; his voice loud in battle went in resounding under the grey stone.

Hate was roused, the treasure-guardian heard the speech of a man; there was no longer time to seek friendship; first the monster's breath, hot sweat of battle, issued out from the stone; the earth resounded.

The warrior, lord of the Geats, swung his shield under the barrow against the dread creature. Then the heart of the coiling dragon was ready to seek strife. The valiant warlike king first brandished the sword, the ancient blade, not dull in its edges. Each of the two hostile-minded ones felt fear of the other. The ruler of friends stood staunchly against his high shield, when the dragon quickly coiled together; he waited in his war-gear. Then striding amid flames, contorted he went, hastening to his fate. The shield guarded life and body well for the famous prince less time than he wished. There then for the first time he had to show his strength without Fate allotting him fame in battle. The lord of the Geats raised up his hand, he struck the dread gleaming monster with the precious sword, so that the bright edge turned on the bone; it bit less keenly than its king, hard pressed by trouble, had need. Then after the battle-stroke the guard-ian of the treasure was in savage mood; he cast forth deadly fire; far leaped the war-flames. The gold-friend of the Geats boasted not of famous victories; the naked battle-blade failed at need, as it should not have done, the long-famous brand. That was no easy step for the famous son of Ecgtheow to consent to yield that ground; against his will he must needs inhabit a dwelling elsewhere; thus must every man forsake fleeting days.

It was not long till the fighters closed again. The treasure-guardian took heart anew. His breast laboured with breathing. He who before held sway over the people suffered anguish, ringed round with fire.

No whit did his comrades, sons of chieftains, stand about him in a band with valour, but they took to the wood, they hid for their lives. In one of them the mind was roused to face sorrows. In him who well considers nothing can ever stifle kinship.

XXXVI

He was called Wiglaf, son of Weohstan, a valued shield-warrior, prince of the Scylfings, kinsman of Ælfhere; he saw his lord suffering the heat under his war-helm. Then he called to mind the favour which formerly he had bestowed on him, the rich dwelling-place of the Wægmundings, all the rights his father possessed. He could not then hold back; his hand seized the shield, the yellow linden wood, drew the ancient sword, that was among men a relic of Eanmund, son of Ohtere. Weohstan slew him in battle with the edge of the sword, a friendless exile, and bore off from his kin the bright gleaming helm, the ringed corslet, the gigantic old sword that Onela gave him, his kinsman's war-trappings, ready battle-equipment. He spoke not of the feud, though he had killed his brother's child. Many years he held the adornments, brand and corslet until his son could achieve mighty deeds like his old father. Then when he departed from life, old in his passing hence, he gave among the Geats an exceeding number of battle-garments.

That was the first time that the young warrior was to stand the rush of battle with his prince. His spirit did not weaken, nor did his father's sword fail in the fight. The dragon discovered that when they had come together. Wiglaf spoke, uttered many fitting words to his comrades; his mind was sad: "I remember that time when we were drinking mead, when in the beer-hall we promised our lord who gave us these rings, that we would requite him for the war-gear, the helms and sharp swords, if need such as this came upon him. He chose us among the host of his own will for this venture, he reminded us of famous deeds and gave me these treasures, the more because he counted us good spear-warriors, bold bearers of helmets, though our lord, the protector of the people, purposed to achieve this mighty task unaided, because among men he had wrought most famous deeds, daring ventures. Now the day has come when our lord needs the strength of valiant warriors. Let us go to help our warlike prince, while the fierce dread flame yet flares. God knows that, as for me, I had much rather the flame should embrace my body with my gold-giver. It does not seem fitting to me, that we should bear shields back to our dwelling, if we cannot first fell the foe, guard the life of the prince of the Weders. I know well that, from his former deeds, he deserves not to suffer affliction alone among the warriors of the Geats, to fall in fight; sword and helmet, corslet and shirt of mail shall be shared by us both."

He went then through the deadly reek, bore his helmet to the aid of the prince, few words he spoke: "Dear Beowulf, achieve all things well, as thou saidst long ago in thy youth, that thou wouldst not let thy repute fail while life lasted; now, resolute chieftain, mighty in deeds, thou must guard thy life with all thy strength; I will help thee."

After these words the dragon came raging once more, the dread evil creature, flashing with surges of flame, to seek out his foes, the hated men. The shield was burnt away to the rim by waves of fire. The corslet could not give help to the young shield-warrior; but the youth fought mightily beneath his kinsman's buckler, when his own was consumed by the flames. Then again the warlike king was mindful of fame; he struck with his battle-sword with mighty strength, so that, urged by the force of hate, it stuck in his head. Nægling burst apart; Beowulf's sword, ancient and grey, failed in fight. It was not granted to him that the edges of swords might aid him in the struggle, when he bore to battle the weapon hardened by blood of wounds; his hand was too strong, he who, as I have heard, tried every sword beyond its strength. He was in evil plight.

Then for the third time the enemy of the people, the bold fire-dragon, was mindful of fighting; he rushed on the mighty man, when a chance offered, hot and fierce in fight; he clutched his whole neck with sharp teeth; Beowulf grew stained with his life-blood; the gore welled out in surges.

XXXVII

Then I heard that, in the peril of the people's prince, the exalted earl showed courage, strength and daring, as was his nature. He guarded not his head, but the brave man's hand burned when he helped his kinsman, so that he, the man in his armour, beat down a little the hostile creature; and the sword sank in, gleaming and plated; and the fire after began to abate. Then once more the king himself was master of his thoughts; he brandished the battle-knife, keen and sharp for the fray, which he wore on his corslet; the protector of the Weders cut through the dragon in the midst. They felled the foe; force drove out his life; and then they both had slain him, the noble kinsmen. Such should a man be, a thane in time of need.

That was the last victory for the prince by his own deeds, the end of his work in the world. Then the wound which erstwhile the earth-dragon dealt him began to burn and swell. He found forthwith that the poison was working with pestilent force within his breast. Then the chieftain went till, taking wise thought, he sat down on a seat by the wall; he gazed on the work of giants, saw how the eternal earth-building held within stone arches, firm fixed by pillars. Then with his hands the exceeding good thane bathed him with water, the blood-stained famous prince, his friendly lord, wearied with battle; and loosed his helm.

Beowulf spoke, he talked of his wound, of the hurt sore unto death; he knew well that he had ended his days, his joy on earth.

Then all his length of days was passed away, death was exceeding close: "Now I would give armour to my son, if it had been so granted that any heir, sprung from my body, should succeed me. I have ruled this people for fifty years. There was no people's king among the nations about who durst come against me with swords, or oppress me with dread. I have lived the appointed span in my land, guarded well my portion, contrived no crafty attacks, nor sworn many oaths unjustly. Stricken with mortal wounds, I can rejoice in all this; wherefore the Ruler of men has no cause to blame me for the slaughter of kinsmen, when my life passes out from my body. Now, dear Wiglaf, do thou go quickly to behold the hoard under the grey stone, now that the dragon lies low, sleeps sorely wounded, spoiled of the treasure. Haste now that I may see the old riches, the golden treasure, may eagerly gaze on the bright gems of artful work, so that, after winning the great store of jewels, I may the more easily leave life and land, which long I have guarded."

XXXVIII

Then I heard that the son of Weohstan after the speeches quickly obeyed his wounded lord, stricken in battle, bore his ringed corslet, his woven shirt of mail, under the roof of the barrow. Then, exulting in victory, the brave kinsman-thane, as he went by the seat, beheld many costly ornaments, gold gleaming along the ground, wondrous work on the wall, and the lair of the dragon, the old flier at twilight; vessels standing, goblets of olden time, lacking a furbisher, reft of their ornaments. There was many a helm, ancient and rusty, many bracelets cunningly bound. Treasure, gold on the ground, may easily madden any man; conceal it who will!

Likewise he saw a banner all gilt lying high above the hoard, greatest of wonders wrought by hand, cunningly woven in stitches. A gleam shone forth from it so that he might see the floor, behold the jewels. There was no trace of the dragon there, for the sword had carried him off. Then I heard that one man rifled the hoard, the old work of giants in the mound, laid in his bosom flagons and dishes at his own will; took also the banner, brightest of beacons. The sword of the old chieftain—its edge was iron—had earlier laid low him who long while was guardian of the treasures; he bore with him to guard the treasure a dread hot flame, blazing out in battle at midnight, till violently he perished. The messenger was in haste, eager to return, urged on by the treasures. Desire was strong on him to know whether he, the courageous one, should find the mortally-wounded prince of the Weders alive in that place where erstwhile he left him.

Then with the treasures he found the famous prince, his lord bleeding, at the end of his life. Again he began to dash water upon him, until speech came from him. Then the warrior spoke, the aged man in his pain; he gazed on the gold:

"I give thanks in words to the Prince, the King of glory, the eternal Lord, for all the adornments which I behold here, that I have been able to win such for my people before my death-day. Now have I sold my old life for the hoard of treasures; attend ye now to the need of my people. No longer may I tarry here. Bid the men famed in battle raise at the sea-headland a gleaming mound after the burning. It shall tower high on Hronesness, a reminder to my people, so that seafarers may afterwards call it Beowulf's barrow when from afar the ships drive over the dark sea."

The prince of brave mind took from his neck a golden ring, gave to the thane, the young spear-warrior, his helm bright with gold, his ring and corslet; bade him use them well: "Thou art the last of our race, of the Wægmundings. Fate has swept all my kinsmen away to their destiny, earls in their might; I must needs follow them."

That was the last word from the old man's thoughts, before he sought the pyre, the hot, fierce surges of flame. His soul passed from his breast to seek the splendour of the saints.

XXXIX

Then was it sorrow for the young man to see on the earth the man he loved best, his life closed, lying there helpless. The slayer also lay low, the dread earth-dragon, reft of life, vanquished by violence. No longer could the coiled dragon keep guard over the treasure-stores, but iron blades, sharp battle-notched swords, forged by hammers, had carried him off, so that the wide-flier sank to the ground near the treasure-house, still from his wounds. No more did he wheel in his flight through the air at midnight, no more made his appearance exulting in costly possessions; but he fell to the earth because of the warrior's handiwork. Few of a truth among men, among those of might in the land, as I have heard, though they were eager for all exploits, have succeeded in rushing against the blast of the venomous foe, or seizing with hands the hall of rings, if they found the guardian on watch dwelling in the barrow. Beowulf had paid with his death for the many costly treasures; each had gone to the end of fleeting life.

It was not long then till the cowards left the wood, weak failers in loyalty, the ten together, who durst not before wield spears in their lord's great need; but shamefully they bore their shields, the war-gear, where the old man lay; they looked at Wiglaf. He, the foot-warrior, sat wearied, hard by the prince's shoulders, tried to recall him with water. No whit did he succeed; he could not, though dearly he wished, keep life in the prince on earth; nor alter the will of the Almighty. The might of God was pleased to show its power over all men by its deeds, as He yet does now.

Then a grim speech came readily from the youth to those who erstwhile had lost their courage. Wiglaf spoke, son of Weohstan, a man sad at heart; he looked at the hated men: "Lo! he, who wishes to tell the truth, can say that the lord who gave you treasures, warlike adornments, wherein ye stand there, when on the ale-bench he often bestowed on men sitting in hall, a prince to his thanes, helmet and corslet, the most excellent he could anywhere find far or near, that doubtless he miserably cast away the garments of war, when battle beset him. The people's king had indeed no cause to boast of his comrades in fight; yet God, the Disposer of victories, granted that he alone with his sword avenged himself, when he had need of might. Small protection to his life could I afford him in the fight, and yet I tried to aid my kinsman beyond my power. When with the sword I smote the deadly foe, he grew ever weaker, his fire surged out less strongly from his breast. Too few protectors pressed round the prince, when the time came upon him. Now the receiving of jewels, giving of swords, all the splendid heritage, and life's necessities, shall pass away from your race. Every man of the people shall wander, stripped of his rights in the land, when chieftains from afar hear of your flight, the inglorious act. Death is better for all earls than a shameful life."

XL

He bade then the battle be proclaimed in the entrenchment, up over the sea-cliff, where that troop of earls, bearing their shields, sat sad in mind the whole morning, expecting both issues, the death and the return of the loved man. He who rode on the headland held back little of the late tidings, but truthfully he told them all:

"Now is the giver of delights among the people of the Weders, the lord of the Geats, fast in his deathbed, he bides in his slaughterous couch by the deeds of the dragon. By his side lies the deadly foe stricken with knife wounds; he could not in any way deal a wound to the monster with a sword. Wiglaf, son of Weohstan, sits over Beowulf, the earl over the other lifeless one; reverently he keeps watch over friend and foe.

"Now there is prospect of a time of strife for the people, when the fall of the king becomes widely known to Franks and Frisians. The harsh strife with the Hugas was brought about when Hygelac went to the land of the Frisians with a navy, where the Hetware laid him low in battle; they did mightily with their greater numbers, so that the corslet-warrior was forced to yield; he fell mid his troops; the prince gave no adornments to his veterans. To us ever since the good will of the Merovingian king has been denied.

"Nor do I expect any peace or good faith from the people of Sweden; for it was widely known that Ongentheow robbed Hæthcyn, son of Hrethel, of life near Ravenswood, when the warlike Scylfings first sought in their pride the people of the Geats. Straightway the aged father of Ohtere, old and terrible, dealt him a blow in return, killed the sea-guide, the old man freed the bride, the wife reft of her gold, the mother of Onela and Ohtere; and then he followed his deadly foes till with difficulty they escaped, leaderless, to Ravenswood. Then he besieged with a mighty host those who had escaped the sword, wearied from wounds; often through the livelong night he threatened the wretched band with misery; he said that in the morning he would do them hurt with the edge of the sword; some on the gallows-tree for the sport of the birds. With dawn came relief again to the woeful, when they heard Hygelac's horn and the blare of the trumpet, when the valiant one came on the track of the warriors of the people.

XLI

"The blood trail of Swedes and Geats, the deadly attack of men, was widely noted, how the men roused strife between one another. Then the valiant one departed with his kinsmen, the old man very sad, to seek his stronghold. The earl Ongentheow went on further; he had heard of Hygelac's skill in battle, of the proud man's war-strength; he relied not on resistance to check the sea-men, to defend treasure, children and wife against the sea-raiders; the aged man turned thence once more behind a rampart. Then chase was given to the men of the Swedes, the banner to Hygelac. Upon that they overran the stronghold after the people of Hrethel had penetrated the fastnesses. There the grey-haired Ongentheow was constrained to tarry by the edge of the sword, so that the people's king had to suffer the might of Eofor alone. Wulf, son of Wonred, struck him with the sword, so that after the blow the blood gushed from the veins under his hair. Yet was he not daunted, the aged Scylfing, but quickly repaid that deadly stroke with a worse in exchange, as soon as he, the people's king, turned thither. The strong son of Wonred could not give a blow in return to the old man, for he first clove his helmet on his head, so that, stained with blood, he had to give back; he fell on the ground; he was not doomed yet, but he revived, though a wound had stricken him. The bold thane of Hygelac, when his brother was laid low, caused his broad sword, old gigantic brand, to crash the massive helmet over the wall of shields; then the king sank down, the protector of the people; he was stricken unto death. Then were there many who bound up his kinsman; they lifted him speedily when space was cleared for them, so that they might hold possession of the battlefield. Then one warrior spoiled another, took from Ongentheow his iron corslet, his sharp hilted sword, and his helm also; bore the trappings of the old man to Hygelac. He received the adornments, and graciously promised him rewards amid the people, and thus did he fulfil it; the lord of the Geats, the son of Hrethel, when he came to his home, rewarded Eofor and Wulf with exceeding rich treasures for that onslaught; to each of them he gave a hundred thousand measures of land and twisted rings; men on earth had no cause to blame him for the gifts, when they fought heroically; and then to Eofor he gave his only daughter, to adorn his dwelling, as a pledge of good-will.

"That is the feud and the hostility, the deadly hatred of man, which I look for, of Swedish men who will come upon us, when they learn that our prince is dead, who erstwhile guarded treasure and kingdom against foes, the bold Scyldings after the fall of heroes, did what was best for the people, and performed heroic deeds more and more.

"Now haste is best, that we should gaze there upon the people's king, and bring him, who gave us rings, on his way to the pyre. No solitary thing shall be consumed with the brave man, but there is store of treasures, untold gold dearly gained, and now, at the last, rings bought with his own life; the flame shall devour them; the earl shall not wear the treasures as a memorial, nor shall the fair maid bear on her neck the adornment of a circlet, but sad in mind, reft of gold, shall walk in a strange land, not once but oftentimes, now that the leader of the host has done with laughter, joy and merriment. Wherefore many a spear, cold in the morning, shall be grasped with fingers, raised aloft with hands; the sound of the harp shall not rouse the warriors, but the dark raven, ready above the fallen, shall speak many things, shall tell the eagle how he sped at the feasting, when with the wolf he spoiled the slain."

Thus the bold man told evil tidings; he lied not at all in his forecasts and words. The troop all rose up, sadly they went under Earnanæss, with tears welling up, to behold the wonder. Then they found him lifeless on the sand, keeping his helpless couch, him who in former times gave them rings. Then the last of days had come to the valiant one, on which the warlike king, the prince of the Weders, perished a wondrous death. First they saw there a stranger creature, the hateful dragon lying opposite on the ground there; the fire-dragon, the grim dread monster, was scorched with flames; he measured fifty feet long as he lay; often he had taken his pleasure in the air at night; he had come down again to visit his lair; and now he was firm bound by death; he had taken his last delight in the earth-caves. By him stood goblets and flagons, dishes lay there and costly swords eaten through by rust, as if they had remained there a thousand years in the earth's embrace. At that time that mighty heritage, gold of men of olden time, had a curse laid upon it, so that none among men might touch that ring-hall, unless God Himself, the true King of victories—He is the helper of heroes—granted to whom He would to lay open the hoard; even to that man who seemed good unto Him.

XLII

Then it was clear that the way of them, who had wrongfully hidden the jewels under the wall, had not prospered. First the guardian slew one; then the feud was fiercely revenged. It is unknown where an earl, mighty in valour, may come to the end of life, when he may no longer sit on the mead-bench with his kinsmen. Thus was it with Beowulf, when he sought out the guardian of the barrow and battle; he knew not himself in what way his passing from the world should come about.

Thus did the famous princes, who stored that there, lay a heavy ban upon it till doomsday, so that the man who should plunder the place should be guilty of sins, confined in cursed places, fast in bonds of hell, smitten with plagues. He would rather not have beheld the gold-treasure, the owner's might.

Wiglaf spoke, son of Weohstan: "Often must many an earl suffer sorrow through the will of one, as has come upon us. We could not counsel the dear prince, the protector of the kingdom, not to approach the guardian of the gold, but to let him lie there, where long he had been; bide in his dwelling till the end of the world. We have suffered sore fortune; the hoard is seen, grimly won; that fate was too hard which drew the people's king thither. I was within and beheld all that, the stores of the building, when the chance was granted me; in no pleasant way was a passage opened to me in under the earth-wall. In haste I seized a mighty burden of precious treasures in my hands; bore them out hither to my king; he was still living then, wise and clear in mind; the old man in his agony spoke many things, and bade me greet you; ordered that ye should raise on the site of the pyre a high barrow, great and famous, befitting his exploits, even as he was among men the most renowned warrior far and wide throughout the earth, whilst he could enjoy wealth in his castle. Let us now hasten to behold and seek once more the heap of rare gems, the wondrous sight beneath the wall. I will guide you, so that ye may see the rings and broad gold near at hand. Let the bier be made ready, speedily wrought, when we come out and bear then our prince, the loved man, where long he shall wait in the Almighty's keeping."

Then the son of Weohstan, the hero bold in battle, bade orders be given to many of the men who were owners of dwellings, that they, the leaders of bands, should bring from afar wood for the funeral-fire to where the valiant man lay: "Now shall the fire consume—the dark flame shall tower up—the ruler of warriors, him who often endured the iron shower when the storm of arrows, urged with might, darted over the shield-wall, when the shaft did its office; fitted with feathers, it followed the arrow."

In truth the wise son of Weohstan called out the king's thanes from the troop, the best seven together; he went with the seven under the hostile roof of the foemen; one who went in front bore in his hand a torch. It was not settled by lot then who plundered that hoard when the men saw any part unguarded remaining in the hall, lying there perishing; little did any of them mourn that they bore out quickly the precious treasures; also they shoved the dragon, the monster, over the cliff; they let the wave take him, the flood embrace the guardian of the treasures. There was twisted gold beyond measure loaded on the waggon; the chieftain, the grey-haired warrior, was borne to Hronesness.

XLIII

Then the people of the Geats made ready for him a pyre firm on the ground, hung round with helmets, battle-targes, bright corslets, as he had craved; then the sorrowing men laid in the midst the famous prince, their loved lord. The warriors began to rouse on the barrow the greatest of funeral-fires; the wood-reek mounted up dark above the smoking glow, the crackling flame, mingled with the cry of weeping—the tumult of the winds ceased—until it had consumed the body, hot to the heart. Sad in heart, they lamented the sorrow of their souls, the slaying of their lord; likewise the woman with bound tresses sang a dirge[2] . . . the sky swallowed up the smoke.

Then the people of the Weders wrought a mound, which was lofty and broad, at the edge of the headland, visible far and wide to seafarers; and in ten days they finished the beacon of the man mighty in battle; the remnant of the pyre they compassed round with a wall, as exceeding wise men might most worthily devise it. They laid on the barrow rings and ornaments, all such adornments as men, eager for combat, had erstwhile taken from the hoard; they let the earth keep the treasure of earls, the gold in the ground, where it yet lies, as useless to men as it was before. Then men bold in battle, sons of chieftains, twelve in all, rode about the mound; they were minded to utter their grief, to lament the king, to make a chant and to speak of the man; they exalted his heroic life and praised his valorous deed with all their strength.

Thus it is fitting that a man should extol his friendly lord in words, should heartily love him, when he must needs depart from his body and pass away. Thus did the men of the Geats, his hearth-companions, bewail the fall of their lord; they said that among the kings of the world he was the mildest of men and most kindly, most gentle to his people and most eager for praise.

---

[2] Words missing in the manuscript.

THE STORY OF MY MISFORTUNES

Peter Abélard

Often neglected by readers fascinated by the story of his doomed romance with Heloise is the fact that Peter Abélard (1079–1142) was the pre-eminent philosopher and theologian of the twelfth century, a crucial time in the development of medieval philosophy. In this classic of medieval literature, this brilliant and daring thinker relates the story of his philosophical and spiritual enlightenment—and the tale of his tragic personal life as well. Peter Abélard paints an absorbing portrait of monastic and scholastic life in twelfth-century Paris, while also recounting the circumstances and consequences of one of history's most famous love stories. "By doubting," he declared, "we come to inquire, and by inquiry we arrive at truth." Here are the first four chapters of Abélard's story.

CHAPTER I

Of the Birthplace of Pierre Abélard and of His Parents

Know, then, that I am come from a certain town which was built on the way into lesser Brittany, distant some eight miles, as I think, eastward from the city of Nantes, and in its own tongue called Palets. Such is the nature of that country, or, it may be, of them who dwell there—for in truth they are quick in fancy—that my mind bent itself easily to the study of letters. Yet more, I had a father who had won some smattering of letters before he had girded on the soldier's belt. And so it came about that long afterwards his love thereof was so strong that he saw to it that each son of his should be taught in letters even earlier than in the management of arms. Thus indeed did it come to pass. And because I was his first born, and for that reason the more dear to him, he sought with double diligence to have me wisely taught. For my part, the more I went forward in the study of letters, and ever more easily, the greater became the ardour of my devotion to them, until in truth I was so enthralled by my passion for learning that, gladly leaving to my brothers the pomp of glory in arms, the right of heritage and all the honours that should have been mine as the eldest born, I fled utterly from the court of Mars that I might win learning in the bosom of Minerva. And since I found the armory of logical reasoning more to my liking than the other forms of philosophy, I exchanged all other weapons for these, and to the prizes of victory in war I preferred the battle of minds in disputation. Thenceforth, journeying through many provinces, and debating as I went, going whithersoever I heard that the study of my chosen art most flourished, I became such an one as the Peripatetics.

CHAPTER II

Of the Persecution He Had from His Master William of Champeaux—
Of His Adventures at Melun, at Corbeil and at Paris—Of His
Withdrawal from the City of the Parisians to Melun, and His Return to
Mont Ste. Geneviève—Of His Journey to His Old Home

I came at length to Paris, where above all in those days the art of dialectics was most flourishing, and there did I meet William of Champeaux, my teacher, a man most distinguished in his science both by his renown and by his true merit. With him I remained for some time, at first indeed well liked of him; but later I brought him great grief, because I undertook to refute certain of his opinions, not infrequently attacking him in disputation, and now and then in these debates I was adjudged victor. Now this, to those among my fellow students who were ranked foremost, seemed all the more insufferable because of my youth and the brief duration of my studies.

Out of this sprang the beginning of my misfortunes, which have followed me even to the present day; the more widely my fame was spread abroad, the more bitter was the envy that was kindled against me. It was given out that I, presuming on my gifts far beyond the warranty of my youth, was aspiring despite my tender years to the leadership of a school; nay, more, that I was making ready the very place in which I would undertake this task, the place being none other than the castle of Melun, at that time a royal seat. My teacher himself had some foreknowledge of this, and tried to remove my school as far as possible from his own. Working in secret, he sought in every way he could before I left his following to bring to nought the school I had planned and the place I had chosen for it. Since, however, in that very place he had many rivals, and some of them men of influence among the great ones of the land, relying on their aid I won to the fulfillment of my wish; the support of many was secured for me by reason of his own unconcealed envy. From this small inception of my school, my fame in the art of dialectics began to spread abroad, so that little by little the renown, not alone of those who had been my fellow students, but of our very teacher himself, grew dim and was like to die out altogether. Thus it came about that, still more confident in myself, I moved my school as soon as I well might to the castle of Corbeil, which is hard by the city of Paris, for there I knew there would be given more frequent chance for my assaults in our battle of disputation.

No long time thereafter I was smitten with a grievous illness, brought upon me by my immoderate zeal for study. This illness forced me to turn homeward to my native province, and thus for some years I was as if cut off from France. And yet, for that very reason, I was sought out all the more eagerly by those whose hearts were troubled by the lore of dialectics. But after a few years had passed, and I was whole again from my sickness, I learned that my teacher, that same William Archdeacon of Paris, had changed his former garb and joined an order of the regular clergy. This he had done, or so men said, in order that he might be deemed more deeply religious, and so might be elevated to a loftier rank in the prelacy, a thing which, in truth, very soon came to pass, for he was made bishop of Châlons. Nevertheless, the garb he had donned by reason of his conversion did nought to keep him away either from the city of Paris or from his wonted study of philosophy; and in the very monastery wherein he had shut himself up for the sake of religion he straightway set to teaching again after the same fashion as before.

To him did I return, for I was eager to learn more of rhetoric from his lips; and in the course of our many arguments on various matters, I compelled him by most potent reasoning first to alter his former opinion on the subject of the universals, and finally to abandon it altogether. Now, the basis of this old concept of his regarding the reality of universal ideas was that the same quality formed the essence alike of the abstract whole and of the individuals which were its parts: in other words, that there could be no essential differences among these individuals, all being alike save for such variety as might grow out of the many accidents of existence. Thereafter, however, he corrected this opinion, no longer maintaining that the same quality was the essence of all things, but that, rather, it manifested itself in them through diverse ways. This problem of universals is ever the most vexed one among logicians, to such a degree, indeed, that even Porphyry, writing in his "Isagoge" regarding universals, dared not attempt a final pronouncement thereon, saying rather: "This is the deepest of all problems of its kind." Wherefore it followed that when William had first revised and then finally abandoned altogether his views on this one subject, his lecturing sank into such a state of negligent reasoning that it could scarce be called lecturing on the science of dialectics at all; it was as if all his science had been bound up in this one question of the nature of universals.

Thus it came about that my teaching won such strength and authority that even those who before had clung most vehemently to my former master, and most bitterly attacked my doctrines, now flocked to my school. The very man who had succeeded to my master's chair in the Paris school offered me his post, in order that he might put himself under my tutelage along with all the rest, and this in the very place where of old his master and mine had reigned. And when, in so short a time, my master saw me directing the study of dialectics there, it is not easy to find words to tell with what envy he was consumed or with what pain he was tormented. He could not long, in truth, bear the anguish of what he felt to be his wrongs, and shrewdly he attacked me that he might drive me forth. And because there was nought in my conduct whereby he could come at me openly, he tried to steal away the school by launching the vilest calumnies against him who had yielded his post to me, and by putting in his place a certain rival of mine. So then I returned to Melun, and set up my school there as before; and the more openly his envy pursued me, the greater was the authority it conferred upon me. Even so held the poet: "Jealousy aims at the peaks; the winds storm the loftiest summits." (Ovid: "Remedy for Love," I, 369.)

Not long thereafter, when William became aware of the fact that almost all his students were holding grave doubts as to his religion, and were whispering earnestly among themselves about his conversion, deeming that he had by no means abandoned this world, he withdrew himself and his brotherhood, together with his students, to a certain estate far distant from the city. Forthwith I returned from Melun to Paris, hoping for peace from him in the future. But since, as I have said, he had caused my place to be occupied by a rival of mine, I pitched the camp, as it were, of my school outside the city on Mont Ste. Geneviève. Thus I was as one laying siege to him who had taken possession of my post. No sooner had my master heard of this than he brazenly returned post haste to the city, bringing back with him such students as he could, and reinstating his brotherhood in their former monastery, much as if he would free his soldiery, whom he had deserted, from my blockade. In truth, though, if it was his purpose to bring them succour, he did nought but hurt them. Before that time my rival had indeed had a certain number of students, of one sort and another, chiefly by reason of his lectures on Priscian, in which he was considered of great authority. After our master had returned, however, he lost nearly all of these followers, and thus was compelled to give up the direction of the school. Not long thereafter, apparently despairing further of worldly fame, he was converted to the monastic life.

Following the return of our master to the city, the combats in disputation which my scholars waged both with him himself and with his pupils, and the successes which fortune gave to us, and above all to me, in these wars, you have long since learned of through your own experience. The boast of Ajax, though I speak it more temperately, I still am bold enough to make:

> ". . . if fain you would learn now
> How victory crowned the battle, by him was
> I never vanquished."
> (Ovid, "Metamorphoses," XIII, 89.)

But even were I to be silent, the fact proclaims itself, and its outcome reveals the truth regarding it.

While these things were happening, it became needful for me again to repair to my old home, by reason of my dear mother, Lucia, for after the conversion of my father, Berengarius, to the monastic life, she so ordered her affairs as to do likewise. When all this had been completed, I returned to France, above all in order that I might study theology, since now my oft-mentioned teacher, William, was active in the episcopate of Châlons. In this field of learning Anselm of Laon, who was his teacher therein, had for long years enjoyed the greatest renown.

CHAPTER III

Of How He Came to Laon to Seek Anselm as Teacher

I sought out, therefore, this same venerable man, whose fame, in truth, was more the result of long-established custom than of the potency of his own talent or intellect. If any one came to him impelled by doubt on any subject, he went away more doubtful still. He was wonderful, indeed, in the eyes of these who only listened to him, but those who asked him questions perforce held him as nought. He had a miraculous flow of words, but they were contemptible in meaning and quite void of reason. When he kindled a fire, he filled his house with smoke and illumined it not at all. He was a tree which seemed noble to those who gazed upon its leaves from afar, but to those who came nearer and examined it more closely was revealed its barrenness. When, therefore, I had come to this tree that I might pluck the fruit thereof, I discovered that it was indeed the fig tree which Our Lord cursed (Matthew xxi, 19; Mark xi, 13), or that ancient oak to which Lucan likened Pompey, saying:

". . . he stands, the shade of a name once mighty,
  Like to the towering oak in the midst of the fruitful field."
          (Lucan, "Pharsalia," IV, 135.)

It was not long before I made this discovery, and stretched myself lazily in the shade of that same tree. I went to his lectures less and less often, a thing which some among his eminent followers took sorely to heart, because they interpreted it as a mark of contempt for so illustrious a teacher. Thenceforth they secretly sought to influence him against me, and by their vile insinuations made me hated of him. It chanced, moreover, that one day, after the exposition of certain texts, we scholars were jesting among ourselves, and one of them, seeking to draw me out, asked me what I thought of the lectures on the Books of Scripture. I, who had as yet studied only the sciences, replied that following such lectures seemed to me most useful in so far as the salvation of the soul was concerned, but that it appeared quite extraordinary to me that educated persons should not be able to understand the sacred books simply by studying them themselves, together with the glosses thereon, and without the aid of any teacher. Most of those who were present mocked at me, and asked whether I myself could do as I had said, or whether I would dare to undertake it. I answered that if they wished, I was ready to try it. Forthwith they cried out and jeered all the more. "Well and good," said they; "we agree to the test. Pick out and give us an exposition of some doubtful passage in the Scriptures, so that we can put this boast of yours to the proof." And they all chose that most obscure prophecy of Ezekiel.

I accepted the challenge, and invited them to attend a lecture on the very next day. Whereupon they undertook to give me good advice, saying that I should by no means make undue haste in so important a matter, but that I ought to devote a much longer space to working out my exposition and offsetting my inexperience by diligent toil. To this I replied indignantly that it was my wont to win success, not by routine, but by ability. I added that I would abandon the test altogether unless they would agree not to put off their attendance at my lecture. In truth at this first lecture of mine only a few were present, for it seemed quite absurd to all of them that I, hitherto so inexperienced in discussing the Scriptures, should attempt the thing so hastily. However, this lecture gave such satisfaction to all those who heard it that they spread its praises abroad with notable enthusiasm, and thus compelled me to continue my interpretation of the sacred text. When word of this was bruited about, those who had stayed away from the first lecture came eagerly, some to the second and more to the third, and all of them were eager to write down the glosses which I had begun on the first day, so as to have them from the very beginning.

CHAPTER IV

Of the Persecution He Had from His Teacher Anselm

Now this venerable man of whom I have spoken was acutely smitten with envy, and straightway incited, as I have already mentioned, by the insinuations of sundry persons, began to persecute me for my lecturing on the Scriptures no less bitterly than my former master, William, had done for my work in philosophy. At that time there were in this old man's school two who were considered far to excel all the others: Alberic of Rheims and Lotulphe the Lombard. The better opinion these two held of themselves, the more they were incensed against me. Chiefly at their suggestion, as it afterwards transpired, yonder venerable coward had the impudence to forbid me to carry on any further in his school the work of preparing glosses which I had thus begun. The pretext he alleged was that if by chance in the course of this work I should write anything containing blunders—as was likely enough in view of my lack of training—the thing might be imputed to him. When this came to the ears of his scholars, they were filled with indignation at so undisguised a manifestation of spite, the like of which had never been directed against any one before. The more obvious this rancour became, the more it redounded to my honour, and his persecution did nought save to make me more famous.

MEDIEVAL LAYS AND LEGENDS

Marie de France

The twelfth-century poet known as Marie de France, the greatest woman writer of the Middle Ages, wrote stories rooted in Celtic and Breton folklore and legends and created works that have always seemed to readers to bring the world of the Middle Ages to life. Little is known of the person who became Marie de France, including her actual name and other details of her life. She was probably born in France and lived in England at the end of the twelfth century. Her style is thought to have influenced Chaucer and other authors. Included here are three of her best-known works, "The Lay of Sir Launfal," and two other romances,"A Story of Beyond the Sea" and "The Chatelaine of Vergi."

VI

The Lay of Sir Launfal

I will tell you the story of another Lay. It relates the adventures of a rich and mighty baron, and the Breton calls it, the Lay of Sir Launfal.

King Arthur—that fearless knight and courteous lord—removed to Wales, and lodged at Caerleon-on-Usk, since the Picts and Scots did much mischief in the land. For it was the wont of the wild people of the north to enter in the realm of Logres, and burn and damage at their will. At the time of Pentecost, the King cried a great feast. Thereat he gave many rich gifts to his counts and barons, and to the Knights of the Round Table. Never were such worship and bounty shown before at any feast, for Arthur bestowed honours and lands on all his servants—save only on one. This lord, who was forgotten and misliked of the King, was named Launfal. He was beloved by many of the Court, because of his beauty and prowess,

142

for he was a worthy knight, open of heart and heavy of hand. These lords, to whom their comrade was dear, felt little joy to see so stout a knight misprized. Sir Launfal was son to a King of high descent, though his heritage was in a distant land. He was of the King's household, but since Arthur gave him naught, and he was of too proud a mind to pray for his due, he had spent all that he had. Right heavy was Sir Launfal, when he considered these things, for he knew himself taken in the toils. Gentles, marvel not overmuch hereat. Ever must the pilgrim go heavily in a strange land, where there is none to counsel and direct him in the path.

Now, on a day, Sir Launfal got him on his horse, that he might take his pleasure for a little. He came forth from the city, alone, attended by neither servant nor squire. He went his way through a green mead, till he stood by a river of clear running water. Sir Launfal would have crossed this stream, without thought of pass or ford, but he might not do so, for reason that his horse was all fearful and trembling. Seeing that he was hindered in this fashion, Launfal unbitted his steed, and let him pasture in that fair meadow, where they had come. Then he folded his cloak to serve him as a pillow, and lay upon the ground. Launfal lay in great misease, because of his heavy thoughts, and the discomfort of his bed. He turned from side to side, and might not sleep. Now as the knight looked towards the river he saw two damsels coming towards him; fairer maidens Launfal had never seen. These two maidens were richly dressed in kirtles closely laced and shapen to their persons and wore mantles of a goodly purple hue. Sweet and dainty were the damsels, alike in raiment and in face. The elder of these ladies carried in her hands a basin of pure gold, cunningly wrought by some crafty smith—very fair and precious was the cup; and the younger bore a towel of soft white linen. These maidens turned neither to the right hand nor to the left, but went directly to the place where Launfal lay. When Launfal saw that their business was with him, he stood upon his feet, like a discreet and courteous gentleman. After they had greeted the knight, one of the maidens delivered the message with which she was charged.

"Sir Launfal, my demoiselle, as gracious as she is fair, prays that you will follow us, her messengers, as she has a certain word to speak with you. We will lead you swiftly to her pavilion, for our lady is very near at hand. If you but lift your eyes you may see where her tent is spread."

Right glad was the knight to do the bidding of the maidens. He gave no heed to his horse, but left him at his provand in the meadow.

All his desire was to go with the damsels, to that pavilion of silk and divers colours, pitched in so fair a place. Certainly neither Semiramis in the days of her most wanton power, nor Octavian, the Emperor of all the West, had so gracious a covering from sun and rain. Above the tent was set an eagle of gold, so rich and precious, that none might count the cost. The cords and fringes thereof were of silken thread, and the lances which bore aloft the pavilion were of refined gold. No King on earth might have so sweet a shelter, not though he gave in fee the value of his realm. Within this pavilion Launfal came upon the Maiden. Whiter she was than any altar lily, and more sweetly flushed than the new born rose in time of summer heat. She lay upon a bed with napery and coverlet of richer worth than could be furnished by a castle's spoil. Very fresh and slender showed the lady in her vesture of spotless linen. About her person she had drawn a mantle of ermine, edged with purple dye from the vats of Alexandria. By reason of the heat her raiment was unfastened for a little, and her throat and the rondure of her bosom showed whiter and more untouched than hawthorn in May. The knight came before the bed, and stood gazing on so sweet a sight. The Maiden beckoned him to draw near, and when he had seated himself at the foot of her couch, spoke her mind.

"Launfal," she said, "fair friend, it is for you that I have come from my own far land. I bring you my love. If you are prudent and discreet, as you are goodly to the view, there is no emperor nor count, nor king, whose day shall be so filled with riches and with mirth as yours."

When Launfal heard these words he rejoiced greatly, for his heart was litten by another's torch.

"Fair lady," he answered, "since it pleases you to be so gracious, and to dower so graceless a knight with your love, there is naught that you may bid me do—right or wrong, evil or good—that I will not do to the utmost of my power. I will observe your commandment, and serve in your quarrels. For you I renounce my father and my father's house. This only I pray, that I may dwell with you in your lodging, and that you will never send me from your side."

When the Maiden heard the words of him whom so fondly she desired to love, she was altogether moved, and granted him forthwith her heart and her tenderness. To her bounty she added another gift besides. Never might Launfal be desirous of aught, but he would have according to his wish. He might waste and spend at will and pleasure, but in his purse ever there was to spare. No more was Launfal sad. Right merry was the pilgrim, since one had set him on the way, with such a gift, that the more pennies he bestowed, the more silver and gold were in his pouch.

But the Maiden had yet a word to say.

"Friend," she said, "hearken to my counsel. I lay this charge upon you, and pray you urgently, that you tell not to any man the secret of our love. If you show this matter, you will lose your friend, for ever and a day. Never again may you see my face. Never again will you have seisin of that body, which is now so tender in your eyes."

Launfal plighted faith, that right strictly he would observe this commandment. So the Maiden granted him her kiss and her embrace, and very sweetly in that fair lodging passed the day till evensong was come.

Right loath was Launfal to depart from the pavilion at the vesper hour, and gladly would he have stayed, had he been able, and his lady wished.

"Fair friend," said she, "rise up, for no longer may you tarry. The hour is come that we must part. But one thing I have to say before you go. When you would speak with me I shall hasten to come before your wish. Well I deem that you will only call your friend where she may be found without reproach or shame of men. You may see me at your pleasure; my voice shall speak softly in your ear at will; but I must never be known of your comrades, nor must they ever learn my speech."

Right joyous was Launfal to hear this thing. He sealed the covenant with a kiss, and stood upon his feet. Then there entered the two maidens who had led him to the pavilion, bringing with them rich raiment, fitting for a knight's apparel. When Launfal had clothed himself therewith, there seemed no goodlier varlet under heaven, for certainly he was fair and true. After these maidens had refreshed him with clear water, and dried his hands upon the napkin, Launfal went to meat. His friend sat at table with him, and small will had he to refuse her courtesy. Very serviceably the damsels bore the meats, and Launfal and the Maiden ate and drank with mirth and content. But one dish was more to the knight's relish than any other. Sweeter than the dainties within his mouth, was the lady's kiss upon his lips.

When supper was ended, Launfal rose from table, for his horse stood waiting without the pavilion. The destrier was newly saddled and bridled, and showed proudly in his rich gay trappings. So Launfal kissed, and bade farewell, and went his way. He rode back towards the city at a slow pace. Often he checked his steed, and looked behind him, for he was filled with amazement, and all bemused concerning this adventure. In his heart he doubted that it was but a dream. He

was altogether astonished, and knew not what to do. He feared that
pavilion and Maiden alike were from the realm of faery.

Launfal returned to his lodging, and was greeted by servitors, clad
no longer in ragged raiment. He fared richly, lay softly, and spent
largely, but never knew how his purse was filled. There was no lord
who had need of a lodging in the town, but Launfal brought him to
his hall, for refreshment and delight. Launfal bestowed rich gifts.
Launfal redeemed the poor captive. Launfal clothed in scarlet the
minstrel. Launfal gave honour where honour was due. Stranger and
friend alike he comforted at need. So, whether by night or by day,
Launfal lived greatly at his ease. His lady, she came at will and pleasure, and, for the rest, all was added unto him.

Now it chanced, the same year, about the feast of St. John, a
company of knights came, for their solace, to an orchard, beneath
that tower where dwelt the Queen. Together with these lords went
Gawain and his cousin, Yvain the fair. Then said Gawain, that goodly
knight, beloved and dear to all,

"Lords, we do wrong to disport ourselves in this pleasaunce without our comrade Launfal. It is not well to slight a prince as brave as
he is courteous, and of a lineage prouder than our own."

Then certain of the lords returned to the city, and finding Launfal
within his hostel, entreated him to take his pastime with them in that
fair meadow. The Queen looked out from a window in her tower,
she and three ladies of her fellowship. They saw the lords at their
pleasure, and Launfal also, whom well they knew. So the Queen
chose of her Court thirty damsels—the sweetest of face and most
dainty of fashion—and commanded that they should descend with
her to take their delight in the garden. When the knights beheld this
gay company of ladies come down the steps of the perron, they rejoiced
beyond measure. They hastened before to lead them by the hand,
and said such words in their ear as were seemly and pleasant to be
spoken. Amongst these merry and courteous lords hasted not Sir
Launfal. He drew apart from the throng, for with him time went
heavily, till he might have clasp and greeting of his friend. The ladies
of the Queen's fellowship seemed but kitchen wenches to his sight,
in comparison with the loveliness of the maiden. When the Queen
marked Launfal go aside, she went his way, and seating herself upon
the herb, called the knight before her. Then she opened out her heart.

"Launfal, I have honoured you for long as a worthy knight, and
have praised and cherished you very dearly. You may receive a
queen's whole love, if such be your care. Be content: he to whom
my heart is given, has small reason to complain him of the alms."

"Lady," answered the knight," grant me leave to go, for this grace is not for me. I am the King's man, and dare not break my troth. Not for the highest lady in the world, not even for her love, will I set this reproach upon my lord."

When the Queen heard this, she was full of wrath, and spoke many hot and bitter words.

"Launfal," she cried, "well I know that you think little of woman and her love. There are sins more black that a man may have upon his soul. Traitor you are, and false. Right evil counsel gave they to my lord, who prayed him to suffer you about his person. You remain only for his harm and loss."

Launfal was very dolent to hear this thing. He was not slow to take up the Queen's glove, and in his haste spake words that he repented long, and with tears.

"Lady," said he, "I am not of that guild of which you speak. Neither am I a despiser of woman, since I love, and am loved, of one who would bear the prize from all the ladies in the land. Dame, know now and be persuaded, that she, whom I serve, is so rich in state, that the very meanest of her maidens, excels you, Lady Queen, as much in clerkly skill and goodness, as in sweetness of body and face, and in every virtue."

The Queen rose straightway to her feet, and fled to her chamber, weeping. Right wrathful and heavy was she, because of the words that had besmirched her. She lay sick upon her bed, from which, she said, she would never rise, till the King had done her justice, and righted this bitter wrong. Now the King that day had taken his pleasure within the woods. He returned from the chase towards evening, and sought the chamber of the Queen. When the lady saw him, she sprang from her bed, and kneeling at his feet, pleaded for grace and pity. Launfal—she said—had shamed her, since he required her love. When she had put him by, very foully had he reviled her, boasting that his love was already set on a lady, so proud and noble, that her meanest wench went more richly, and smiled more sweetly, than the Queen. Thereat the King waxed marvellously wrathful, and swore a great oath that he would set Launfal within a fire, or hang him from a tree, if he could not deny this thing, before his peers.

Arthur came forth from the Queen's chamber, and called to him three of his lords. These he sent to seek the knight who so evilly had entreated the Queen. Launfal, for his part, had returned to his lodging, in a sad and sorrowful case. He saw very clearly that he had lost his friend, since he had declared their love to men. Launfal sat within his chamber, sick and heavy of thought. Often he called upon his friend, but the lady would not hear his voice. He bewailed his evil lot, with tears; for grief he came nigh to swoon; a hundred times he implored the Maiden that she would deign to speak with her knight. Then, since the lady yet refrained from speech, Launfal cursed his hot and unruly tongue. Very near he came to ending all this trouble with his knife. Naught he found to do but to wring his hands, and call upon the Maiden, begging her to forgive his trespass, and to talk with him again, as friend to friend.

But little peace is there for him who is harassed by a King. There came presently to Launfal's hostel those three barons from the Court. These bade the knight forthwith to go with them to Arthur's presence, to acquit him of this wrong against the Queen. Launfal went forth, to his own deep sorrow. Had any man slain him on the road, he would have counted him his friend. He stood before the King, downcast and speechless, being dumb by reason of that great grief, of which he showed the picture and image.

Arthur looked upon his captive very evilly.

"Vassal," said he, harshly, "you have done me a bitter wrong. It was a foul deed to seek to shame me in this ugly fashion, and to smirch the honour of the Queen. Is it folly or lightness which leads you to boast of that lady, the least of whose maidens is fairer, and goes more richly, than the Queen?"

Launfal protested that never had he set such shame upon his lord. Word by word he told the tale of how he denied the Queen, within the orchard. But concerning that which he had spoken of the lady, he owned the truth, and his folly. The love of which he bragged was now lost to him, by his own exceeding fault. He cared little for his life, and was content to obey the judgment of the Court.

Right wrathful was the King at Launfal's words. He conjured his barons to give him such wise counsel herein, that wrong might be done to none. The lords did the King's bidding, whether good came of the matter, or evil. They gathered themselves together, and appointed a certain day that Launfal should abide the judgment of his peers. For his part Launfal must give pledge and surety to his lord, that he would come before this judgment in his own body. If he might not give such surety then he should be held captive till the appointed day. When the lords of the King's household returned to tell him of their counsel, Arthur demanded that Launfal should put such pledge in his hand, as they had said. Launfal was altogether mazed and bewildered at this judgment, for he had neither friend nor kindred in the land. He would have been set in prison, but

Gawain came first to offer himself as his surety, and with him, all the knights of his fellowship. These gave into the King's hand as pledge, the fiefs and lands that they held of his Crown. The King having taken pledges from the sureties, Launfal returned to his lodging, and with him certain knights of his company. They blamed him greatly because of his foolish love, and chastened him grievously by reason of the sorrow he made before men. Every day they came to his chamber, to know of his meat and drink, for much they feared that presently he would become mad.

The lords of the household came together on the day appointed for this judgment. The King was on his chair, with the Queen sitting at his side. The sureties brought Launfal within the hall, and rendered him into the hands of his peers. Right sorrowful were they because of his plight. A great company of his fellowship did all that they were able to acquit him of this charge. When all was set out, the King demanded the judgment of the Court, according to the accusation and the answer. The barons went forth in much trouble and thought to consider this matter. Many amongst them grieved for the peril of a good knight in a strange land; others held that it were well for Launfal to suffer, because of the wish and malice of their lord. Whilst they were thus perplexed, the Duke of Cornwall rose in the council, and said,

"Lords, the King pursues Launfal as a traitor, and would slay him with the sword, by reason that he bragged of the beauty of his maiden, and roused the jealousy of the Queen. By the faith that I owe this company, none complains of Launfal, save only the King. For our part we would know the truth of this business, and do justice between the King and his man. We would also show proper reverence to our own liege lord. Now, if it be according to Arthur's will, let us take oath of Launfal, that he seek this lady, who has put such strife between him and the Queen. If her beauty be such as he has told us, the Queen will have no cause for wrath. She must pardon Launfal for his rudeness, since it will be plain that he did not speak out of a malicious heart. Should Launfal fail his word, and not return with the lady, or should her fairness fall beneath his boast, then let him be cast off from our fellowship, and be sent forth from the service of the King."

This counsel seemed good to the lords of the household. They sent certain of his friends to Launfal, to acquaint him with their judgment, bidding him to pray his damsel to the Court, that he might be acquitted of this blame. The knight made answer that in no wise could he do this thing. So the sureties returned before the judges, saying that Launfal hoped neither for refuge nor for succour from the lady, and Arthur urged them to a speedy ending, because of the prompting of the Queen.

The judges were about to give sentence upon Launfal, when they saw two maidens come riding towards the palace, upon two white ambling palfreys. Very sweet and dainty were these maidens, and richly clothed in garments of crimson sendal, closely girt and fashioned to their bodies. All men, old and young, looked willingly upon them, for fair they were to see. Gawain, and three knights of his company, went straight to Launfal, and showed him these maidens, praying him to say which of them was his friend. But he answered never a word. The maidens dismounted from their palfreys, and coming before the daïs where the King was seated, spake him fairly, as they were fair.

"Sire, prepare now a chamber, hung with silken cloths, where it is seemly for my lady to dwell; for she would lodge with you awhile."

This gift the King granted gladly. He called to him two knights of his household, and bade them bestow the maidens in such chambers as were fitting to their degree. The maidens being gone, the King required of his barons to proceed with their judgment, saying that he had sore displeasure at the slowness of the cause.

"Sire," replied the barons, "we rose from Council, because of the damsels who entered in the hall. We will at once resume the sitting, and give our judgment without more delay."

The barons again were gathered together, in much thought and trouble, to consider this matter. There was great strife and dissension amongst them, for they knew not what to do. In the midst of all this noise and tumult, there came two other damsels riding to the hall on two Spanish mules. Very richly arrayed were these damsels in raiment of fine needlework, and their kirtles were covered by fresh fair mantles, embroidered with gold. Great joy had Launfal's comrades when they marked these ladies. They said between themselves that doubtless they came for the succour of the good knight. Gawain, and certain of his company, made haste to Launfal, and said,

"Sir, be not cast down. Two ladies are near at hand, right dainty of dress, and gracious of person. Tell us truly, for the love of God, is one of these your friend?"

But Launfal answered very simply that never before had he seen these damsels with his eyes, nor known and loved them in his heart.

The maidens dismounted from their mules, and stood before Arthur, in the sight of all. Greatly were they praised of many, because of their beauty, and of the colour of their face and hair. Some there were who deemed already that the Queen was overborne.

The elder of the damsels carried herself modestly and well, and sweetly told over the message wherewith she was charged.

"Sire, make ready for us chambers, where we may abide with our lady, for even now she comes to speak with thee."

The King commanded that the ladies should be led to their companions, and bestowed in the same honourable fashion as they. Then he bade the lords of his household to consider their judgment, since he would endure no further respite. The Court already had given too much time to the business, and the Queen was growing wrathful, because of the blame that was hers. Now the judges were about to proclaim their sentence, when, amidst the tumult of the town, there came riding to the palace the flower of all the ladies of the world. She came mounted upon a palfrey, white as snow, which carried her softly, as though she loved her burthen. Beneath the sky was no goodlier steed, nor one more gentle to the hand. The harness of the palfrey was so rich, that no king on earth might hope to buy trappings so precious, unless he sold or set his realm in pledge. The Maiden herself showed such as I will tell you. Passing slim was the lady, sweet of bodice and slender of girdle. Her throat was whiter than snow on branch, and her eyes were like flowers in the pallor of her face. She had a witching mouth, a dainty nose, and an open brow. Her eyebrows were brown, and her golden hair parted in two soft waves upon her head. She was clad in a shift of spotless linen, and above her snowy kirtle was set a mantle of royal purple, clasped upon her breast. She carried a hooded falcon upon her glove, and a greyhound followed closely after. As the Maiden rode at a slow pace through the streets of the city, there was none, neither great nor small, youth nor sergeant, but ran forth from his house, that he might content his heart with so great beauty. Every man that saw her with his eyes, marvelled at a fairness beyond that of any earthly woman. Little he cared for any mortal maiden, after he had seen this sight. The friends of Sir Launfal hastened to the knight, to tell him of his lady's succour, if so it were according to God's will.

"Sir comrade, truly is not this your friend? This lady is neither black nor golden, mean nor tall. She is only the most lovely thing in all the world."

When Launfal heard this, he sighed, for by their words he knew again his friend. He raised his head, and as the blood rushed to his face, speech flowed from his lips.

"By my faith," cried he, "yes, she is indeed my friend. It is a small matter now whether men slay me, or set me free; for I am made whole of my hurt just by looking on her face."

The Maiden entered in the palace—where none so fair had come before—and stood before the King, in the presence of his household. She loosed the clasp of her mantle, so that men might the more easily perceive the grace of her person. The courteous King advanced to meet her, and all the Court got them on their feet, and pained themselves in her service. When the lords had gazed upon her for a space, and praised the sum of her beauty, the lady spake to Arthur in this fashion, for she was anxious to begone.

"Sire, I have loved one of thy vassals,—the knight who stands in bonds, Sir Launfal. He was always misprized in thy Court, and his every action turned to blame. What he said, that thou knowest; for over hasty was his tongue before the Queen. But he never craved her in love, however loud his boasting. I cannot choose that he should come to hurt or harm by me. In the hope of freeing Launfal from his bonds, I have obeyed thy summons. Let now thy barons look boldly upon my face, and deal justly in this quarrel between the Queen and me."

The King commanded that this should be done, and looking upon her eyes, not one of the judges but was persuaded that her favour exceeded that of the Queen.

Since then Launfal had not spoken in malice against his lady, the lords of the household gave him again his sword. When the trial had come thus to an end the Maiden took her leave of the King, and made her ready to depart. Gladly would Arthur have had her lodge with him for a little, and many a lord would have rejoiced in her service, but she might not tarry. Now without the hall stood a great stone of dull marble, where it was the wont of lords, departing from the Court, to climb into the saddle, and Launfal by the stone. The Maiden came forth from the doors of the palace, and mounting on the stone, seated herself on the palfrey, behind her friend. Then they rode across the plain together, and were no more seen.

The Bretons tell that the knight was ravished by his lady to an island, very dim and very fair, known as Avalon. But none has had speech with Launfal and his faery love since then, and for my part I can tell you no more of the matter.

XVI

A Story of Beyond the Sea

In times gone by there lived a Count of Ponthieu, who loved chivalry and the pleasures of the world beyond measure, and moreover was a stout knight and a gallant gentleman. In the self-same day there lived a Count of St. Pol, who was lord of much land, and a right worthy man. One grief he had, that there was no heir of his body; but a sister was his, a prudent woman and a passing good gentlewoman, who was dame of Dommare in Ponthieu. This lady had a son, Thibault by name, who was heir to this County of St. Pol, but he was a poor man so long as his uncle lived. He was a prudent knight, valiant and skilled with the spear, noble and fair. Greatly was he loved and honoured of all honest people, for he was of high race and gentle birth.

The Count of Ponthieu, of whom the tale hath spoken, had to wife a very worthy lady. He and his dame had but one child, a daughter, very good and gracious, who increased with her days in favour and in virtues; and the maid was of some sixteen years. The third year after her birth her mother died, whereof she was sorely troubled and right heavy. The Count, her father, took to himself another wife with no long tarrying, a dame of gentle race and breeding. Of this lady he got him quickly a son; very near was the boy to his father's heart. The lad grew with his years in stature and in valour, and gave promise to increase in all good qualities.

The Count of Ponthieu marked my lord Thibault of Dommare. He summoned the knight to his castle, and made him of his house for guerdon. When Sir Thibault was of his fellowship he rejoiced greatly, for the Count prospered in goods and in praise by reason of his servant's deeds. As they came from a tournament on a day, the Count and my lord Thibault together, the Count required of his companion and said,

"Thibault, by the aid of God tell me truly which jewel of my crown shines the fairest in your eyes!"

"Sir," replied Messire Thibault, "I am only a beggar, but so help me God, of all the jewels in your crown I love and covet none, save only my demoiselle, your daughter."

When he heard this thing the Count had great content. He laughed in his heart and said,

"Thibault, I will grant her to the beggar, if it be to her mind."

"Sir," answered he, "thanks and gramercy. May God make it up to you."

Then went the Count to his daughter, and said,

"Fair daughter, I have promised you in marriage, so it go not against your heart."

"Sir," inquired the maid, "to whom?"

"In the name of God, to a loyal man, and a true man, of whom much is hoped; to a knight of my own household, Thibault of Dommare."

"Dear sir," answered the maiden sweetly, "if your county were a kingdom, and I were the king's only child, I would choose him as my husband, and gladly give him all that I had."

"Daughter," said the Count, "blessed be your pretty person, and the hour that you were born."

Thus was this marriage made. The Count of Ponthieu and the Count of St. Pol were at the feast, and many another honourable man besides. Great was the joy in which they met, fair was the worship, and marvellous the delight. The bride and groom lived together in all happiness for five years. This was their only sorrow, that it pleased not our Lord Jesus Christ that they should have an heir to their flesh.

On a night Sir Thibault lay in his bed. He considered within himself and said,

"Lord, whence cometh it that I love this dame so fondly, and she me, yet we may have no heir of our bodies to serve God and to do a little good in the world?"

Then he remembered my lord St. James, the Apostle of Spain, who gives to the fervent supplicant that which rightly he desires. Earnestly, to his own heart, he promised that he would walk a pilgrim in his way. His wife lay sleeping at his side, but when she came from out her sleep, he took her softly in his arms, and required of her that she would bestow on him a gift.

"Sir," said the lady, "what gift would you have?"

"Wife," he made answer, "that you shall know when it is mine."

"Husband," said she, "if it be mine to grant, I will give it you, whatever the price."

"Wife," he said, "I pray you to grant me leave to seek my lord St. James the Apostle, that he may intercede with our Lord Jesus Christ to bestow on us an heir of our flesh, whereby God may be served in this world and Holy Church glorified."

"Sir," cried the lady, "sweet and dear it is that you should crave such bounty, and I grant the permission you desire right willingly."

Deep and long was the tenderness that fell betwixt these twain. Thus passed a day, and another day, and yet a third. On this third day it chanced that they lay together in their bed, and it was night. Then said the dame,

"Husband, I pray and require of you a gift."

"Wife," he replied, "ask, and I will give it you, if by any means I can."

"Husband," she said, "I require leave to come with you on this errand and journey."

When Messire Thibault heard this thing he was right sorrowful, and said,

"Wife, grievous would be the journey to your body, for the way is very long, and the land right strange and perilous."

Said she,

"Husband, be not in doubt because of me. You shall be more hindered of your squire than of your wife."

"Dame," said he, "as God wills and as you wish."

The days went, and these tidings were so noised abroad that the Count of Ponthieu heard thereof. He commanded my lord Sir Thibault to his house, and said,

"Thibault, you are a vowed pilgrim, as I hear, and my daughter too!"

"Sir," answered he, "that is verily and truly so."

"Thibault," replied the Count, "as to yourself what pleases you is to my mind also, but concerning my daughter that is another matter."

"Sir," made answer Sir Thibault, "go she must, and I cannot deny her."

"Since this is so," said the Count, "part when you will. Make ready for the road your steeds, your palfreys, and the pack horses, and I will give you riches and gear enough for the journey."

"Sir," said Messire Thibault, "thanks and gramercy."

Thus these pilgrims arrayed them, and sought that shrine with marvellous joy. They fared so speedily upon the way, that at length they came near to my lord St. James, by less than two days faring. That night they drew to a goodly town. After they had eaten in the hostel, Sir Thibault called for the host and inquired of him the road for the morrow, how it ran, and whether it were smooth.

"Fair sir," replied the innkeeper to the knight, "at the gate of this town you will find a little wood. Beyond the wood a strong smooth road runs for the whole day's journey."

Hearing this they asked no more questions, but the beds being laid down, they went to their rest. The morrow broke full sweetly.

The pilgrims rose lightly from their beds as soon as it was day, and made much stir and merriment. Sir Thibault rose also, since he might not sleep, but his head was heavy. He therefore called his chamberlain, and said,

"Rise quickly, and bid the company to pack the horses and go their way. Thou shalt remain with me, and make ready our harness, for I am a little heavy and disquieted."

The chamberlain made known to the sergeants the pleasure of their lord, so that presently they took the road. In no great while Messire Thibault and his dame got them from the bed, and arraying their persons, followed after their household. The chamberlain folded the bed linen, and it was yet but dawn, though warm and fair. The three went forth through the gate of the city, those three together, with no other companion save God alone, and drew near to the forest. When they came close they found two roads, the one good, the other ill; so that Sir Thibault said to his chamberlain,

"Put spurs to your horse, and ride swiftly after our people. Bid them await our coming, for foul it is for lady and knight to pass through this wood with so little company."

The servitor went speedily, and Messire Thibault entered the forest. He drew rein beside the two roads, for he knew not which to follow.

"Wife," he said, "which way is ours?"

"Please God, the good," she answered.

Now in this wood were robbers, who spoiled the fair way, and made wide and smooth the false, so that pilgrims should mistake and wander from the path. Messire Thibault lighted from his horse. He looked from one to the other, and finding the wrong way broader and more smooth than the true, he cried,

"Wife, come now; in the name of God, this."

They had proceeded along this road for some quarter of a mile when the path grew strict and narrow, and boughs made dark the way.

"Wife," said the knight, "I fear that we fare but ill."

When he had thus spoken he looked before him, and marked four armed thieves, seated on four strong horses, and each bore lance in hand. Thereupon he glanced behind him, and, lo, four other robbers, armed and set in ambush, so he said,

"Dame, be not affrighted of aught that you may see from now."

Right courteously Sir Thibault saluted the robbers in his path, but they gave no answer to his greeting. Afterwards he sought of them what was in their mind, and one replied that he should know anon. The thief, who had thus spoken, drew towards my lord Thibault, with outstretched sword, thinking to smite him in the middle. Messire

Thibault saw the blow about to fall, and it was no marvel if he feared greatly. He sprang forward nimbly, as best he might, so that the glaive smote the air. Then as the robber staggered by, Sir Thibault seized him fiercely, and wrested the sword from his hand. The knight advanced stoutly against those three from whom the thief had come. He struck the foremost amidst the bowels, so that he perished miserably. Then he turned and went again to that one who had first come against him with the sword, and slew him also. Now it was decreed of God that after the knight had slain three of this company of robbers, that the five who were left, encompassed him round about, and killed his palfrey. Sir Thibault tumbled flat upon his back, although he was not wounded to his hurt. Since he had neither sword nor other harness he could do no more. The thieves therefore stripped him to his very shirt, his boots and hosen, and binding him hand and foot with a baldrick, cast him into a thorn bush, right thick and sharp. When they had done this they hastened to the lady. From her they took her palfrey and her vesture, even to the shift. Passing fair was the lady; she wept full piteously, and never was dame more sorrowful than she. Now one of these bold robbers stared upon the lady, and saw that she was very fair. He spoke to his companions in this fashion,

"Comrades, I have lost my brother in this broil. I will take this woman for his blood money."

But the others made answer,

"I, too, have lost my kin. I claim as much as you, and my right is good as yours."

So said a third, and a fourth, and a fifth. Then spake yet another.

"In keeping of the lady will be found neither peace nor profit. Rather let us lead her from here within the forest, there do our pleasure upon her, and then put her again upon the path, so that she may go her way."

Thus they did as they had devised together, and left her on the road.

Right sick at heart was Messire Thibault when he saw her so entreated, but nothing could he do. He bore no malice against his wife by reason of that which had befallen, for well he knew that it was by force, and not according to her will. When he saw her again, weeping bitterly and altogether shamed, he called to her, and said,

"Wife, for God's love unloose me from these bonds, and deliver me from the torment that I suffer, for these thorns are sharper than I can endure."

The lady hastened to the place where Sir Thibault lay, and marked a sword flung behind the bush, belonging to one of those felons that were slain. She took the glaive, and went towards her lord, filled full of wrath and evil thoughts because of what had chanced to her. She feared greatly lest her husband should bear malice for that which he had seen, reproaching her upon a day, and taunting her for what was past. She said,

"Sir, you are out of your pain already."

She raised the sword, and came towards her husband, thinking to strike him midmost the body. When he marked the falling glaive he deemed that his day had come, for he was a naked man, clad in nought but his shirt and hosen. He trembled so sorely that his bonds were loosed, and the lady struck so feebly that she wounded him but little, severing that baldrick with which his hands were made fast. Thereat the knight brake the cords about his legs, and leaping upon his feet, cried,

"Dame, by the grace of God it is not to-day that you shall slay me with the sword."

Then she made answer,

"Truly, sir, the sorer grief is mine."

Sir Thibault took the sword, and set it again in the sheath, afterwards he put his hand upon the lady's shoulder, and brought her back by the path they had fared. At the fringe of the woodland he found a large part of his fellowship, who were come to meet him. When these saw their lord and lady so spoiled and disarrayed they inquired of them,

"Sir, who hath put you in this case?"

He set them by, saying that they had fallen amongst felons who had done them much mischief.

Mightily the sergeants lamented; but presently they fetched raiment from the packs, and arrayed them, for enough they had and to spare. So they climbed into the saddle, and continued their journey.

They rode that day, nor for aught that had chanced did Messire Thibault show sourer countenance to the lady. At nightfall they came to a goodly town, and there took shelter in an inn. Messire Thibault sought of his host if there was any convent of nuns in those parts where a lady might repose her. The host made answer to him,

"Sir, you are served to your wish. Just beyond the walls is a right fair religious house, with many holy women."

On the morrow Messire Thibault went to this house, and heard Mass. Afterwards he spoke to the Abbess and her chapter, praying that he might leave his lady in their charge, until his return; and this they accorded very willingly. Messire Thibault bestowed the lady in this convent, with certain of his house to do her service, and went his way to bring his pilgrimage to a fair end. When he had knelt before the shrine, and honoured the Saint, he came again to the convent and the lady. He gave freely of his wealth to the house, and taking to himself his wife, returned with her to their own land, in the same joy and honour as he had brought her forth, save only that they lay not together.

Great was the gladness of the folk of that realm when Sir Thibault returned to his home. The Count of Ponthieu, the father of his wife was there, and there, too, was his uncle the Count of St. Pol. Many worthy and valiant gentlemen came for his welcome, and a fair company of dames and maidens likewise honoured the lady. That day the Count of Ponthieu sat at meat with my lord Thibault, and ate from the same dish, the two together. Then it happed that the Count spake to him,

"Thibault, fair son, he who journeys far hears many a strange matter and sees many strange sights, which are hidden from those who sit over the fire. Tell me therefore, of your favour, something of all you have seen and heard since you went from amongst us."

Messire Thibault answered shortly that he knew no tale worth the telling. The Count would take no denial, but plagued him so sorely, begging him of his courtesy to tell over some adventure, that at the last he was overborne.

"Sir, I will narrate a story, since talk I must; but at least let it be in your private ear, if you please, and not for the mirth of all."

The Count replied that his pleasure was the same. After meat, when men had eaten their fill, the Count rose in his chair, and taking my lord Thibault by the hand, entreated,

"Tell me now, I pray, that which it pleases you to tell, for there are few of the household left in hall."

Then Messire Thibault began to relate that which chanced to a knight and a dame, even as it has been rehearsed before you in this tale; only he named not the persons to whom this lot was appointed. The Count, who was wise and sober of counsel, inquired what the knight had done with the lady. Thibault made answer that the knight had brought the lady back by the way she went, with the same joy and worship as he led her forth, save only that they slept not together.

"Thibault," said the Count, "your knight walked another road than I had trod. By my faith in God and my love for you, I had hanged this dame by her tresses to a tree. The laces of her gown would suffice if I could find no other cord."

"Sir," said Messire Thibault, "you have but my word. The truth can only be assured if the lady might bear witness and testify with her own mouth."

"Thibault," said the Count, "know you the name of this knight?"

"Sir," cried Messire Thibault, "I beg you again to exempt me from naming the knight to whom this sorrow befell. Know of a truth that his name will bring no profit."

"Thibault," said the Count, "it is my pleasure that his name should not be hid."

"Sir," answered Thibault, "tell I must, as you will not acquit me; but I take you to witness that I speak only under compulsion, since gladly I would have kept silence, had this been your pleasure, for in the telling there is neither worship nor honour."

"Thibault," replied the Count, "without more words I would know forthwith who was the knight to whom this adventure chanced. By the faith that you owe to your God and to me, I conjure you to tell me his name, since it is in your mind."

"Sir," replied Messire Thibault, "I will answer by the faith I owe my God and you, since you lay this charge upon me. Know well, and be persuaded, that I am the knight on whom this sorrow lighted. Hold it for truth that I was sorely troubled and sick of heart. Be assured that never before have I spoken to any living man about the business, and moreover that gladly would I have held my peace, had such been your will."

When the Count heard this adventure he was sore astonied, and altogether cast down. He kept silence for a great space, speaking never a word. At the last he said,

"Thibault, was it indeed my child who did this thing?"

"Sir, it is verily and truly so."

"Thibault," said the Count, "sweet shall be your vengeance, since you have given her again to my hand."

Because of his exceeding wrath the Count sent straightway for his daughter, and demanded of her if those things were true of which Messire Thibault had spoken. She inquired of the accusation, and her father answered,

"That you would have slain him with the sword, even as he has told me?"

"Sir, of a surety."

"And wherefore would you slay your husband?"

"Sir, for reason that I am yet heavy that he is not dead."

When the Count heard the lady speak in this fashion, he answered her nothing, but suffered in silence until the guests had departed.

After these were gone, the Count came on a day to Rue-sur-Mer, and Messire Thibault with him, and the Count's son. With them also went the lady. Then the Count caused a ship to be got ready, very stout and speedy, and he made the dame to enter in the boat. He set also on the ship an untouched barrel, very high and strong. These three lords climbed into the nave, with no other company, save those sailors who should labour at the oar. The Count commanded the mariners to put the ship to sea, and all marvelled greatly as to what he purposed, but there was none so bold as to ask him any questions. When they had rowed a great way from the land, the Count bade them to strike the head from out the barrel. He took that dame, his own child, who was so dainty and so fair, and thrust her in the tun, whether she would or whether she would not. This being done he caused the cask to be made fast again with staves and wood, so that the water might in no manner enter therein. Afterwards he dragged the barrel to the edge of the deck, and with his own hand cast it into the sea, saying,

"I commend thee to the wind and waves."

Passing heavy was Messire Thibault at this, and the lady's brother also, and all who saw. They fell at the Count's feet, praying him of his grace that she might be delivered from the barrel. So hot was his wrath that he would not grant their prayer, for aught that they might do or say. They therefore left him to his rage, and turning to the Heavenly Father, besought our Lord Jesus Christ that of His most sweet pity He would have mercy on her soul, and give her pardon for her sins.

The ship came again to land, leaving the lady in sore peril and trouble, even as the tale has told you. But our Lord Jesus Christ, who is Lord and Father of all, and desireth not the death of a sinner, but rather that he should turn from his wickedness and live—as each day He showeth us openly by deed, by example and by miracle—sent succour to this lady, even as you shall hear. For a ship from Flanders, laden with merchandise, marked this barrel drifting at the mercy of winds and waters, before ever the Count and his companions were come ashore. One of the merchants said to his comrades,

"Friends, behold a barrel drifting in our course. If we may reach it, perchance we may find it to our gain."

This ship was wont to traffic with the Saracens in their country, so the sailors rowed towards the barrel, and partly by cunning and partly by strength, at the last got it safely upon the deck. The merchants looked long at the cask. They wondered greatly what it could be, and wondering, they saw that the head of the barrel was newly closed. They opened the cask, and found therein a woman at the point of death, for air had failed her. Her body was gross, her visage swollen, and the eyes started horribly from her head. When she breathed the fresh air and felt the wind blow upon her, she sighed a little, so that the merchants standing by, spoke comfortably to her, but she might not answer them a word. In the end, heart and speech came again to her. She spoke to the chapmen and the sailors who pressed about her, and much she marvelled how she found herself amongst them. When she perceived that she was with merchants and Christian men she was the more easy, and fervently she praised Jesus Christ in her heart, thanking Him for the lovingkindness which had kept her from death. For this lady was altogether contrite in heart, and earnestly desired to amend her life towards God, repenting the trespass she had done to others, and fearing the judgment that was rightly her due. The merchants inquired of the lady whence she came, and she told them the truth, saying that she was a miserable wretch and a poor sinner, as they could see for themselves. She related the cruel adventure which had chanced to her, and prayed them to take pity on a most unhappy lady, and they answered that mercy they would show. So with meat and drink her former beauty came to her again.

Now this merchant ship fared so far that she came to the land of the Paynims, and cast anchor in the port of Aumarie. Galleys of these Saracens came to know their business, and they answered that they were traffickers in divers merchandise in many a realm. They showed them also the safe conduct they carried of princes and mighty lords that they might pass in safety through their countries to buy and sell their goods. The merchants got them to land in this port, taking the lady with them. They sought counsel one of the other to know what it were best to do with her. One was for selling her as a slave, but his companion proposed to give her as a sop to the rich Soudan of Aumarie, that their business should be the less hindered. To this they all agreed. They arrayed the lady freshly in broidered raiment, and carried her before the Soudan, who was a lusty young man. He accepted their gift, receiving the lady with a right glad heart, for she was passing fair. The Soudan inquired of them as to who she was.

"Sire," answered the merchants, "we know no more than you, but marvellous was the fashion in which she came to our hands."

The gift was so greatly to the Soudan's mind that he served the chapmen to the utmost of his power. He loved the lady very tenderly, and entreated her in all honour. He held and tended her so well, that her sweet colour came again to her, and her beauty increased beyond measure. The Soudan sought to know by those who had the gift of tongues as to the lady's home and race, but these she would not reveal to any. He was the more thoughtful therefore, because he might see that she was a dame of birth and lineage. He inquired of her as to whether she were a Christian woman, promising that if she would deny her faith, he would take her as his wife, since he was yet unwed. The lady saw clearly that it were better to be converted by love than perforce; so she answered that her religion was to do her master's pleasure. When she had renounced her faith, and rejected the Christian law, the Soudan made her his dame according to the use and wont of this country of the Paynim. He held her very dear, cherishing her in all honour, for his love waxed deeper as the days wore on.

In due time it was with this lady after the manner of women, and she came to bed of a son. The Soudan rejoiced greatly, being altogether merry and content. The lady, for her part, lived in fair fellowship with the folk of her husband's realm. Very courteous was she, and very serviceable, so that presently she was instructed in the Saracen tongue. In no long while after the birth of her son she conceived of a maid, who in the years that befell grew passing sweet and fair, and richly was she nurtured as became the daughter of so high a prince. Thus for two years and a half the lady dwelt with the Paynim in much softness and delight.

Now the story keeps silence as to the lady and the Soudan, her husband, till later, as you may hear, and returns to the Count of Ponthieu, the son of the Count, and to my lord Thibault of Dommare, who were left grieving for the dame who was flung into the sea, as you have heard, nor knew aught of her tidings, but deemed that she were rather dead than alive. Now tells the story—and the truth bears witness to itself and is its own confirmation—that the Count was in Ponthieu, together with his son, and Messire Thibault. Very heavy was the Count, for in no wise could he get his daughter from his mind, and grievously he lamented the wrong that he had done her. Messire Thibault dared not take to himself another wife, because of the anguish of his friend. The son of the Count might not wed also; neither durst he to become knight, though he was come to an age when such things are greatly to a young man's mind.

On a day the Count considered deeply the sin that he had committed against his own flesh. He sought the Archbishop of Rheims in confession, and opened out his grief, telling in his ear the crime that he had wrought. He determined to seek those holy fields beyond the sea, and sewed the Cross upon his mantle. When Messire Thibault knew that his lord, the Count, had taken the Cross, he confessed him, and did likewise. And when the Count's son was assured of the purpose of his sire and of Messire Thibault, whom he loved dearly, he took the Cross with them. Passing heavy was the Count to mark the Sign upon his son's raiment.

"Fair son, what is this you have done; for now the land remains without a lord!"

The son answered, and said,

"Father, I wear the Sign first and foremost for the love of God; afterwards for the saving of my soul, and by reason that I would serve and honour Him to the utmost of my power, so long as I have life in my body."

The Count put his realm in ward full wisely. He used diligence in making all things ready, and bade farewell to his friends. Messire Thibault and the son of the Count ordered their business, and the three set forth together, with a fair company. They came to that holy land beyond the sea, safe of person and of gear. There they made devout pilgrimage to every place where they were persuaded it was meet to go, and God might be served. When the Count had done all that he was able, he deemed that there was yet one thing to do. He gave himself and his fellowship to the service of the Temple for one year; and at the end of this term he purposed to seek his country and his home. He sent to Acre, and made ready a ship against his voyage. He took his leave of the Knights Templar, and other lords of that land, and greatly they praised him for the worship that he had brought them. When the Count and his company were come to Acre they entered in the ship, and departed from the haven with a fair wind. But little was their solace. For when they drew to the open sea a strong and horrible tempest sprang suddenly upon them, so that the sailors knew not where they went, and feared each hour that all would be drowned. So piteous was their plight that, with ropes, they bound themselves one to another, the son to the father, the uncle to the nephew, according as they stood. The Count, his son, and Messire Thibault for their part, fastened themselves together, so that the same end should chance to all. In no long time after this was done they saw land, and inquired of the shipmen whither they were come. The mariners answered that this realm belonged to the Paynim, and was called the Land of Aumarie. They asked of the Count,

"Sire, what is your will that we do? If we seek the shore, doubtless we shall be made captives, and fall into the hands of the Saracen."

The Count made answer,

"Not my will, but the will of Jesus Christ be done. Let the ship go as He thinks best. We will commit our bodies and our lives to

His good keeping, for a fouler and an uglier death we cannot die, than to perish in this sea."

They drove with the wind along the coast of Aumarie, and the galleys and warships of the Saracens put out to meet them. Be assured that this was no fair meeting, for the Paynims took them and led them before the Soudan, who was lord of that realm. There they gave him the goods and the bodies of these Christians as a gift. The Soudan sundered this fair fellowship, setting them in many places and in divers prisons; but since the Count, his son, and Messire Thibault were so securely bound together, he commanded that they should be cast into a dungeon by themselves, and fed upon the bread of affliction and the water of affliction. So it was done, even as he commanded. In this prison they lay for a space, till such time as the Count's son fell sick. His sickness was so grievous that the Count and Messire Thibault feared greatly that this sorrow was to death.

Now it came to pass that the Soudan held high Court because of the day of his birth, for such was the custom of the Saracens. After they had well eaten, the Saracens stood before the Soudan, and said,

"Sire, we require of you our right."

He inquired of what right they were speaking, and they answered,

"Sire, a Christian captive to set as a mark for our arrows."

When the Soudan heard this he gave no thought to such a trifle, but made reply,

"Get you to the prison, and take out that captive who has the least of life in him."

The Paynim hastened to the dungeon, and brought forth the Count, bearded, unkempt and foredone. The Soudan marked his melancholy case, so he said to them,

"This man has not long to live; take him hence, and do your will on him."

The wife of the Soudan, of whom you have heard, the daughter of this very Count, was in the hall, when they brought forth her father to slay him. Immediately that her eyes fell upon him the blood in her veins turned to water; not so much that she knew him as her sire, but rather that Nature tugged at her heart strings. Then spake the dame to the Soudan,

"Husband, I, too, am French, and would gladly speak with this poor wretch ere he die, if so I may."

"Wife," answered the Soudan, "truly, yes; it pleases me well."

The lady came to the Count. She took him apart, and bidding the Saracens fall back, she inquired of him whence he was.

"Lady, I am from the kingdom of France, of a county that men call Ponthieu."

When the lady heard this her bowels were moved. Earnestly she demanded his name and race.

"Of a truth, lady, I have long forgotten my father's house, for I have suffered such pain and anguish since I departed, that I would rather die than live. But this you may know, that I—even the man who speaks to you—was once the Count of Ponthieu."

The lady hearkened to this, but yet she made no sign. She went from the Count, and coming to the Soudan, said,

"Husband, give me this captive as a gift, if such be your pleasure. He knows chess and draughts and many fair tales to bring solace to the hearer. He shall play before you, and we will make our pastime of his skill."

"Wife," answered the Soudan, "I grant him to you very willingly; do with him as you wish."

The lady took the captive, and bestowed him in her chamber. The gaolers sought another in his stead, and brought forth my lord Thibault, the husband to the dame. He came out in tatters, for he was clothed rather in his long hair and great beard, than in raiment. His body was lean and bony, and he seemed as one who had endured pain and sorrow enough, and to spare. When the lady saw him she said to the Soudan,

"Husband, with this one also would I gladly speak, if so I may."

"Wife," answered the Soudan, "it pleases me well."

The lady came to my lord Thibault, and inquired of him whence he was.

"Lady, I am of the realm of that ancient gentleman who was taken from prison before me. I had his daughter to wife, and am his knight."

The lady knew well her lord, so she returned to the Soudan, and said to him,

"Husband, great kindness will you show me, if you give me this captive also."

"Wife," said the Soudan, "I grant him to you very willingly."

She thanked him sweetly, and bestowed the gift in her chamber, with the other.

The archers hastened together, and drawing before the Soudan said,

"Sire, you do us wrong, for the day is far spent."

They went straight to the prison, and brought forth the son of the Count, shagged and filthy, as one who had not known of water for many a day. He was a young man, so young that his beard had not come on him, but for all his youth he was so thin and sick and weak, that he scarce could stand upon his feet. When the lady saw him she had compassion upon him. She came to him asking whose son he was and of his home, and he replied that he was son to that gentleman, who was first brought out of the dungeon. She knew well that this was her brother, but she made herself strange unto him.

"Husband," said she to the Soudan, "verily you will shew kindness to your wife beyond measure if you grant me this captive. He knows chess and draughts and other delights passing fair to see and hear."

And the Soudan made answer,

"Wife, by our holy law if they were a hundred I would give them all to you gladly."

The lady thanked him tenderly, and bestowed the captive swiftly in her chamber. The Saracens went again to the prison and fetched out another, but the lady left him to his fate, when she looked upon his face. So he won a martyr's crown, and our Lord Jesus Christ received his soul. As for the dame, she hid herself from the sight, for it gave her little joy, this slaying of the Christian by the Paynims.

The lady came to her chamber, and at her coming the captives would have got them to their feet, but she made signs that they should remain seated. Drawing close she made gestures of friendship. The Count, who was very shrewd, asked at this,

"Lady, when will they slay us?"

She answered that their time had not yet come.

"Lady," said he, "the sorer grief is ours, for we are so anhungered, that for a little our souls would leave our bodies."

The lady went out, and bade meat to be made ready. This she carried in, giving to each a little, and to each a little drink. When they had eaten, they had yet greater hunger than before. In this manner she fed them, little by little, ten times a day, for she deemed that should they eat to their desire, they would die of repletion. For this reason she caused them to break their fast temperately. Thus the good lady dealt with them for the first seven days, and at nights, by her grace, they lay softly at their ease. She did away with their rags, and clad them in seemly apparel. When the week was done she set before them meat and drink to their heart's desire, so that their strength returned to them again. They had chess and draughts, and played these games to their great content. The Soudan was often with them. He watched the play, and took pleasure in their gladness. But the lady refrained, so that none might conceive, either by speech or fashion, that he had known her before.

Now a short while after this matter of the captives, the story tells that the Soudan had business enough of his own, for a mighty Sultan laid waste his realm, and sought to do him much mischief. To avenge his wrong the Soudan commanded his vassals from every place, and assembled a great host. When the lady knew this, she entered the chamber where the captives lay, and sitting amidst them lifted her hand, and said,

"Sirs, you have told me somewhat of your business; now will I be assured whether you are true men or not. You told me that in your own land you were once the Count of Ponthieu, that this man was wedded to your daughter, and that this other was your son. Know that I am a Saracen, having the science of astrology; so I tell you plainly that you were never so near to a shameful death, as you are now, if you hide from me the truth. What chanced to your daughter, the wife of this knight?"

"Lady," replied the Count, "I deem her to be dead."

"How came she to her death?"

"Certes, lady," said the Count, "because for once she received her deserts."

"Tell me of these deservings," said the dame.

Then the Count began to tell, with tears, of how she was wedded, but was yet a barren wife; how the good knight vowed pilgrimage to my lord St. James in Galicia, and how the lady prayed that she might go with him, which prayer he granted willingly. He told how they went their way with joy, till alone, in the deep wood, they met with sturdy felons who set upon them. The good knight might do nothing against so many, for he was a naked man; but despite of all, he slew three, and five were left, who killed his palfrey, and spoiling him to the very shirt, bound him hands and feet, and flung him into a thorn bush. They spoiled the lady also and stole her palfrey from her. When they looked upon her, and saw that she was fair, each would have taken her. Afterwards they accorded that she should be to all, and having had their will in her despite, they departed and left her weeping bitterly. This the good knight saw, so he besought her courteously to unloose his hands, that they might get them from the wood. But the lady marked a sword belonging to one of these felons that were slain. She handselled it, and hastening where he lay, cried in furious fashion, "You are unbound already." Then she raised the naked sword, and struck at his body. But by the loving kindness of God, and the vigour of the knight, she but sundered the bonds that bound him, so that he sprang forth, and wounded as he was, cried,

"Dame, by the grace of God it is not to-day that you shall kill me with the sword."

At this word that fair lady, the wife of the Soudan, spoke suddenly, and said,

"Ah, sir, you have told the tale honestly, and very clear it is why she would have slain him."

"For what reason, lady?"

"Certes," answered she, "for reason of the great shame which had befallen her."

When Messire Thibault heard this he wept right tenderly, and said,

"Alas, what part had she in this wickedness! May God keep shut the doors of my prison if I had shown her the sourer face therefore, seeing that her will was not in the deed."

"Sir," said the lady, "she feared your reproach. But tell me which is the more likely, that she be alive or dead?"

"Lady," said Thibault, "we know not what to think."

"Well I know," cried the Count, "of the great anguish we have suffered, by reason of the sin I sinned against her."

"If it pleased God that she were yet living," inquired the lady, "and tidings were brought which you could not doubt, what would you have to say?"

"Lady," said the Count, "I should be happier than if I were taken from this prison, or were granted more wealth than ever I have had in my life."

"Lady," said Messire Thibault, "so God give me no joy of my heart's dearest wish, if I had not more solace than if men crowned me King of France."

"Certes, lady," said the dansellon, who was her brother, "none could give or promise me aught so sweet, as the life of that sister, who was so fair and good."

When the lady hearkened to these words her heart yearned with tenderness. She praised God, rendering Him thanks, and said to them,

"Be sure that you speak with unfeigned lips."

And they answered and said that they spoke with unfeigned lips. Then the lady began to weep with happy tears, and said to them,

"Sir, now may you truly say that you are my father, for I am that daughter on whom you wrought such bitter justice. And you, Messire Thibault, are my lord and husband; and you, sir dansellon, are my brother."

Then she rehearsed to them in what manner she was found of the chapmen, and how they bestowed her as a gift on the Soudan. They were very glad, and rejoiced mightily, humbling themselves before her, but she forbade them to show their mirth, saying,

"I am a Saracen, and have renounced the faith; otherwise I should not be here, but were dead already. Therefore I pray and beseech you as you love your lives and would prolong your days, whatever you may see or hear, not to show me any affection, but keep yourselves strange to me, and leave me to unravel the coil. Now I will tell why I have revealed myself to you. My husband, the Soudan, rides presently to battle. I know well, Messire Thibault, that you are a hardy knight, and I will pray the Soudan to take you with him. If ever you were brave, now is the time to make it plain. See to it that you do him such service that he have no grievance against you."

The lady departed forthwith, and coming before the Soudan, said,

"Husband, one of my captives desires greatly to go with you, if such be your pleasure."

"Wife," answered he, "I dare not put myself in his hand, for fear that he may do me a mischief."

"Husband, he will not dare to be false, since I hold his companions as hostages."

"Wife," said he, "I will take him with me, because of your counsel, and I will deliver him a good horse and harness, and all that warrior may require."

The lady returned straightway to the chamber. She said to Messire Thibault,

"I have persuaded the Soudan to bring you to the battle. Act therefore manfully."

At this her brother knelt at her knee, praying her to plead with the Soudan that he might go also.

"That I may not do," said she, "or the thing will be too clear."

The Soudan ordered his business, and went forth, Messire Thibault being with him, and came upon the enemy. According to his word, the Soudan had given to the knight both horse and harness. By the will of Jesus Christ, who faileth never such as have faith and affiance in Him, Messire Thibault did such things in arms that in a short space the enemies of the Soudan were put under his feet. The Soudan rejoiced greatly at his knight's deeds and his victory, and returned bringing many captives with him. He went straight to the dame, and said,

"Wife, by my law I have naught but good to tell of your prisoner, for he has done me faithful service. So he deny his faith, and receive our holy religion, I will grant him broad lands, and find him a rich heiress in marriage."

"Husband, I know not, but I doubt if he will do this thing."

No more was spoken of the matter; but the lady set her house in order, as best she was able, and coming to her captives said,

"Sirs, go warily, so that the Saracens see nothing of what is in our mind; for, please God, we shall yet win to France and the county of Ponthieu."

On a day the lady came before the Soudan. She went in torment, and lamented very grievously.

"Husband, it is with me as it was before. Well I know it, for I have fallen into sore sickness, and my food has no relish in my mouth, no, not since you went to the battle."

"Wife, I am right glad to hear that you are with child, although your infirmity is very grievous unto me. Consider and tell me those things that you deem will be to your healing, and I will seek and procure them whatever the cost."

When the lady heard this, her heart beat lightly in her breast. She showed no semblance of joy, save this only, that she said,

"Husband, my old captive tells me that unless I breathe for awhile such air as that of my native land, and that quickly, I am but dead, for in nowise have I long to live."

"Wife," said the Soudan, "your death shall not be on my conscience. Consider and show me where you would go, and there I will cause you to be taken."

"Husband, it is all one to me, so I be out of this city."

Then the Soudan made ready a ship, both fair and strong, and garnished her plenteously with wines and meats.

"Husband," said the lady to the Soudan, "I will take of my captives the aged and the young, that they may play chess and draughts at my bidding, and I will carry with me my son for my delight."

"Wife," answered he, "your will is my pleasure. But what shall be done with the third captive?"

"Husband, deal with him after your desire."

"Wife, I desire that you take him on the ship; for he is a brave man, and will keep you well, both on land and sea, if you have need of his sword."

The lady took leave of the Soudan, bidding him farewell, and urgently he prayed her to return so soon as she was healed of her sickness. The stores being put upon the ship and all things made ready, they entered therein and set sail from the haven. With a fair wind they went very swiftly, so that the shipmen sought the lady, saying,

"Madam, this wind is driving the boat to Brindisi. Is it your pleasure to take refuge there, or to go elsewhere?"

"Let the ship keep boldly on her course," answered the lady to them, "for I speak French featly and other tongues also, so I will bring you to a good end."

They made such swift passage by day and by night, that according to the will of Our Lord they came quickly to Brindisi. The ship cast anchor safely in the harbour, and they lighted on the shore, being welcomed gladly by the folk of that country. The lady, who was very shrewd, drew her captives apart, and said,

"Sirs, I desire you to call to mind the pledge and the covenant you have made. I must now be certain that you are true men, remembering your oaths and plighted words. I pray you to let me know, by all that you deem of God, whether you will abide or not by our covenant together; for it is yet not too late to return to my home."

They answered,

"Lady, know beyond question that the bargain we have made we will carry out loyally. By our faith in God and as christened men we will abide by this covenant; so be in no doubt of our assurance."

"I trust you wholly," replied the lady; "but, sirs, see here my son, whom I had of the Soudan, what shall we do with him?"

"Lady, the boy is right welcome, and to great honour shall he come in our own land."

"Sirs," said the dame, "I have dealt mischievously with the Soudan, for I have stolen my person from him, and the son who was so dear to his heart."

The lady went again to the shipmen, and lifting her hand, said to them,

"Sirs, return to the Soudan whence you came, and greet him with this message. Tell him that I have taken from him my body and the son he loved so well, that I might deliver my father, my lord, and my brother from the prison where they were captive."

When the sailors heard this they were very dolent, but there was naught that they might do. They set sail for their own country, sad and very heavy by reason of the lady, of the young lad, whom they loved greatly, and of the captives who were escaped altogether from their hand.

For his part the Count arrayed himself meetly by grace of merchants and Templars, who lent him gladly of their wealth. He abode in the town, together with his fellowship, for their solace, till they made them ready for the journey, and took the road to Rome. The Count sought the Pontiff, and his company with him. Each confessed him of the secrets of his heart, and when the Bishop heard thereof, he accepted their devotion, and comforted them right tenderly. He baptised the child, who was named William. He reconciled the lady with Holy Church, and confirmed the lady and Messire Thibault her lord, in their marriage bond, reknitting them together, giving penance to each, and absolution for their sins. After this they made no long sojourn in Rome, but took their leave of the Apostle who had honoured them so greatly. He granted them his benison, and commended them to God. So they went their way in great solace and delight, praising God and His Mother, and all the calendar of saints, and rendering thanks for the mercies which had been vouchsafed to them. Journeying thus they came at last to the country of their birth, and were met by a fair procession of bishops and abbots, monks and priests, who had desired them fervently. But of all these welcomes they welcomed most gladly her who was recovered from death, and had delivered her sire, her lord, and her brother from the hands of the Paynim, even as you have heard. There we leave them for awhile, and will tell you of the shipmen and Saracens who had fared with them across the sea.

The sailors and Saracens who had carried them to Brindisi, returned as quickly as they were able, and with a fair wind cast anchor before Aumarie. They got them to land, very sad and heavy, and told their tidings to the Soudan.

Right sorrowful was the Soudan, and neither for time nor reason could he forget his grief. Because of this mischief he loved that daughter the less who tarried with him, and showed her the less courtesy. Nevertheless the maiden increased in virtue and in wisdom, so that the Paynim held her in love and honour, praising her for the good that was known of her. But now the story is silent as to that Soudan who was so tormented by reason of the flight of his dame and captives; and comes again to the Count of Ponthieu, who was welcomed to his realm with such pomp and worship, as became a lord of his degree.

In no long while after his return the son of the Count was dubbed knight, and rich was the feast. He became a knight both chivalrous and brave. Greatly he loved all honourable men, and gladly he bestowed fair gifts on the poor knights and poor gentlewomen of the country. Much was he esteemed of lord and hind, for he was a worthy knight, generous, valiant and debonair, proud only to his foes. Yet his days on earth were but a span, which was the sorer pity, for he died lamented of all.

Now it befell that the Count held high Court, and many a knight and lord sat with him at the feast. Amongst these came a very noble

man and knight, of great place in Normandy, named my lord Raoul
des Preaux. This Raoul had a daughter, passing sweet and fair. The
Count spoke so urgently to Raoul and to the maiden's kin that a
marriage was accorded between William, his grandson, the son of the
Soudan of Aumarie, and the daughter of my lord Raoul, the heiress
to all his wealth. William wedded the damsel with every rich observance, and in right of his wife this William became Lord of Preaux.

For a long while the realm had peace from its foes. Messire Thibault
dwelt with the lady, and had of her two sons, who in later days were
worthy gentlemen of great worship. The son of the Count of Ponthieu,
of whom we have spoken much and naught but good, died shortly
after, to the grief of all the land. The Count of St. Pol was yet alive;
therefore the two sons of my lord Thibault were heirs to both these
realms, and attained thereto in the end. That devout lady, their
mother, because of her contrite heart, gave largely to the poor; and
Messire Thibault, like the honourable gentleman he was, abounded
in good works so long as he was quick.

Now it chanced that the daughter of the lady, who abode with
the Soudan her father, increased greatly in favour and in virtue. She
was called The Fair Captive, by reason that her mother had left her
in the Soudan's keeping, as you have heard. A certain brave Turk in
the service of the Soudan—Malakin of Baudas by name—saw this
damsel, so fair and gracious, and desired her dearly in his heart,
because of the good men told of her. He came before his master,
and said to him,

"Sire, in return for his labour your servant craves a gift."

"Malakin," returned the Soudan, "what gift would you have?"

"Sire, I would dare to tell it to your face, if only she were not so
high above my reach."

The Sultan who was both shrewd and quick witted made reply,

"Say out boldly what is in your mind, for I hold you dear, and
remember what you have done. If there is aught it beseems me to
grant—saving only my honour—be assured that it is yours."

"Sire, well I know that your honour is without spot, nor would
I seek anything against it. I pray you to bestow on your servant—if
so it be your pleasure—my lady your daughter, for she is the gift I
covet most in all the world."

The Soudan kept silence, and considered for a space. He knew
well that Malakin was both valiant and wise, and might easily come
to great honour and degree. Since the servant was worthy of his high
desire, the Soudan said,

"By my law you have required of me a great thing, for I love my daughter dearly, and have no other heir. You know well, and it is the simple truth, that she comes of the best and bravest blood in France, for her mother is the child of the Count of Ponthieu. But since you too are valiant, and have done me loyal service, for my part I will give her to you willingly, save only that it be to the maiden's mind."

"Sire," said Malakin, "I would not take her against her wish."

The Soudan bade the girl be summoned. When she came, he said, "Fair daughter, I have granted you in marriage, if it pleases you."

"Sir," answered the maiden, "my pleasure is in your will."

The Soudan took her by the hand, saying,

"Take her, Malakin, the maid is yours."

Malakin received her with a glad heart, and wedded her according to the Paynim rite, bringing her to his house right joyously, with the countenance of all his friends. Afterwards he returned with her to his own land. The Soudan escorted them upon their way, with such a fair company of his household as seemed good to him. Then he bade farewell to his child and her lord, and returned to his home. But a great part of his fellowship he commanded to go with her for their service.

Malakin came back to his own land, where he was welcomed right gladly of his friends, and served and honoured by all the folk of his realm. He lived long and tenderly with his wife, neither were they childless, as this story testifies. For of this lady, who was called the Fair Captive, was born the mother of that courteous Turk, the Sultan Saladin, an honourable, a wise, and a conquering lord.

XVII

The Chatelaine of Vergi

There are divers men who make a great show of loyalty, and pretend to such discretion in the hidden things they hear, that at the end folk come to put faith in them. When by their false seeming they have persuaded the simple to open out to them their love and their deeds, then they noise the matter about the country, and make it their song and their mirth. Thus it chances that the lesser joy is his who has bared to them his heart. For the sweeter the love, the more bitter is the pang that lovers know, when each deems the other to

have bruited abroad the secret he should conceal. Oftentimes these
blabbers do such mischief with their tongue, that the love they spoil
comes to its close in sorrow and in care. This indeed happened in
Burgundy to a brave and worthy knight, and to the Lady of Vergi.
This knight loved his lady so dearly that she granted him her tenderness, on such covenant as this—that the day he showed her favour
to any, that very hour he would lose the love and the grace she
bestowed on him. To seal this bond they devised together that the
knight should come a days to an orchard, at such hour as seemed
good to his friend. He must remain coy in his nook within the wall
till he might see the lady's lapdog run across the orchard. Then
without further tarrying he should enter her chamber, knowing full
well she was alone, whom so fondly he desired to greet. This he did,
and in this fashion they met together for a great while, none being
privy to their sweet and stolen love, save themselves alone.

The knight was courteous and fair, and by reason of his courage
was right welcome to that Duke who was lord of Burgundy. He
came and went about the Court, and that so often that the Duchess
set her mind upon him. She cared so little to hide her thought, that
had his heart not been in another's keeping, he must surely have
perceived in her eyes that she loved him. But however tender her
semblance the knight showed no kindness in return, for he marked
nothing of her inclination. Passing troubled was the dame that he
should treat her thus; so that on a day she took him apart, and sought
to make him of her counsel.

"Sir, as men report, you are a brave and worthy knight, for the
which give God thanks. It would not be more than your deserts,
if you had for friend a lady in so high a place that her love would
bring to you both honour and profit. How richly could such a lady
serve you!"

"Lady," said he, "I have never yet had this in my thought."

"By my faith," she answered, "it seems to me that the longer you
wait, the less is your hope. Perchance the lady will stoop very readily from her throne, if you but kneel at her knee."

The knight replied,

"Lady, by my faith, I know little why you speak such words, and
I understand their meaning not at all. I am neither duke nor count
to dare to set my love in so high a seat. There is nought in me to
gain the love of so sovereign a dame, pain me how I may."

"Such things have been," said she, "and so may chance again.
Many more marvellous works have been wrought than this, and the

day of miracles is not yet past. Tell me, know you not yet that you have gained the love of some high princess, even mine?"

The knight made answer forthwith,

"Lady, I know it not. I would desire to have your love in a fair and honourable fashion; but may God keep me from such love between us, as would put shame upon my lord. In no manner, nor for any reason, will I enter on such a business as would lead me to deal my true and lawful lord so shrewd and foul a wrong."

Bitter at heart was the dame to see her love so scorned.

"Fie upon you," she cried, "and who required of you any such thing?"

"Ah, lady, to God be the praise; you have said enough to make your meaning passing plain."

The lady strove no more to show herself kind to him. Great was the wrath and sharp the malice that she hid within her heart, and well she purposed that, if she might, she would avenge herself speedily. All the day she considered her anger. That night as she lay beside the Duke she began to sigh, and afterwards to weep. Presently the Duke inquired of her grief, bidding her show it him forthwith.

"Certes," said the dame, "I make this great sorrow because no prince can tell who is his faithful servant, and who is not. Often he gives the more honour and wealth to those who are traitors rather than friends, and sees nothing of their wrong."

"In faith, wife," answered the Duke, "I know not why you speak these words. At least I am free of such blame as this, for in nowise would I nourish a traitor, if only a traitor I knew him to be."

"Hate then this traitor," cried she,—and she named a name— "who gives me no peace, praying and requiring me the livelong day that I should grant him my love. For a great while he had been in this mind—as he says—but did not dare to speak his thoughts. I considered the whole matter, fair lord, and resolved to show it you at once. It is likely enough to be true that he cherished this hope, for we have never heard that he loves elsewhere. I entreat you in guerdon, to look well to your own honour, since this, as you know, is your duty and right."

Passing grievous was this business to the Duke. He answered to the lady,

"I will bring it to a head, and very quickly, as I deem."

That night the Duke lay upon a bed of little ease. He could neither sleep nor rest, by reason of that lord, his friend, who, he was persuaded, had done him such bitter wrong as justly to have forfeited his love. Because of this he kept vigil the whole night through. He rose very early on the morrow, and bade him come whom his wife had put to blame, although he had done nothing blameworthy. Then he took him to task, man to man, when there were but these two together.

"Certes," he said, "it is a heavy grief that you who are so comely and brave, should yet have no honour in you. You have deceived me the more, for I have long believed you to be a man of good faith, giving loyalty, at least, to me, in return for the love I have given to you. I know not how you can have harboured such a felon's wish, as to pray and require the Duchess to grant you her grace. You are guilty of such treachery that conduct more vile it would be far to seek. Get you hence from my realm. You have my leave to part, and it is denied to you for ever. If you return here it will be at your utmost peril, for I warn you beforehand that if I lay hands upon you, you will die a shameful death."

When the knight heard this judgment, such wrath and mortification were his that his members trembled beneath him. He called to mind his friend, of whom he would have no joy, if he might not come and go and sojourn in that realm from which the Duke had banished him. Moreover he was sick at heart that his lord should deem him a disloyal traitor, without just cause. He knew such sore discomfort that he held himself as dead and betrayed.

"Sire," said he, "for the love of God believe this never, neither think that I have been so bold. To do that of which you wrongfully charge me, has never entered my mind, not one day, nor for one single hour. Who has told you this lie has wrought a great ill."

"You gain nothing by such denials," answered the Duke, "for of a surety the thing is true. I have heard from her own lips the very guise and fashion in which you prayed and required her love, like the envious traitor that you are. Many another word it may well be that you spoke, as to which the lady of her courtesy keeps silence."

"My lady says what it pleases her to say," replied the dolorous knight, "and my denials are lighter than her word. Naught is there for me to say; nothing is left for me to do, so that I may be believed that this adventure never happened."

"Happen it did, by my soul," said the Duke, remembering certain words of his wife. Well he deemed that he might be assured of the truth, if but the lady's testimony were true that this lord had never loved otherwise. Therefore the Duke said to the knight,

"If you will pledge your faith to answer truly what I may ask, I shall be certified by your words whether or not you have done this deed of which I misdoubt you."

The knight had but one desire—to turn aside his lord's wrath, which had so wrongfully fallen upon him. He feared only lest he should be driven from the land where lodged the dame who was the closest to his mind. Knowing nothing of what was in the Duke's thought, he considered that his question could only concern the one matter; so he replied that without fraud or concealment he would do as his lord had said. Thus he pledged his faith, and the Duke accepted his affiance.

When this was done the Duke made question,

"I have loved you so dearly that at the bottom of my heart I cannot believe you guilty of such shameless misdoing as the Duchess tells me. I would not credit it a moment, if you yourself were not the cause of my doubtfulness. From your face, the care you bestow upon your person, and a score of trifles, any who would know, can readily see that you are in love with some lady. Since none about the Court perceives damsel or dame on whom you have set your heart, I ask myself whether indeed it may not be my wife, who tells me that you have entreated her for love. Nothing that any one may do can take this suspicion from my mind, except you tell me yourself that you love elsewhere, making it so plain that I am left without doubt that I know the naked truth. If you refuse her name you will have broken your oath, and forth from my realm you go as an outlawed man."

The knight had none to give him counsel. To himself he seemed to stand at the parting of two ways, both one and the other leading to death. If he spoke the simple truth (and tell he must if he would not be a perjurer) then was he as good as dead; for if he did such wrong as to sin against the covenant with his lady and his friend, certainly he would lose her love, so it came to her knowledge. But if he concealed the truth from the Duke, then he was false to his oath, and had lost both country and friend. But little he recked of country, so only he might keep his Love, since of all his riches she was the most dear. The knight called to heart and remembrance the fair joy and the solace that were his when he had this lady between his arms. He considered within himself that if by reason of his misdoing she came to harm, or were lost to him, since he might not take her where he went, how could he live without her. It would be with

him also, as erst with the Castellan of Couci, who having his Love
fast only in his heart, told over in his song,

> Ah, God, strong Love, I sit and weep alone,
>   Remembering the solace that was given;
> The tender guise, the semblance that was shown
>   By her, my friend, my comrade, and my Heaven.
>
> When grief brings back the joy that was mine own,
>   I would the heart from out my breast were riven.
> Ah, Lord, the sweet words hushed, the beauty flown;
>   Would God that I were dead, and low, and shriven.

The knight was in anguish such as this, for he knew not whether
to make clear the truth, or to lie and be banished from the country.

Whilst he was deep in thought, turning over in his mind what it
were best to do, tears rose in his heart and flowed from his eyes, so
that his face was wet, by reason of the sorrow that he suffered. The
Duke had no more mirth than the knight, deeming that his secret
was so heavy that he dared not make it plain. The Duke spoke swiftly
to his friend,

"I see clearly that you fear to trust me wholly, as a knight should
trust his lord. If you confess your counsel privily to me, you cannot
think that I shall show the matter to any man. I would rather have
my teeth drawn one by one, than speak a word."

"Ah," cried the knight, "for God's love, have pity, Sire. I know
not what I ought to say, nor what will become of me; but I would
rather die than lose what lose I shall if she only hears that you have
the truth, and that you heard it from my lips, whilst I am a living
man."

The Duke made answer,

"I swear to you by my body and my soul, and on the faith and
love I owe you again by reason of your homage, that never in my
life will I tell the tale to any creature born, or even breathe a word
or make a sign about the business."

With the tears yet running down his face the knight said to him,

"Sire, right or wrong, now will I show my secret. I love your
niece of Vergi, and she loves me, so that no friends can love more
fondly."

"If you wish to be believed," replied the Duke, "tell me now, if
any, save you two alone, knows anything of this joy?"

And the knight made answer to him,

"Nay, not a creature in the world."

Then said the Duke,

"No love is so privy as that. If none has heard thereof, how do you meet together, and how devise time and place?"

"By my faith, Sire, I will tell you all, and keep back nothing, since you know so much of our counsel."

So he related the whole story of his goings to and fro within the pleasaunce; of that first covenant with his friend, and of the office of the little dog.

Then said the Duke,

"I require of you that I may be your comrade at such fair meeting. When you go again to the orchard, I too, would enter therein, and mark for myself the success of your device. As for my niece she shall perceive naught."

"Sire, if it be your will it is my pleasure also; save, only, that you find it not heavy or burdensome. Know well that I go this very night."

The Duke said that he would go with him, for the vigil would in no wise be burdensome, but rather a frolic and a game. They accorded between them a place of meeting, where they would draw together on foot, and alone. When nightfall was come they fared to the hostel of the Duke's niece, for her dwelling was near at hand. They had not tarried long in the garden, when the Duke saw his niece's lapdog run straight to that end of the orchard where the knight was hidden. Wondrous kindness showed the knight to his lady's dog. Immediately he took his way to her lodging, and left his master in his nook by the wall. The Duke followed after till he drew near the chamber, and held himself coy, concealing him as best he might. It was easy enough to do this, for a great tree stood there, high and leafy, so that he was covered close as by a shield. From this place he marked the little dog enter the chamber, and presently saw his niece issue therefrom, and hurry forth to meet her lover in the pleasaunce. He was so close that he could see and hear the solace of that greeting, the salutation of her mouth and of her hands. She embraced him closely in her fair white arms, kissing him more than a hundred times, whilst she spoke many comforting words. The knight for his part kissed her again, and held her fast, praising her with many tender names.

"My lady, my friend, my love," said he, "heart and mistress and hope, and the sum of all that I hold dear, know well that I have yearned to be with you as we are now, every day and all day long since we met."

"Sweet lord, sweet friend, sweet love," replied the lady, "never has a day nor an hour gone by but I was awearied of its length. But I grieve no longer over the past, for I have my heart's desire when you are with me, joyous and well. Right welcome are you to your friend."

And the knight made answer,

"Love, you are welcome and wellmet."

From his place of hiding, near the entrance to the chamber, the Duke hearkened to every word. His niece's voice and face were so familiar to him, that he could not doubt that the Duchess had lied. Greatly was he content, for he was now assured that his friend had not done amiss in that of which he had misdoubted him. All through the night he kept watch and ward. But during his vigil the dame and the knight, close and sleepless in the chamber, knew such joy and tenderness as it is not seemly should be told or heard, save of those who hope themselves to attain such solace, when Love grants them recompense for all their pains. For he who desires nothing of this joy and quittance, even if it were told him, would but listen to a tongue he could not understand, since his heart is not turned to Love, and none can know the wealth of such riches, except Love whisper it in his ear. Of such kingdom not all are worthy: for there joy goes without anger, and solace is crowned with fruition. But so fleet are things sweet, that to the lover his joy seems to find but a brief content. So pleasant is the life he passes that he wishes his night a week, his week to stretch to a month, the month become a year, and one year three, and three years twenty, and the twenty attain to a hundred. Yea, when the term and end were reached, he would that the dusk were closing, rather than the dawn had come.

This was the case with the lover whom the Duke awaited in the orchard. When day was breaking, and he durst remain no longer, he came with his lady to the door. The Duke marked the fashion of their leave-taking, the kisses given and granted, the sighs and the weeping as they bade farewell. When they had wept many tears, and devised an hour for their next meeting, the knight departed in this fashion, and the lady shut the door. But so long as she might see him, she followed his going with her pretty eyes, since there was nothing better she could do.

When the Duke knew the postern was made fast, he hastened on his road until he overtook the knight, who to himself was making his complaint of the season, that all too short was his hour. The same thought and the self same words were hers from whom he had parted, for the briefness of the time had betrayed her delight, and she had no praises for the dawn. The knight was deep in his thought and speech, when he was overtaken by the Duke. The Duke embraced his friend, greeting him very tenderly. Then he said to him,

"I pledge my faith that I will love you all the days of my life, never on any day seeking to do you a mischief, for you have told me the very truth, and have not lied to me by a single word."

"Sire," he made answer, "thanks and gramercy. But for the love of God I require and pray of you that it be your pleasure to hide this counsel; for I should lose my love, and the peace and comfort of my life—yea, and should die without sin of my own, if I deemed that any other in this realm than yourself knew aught of the business."

"Now speak of it never," replied the Duke. "Know that the counsel shall be kept so hidden, that by me shall not a syllable be spoken."

On this covenant they came again whence they had set forth together. That day, when men sat at meat, the Duke showed to his knight a friendlier semblance and a fairer courtesy than ever he had done before. The Duchess felt such wrath and despitefulness at this, that—without any leasing—she rose from the table, and making pretence of sudden sickness, went to lie upon her bed, where she found little softness. When the Duke had eaten and washed and made merry, he afterwards sought his wife's chamber, and causing her to be seated on her bed, commanded that none should remain, save himself. So all men went forth at his word, even as he had bidden. Thereupon the Duke inquired of the lady how this evil had come to her, and of what she was sick. She made answer,

"As God hears me, never till I ate at table did I deem that you had so little sense or decency, as when I saw you making much of him, who, I have told you already, strove to bring shame and disgrace on me. When I watched you entreat him with more favour than even was your wont, such great sorrow and such great anger took hold on me, that I could not contain myself in the hall."

"Sweet friend," replied the Duke, "know that I shall never believe—either from your lips or from those of any creature in the world—that the story ever happened as you rehearsed it. I am so deep in his counsel that he has my quittance, for I have full assurance that he never dreamed of such a deed. But as to this you must ask of me no more."

The Duke went straightway from the chamber, leaving the lady sunk in thought. However long she had to live, never might she know an hour's comfort, till she had learnt something of that secret of which the Duke forbade her to seek further. No denial could now stand in her way, for in her heart swiftly she devised a means to unriddle this counsel, so only she might endure until the evening, and the Duke was in her arms. She was persuaded that, beyond doubt, such solace would win her wish more surely than wrath or tears. For this purpose she held herself coy, and when the Duke came to lie at her side she betook herself to the further side of the bed, making semblance that his company gave her no pleasure. Well she knew that such show of anger was the device to put her lord beneath her feet. Therefore she turned her back upon him, that the Duke might the more easily be drawn by the cords of her wrath. For this same reason when he had no more than kissed her, she burst out,

"Right false and treacherous and disloyal are you to make such a pretence of affection, who yet have never loved me truly one single day. All these years of our wedded life I have been foolish enough to believe, what you took such pains in the telling, that you loved me with a loyal heart. To-day I see plainly that I was the more deceived."

"In what are you deceived?" inquired the Duke.

"By my faith," cried she, who was sick of her desire, "you warn me that I be not so bold as to ask aught of that of which you know the secret."

"In God's name, sweet wife, of what would you know?"

"Of all that he has told you, the lies and the follies he has put in your mind, and led you to believe. But it matters little now whether I hear it or not, for I remember how small is my gain in being your true and loving wife. For good or for ill I have shown you all my counsel. There was nothing that was known and seen of my heart that you were not told at once; and of your courtesy you repay me by concealing your mind. Know, now, without doubt, that never again shall I have in you such affiance, nor grant you my love with such sweetness, as I have bestowed them in the past."

Thereat the Duchess began to weep and sigh, making the most tender sorrow that she was able. The Duke felt such pity for her grief that he said to her,

"Fairest and dearest, your wrath and anger are more heavy than I can bear; but learn that I cannot tell what you wish me to say without sinning against my honour too grievously."

Then she replied forthwith,

"Husband, if you do not tell me, the reason can only be that you do not trust me to keep silence in the business. I wonder the more sorely at this, because there is no matter, either great or small, that you have told me, which has been published by me. I tell you honestly that never in my life could I be so indiscreet."

When she had said this, she betook her again to her tears. The Duke kissed and embraced her, and was so sick of heart that strength failed him to keep his purpose.

"Fair wife," he said to her, "by my soul I am at my wits' end. I have such trust and faith in you that [deem I should hide nothing, but show you all that I know. Yet I dread that you will let fall some word. Know, wife—and I tell it you again—that if ever you betray this counsel you will get death for your payment."

The Duchess made answer,

"I agree to the bargain, for it is not possible that I should deal you so shrewd a wrong."

Then he who loved her, because of his faith and his credence in her word, told all this story of his niece, even as he had learned it from the knight. He told how those two were alone together in the shadow of the wall, when the little dog ran to them. He showed plainly of that coming forth from the chamber, and of the entering in; nothing was hid, he concealed naught of that he had heard and seen. When the Duchess understood that the love of a mighty dame was despised for the sake of a lowly gentlewoman, her humiliation was bitter in her mouth as death. She showed no semblance of despitefulness, but made covenant and promise with the Duke to keep the matter close, saying that should she repeat his tale he might hang her from a tree.

Time went very heavily with the lady, till she could get speech with her, whom she hated from the hour she knew her to be the friend of him who had caused her such shame and grief. She was persuaded that for this reason he would not give her love, in return for that she set on him. She confirmed herself in her purpose, that at such time and place she saw the Duke speaking with his niece, she would go swiftly to the lady, and tell out all her mind, hiding nothing because it was evil. Neither time nor place was met, till Pentecost was come, and the Duke held high Court, commanding to the feast all the ladies of his realm, amongst the first that lady, his niece, who was the Chatelaine of Vergi. When the Duchess looked on her, the blood pricked in her veins, for reason that she hated her more than aught else in the world. She had the courage to hide her malice, and greeted the lady more gladly than ever she had done before. But she yearned to show openly the anger that burned in her heart, and the delay was much against her mind. On Pentecost, whilst the tables were removed, the Duchess brought the ladies to her chamber with her, that, apart from the throng, they might the more graciously attire them for the dance. She deemed her hour had come, and having no longer the power to refrain her lips, she said gaily, as if in jest,

"Chatelaine, array yourself very sweetly, since there is a fair and worthy lord you have to please."

The lady answered right simply,

"In truth, madam, I know not what you are thinking of; but for my part I wish for no such friendship as may not be altogether according to my honour and to that of my lord."

"I grant that readily," replied the Duchess, "you are a good mistress, and have an apt pupil in your little dog."

The ladies returned with the Duchess to the hall, where the dances were already set. They had listened to the tale, but could not mark the jest. The chatelaine remained in the chamber. Her colour came and went, and because of her wrath and trouble the heart throbbed thickly in her breast. She passed within a tiring chamber, where a little maiden was lying at the foot of the bed; but for grief she might not perceive her. The chatelaine flung herself upon the bed, bewailing her evil plight, for she was exceedingly sorrowful. She said,

"Ah, Lord God, take pity on me! What may this mean, that I have listened to my lady's reproaches because of the training of my little dog! This she can have learned from none—as well I know—save from him whom I have loved, and who has betrayed me. He would never have shown her this thing, except that he was her familiar friend, and doubtless loves her more dearly than me, whom he has betrayed. I see now the value of his oaths, since he finds it so easy to fail in his covenant. Sweet God, and I loved him so fondly, more fondly than any woman has loved before; who never had him from my thoughts one single hour, whether it were night or day. For he was my mirth and my carol; in him were my joy and my pleasure; he alone was my solace and comfort. Ah, my friend, how can this have come; you who were always with me, even when I might not see you with my eyes! What ill has befallen you, that you durst prove false to me? I deemed you more faithful—God take me in His keeping—than ever was Tristan to Isoude. May God pity a poor fool, I loved you half as much again than I had love for myself. From the first to the last of our friendship, never by thought, or by word, or by deed, have I done amiss; there is no wrong doing, trifling or great, to make plain your hatred, or to excuse so vile a betrayal as this scorning of our love for a fresher face, this desertion of me, this proclaiming of our secret. Alas, my friend, I marvel greatly; for as God is my witness my heart was not thus towards you. If God had offered me all the kingdoms of the world, yea, and His Heaven and its Paradise besides, I would have refused them gladly, had my gain meant the losing of you. For you were my wealth and my song and my health, and nothing can hurt me any more, since my heart has learnt that yours no longer loves me. Ah, lasting, precious love! Who could have guessed that he would deal this blow, to whom I gave the grace of my tenderness—who said that I was his lady both in body and in soul, and he the slave at my bidding. Yea, he told it over so sweetly, that I believed him faithfully, nor thought in any wise that his heart would bear wrath and malice against me, whether for Duchess or for Queen. How good was this love, since the heart in my breast must always cleave to his! I counted him to be my friend, in age as in youth, our lives together; for well I knew that if he died first I should not dare to endure long without him, because of the greatness of my love. The grave, with him, would be fairer, than life in a world where I might never see him with my eyes. Ah, lasting, precious love! Is it then seemly that he should publish our counsel, and destroy her who had done him no wrong? When I gave him my love without grudging, I warned him plainly, and made covenant with him, that he would lose me the self same hour that he made our tenderness a song. Since part we must, I may not live after so bitter a sorrow; nor would I choose to live, even if I were able. Fie upon life, it has no savour in it. Since it pleases me naught, I pray to God to grant me death, and—so truly as I have loved him who requites me thus—to have mercy on my soul. I forgive him his wrong, and may God give honour and life to him who has betrayed and delivered me to death. Since it comes from his hand, death, meseems, is no bitter potion; and when I remember his love, to die for his sake is no grievous thing."

When the chatelaine had thus spoken she kept silence, save only that she said in sighing,

"Sweet friend, I commend you to God."

With these words she strained her arms tightly across her breast, the heart failed her, and her face lost its fair colour. She swooned in her anguish, and lay back, pale and discoloured in the middle of the bed, without life or breath.

Of this her friend knew nothing, for he sought his delight in the hall, at carol and dance and play. But amongst all those ladies he had no pleasure in any that he saw, since he might not perceive her to whom his heart was given, and much he marvelled thereat. He took the Duke apart, and said in his ear,

"Sire, whence is this that your niece tarries so long, and comes not to the dancing? Have you put her in prison?"

The Duke looked upon the dancers, for he had not concerned himself with the revels. He took his friend by the hand, and led him directly to his wife's chamber. When he might not find her there he bade the knight seek her boldly in the tiring chamber; and this he did of his courtesy that these two lovers might solace themselves with clasp and kiss. The knight thanked his lord sweetly, and entered softly in the chamber, where his friend lay dark and discoloured upon the bed. Time and place being met together, he took her in his arms and touched her lips. But when he found how cold was her mouth, how pale and rigid her person, he knew by the semblance of all her body that she was quite dead. In his amazement he cried out swiftly,

"What is this? Alas, is my dear one dead?"

The maiden started from the foot of the bed where she still lay, making answer,

"Sir, I deem truly that she be dead. Since she came to this room she has done nothing but call upon death, by reason of her friend's falsehood, whereof my lady assured her, and because of a little dog, whereof my lady made her jest. This sorrow brought her to her death."

When the knight understood from this that the words he had spoken to the Duke had slain his friend, he was discomforted beyond measure.

"Alas," said he, "sweet love, the most gracious and the best that ever knight had, loyal and true, how have I slain you, like the faithless traitor that I am! It were only just that I should receive the wages for my deed, so that you could have gone free of blame. But you were so faithful of heart that you took it on yourself to pay the price. Then I will do justice on myself for the treason I have wrought."

The knight drew from its sheath a sword that was hanging from the wall, and thrust it throught his heart. He pained himself to fall upon his lady's body; and because of the mightiness of his hurt, bled swiftly to death. The maiden fled forth from the chamber, when she marked these lifeless lovers, for she was all adread at what she saw. She lighted on the Duke, and told him all that she had heard and seen, keeping back nothing. She showed him the beginning of the matter, and also of the little dog, whereof the Duchess had spoken.

Hearken all to what befell. The Duke went straightway to the tiring chamber, and drew from out the wound that sword by which the knight lay slain. He said no word, but hastened forthwith to the hall where the guests were yet at their dancing. Entering there he acquitted himself of his promise, for he smote the Duchess on the head with the naked sword he carried in his hand. He struck the blow without one word, since his wrath was too deep for speech. The Duchess fell at his feet, in the sight of the barons of his realm, whereat the feast was sorely troubled, for in place of mirth and carol, now were blood and death. Then the Duke told loudly and swiftly, before all who cared to hear, this pitiful story, in the midst of his Court. There was not one but wept, and his tears were the more piteous when he beheld those two lovers who lay dead in the chamber, and the Duchess in her hall. So the Court broke up in dole and anger, for of this deed came mighty mischief. On the morrow the Duke caused the lovers to be laid in one tomb, and the Duchess in a place apart. But of this adventure the Duke had such bitterness that never was he known to laugh again. He took the Cross, and went beyond the sea, where joining himself to the Knights Templar, he never returned to his own realm.

Ah, God! all this mischief and encumbrance chanced to the knight by reason of his making plain that he should have hid, and of publishing what his friend forbade him to speak, if he would keep her love. From this ensample we may learn that it is not seemly to love, and tell. He who blabs and blazons his friendship gets not one kiss the more; but he who goes discreetly preserves life and love and fame. For the friendship of the discreet lover falls not before the mine of such false and felon pryers as burrow privily into their neighbour's secret love.

THE MABINOGION

Lady Charlotte E. Guest

The Mabinogion is a collection of prose stories composed in Middle Welsh in the twelfth and thirteenth centuries from older oral traditions and represents the oldest prose literature in British history. Reprinted here are "The Dream of Rhonabwy" and an Arthurian romance, "The Lady of the Fountain," from the justly famous translation of Lady Charlotte E. Guest, first published by Longmans, London, in three volumes between 1841 and 1850, and frequently reprinted since then.

THE DREAM OF RHONABWY

Madawc the son of Maredudd possessed Powys within its boundaries, from Porfoed to Gwauan in the uplands of Arwystli. And at that time he had a brother, Iorwerth the son of Maredudd, in rank not equal to himself. And Iorwerth had great sorrow and heaviness because of the honour and power that his brother enjoyed, which he shared not. And he sought his fellows and his foster-brothers, and took counsel with them what he should do in this matter. And they resolved to dispatch some of their number to go and seek a maintenance for him. Then Madawc offered him to become Master of the Household and to have horses, and arms, and honour, and to fare like as himself. But Iorwerth refused this.

And Iorwerth made an inroad into Loegria, slaying the inhabitants, and burning houses, and carrying away prisoners. And Madawc took counsel with the men of Powys, and they determined to place an hundred men in each of the three Commots of Powys to seek for him. And thus did they in the plains of Powys from Aber Ceirawc, and in Allictwn Ver, and in Rhyd Wilure, on the Vyrnwy, the three best Commots of Powys. So he was none the better, he nor his household, in Powys, nor in the plains thereof. And they spread these men over the plains as far as Nillystwn Trevan.

Now one of the men who was upon this quest was called Rhonabwy. And Rhonabwy and Kynwrig Vrychgoch, a man of Mawddwy, and Cadwgan Vras, a man of Moelvre in Kynlleith, came together to the house of Heilyn Goch the son of Cadwgan the son of Iddon. And when they came near to the house, they saw an old hall, very black and having an upright gable, whence issued a great smoke; and on entering, they found the floor full of puddles and mounds; and it was difficult to stand thereon, so slippery was it with the mire of cattle. And where the puddles were, a man might go up to his ankles in water and dirt. And there were boughs of holly spread over the floor, whereof the cattle had browsed the sprigs. When they came to the hall of the house, they beheld cells full of dust, and very gloomy, and on one side an old hag making a fire. And whenever she felt cold, she cast a lapful of chaff upon the fire, and raised such a smoke, that it was scarcely to be borne, as it rose up the nostrils. And on the other side was a yellow calf-skin on the floor; a main privilege was it to any one who should get upon that hide.

And when they had sat down, they asked the hag where were the people of the house. And the hag spoke not, but muttered. Thereupon behold the people of the house entered; a ruddy, clownish, curly-headed man, with a burthen of faggots on his back, and a pale slender woman, also carrying a bundle under her arm. And they barely welcomed the men, and kindled a fire with the boughs. And the woman cooked something, and gave them to eat, barley bread, and cheese, and milk and water.

And there arose a storm of wind and rain, so that it was hardly possible to go forth with safety. And being weary with their journey, they laid themselves down and sought to sleep. And when they looked at the couch, it seemed to be made but of a little coarse straw full of dust and vermin, with the stems of boughs sticking up there-through, for the cattle had eaten all the straw that was placed at the head and the foot. And upon it was stretched an old russet-coloured rug, threadbare and ragged; and a coarse sheet, full of slits, was upon the rug, and an ill-stuffed pillow, and a worn-out cover upon the sheet. And after much suffering from the vermin, and from the discomfort of their couch, a heavy sleep fell on Rhonabwy's companions. But Rhonabwy, not being able either to sleep or to rest, thought he should suffer less if he went to lie upon the yellow calf-skin that was stretched out on the floor. And there he slept.

As soon as sleep had come upon his eyes, it seemed to him that he was journeying with his companions across the plain of Argyngroeg, and he thought that he went towards Rhyd y Groes on the Severn. As he journeyed, he heard a mighty noise, the like whereof heard he never before; and looking behind him, he beheld a youth with yellow curling hair, and with his beard newly trimmed, mounted on a chestnut horse, whereof the legs were grey from the top of the forelegs, and from the bend of the hindlegs downwards. And the rider wore a coat of yellow satin sewn with green silk, and on his thigh was a gold-hilted sword, with a scabbard of new leather of Cordova, belted with the skin of the deer, and clasped with gold. And over this was a scarf of yellow satin wrought with green silk, the borders whereof were likewise green. And the green of the caparison of the horse, and of his rider, was as green as the leaves of the fir-tree, and the yellow was as yellow as the blossom of the broom. So fierce was the aspect of the knight, that fear seized upon them, and they began to flee. And the knight pursued them. And when the horse breathed forth, the men became distant from him, and when he drew in his breath, they were drawn near to him, even to the horse's chest. And when he had overtaken them, they besought his mercy. "You have it gladly," said he, "fear nought." "Ha, chieftain, since thou hast mercy upon me, tell me also who thou art," said Rhonabwy. "I will not conceal my lineage from thee, I am Iddawc the son of Mynyo, yet not by my name, but by my nickname am I best known." "And wilt thou tell us what thy nickname is?" "I will tell you; it is Iddawc Cordd Prydain." "Ha, chieftain," said Rhonabwy, "why art thou called thus?" "I will tell thee. I was one of the messengers between Arthur and Medrawd his nephew, at the battle of Camlan; and I was then a reckless youth, and through my desire for battle, I kindled strife between them, and stirred up wrath, when I was sent by Arthur the Emperor to reason with Medrawd, and to show him, that he was his foster-father and his uncle, and to seek for peace, lest the sons of the Kings of the Island of Britain, and of the nobles, should be slain. And whereas Arthur charged me with the fairest sayings he could think of, I uttered unto Medrawd the harshest I could devise. And therefore am I called Iddawc Cordd Prydain, for from this did the battle of Camlan ensue. And three nights before the end of the battle of Camlan I left them, and went to the Llech Las in North Britain to do penance. And there I remained doing penance seven years, and after that I gained pardon."

Then lo! they heard a mighty sound which was much louder than that which they had heard before, and when they looked round towards the sound, they beheld a ruddy youth, without beard or whiskers, noble of mien, and mounted on a stately courser. And from the shoulders and the front of the knees downwards the horse was bay. And upon the man was a dress of red satin wrought with yellow silk, and yellow were the borders of his scarf. And such parts of his apparel and of the trappings of his horse as were yellow, as yellow were they as the blossom of the broom, and such as were red, were as ruddy as the ruddiest blood in the world.

Then, behold the horseman overtook them, and he asked of Iddawc a share of the little men that were with him. "That which is fitting for me to grant I will grant, and thou shalt be a companion to them as I have been." And the horseman went away. "Iddawc," inquired Rhonabwy, "who was that horseman?" "Rhuvawn Pebyr the son of Prince Deorthach."

And they journeyed over the plain of Argyngroeg as far as the ford of Rhyd y Groes on the Severn. And for a mile around the ford on both sides of the road, they saw tents and encampments, and there was the clamour of a mighty host. And they came to the edge of the ford, and there they beheld Arthur sitting on a flat island below the ford, having Bedwini the Bishop on one side of him, and Gwarthegyd the son of Kaw on the other. And a tall, auburn-haired youth stood before him, with his sheathed sword in his hand, and clad in a coat and cap of jet-black satin. And his face was white as ivory, and his eyebrows black as jet, and such part of his wrist as could be seen between his glove and his sleeve, was whiter than the lily, and thicker than a warrior's ankle.

Then came Iddawc and they that were with him, and stood before Arthur and saluted him. "Heaven grant thee good," said Arthur. "And where, Iddawc, didst thou find these little men?" "I found them, lord, up yonder on the road." Then the Emperor smiled. "Lord," said Iddawc, "wherefore dost thou laugh?" "Iddawc," replied Arthur, "I laugh not; but it pitieth me that men of such stature as these should have this island in their keeping, after the men that guarded it of yore." Then said Iddawc, "Rhonabwy, dost thou see the ring with a stone set in it, that is upon the Emperor's hand?" "I see it," he answered. "It is one of the properties of that stone to enable thee to remember that thou seest here to-night, and hadst thou not seen the stone, thou wouldest never have been able to remember aught thereof."

After this they saw a troop coming towards the ford. "Iddawc," inquired Rhonabwy, "to whom does yonder troop belong?" "They are the fellows of Rhuvawn Pebyr the son of Prince Deorthach. And these men are honourably served with mead and bragget, and are freely beloved by the daughters of the kings of the Island of Britain. And this they merit, for they were ever in the front and the rear in every peril." And he saw but one hue upon the men and the horses of this troop, for they were all as red as blood. And when one of the knights rode forth from the troop, he looked like a pillar of fire glancing athwart the sky. And this troop encamped above the ford.

Then they beheld another troop coming towards the ford, and these from their horses' chests upwards were whiter than the lily, and below blacker than jet. And they saw one of these knights go before the rest, and spur his horse into the ford in such a manner that the water dashed over Arthur and the Bishop, and those holding counsel with them, so that they were as wet as if they had been drenched in the river. And as he turned the head of his horse, the youth who stood before Arthur struck the horse over the nostrils with his sheathed sword, so that, had it been with the bare blade, it would have been a marvel if the bone had not been wounded as well as the flesh. And the knight drew his sword half out of the scabbard, and asked of him, "Wherefore didst thou strike my horse? Whether was it in insult or in counsel unto me?" "Thou dost indeed lack counsel. What madness caused thee to ride so furiously as to dash the water of the ford over Arthur, and the consecrated Bishop, and their counsellors, so that they were as wet as if they had been dragged out of the river?" "As counsel then will I take it." So he turned his horse's head round towards his army.

"Iddawc," said Rhonabwy, "who was yonder knight?" "The most eloquent and the wisest youth that is in this island; Adaon, the son of Taliesin." "Who was the man that struck his horse?" "A youth of froward nature; Elphin, the son of Gwyddno."

Then spake a tall and stately man, of noble and flowing speech, saying that it was a marvel that so vast a host should be assembled in so narrow a space, and that it was a still greater marvel that those should be there at that time who had promised to be by mid-day in the battle of Badon, fighting with Osla Gyllellvawr. "Whether thou mayest choose to proceed or not, I will proceed." "Thou sayest well," said Arthur, "and we will go altogether." "Iddawc," said Rhonabwy, "who was the man who spoke so marvellously unto Arthur erewhile?" "A man who may speak as boldly as he listeth, Caradawc Vreichvras, the son of Llyr Marini, his chief counsellor and his cousin."

Then Iddawc took Rhonabwy behind him on his horse, and that mighty host moved forward, each troop in its order, towards Cevndigoll. And when they came to the middle of the ford of the Severn, Iddawc turned his horse's head, and Rhonabwy looked along the valley of the Severn. And he beheld two fair troops coming towards the ford. One troop there came of brilliant white, whereof every one of the men had a scarf of white satin with jet-black borders. And the knees and the tops of the shoulders of their horses were jet-black, though they were of a pure white in every other part. And their banners were pure white, with black points to them all.

"Iddawc," said Rhonabwy, "who are yonder pure white troop?" "They are the men of Norway, and March the son of Meirchion is their prince. And he is cousin unto Arthur." And further on he saw a troop, whereof each man wore garments of jet-black, with borders of pure white to every scarf; and the tops of the shoulders and the knees of their horses were pure white. And their banners were jet-black with pure white at the point of each.

"Iddawc," said Rhonabwy, "who are the jet-black troop yonder?" "They are the men of Denmark, and Edeyrn the son of Nudd is their prince."

And when they had overtaken the host, Arthur and his army of mighty ones dismounted below Caer Badou, and he perceived that he and Iddawc journeyed the same road as Arthur. And after they had dismounted he heard a great tumult and confusion amongst the host, and such as were then at the flanks turned to the centre, and such as had been in the centre moved to the flanks. And then, behold, he saw a knight coming, clad, both he and his horse, in mail, of which the rings were whiter than the whitest lily, and the rivets redder than the ruddiest blood. And he rode amongst the host.

"Iddawc," said Rhonabwy, "will yonder host flee?" "King Arthur never fled, and if this discourse of thine were heard, thou wert a lost man. But as to the knight whom thou seest yonder, it is Kai. The fairest horseman is Kai in all Arthur's Court; and the men who are at the front of the army hasten to the rear to see Kai ride, and the men who are in the centre flee to the side, from the shock of his horse. And this is the cause of the confusion of the host."

Thereupon they heard a call made for Kadwr, Earl of Cornwall, and behold he arose with the sword of Arthur in his hand. And the similitude of two serpents was upon the sword in gold. And when the sword was drawn from its scabbard, it seemed as if two flames of fire burst forth from the jaws of the serpents, and then, so wonderful was the sword, that it was hard for any one to look upon it. And the host became still, and the tumult ceased, and the Earl returned to the tent.

"Iddawc," said Rhonabwy, "who is the man who bore the sword of Arthur?" "Kadwr, the Earl of Cornwall, whose duty it is to arm the King on the days of battle and warfare."

And they heard a call made for Eirynwych Amheibyn, Arthur's servant, a red, rough, ill-favoured man, having red whiskers with bristly hairs. And behold he came upon a tall red horse with the mane parted on each side, and he brought with him a large and beautiful sumpter pack. And the huge red youth dismounted before Arthur, and he drew a golden chair out of the pack, and a carpet of diapered satin. And he spread the carpet before Arthur, and there was an apple of ruddy gold at each corner thereof, and he placed the chair upon the carpet. And so large was the chair that three armed warriors might have sat therein. Gwenn was the name of the carpet, and it was one of its properties that whoever was upon it no one could see him, and he could see every one. And it would retain no colour but its own.

And Arthur sat within the carpet, and Owain the son of Urien was standing before him. "Owain," said Arthur, "wilt thou play chess?" "I will, Lord," said Owain. And the red youth brought the chess for Arthur and Owain; golden pieces and a board of silver. And they began to play.

And while they were thus, and when they were best amused with their game, behold they saw a white tent with a red canopy, and the figure of a jet-black serpent on the top of the tent, and red glaring venomous eyes in the head of the serpent, and a red flaming tongue. And there came a young page with yellow curling hair, and blue eyes, and a newly-springing beard, wearing a coat and a surcoat of yellow satin, and hose of thin greenish-yellow cloth upon his feet, and over his hose shoes of parti-coloured leather, fastened at the insteps with golden clasps. And he bore a heavy three-edged sword with a golden hilt, in a scabbard of black leather tipped with fine gold. And he came to the place where the Emperor and Owain were playing at chess.

And the youth saluted Owain. And Owain marvelled that the youth should salute him and should not have saluted the Emperor

Arthur. And Arthur knew what was in Owain's thought. And he said to Owain, "Marvel not that the youth salutes thee now, for he saluted me erewhile; and it is unto thee that his errand is." Then said the youth unto Owain, "Lord, is it with thy leave that the young pages and attendants of the Emperor harass and torment and worry thy Ravens? And if it be not with thy leave, cause the Emperor to forbid them." "Lord," said Owain, "thou hearest what the youth says; if it seem good to thee, forbid them from my Ravens." "Play thy game," said he. Then the youth returned to the tent.

That game did they finish, and another they began, and when they were in the midst of the game, behold, a ruddy young man with auburn curling hair and large eyes, well-grown, and having his beard new-shorn, came forth from a bright yellow tent, upon the summit of which was the figure of a bright red lion. And he was clad in a coat of yellow satin, falling as low as the small of his leg, and embroidered with threads of red silk. And on his feet were hose of fine white buckram, and buskins of black leather were over his hose, whereon were golden clasps. And in his hand a huge, heavy, three-edged sword, with a scabbard of red deer-hide, tipped with gold. And he came to the place where Arthur and Owain were playing at chess. And he saluted him. And Owain was troubled at his salutation, but Arthur minded it no more than before. And the youth said unto Owain, "Is it not against thy will that the attendants of the Emperor harass thy Ravens, killing some and worrying others? If against thy will it be, beseech him to forbid them." "Lord," said Owain, "forbid thy men, if it seem good to thee." "Play thy game," said the Emperor. And the youth returned to the tent.

And that game was ended and another begun. And as they were beginning the first move of the game, they beheld at a small distance from them a tent speckled yellow, the largest ever seen, and the figure of an eagle of gold upon it, and a precious stone on the eagle's head. And coming out of the tent, they saw a youth with thick yellow hair upon his head, fair and comely, and a scarf of blue satin upon him, and a brooch of gold in the scarf upon his right shoulder as large as a warrior's middle finger. And upon his feet were hose of fine Totness, and shoes of particoloured leather, clasped with gold, and the youth was of noble bearing, fair of face, with ruddy cheeks and large hawk's eyes. In the hand of the youth was a mighty lance, speckled yellow, with a newly-sharpened head; and upon the lance a banner displayed.

Fiercely angry, and with rapid pace, came the youth to the place where Arthur was playing at chess with Owain. And they perceived that he was wroth. And thereupon he saluted Owain, and told him that his Ravens had been killed, the chief part of them, and that such of them as were not slain were so wounded and bruised that not one of them could raise its wings a single fathom above the earth. "Lord," said Owain, "forbid thy men." "Play," said he, "if it please thee." Then said Owain to the youth, "Go back, and wherever thou findest the strife at the thickest, there lift up the banner, and let come what pleases Heaven."

So the youth returned back to the place where the strife bore hardest upon the Ravens, and he lifted up the banner; and as he did so they all rose up in the air, wrathful and fierce and high of spirit, clapping their wings in the wind, and shaking off the weariness that was upon them. And recovering their energy and courage, furiously and with exultation did they, with one sweep, descend upon the heads of the men, who had erewhile caused them anger and pain and damage, and they seized some by the heads and others by the eyes, and some by the ears, and others by the arms, and carried them up into the air; and in the air there was a mighty tumult with the flapping of the wings of the triumphant Ravens, and with their croaking; and there was another mighty tumult with the groaning of the men, that were being torn and wounded, and some of whom were slain.

And Arthur and Owain marvelled at the tumult as they played at chess; and, looking, they perceived a knight upon a dun-coloured horse coming towards them. And marvellous was the hue of the dun horse. Bright red was his right shoulder, and from the top of his legs to the centre of his hoof was bright yellow. Both the knight and his horse were fully equipped with heavy foreign armour. The clothing of the horse from the front opening upwards was of bright red sendal, and from thence opening downwards was of bright yellow sendal. A large gold-hilted one-edged sword had the youth upon his thigh, in a scabbard of light blue, and tipped with Spanish laton. The belt of the sword was of dark green leather with golden slides and a clasp of ivory upon it, and a buckle of jet-black upon the clasp. A helmet of gold was on the head of the knight, set with precious stones of great virtue, and at the top of the helmet was the image of a flame-coloured leopard with two ruby-red stones in its head, so that it was astounding for a warrior, however stout his heart, to look at the face of the leopard, much more at the face of the knight. He had in his

hand a blue-shafted lance, but from the haft to the point it was stained
crimson-red with the blood of the Ravens and their plumage.

The knight came to the place where Arthur and Owain were
seated at chess. And they perceived that he was harassed and vexed
and weary as he came towards them. And the youth saluted Arthur,
and told him that the Ravens of Owain were slaying his young
men and attendants. And Arthur looked at Owain and said, "Forbid
thy Ravens." "Lord," answered Owain, "play thy game." And they
played. And the knight returned back towards the strife, and the
Ravens were not forbidden any more than before.

And when they had played awhile, they heard a mighty tumult,
and a wailing of men, and a croaking of Ravens, as they carried the
men in their strength into the air, and, tearing them betwixt them,
let them fall piecemeal to the earth. And during the tumult they saw
a knight coming towards them, on a light grey horse, and the left
foreleg of the horse was jet-black to the centre of his hoof. And the
knight and the horse were fully accoutred with huge heavy blue
armour. And a robe of honour of yellow diapered satin was upon
the knight, and the borders of the robe were blue. And the housings
of the horse were jet-black, with borders of bright yellow. And on
the thigh of the youth was a sword, long, and three-edged, and heavy.
And the scabbard was of red cut leather, and the belt of new red
deer-skin, having upon it many golden slides and a buckle of the
bone of the seahorse, the tongue of which was jet-black. A golden
helmet was upon the head of the knight, wherein were set sapphire-
stones of great virtue. And at the top of the helmet was the figure of
a flame-coloured lion, with a fiery-red tongue, issuing above a foot
from his mouth, and with venomous eyes, crimson-red, in his head.
And the knight came, bearing in his hand a thick ashen lance, the
head whereof, which had been newly steeped in blood, was overlaid
with silver.

And the youth saluted the Emperor: "Lord," said he, "carest thou
not for the slaying of thy pages, and thy young men, and the sons of
the nobles of the Island of Britain, whereby it will be difficult to
defend this island from henceforward for ever?" "Owain," said Arthur,
"forbid thy Ravens." "Play this game, Lord," said Owain.

So they finished the game and began another; and as they were
finishing that game, lo, they heard a great tumult and a clamour of
armed men, and a croaking of Ravens, and a flapping of wings in
the air, as they flung down the armour entire to the ground, and the
men and the horses piecemeal. Then they saw coming a knight on

a lofty-headed piebald horse. And the left shoulder of the horse was of bright red, and its right leg from the chest to the hollow of the hoof was pure white. And the knight and horse were equipped with arms of speckled yellow, variegated with Spanish laton. And there was a robe of honour upon him, and upon his horse, divided in two parts, white and black, and the borders of the robe of honour were of golden purple. And above the robe he wore a sword three-edged and bright, with a golden hilt. And the belt of the sword was of yellow goldwork, having a clasp upon it of the eyelid of a black seahorse, and a tongue of yellow gold to the clasp. Upon the head of the knight was a bright helmet of yellow laton, with sparkling stones of crystal in it, and at the crest of the helmet was the figure of a griffin, with a stone of many virtues in its head. And he had an ashen spear in his hand, with a round shaft, coloured with azure blue. And the head of the spear was newly stained with blood, and was overlaid with fine silver.

Wrathfully came the knight to the place where Arthur was, and he told him that the Ravens had slain his household and the sons of the chief men of this island, and he besought him to cause Owain to forbid his Ravens. And Arthur besought Owain to forbid them. Then Arthur took the golden chessmen that were upon the board, and crushed them until they became as dust. Then Owain ordered Gwres the son of Rheged to lower his banner. So it was lowered, and all was peace.

Then Rhonabwy inquired of Iddawc who were the first three men that came to Owain, to tell him his Ravens were being slain. Said Iddawc, "They were men who grieved that Owain should suffer loss, his fellow-chieftains and companions, Selyv the son of Kynan Garwyn of Powys, and Gwgawn Gleddyvrudd, and Gwres the son of Rheged, he who bears the banner in the day of battle and strife." "Who," said Rhonabwy, "were the last three men who came to Arthur, and told him that the Ravens were slaughtering his men?" "The best of men," said Iddawc, "and the bravest, and who would grieve exceedingly that Arthur should have damage in aught; Blathaon the son of Mawrheth, and Rhuvawn Pebyr the son of Prince Deorthach, and Hyveidd Unllenn."

And with that behold four-and-twenty knights came from Osla Gyllellvawr, to crave a truce of Arthur for a fortnight and a month. And Arthur rose and went to take counsel. And he came to where a tall, auburn, curly-headed man was a little way off, and there he assembled his counsellors. Bedwini, the Bishop, and Gwarthegyd the

son of Kaw, and March the son of Meirchawn, and Caradawc
Vreichvras, and Gwalchmai the son of Gwyar, and Edeyrn the son
of Nudd, and Rhuvawn Pebyr the son of Prince Deorthach, and
Rhiogan the son of the King of Ireland, and Gwenwynwyn the son
of Nav, Howel the son of Emyr Llydaw, Gwilym the son of Rhwyf
Freinc, and Daned the son of Ath, and Goreu Custennin, and Mabon
the son of Modron, and Peredur Paladyr Hir, and Hyveidd Unllenn,
and Twrch the son of Perif, and Nerth the son of Kadarn, and Gobrwy
the son of Echel Vorddwyttwll, Gwair the son of Gwestyl, and Gadwy
the son of Geraint, Trystan the son of Tallwch, Moryen Manawc,
Granwen the son of Llyr, and Llacheu the son of Arthur, and
Llawvrodedd Varvawc, and Kadwr Earl of Cornwall, Morvran the
son of Tegid, and Rhyawd the son of Morgant, and Dyvyr the son
of Alun Dyved, Gwrhyr Gwalstawd Ieithoedd, Adaon the son of
Taliesin, Llary the son of Kasnar Wledig, and Fflewddvr Fflam, and
Greidawl Galldovydd, Gilbert the son of Kadgyffro, Menw the son
of Teirgwaedd, Gwrthmwl Wledig, Cawrdav the son of Caradawc
Vreichvras, Gildas the son of Kaw, Kadyriaith the son of Saidi, and
many of the men of Norway and Denmark, and many of the men
of Greece, and a crowd of the men of the host came to that council.

"Iddawc," said Rhonabwy, "who was the auburn-haired man to
whom they came just now?" "Rhun the son of Maelgwn Gwynedd,
a man whose prerogative it is, that he may join in counsel with all."
"And wherefore did they admit into counsel with men of such dignity as are yonder a stripling so young as Kadyriaith the son of Saidi?"
"Because there is not throughout Britain a man better skilled in
counsel than he."

Thereupon, behold, bards came and recited verses before Arthur,
and no man understood those verses but Kadyriaith only, save that
they were in Arthur's praise.

And lo, there came four-and-twenty asses with their burdens of
gold and of silver, and a tired way-worn man with each of them,
bringing tribute to Arthur from the Islands of Greece. Then Kadyriaith
the son of Saidi besought that a truce might be granted to Osla
Gyllellvąwr for the space of a fortnight and a month, and that the
asses and the burdens they carried might be given to the bards, to be
to them as the reward for their stay and that their verse might be
recompensed during the time of the truce. And thus it was settled.

"Rhonabwy," said Iddawc, "would it not be wrong to forbid a
youth who can give counsel so liberal as this from coming to the
councils of his Lord?"

Then Kai arose, and he said, "Whosoever will follow Arthur, let him be with him to-night in Cornwall, and whosoever will not, let him be opposed to Arthur even during the truce." And through the greatness of the tumult that ensued, Rhonabwy awoke. And when he awoke he was upon the yellow calf-skin, having slept three nights and three days.

And this tale is called the Dream of Rhonabwy. And this is the reason that no one knows the dream without a book, neither bard nor gifted seer; because of the various colours that were upon the horses, and the many wondrous colours of the arms and of the panoply, and of the precious scarfs, and of the virtue-bearing stones.

THE LADY OF THE FOUNTAIN

King Arthur was at Caerlleon upon Usk; and one day he sat in his chamber; and with him were Owain the son of Urien, and Kynon the son of Clydno, and Kai the son of Kyner; and Gwenhwyvar and her handmaidens at needlework by the window. And if it should be said that there was a porter at Arthur's palace, there was none. Glewlwyd Gavaelvawr was there, acting as porter, to welcome guests and strangers, and to receive them with honour, and to inform them of the manners and customs of the Court; and to direct those who came to the Hall or to the presence-chamber, and those who came to take up their lodging.

In the centre of the chamber King Arthur sat upon a seat of green rushes, over which was spread a covering of flame-coloured satin, and a cushion of red satin was under his elbow.

Then Arthur spoke, "If I thought you would not disparage me," said he, "I would sleep while I wait for my repast; and you can entertain one another with relating tales, and can obtain a flagon of mead and some meat from Kai." And the King went to sleep. And Kynon the son of Clydno asked Kai for that which Arthur had promised them. "I, too, will have the good tale which he promised to me," said Kai. "Nay," answered Kynon, "fairer will it be for thee to fulfill Arthur's behest, in the first place, and then we will tell thee the best tale that we know." So Kai went to the kitchen and to the mead-cellar, and returned bearing a flagon of mead and a golden goblet, and a handful of skewers, upon which were broiled collops of meat. Then they ate the collops and began to drink the mead. "Now," said Kai, "it is time for you to give me my story." "Kynon," said Owain, "do thou pay to Kai the tale that is his due." "Truly," said Kynon, "thou are older, and art a better teller of tales, and hast seen more marvellous things than I; do thou therefore pay Kai his tale." "Begin thyself," quoth Owain, "with the best that thou knowest." "I will do so," answered Kynon.

"I was the only son of my mother and father, and I was exceedingly aspiring, and my daring was very great. I thought there was no enterprise in the world too mighty for me, and after I had achieved all the adventures that were in my own country, I equipped myself, and set forth to journey through deserts and distant regions. And at length it chanced that I came to the fairest valley in the world, wherein were trees of equal growth; and a river ran through the valley, and a path was by the side of the river. And I followed the path until mid-day, and continued my journey along the remainder of the valley until the evening; and at the extremity of a plain I came to a large and lustrous Castle, at the foot of which was a torrent. And I approached the Castle, and there I beheld two youths with yellow curling hair, each with a frontlet of gold upon his head, and clad in a garment of yellow satin, and they had gold clasps upon their insteps. In the hand of each of them was an ivory bow, strung with the sinews of the stag; and their arrows had shafts of the bone of the whale, and were winged with peacock's feathers; the shafts also had golden heads. And they had daggers with blades of gold, and with hilts of the bone of the whale. And they were shooting their daggers.

"And a little way from them I saw a man in the prime of life, with his beard newly shorn, clad in a robe and a mantle of yellow satin; and round the top of his mantle was a band of gold lace. On his feet were shoes of variegated leather, fastened by two bosses of gold. When I saw him, I went towards him and saluted him, and such was his courtesy that he no sooner received my greeting than he returned it. And he went with me towards the Castle. Now there were no dwellers in the Castle except those who were in one hall. And there I saw four-and-twenty damsels, embroidering satin at a window. And this I tell thee, Kai, that the least fair of them was fairer than the fairest maid thou hast ever beheld in the Island of Britain, and the least lovely of them was more lovely than Gwenhwyvar, the wife of Arthur, when she has appeared loveliest at the Offering, on the day of the Nativity, or at the feast of Easter. They rose up at my coming, and six of them took my horse, and divested me of my armour; and six others took my arms, and washed them in a vessel until they were perfectly bright. And the third six spread cloths upon the tables and prepared meat. And the fourth six took off my soiled garments, and placed others upon me; namely, an under-vest and a doublet of fine linen, and a robe, and a surcoat, and a mantle of yellow satin with a broad gold band upon the mantle. And they placed cushions both beneath and around me, with coverings of red linen; and I sat down. Now the six maidens who had taken my horse, unharnessed him, as well as if they had been the best squires in the Island of Britain. Then, behold, they brought bowls of silver wherein was water to wash, and towels of linen, some green and some white; and I washed. And in a little while the man sat down to the table. And I sat next to him, and below me sat all the maidens, except those who waited on us. And the table was of silver, and the cloths upon the table were of linen; and no vessel was served upon the table that was not either of gold or of silver, or of buffalo-horn. And our meat was brought to us. And verily, Kai, I saw there every sort of meat and every sort of liquor that I have ever seen elsewhere; but the meat and the liquor were better served there than I have ever seen them in any other place.

"Until the repast was half over, neither the man nor any one of the damsels spoke a single word to me; but when the man perceived that it would be more agreeable to me to converse than to eat any more, he began to inquire of me who I was. I said I was glad to find that there was some one who would discourse with me, and that it was not considered so great a crime at that Court for people to hold converse together. 'Chieftain,' said the man, 'we would have talked to thee sooner, but we feared to disturb thee during thy repast; now, however, we will discourse.' Then I told the man who I was, and what was the cause of my journey; and said that I was seeking whether any one was superior to me, or whether I could gain the mastery over all. The man looked upon me, and he smiled and said, 'If I did not fear to distress thee too much, I would show thee that which thou seekest.' Upon this I became anxious and sorrowful, and when the man perceived it, he said, 'If thou wouldest rather that I should show thee thy disadvantage than thine advantage, I will do so. Sleep here to-night, and in the morning arise early, and take the road upwards through the valley until thou reachest the wood through which thou camest hither. A little way within the wood thou wilt meet with a road branching off to the right, by which thou must proceed, until thou comest to a large sheltered glade with a mound in the centre. And thou wilt see a black man of great stature on the top of the mound. He is not smaller in size than two of the men of this world. He has but one foot; and one eye in the middle of his forehead. And he has a club of iron, and it is certain that there are no two men in the world who would not find their burden in that club. And he is not a comely man, but on the contrary he is exceedingly ill-favoured; and he is the woodward of that wood. And thou wilt see a thousand wild animals grazing around him. Inquire of him the way out of the glade, and he will reply to thee briefly, and will point out the road by which thou shalt find that which thou art in quest of.'

"And long seemed that night to me. And the next morning I arose and equipped myself, and mounted my horse, and proceeded straight through the valley to the wood; and I followed the cross-road which the man had pointed out to me, till at length I arrived at the glade. And there was I three times more astonished at the number of wild animals that I beheld, than the man had said I should be. And the black man was there, sitting upon the top of the mound. Huge of stature as the man had told me that he was, I found him to exceed by far the description he had given me of him. As for the iron club which the man had told me was a burden for two men, I am certain, Kai, that it would be a heavy weight for four warriors to lift; and this was in the black man's hand. And he only spoke to me in answer to my questions. Then I asked him what power he held over those animals. 'I will show thee, little man,' said he. And he took his club in his hand, and with it he struck a stag a great blow so that he brayed vehemently, and at his braying the animals came together, as numerous as the stars in the sky, so that it was difficult for me to find room in the glade to stand among them. There were serpents, and dragons, and divers sorts of animals. And he looked at them, and bade them go and feed; and they bowed their heads, and did him homage as vassals to their lord.

"Then the black man said to me, 'Seest thou now, little man, what power I hold over these animals?' Then I inquired of him the way, and he became very rough in his manner to me; however, he asked me whither I would go? And when I told him who I was and what I sought, he directed me. 'Take,' said he, 'that path that leads towards the head of the glade, and ascend the wooded steep until thou comest to its summit; and there thou wilt find an open space like to a large valley, and in the midst of it a tall tree, whose branches are greener than the greenest pine-trees. Under this tree is a fountain, and by the side of the fountain a marble slab, and on the marble slab a silver bowl, attached by a chain of silver, so that it may not be carried away.

Take the bowl and throw a bowlful of water upon the slab, and thou wilt hear a mighty peal of thunder, so that thou wilt think that heaven and earth are trembling with its fury. With the thunder there will come a shower so severe that it will be scarce possible for thee to endure it and live. And the shower will be of hailstones; and after the shower, the weather will become fair, but every leaf that was upon the tree will have been carried away by the shower. Then a flight of birds will come and alight upon the tree; and in thine own country thou didst never hear a strain so sweet as that which they will sing. And at the moment thou art most delighted with the song of the birds, thou wilt hear a murmuring and complaining coming towards thee along the valley. And thou wilt see a knight upon a coal-black horse, clothed in black velvet, and with a pennon of black linen upon his lance; and he will ride unto thee to encounter thee with the utmost speed. If thou fleest from him he will overtake thee, and if thou abidest there, as sure as thou art a mounted knight, he will leave thee on foot. And if thou dost not find trouble in that adventure, thou needest not seek it during the rest of thy life.'

"So I journeyed on, until I reached the summit of the steep, and there I found everything as the black man had described it to me. And I went up to the tree, and beneath it I saw the fountain, and by its side the marble slab, and the silver bowl fastened by the chain. Then I took the bowl, and cast a bowlful of water upon the slab; and thereupon, behold, the thunder came, much more violent than the black man had led me to expect; and after the thunder came the shower; and of a truth I tell thee, Kai, that there is neither man nor beast that can endure that shower and live. For not one of those hailstones would be stopped, either by the flesh or by the skin, until it had reached the bone. I turned my horse's flank towards the shower, and placed the beak of my shield over his head and neck, while I held the upper part of it over my own head. And thus I withstood the shower. When I looked on the tree there was not a single leaf upon it, and then the sky became clear, and with that, behold the birds lighted upon the tree, and sang. And truly, Kai, I never heard any melody equal to that, either before or since. And when I was most charmed with listening to the birds, lo, a murmuring voice was heard through the valley, approaching me and saying, 'Oh, Knight, what has brought thee hither? What evil have I done to thee, that thou shouldst act towards me and my possessions as thou hast this day? Dost thou not know that the shower to-day has left in my dominions neither man nor beast alive that was exposed to it?' And thereupon, behold, a Knight on a black horse appeared, clothed in jet-black velvet, and with a tabard of black linen about him. And we charged each other, and, as the onset was furious, it was not long before I was overthrown. Then the Knight passed the shaft of his lance through the bridle rein of my horse, and rode off with the two horses, leaving me where I was. And he did not even bestow so much notice upon me as to imprison me, nor did he despoil me of my arms. So I returned along the road by which I had come. And when I reached the glade where the black man was, I confess to thee, Kai, it is a marvel that I did not melt down into a liquid pool, through the shame that I felt at the black man's derision. And that night I came to the same castle where I had spent the night preceding. And I was more agreeably entertained that night than I had been the night before; and I was better feasted, and I conversed freely with the inmates of the castle, and none of them alluded to my expedition to the fountain, neither did I mention it to any; and I remained there that night. When I arose on the morrow, I found, ready saddled, a dark bay palfrey, with nostrils as red as scarlet; and after putting on my armour, and leaving there my blessing, I returned to my own Court. And that horse I still possess, and he is in the stable yonder. And I declare that I would not part with him for the best palfrey in the Island of Britain.

"Now of a truth, Kai, no man ever before confessed to an adventure so much to his own discredit, and verily it seems strange to me, that neither before nor since have I heard of any person besides myself who knew of this adventure, and that the subject of it should exist within King Arthur's dominions, without any other person lighting upon it."

"Now," quoth Owain, "would it not be well to go and endeavour to discover that place?"

"By the hand of my friend," said Kai, "often dost thou utter that with thy tongue which thou wouldst not make good with thy deeds."

"In very truth," said Gwenhwyvar, "it were better thou wert hanged, Kai, than to use such uncourteous speech towards a man like Owain."

"By the hand of my friend, good Lady," said Kai, "thy praise of Owain is not greater than mine."

With that Arthur awoke, and asked if he had not been sleeping a little.

"Yes, Lord," answered Owain, "thou hast slept awhile."

"Is it time for us to go to meat?"

"It is, Lord," said Owain.

Then the horn for washing was sounded, and the King and all his household sat down to eat. And when the meal was ended, Owain withdrew to his lodging, and made ready his horse and his arms.

On the morrow, with the dawn of day, he put on his armour, and mounted his charger, and travelled through distant lands and over desert mountains. And at length he arrived at the valley which Kynon had described to him; and he was certain that it was the same that he sought. And journeying along the valley by the side of the river, he followed its course till he came to the plain and within sight of the Castle. When he approached the Castle, he saw the youths shooting their daggers in the place where Kynon had seen them, and the yellow man, to whom the Castle belonged, standing hard by. And no sooner had Owain saluted the yellow man than he was saluted by him in return.

And he went forward towards the Castle, and there he saw the chamber, and when he had entered the chamber he beheld the maidens working at satin embroidery, in chairs of gold. And their beauty and their comeliness seemed to Owain far greater than Kynon had represented to him. And they rose to wait upon Owain, as they had done to Kynon, and the meal which they set before him gave more satisfaction to Owain than it had done to Kynon.

About the middle of the repast, the yellow man asked Owain the object of his journey. And Owain made it known to him, and said, "I am in quest of the Knight who guards the fountain." Upon this the yellow man smiled, and said that he was as loth to point out that adventure to Owain as he had been to Kynon. However, he described the whole to Owain, and they retired to rest.

The next morning Owain found his horse made ready for him by the damsels, and he set forward and came to the glade where the black man was. And the stature of the black man seemed more wonderful to Owain than it had done to Kynon, and Owain asked of him his road, and he showed it to him. And Owain followed the road, as Kynon had done, till he came to the green tree; and he beheld the fountain, and the slab beside the fountain, with the bowl upon it. And Owain took the bowl, and threw a bowlful of water upon the slab. And, lo, the thunder was heard, and after the thunder came the shower, much more violent than Kynon had described, and after the shower the sky became bright. And when Owain looked at the tree, there was not one leaf upon it. And immediately the birds came, and settled upon the tree, and sang. And when their song was most pleasing to Owain, he beheld a Knight coming towards him through the valley, and he prepared to receive him; and encountered him violently. Having broken both their lances, they drew their swords, and fought blade to blade. Then Owain struck the Knight a blow through his helmet, head-piece and visor, and through the skin, and the flesh, and the bone, until it wounded the very brain. Then the black Knight felt that he had received a mortal wound, upon which he turned his horse's head, and fled. And Owain pursued him, and followed close upon him, although he was not near enough to strike him with his sword. Thereupon Owain descried a vast and resplendent Castle. And they came to the Castle gate. And the black Knight was allowed to enter, and the portcullis was let fall upon Owain; and it struck his horse behind the saddle, and cut him in two, and carried away the rowels of the spurs that were upon Owain's heels. And the portcullis descended to the floor. And the rowels of the spurs and part of the horse were without, and Owain with the other part of the horse remained between the two gates, and the inner gate was closed, so that Owain could not go thence; and Owain was in a perplexing situation. And while he was in this state, he could see through an aperture in the gate, a street facing him, with a row of houses on each side. And he beheld a maiden, with yellow curling hair, and a frontlet of gold upon her head; and she was clad in a dress of yellow satin, and on her feet were shoes of variegated leather. And she approached the gate, and desired that it should be opened. "Heaven knows, Lady," said Owain, "it is no more possible for me to open to thee from hence, than it is for thee to set me free." "Truly," said the damsel, "it is very sad that thou canst not be released, and every woman ought to succour thee, for I never saw one more faithful in the service of ladies than thou. As a friend thou art the most sincere, and as a lover the most devoted. Therefore," quoth she, "whatever is in my power to do for thy release, I will do it. Take this ring and put it on thy finger, with the stone inside thy hand; and close thy hand upon the stone. And as long as thou concealest it, it will conceal thee. When they have consulted together, they will come forth to fetch thee, in order to put thee to death; and they will be much grieved that they cannot find thee. And I will await thee on the horseblock yonder; and thou wilt be able to see me, though I cannot see thee; therefore come and place thy hand upon my shoulder, that I may know that thou art near me. And by the way that I go hence, do thou accompany me."

Then she went away from Owain, and he did all that the maiden had told him. And the people of the Castle came to seek Owain, to put him to death, and when they found nothing but the half of his horse, they were sorely grieved.

And Owain vanished from among them, and went to the maiden, and placed his hand upon her shoulder; whereupon she set off, and Owain followed her, until they came to the door of a large and beautiful chamber, and the maiden opened it, and they went in, and closed the door. And Owain looked around the chamber, and behold there was not even a single nail in it that was not painted with gorgeous colours; and there was not a single panel that had not sundry images in gold portrayed upon it.

The maiden kindled a fire, and took water in a silver bowl, and put a towel of white linen on her shoulder, and gave Owain water to wash. Then she placed before him a silver table, inlaid with gold; upon which was a cloth of yellow linen; and she brought him food. And of a truth, Owain had never seen any kind of meat that was not there in abundance, but it was better cooked there than he had ever found it in any other place. Nor did he ever see so excellent a display of meat and drink, as there. And there was not one vessel from which he was served, that was not of gold or of silver. And Owain ate and drank, until late in the afternoon, when lo, they heard a mighty clamour in the Castle; and Owain asked the maiden what that outcry was. "They are administering extreme unction," said she, "to the Nobleman who owns the Castle." And Owain went to sleep.

The couch which the maiden had prepared for him was meet for Arthur himself; it was of scarlet, and fur, and satin, and sendal, and fine linen. In the middle of the night they heard a woeful outcry. "What outcry again is this?" said Owain. "The Nobleman who owned the Castle is now dead," said the maiden. And a little after daybreak, they heard an exceeding loud clamour and wailing. And Owain asked the maiden what was the cause of it. "They are bearing to the church the body of the Nobleman who owned the Castle."

And Owain rose up, and clothed himself, and opened a window of the chamber, and looked towards the Castle; and he could see neither the bounds, nor the extent of the hosts that filled the streets. And they were fully armed; and a vast number of women were with them, both on horseback and on foot; and all the ecclesiastics in the city, singing. And it seemed to Owain that the sky resounded with the vehemence of their cries, and with the noise of the trumpets, and with the singing of the ecclesiastics. In the midst of the throng,

he beheld the bier, over which was a veil of white linen; and wax
tapers were burning beside and around it, and none that supported
the bier was lower in rank than a powerful Baron.

Never did Owain see an assemblage so gorgeous with satin, and
silk, and sendal. And following the train, he beheld a lady with yellow hair falling over her shoulders, and stained with blood; and about
her a dress of yellow satin, which was torn. Upon her feet were shoes
of variegated leather. And it was a marvel that the ends of her fingers
were not bruised, from the violence with which she smote her hands
together. Truly she would have been the fairest lady Owain ever
saw, had she been in her usual guise. And her cry was louder than
the shout of the men, or the clamour of the trumpets. No sooner
had he beheld the lady, than he became inflamed with her love, so
that it took entire possession of him.

Then he inquired of the maiden who the lady was. "Heaven
knows," replied the maiden, "she may be said to be the fairest, and
the most chaste, and the most liberal, and the wisest, and the most
noble of women. And she is my mistress; and she is called the Countess
of the Fountain, the wife of him whom thou didst slay yesterday."
"Verily," said Owain, "she is the woman that I love best." "Verily,"
said the maiden, "she shall also love thee not a little."

And with that the maid arose, and kindled a fire, and filled a pot
with water, and placed it to warm; and she brought a towel of white
linen, and placed it around Owain's neck; and she took a goblet of
ivory, and a silver basin, and filled them with warm water, wherewith
she washed Owain's head. Then she opened a wooden casket, and
drew forth a razor, whose haft was of ivory, and upon which were
two rivets of gold. And she shaved his beard, and she dried his head,
and his throat, with the towel. Then she rose up from before Owain,
and brought him to eat. And truly Owain had never so good a meal,
nor was he ever so well served.

When he had finished his repast, the maiden arranged his couch.
"Come here," said she, "and sleep, and I will go and woo for thee."
And Owain went to sleep, and the maiden shut the door of the
chamber after her, and went towards the Castle. When she came
there, she found nothing but mourning, and sorrow; and the Countess
in her chamber could not bear the sight of any one through grief.
Luned came and saluted her, but the Countess answered her not.
And the maiden bent down towards her, and said, "What aileth thee,
that thou answerest no one to-day?" "Luned," said the Countess,
"what change hath befallen thee, that thou hast not come to visit me

in my grief? It was wrong in thee, and I having made thee rich; it was wrong in thee that thou didst not come to see me in my distress. That was wrong in thee." "Truly," said Luned, "I thought thy good sense was greater than I find it to be. Is it well for thee to mourn after that good man, or for anything else, that thou canst not have?" "I declare to heaven," said the Countess, "that in the whole world there is not a man equal to him." "Not so," said Luned, "for an ugly man would be as good as, or better than he." "I declare to heaven," said the Countess, "that were it not repugnant to me to cause to be put to death one whom I have brought up, I would have thee executed, for making such a comparison to me. As it is, I will banish thee." "I am glad," said Luned, "that thou hast no other cause to do so, than that I would have been of service to thee where thou didst not know what was to thine advantage. And henceforth evil betide whichever of us shall make the first advance towards reconciliation to the other; whether I should seek an invitation from thee, or thou of thine own accord shouldst send to invite me."

With that Luned went forth: and the Countess arose and followed her to the door of the chamber, and began coughing loudly. And when Luned looked back, the Countess beckoned to her; and she returned to the Countess. "In truth," said the Countess, "evil is thy disposition; but if thou knowest what is to my advantage, declare it to me." "I will do so," quoth she.

"Thou knowest that except by warfare and arms it is impossible for thee to preserve thy possessions; delay not, therefore, to seek some one who can defend them." "And how can I do that?" said the Countess. "I will tell thee," said Luned. "Unless thou canst defend the fountain, thou canst not maintain thy dominions; and no one can defend the fountain, except it be a knight of Arthur's household; and I will go to Arthur's Court, and ill betide me, if I return thence without a warrior who can guard the fountain as well as, or even better than, he who defended it formerly." "That will be hard to perform," said the Countess. "Go, however, and make proof of that which thou hast promised."

Luned set out, under the pretence of going to Arthur's Court; but she went back to the chamber where she had left Owain; and she tarried there with him as long as it might have taken her to have travelled to the Court of King Arthur. And at the end of that time, she apparelled herself and went to visit the Countess. And the Countess was much rejoiced when she saw her, and inquired what news she brought from the Court. "I bring thee the best of news," said Luned, "for I have compassed the object of my mission. When wilt thou, that I should present to thee the chieftain who has come with me hither?" "Bring him here to visit me to-morrow, at mid-day," said the Countess, "and I will cause the town to be assembled by that time."

And Luned returned home. And the next day, at noon, Owain arrayed himself in a coat, and a surcoat, and a mantle of yellow satin, upon which was a broad band of gold lace; and on his feet were high shoes of variegated leather, which were fastened by golden clasps, in the form of lions. And they proceeded to the chamber of the Countess.

Right glad was the Countess of their coming, and she gazed stead-fastly upon Owain, and said, "Luned, this knight has not the look of a traveller." "What harm is there in that, lady?" said Luned. "I am certain," said the Countess, "that no other man than this chased the soul from the body of my lord." "So much the better for thee, lady," said Luned, "for had he not been stronger than thy lord he could not have deprived him of life. There is no remedy for that which is past, be it as it may." "Go back to thine abode," said the Countess, "and I will take counsel."

The next day the Countess caused all her subjects to assemble, and showed them that her earldom was left defenceless, and that it could not be protected but with horse and arms, and military skill. "Therefore," said she, "this is what I offer for your choice: either let one of you take me, or give your consent for me to take a husband from elsewhere to defend my dominions."

So they came to the determination that it was better that she should have permission to marry some one from elsewhere; and, thereupon, she sent for the bishops and archbishops to celebrate her nuptials with Owain. And the men of the earldom did Owain homage.

And Owain defended the Fountain with lance and sword. And this is the manner in which he defended it: Whensoever a knight came there he overthrew him, and sold him for his full worth, and what he thus gained he divided among his barons and his knights; and no man in the whole world could be more beloved than he was by his subjects. And it was thus for the space of three years.

It befell that as Gwalchmai went forth one day with King Arthur, he perceived him to be very sad and sorrowful. And Gwalchmai was much grieved to see Arthur in this state; and he questioned him, saying, "Oh, my lord! what has befallen thee?" "In sooth, Gwalchmai," said Arthur, "I am grieved concerning Owain, whom I have lost these three years, and I shall certainly die if the fourth year passes without my seeing him. Now I am sure, that it is through the tale which Kynon the son of Clydno related, that I have lost Owain." "There is no need for thee," said Gwalchmai, "to summon to arms thy whole dominions on this account, for thou thyself and the men of thy household will be able to avenge Owain, if he be slain; or to set him free, if he be in prison; and, if alive, to bring him back with thee." And it was settled according to what Gwalchmai had said.

Then Arthur and the men of his household prepared to go and seek Owain, and their number was three thousand, besides their attendants. And Kynon the son of Clydno acted as their guide. And Arthur came to the Castle where Kynon had been before, and when he came there the youths were shooting in the same place, and the yellow man was standing hard by. When the yellow man saw Arthur he greeted him, and invited him to the Castle; and Arthur accepted his invitation, and they entered the Castle together. And great as was the number of his retinue, their presence was scarcely observed in the Castle, so vast was its extent. And the maidens rose up to wait on them, and the service of the maidens appeared to them all to excel any attendance they had ever met with; and even the pages who had charge of the horses were no worse served, that night, than Arthur himself would have been in his own palace.

The next morning Arthur set out thence, with Kynon for his guide, and came to the place where the black man was. And the stature of the black man was more surprising to Arthur than it had been represented to him. And they came to the top of the wooded steep, and traversed the valley till they reached the green tree, where they saw the fountain, and the bowl, and the slab. And upon that, Kai came to Arthur and spoke to him. "My lord," said he, "I know the meaning of all this, and my request is, that thou wilt permit me to throw the water on the slab, and to receive the first adventure that may befall." And Arthur gave him leave.

Then Kai threw a bowlful of water upon the slab, and immediately there came the thunder, and after the thunder the shower. And such a thunderstorm they had never known before, and many of the attendants who were in Arthur's train were killed by the shower. After the shower had ceased the sky became clear; and on looking at the tree they beheld it completely leafless. Then the birds descended upon the tree, and the song of the birds was far sweeter than any strain they had ever heard before. Then they beheld a knight on a coal-black horse, clothed in black satin, coming rapidly towards them.

And Kai met him and encountered him, and it was not long before Kai was overthrown. And the knight withdrew, and Arthur and his host encamped for the night.

And when they arose in the morning, they perceived the signal of combat upon the lance of the Knight. And Kai came to Arthur, and spoke to him: "My lord," said he, "though I was overthrown yesterday, if it seem good to thee, I would gladly meet the Knight again to-day." "Thou mayst do so," said Arthur. And Kai went towards the Knight. And on the spot he overthrew Kai, and struck him with the head of his lance in the forehead, so that it broke his helmet and the head-piece, and pierced the skin and the flesh, the breadth of the spear-head, even to the bone. And Kai returned to his companions.

After this, all the household of Arthur went forth, one after the other, to combat the Knight, until there was not one that was not overthrown by him, except Arthur and Gwalchmai. And Arthur armed himself to encounter the Knight. "Oh, my lord," said Gwalchmai, "permit me to fight with him first." And Arthur permitted him. And he went forth to meet the Knight, having over himself and his horse a satin robe of honour which had been sent him by the daughter of the Earl of Rhangyw, and in this dress he was not known by any of the host. And they charged each other, and fought all that day until the evening, and neither of them was able to unhorse the other.

The next day they fought with strong lances, and neither of them could obtain the mastery.

And the third day they fought with exceeding strong lances. And they were incensed with rage, and fought furiously, even until noon. And they gave each other such a shock that the girths of their horses were broken, so that they fell over their horses' cruppers to the ground. And they rose up speedily, and drew their swords, and resumed the combat; and the multitude that witnessed their encounter felt assured that they had never before seen two men so valiant or so powerful. And had it been midnight, it would have been light from the fire that flashed from their weapons. And the Knight gave Gwalchmai a blow that turned his helmet from off his face, so that the Knight knew that it was Gwalchmai. Then Owain said, "My lord Gwalchmai, I did not know thee for my cousin, owing to the robe of honour that enveloped thee; take my sword and my arms." Said Gwalchmai, "Thou, Owain, art the victor; take thou my sword." And with that Arthur saw that they were conversing, and advanced towards them. "My lord Arthur," said Gwalchmai, "here is Owain, who has vanquished me, and will not take my arms." "My lord," said Owain, "it is he that has vanquished me, and he will not take my sword." "Give me your swords," said Arthur, "and then neither of you has vanquished the other." Then Owain put his arms around Arthur's neck, and they embraced. And all the host hurried forward to see Owain, and to embrace him; and there was nigh being a loss of life, so great was the press.

And they retired that night, and the next day Arthur prepared to depart. "My lord," said Owain, "this is not well of thee; for I have been absent from thee these three years, and during all that time, up to this very day, I have been preparing a banquet for thee, knowing that thou wouldst come to seek me. Tarry with me, therefore, until thou and thy attendants have recovered the fatigues of the journey, and have been anointed."

And they all proceeded to the Castle of the Countess of the Fountain, and the banquet which had been three years preparing was consumed in three months. Never had they a more delicious or agreeable banquet. And Arthur prepared to depart. Then he sent an embassy to the Countess, to beseech her to permit Owain to go with him for the space of three months, that he might show him to the nobles and the fair dames of the Island of Britain. And the Countess gave her consent, although it was very painful to her. So Owain came with Arthur to the Island of Britain. And when he was once more amongst his kindred and friends, he remained three years, instead of three months, with them.

And as Owain one day sat at meat, in the city of Caerlleon upon Usk, behold a damsel entered upon a bay horse, with a curling mane and covered with foam, and the bridle and so much as was seen of the saddle were of gold. And the damsel was arrayed in a dress of yellow satin. And she came up to Owain, and took the ring from off his hand. "Thus," said she, "shall be treated the deceiver, the traitor, the faithless, the disgraced, and the beardless." And she turned her horse's head and departed.

Then his adventure came to Owain's remembrance, and he was sorrowful; and having finished eating he went to his own abode and made preparations that night. And the next day he arose but did not go to the Court, but wandered to the distant parts of the earth and to uncultivated mountains. And he remained there until all his apparel was worn out, and his body was wasted away, and his hair was grown long. And he went about with the wild beasts and fed with them, until they became familiar with him; but at length he grew so weak that he could no longer bear them company. Then he descended from the mountains to the valley, and came to a park that was the fairest in the world, and belonged to a widowed Countess.

One day the Countess and her maidens went forth to walk by a lake, that was in the middle of the park. And they saw the form of a man. And they were terrified. Nevertheless they went near him, and touched him, and looked at him. And they saw that there was life in him, though he was exhausted by the heat of the sun. And the Countess returned to the Castle, and took a flask full of precious ointment, and gave it to one of her maidens. "Go with this," said she, "and take with thee yonder horse and clothing, and place them near the man we saw just now. And anoint him with this balsam, near his heart; and if there is life in him, he will arise through the efficacy of this balsam. Then watch what he will do."

And the maiden departed from her, and poured the whole of the balsam upon Owain, and left the horse and the garments hard by, and went a little way off, and hid herself to watch him. In a short time she saw him begin to move his arms; and he rose up, and looked at his person, and became ashamed of the unseemliness of his appearance. Then he perceived the horse and the garments that were near him. And he crept forward till he was able to draw the garments to him from off the saddle. And he clothed himself, and with difficulty mounted the horse. Then the damsel discovered herself to him, and saluted him. And he was rejoiced when he saw her, and inquired of her, what land and what territory that was. "Truly," said the maiden, "a widowed Countess owns yonder Castle; at the death of her husband, he left her two Earldoms, but at this day she has but this one dwelling that has not been wrested from her by a young Earl, who is her neighbour, because she refused to become his wife." "That is a pity," said Owain. And he and the maiden proceeded to the Castle; and he alighted there, and the maiden conducted him to a pleasant chamber, and kindled a fire and left him.

And the maiden came to the Countess, and gave the flask into her hand. "Ha! maiden," said the Countess, "where is all the balsam?" "Have I not used it all?" said she. "Oh, maiden," said the Countess, "I cannot easily forgive thee this; it is sad for me to have wasted seven-score pounds' worth of precious ointment upon a stranger whom I know not. However, maiden, wait thou upon him, until he is quite recovered."

And the maiden did so, and furnished him with meat and drink, and fire, and lodging, and medicaments, until he was well again. And in three months he was restored to his former guise, and became even more comely than he had ever been before.

One day Owain heard a great tumult, and a sound of arms in the Castle, and he inquired of the maiden the cause thereof. "The Earl," said she, "whom I mentioned to thee, has come before the Castle, with a numerous army, to subdue the Countess." And Owain inquired of her whether the Countess had a horse and arms in her possession. "She has the best in the world," said the maiden. "Wilt thou go and request the loan of a horse and arms for me," said Owain, "that I may go and look at this army?" "I will," said the maiden.

And she came to the Countess, and told her what Owain had said. And the Countess laughed. "Truly," said she, "I will even give him a horse and arms for ever; such a horse and such arms had he never yet, and I am glad that they should be taken by him to-day, lest my enemies should have them against my will to-morrow. Yet I know not what he would do with them."

The Countess bade them bring out a beautiful black steed, upon which was a beechen saddle, and a suit of armour, for man and horse. And Owain armed himself, and mounted the horse, and went forth, attended by two pages completely equipped, with horses and arms. And when they came near to the Earl's army, they could see neither its extent nor its extremity. And Owain asked the pages in which troop the Earl was. "In yonder troop," said they, "in which are four yellow standards. Two of them are before, and two behind him." "Now," said Owain, "do you return and await me near the portal of the Castle." So they returned, and Owain pressed forward until he met the Earl. And Owain drew him completely out of his saddle, and turned his horse's head towards the Castle, and though it was with difficulty, he brought the Earl to the portal, where the pages awaited him. And in they came. And Owain presented the Earl as a gift to the Countess. And said to her, "Behold a requital to thee for thy blessed balsam."

The army encamped around the Castle. And the Earl restored to the Countess the two Earldoms he had taken from her, as a ransom for his life; and for his freedom he gave her the half of his own dominions, and all his gold, and his silver, and his jewels, besides hostages.

And Owain took his departure. And the Countess and all her subjects besought him to remain, but Owain chose rather to wander through distant lands and deserts.

And as he journeyed, he heard a loud yelling in a wood. And it was repeated a second and a third time. And Owain went towards the spot, and beheld a huge craggy mound, in the middle of the wood; on the side of which was a grey rock. And there was a cleft in the rock, and a serpent was within the cleft. And near the rock stood a black lion, and every time the lion sought to go thence, the serpent darted towards him to attack him. And Owain unsheathed his sword, and drew near to the rock; and as the serpent sprang out, he struck him with his sword, and cut him in two. And he dried his sword, and went on his way, as before. But behold the lion followed him, and played about him, as though it had been a greyhound that he had reared.

They proceeded thus throughout the day, until the evening. And when it was time for Owain to take his rest, he dismounted, and turned his horse loose in a flat and wooded meadow. And he struck fire, and when the fire was kindled, the lion brought him fuel enough to last for three nights. And the lion disappeared. And presently the lion returned, bearing a fine large roebuck. And he threw it down before Owain, who went towards the fire with it.

And Owain took the roebuck, and skinned it, and placed collops of its flesh upon skewers, around the fire. The rest of the buck he gave to the lion to devour. While he was doing this, he heard a deep sigh near him, and a second, and a third. And Owain called out to know whether the sigh he heard proceeded from a mortal; and he received answer that it did. "Who art thou?" said Owain. "Truly," said the voice, "I am Luned, the handmaiden of the Countess of the Fountain." "And what dost thou here?" said Owain. "I am imprisoned," said she, "on account of the knight who came from Arthur's Court, and married the Countess. And he stayed a short time with her, but he afterwards departed for the Court of Arthur, and has not returned since. And he was the friend I loved best in the world. And two of the pages in the Countess's chamber traduced him, and called him a deceiver. And I told them that they two were not a match for him alone. So they imprisoned me in the stone vault, and said that I should be put to death, unless he came himself to deliver me, by a certain day; and that is no further off than the day after to-morrow. And I have no one to send to seek him for me. And his name is Owain the son of Urien." "And art thou certain that if that knight knew all this, he would come to thy rescue?" "I am most certain of it," said she.

When the collops were cooked, Owain divided them into two parts, between himself and the maiden; and after they had eaten, they talked together, until the day dawned. And the next morning Owain inquired of the damsel, if there was any place where he could get food and entertainment for that night. "There is, Lord," said she; "cross over yonder, and go along the side of the river, and in a short time thou wilt see a great Castle, in which are many towers, and the Earl who owns that Castle is the most hospitable man in the world. There thou mayst spend the night."

Never did sentinel keep stricter watch over his lord, than the lion that night over Owain.

And Owain accoutred his horse, and passed across by the ford, and came in sight of the Castle. And he entered it, and was honourably received. And his horse was well cared for, and plenty of fodder was placed before him. Then the lion went and lay down in the horse's manger; so that none of the people of the Castle dared to approach him. The treatment which Owain met with there was such as he had never known elsewhere, for every one was as sorrowful as though death had been upon him. And they went to meat; and the Earl sat upon one side of Owain, and on the other side his only daughter. And Owain had never seen any more lovely than she. Then the lion came and placed himself between Owain's feet, and he fed him with every kind of food that he took himself. And he never saw anything equal to the sadness of the people.

In the middle of the repast the Earl began to bid Owain welcome. "Then," said Owain, "behold, it is time for thee to be cheerful." "Heaven knows," said the Earl, "that it is not thy coming that makes us sorrowful, but we have cause enough for sadness and care." "What is that?" said Owain. "I have two sons," replied the Earl, "and yesterday they went to the mountains to hunt. Now there is on the mountain a monster who kills men and devours them, and he seized my sons; and to-morrow is the time he has fixed to be here, and he threatens that he will then slay my sons before my eyes, unless I will deliver into his hands this my daughter. He has the form of a man, but in stature he is no less than a giant."

"Truly," said Owain, "that is lamentable. And which wilt thou do?" "Heaven knows," said the Earl, "it will be better that my sons should be slain against my will, than that I should voluntarily give up my daughter to him to ill-treat and destroy." Then they talked about other things, and Owain stayed there that night.

The next morning they heard an exceeding great clamour, which was caused by the coming of the giant with the two youths. And the Earl was anxious both to protect his Castle and to release his two sons. Then Owain put on his armour and went forth to encounter the giant, and the lion followed him. And when the giant saw that Owain was armed, he rushed towards him and attacked him. And the lion fought with the giant much more fiercely than Owain did. "Truly," said the giant, "I should find no difficulty in fighting with thee, were it not for the animal that is with thee." Upon that Owain took the lion back to the Castle and shut the gate upon him, and then he returned to fight the giant, as before. And the lion roared very loud, for he heard that it went hard with Owain. And he climbed up till he reached the top of the Earl's hall, and thence he got to the top of the Castle, and he sprang down from the walls and went and joined Owain. And the lion gave the giant a stroke with his paw, which tore him from his shoulder to his hip, and his heart was laid bare, and the giant fell down dead. Then Owain restored the two youths to their father.

The Earl besought Owain to remain with him, and he would not, but set forward towards the meadow where Luned was. And when he came there he saw a great fire kindled, and two youths with beautiful curling auburn hair were leading the maiden to cast her into the fire. And Owain asked them what charge they had against her. And they told him of the compact that was between them, as the maiden had done the night before. "And," said they, "Owain has failed her, therefore we are taking her to be burnt." "Truly," said Owain, "he is a good knight, and if he knew that the maiden was in such peril, I marvel that he came not to her rescue; but if you will accept me in his stead, I will do battle with you." "We will," said the youths, "by him who made us."

And they attacked Owain, and he was hard beset by them. And with that the lion came to Owain's assistance, and they two got the better of the young men. And they said to him, "Chieftain, it was not agreed that we should fight save with thyself alone, and it is harder for us to contend with yonder animal than with thee." And Owain put the lion in the place where the maiden had been imprisoned, and blocked up the door with stones, and he went to fight with the young men, as before. But Owain had not his usual strength, and the two youths pressed hard upon him. And the lion roared incessantly at seeing Owain in trouble; and he burst through the wall until he found a way out, and rushed upon the young men, and instantly slew them. So Luned was saved from being burned.

Then Owain returned with Luned to the dominions of the Countess of the Fountain. And when he went thence he took the

Countess with him to Arthur's Court, and she was his wife as long as she lived.

And then he took the road that led to the Court of the savage black man, and Owain fought with him, and the lion did not quit Owain until he had vanquished him. And when he reached the Court of the savage black man he entered the hall, and beheld four-and-twenty ladies, the fairest that could be seen. And the garments which they had on were not worth four-and-twenty pence, and they were as sorrowful as death. And Owain asked them the cause of their sadness. And they said, "We are the daughters of Earls, and we all came here with our husbands, whom we dearly loved. And we were received with honour and rejoicing. And we were thrown into a state of stupor, and while we were thus, the demon who owns this Castle slew all our husbands, and took from us our horses, and our raiment, and our gold, and our silver; and the corpses of our husbands are still in this house, and many others with them. And this, Chieftain, is the cause of our grief, and we are sorry that thou art come hither, lest harm should befall thee."

And Owain was grieved when he heard this. And he went forth from the Castle, and he beheld a knight approaching him, who saluted him in a friendly and cheerful manner, as if he had been a brother. And this was the savage black man. "In very sooth," said Owain, "it is not to seek thy friendship that I am here." "In sooth," said he, "thou shalt find it then." And with that they charged each other, and fought furiously. And Owain overcame him, and bound his hands behind his back. Then the black savage besought Owain to spare his life, and spoke thus: "My lord Owain," said he, "it was foretold that thou shouldst come hither and vanquish me, and thou hast done so. I was a robber here, and my house was a house of spoil; but grant me my life, and I will become the keeper of an Hospice, and I will maintain this house as an Hospice for weak and for strong, as long as I live, for the good of thy soul." And Owain accepted this proposal of him, and remained there that night.

And the next day he took the four-and-twenty ladies, and their horses, and their raiment, and what they possessed of goods and jewels, and proceeded with them to Arthur's Court. And if Arthur was rejoiced when he saw him, after he had lost him the first time, his joy was now much greater. And of those ladies, such as wished to remain in Arthur's Court remained there, and such as wished to depart departed.

And thenceforward Owain dwelt at Arthur's Court greatly beloved, as the head of his household, until he went away with his followers; and those were the army of three hundred ravens which Kenverchyn had left him. And wherever Owain went with these he was victorious.

And this is the tale of the Lady of the Fountain.

THE DECAMERON

Giovanni Boccaccio

The Decameron *of Giovanni Boccaccio (1313–1375), the Florentine* counterpart *to* The Canterbury Tales, *relates the amusing and enter- taining stories told to each other by a group of young people—seven young women and three young men—who took refuge from an outbreak of the Black Death in a villa outside Florence while the disease ravaged the city. There are imperishable stories of murder, revenge, passionate love, good fortune and bad, and disastrous and/or amazing beneficial coincidence. The three tales selected here will speak for the other ninety-seven that make up* The Decameron, *a timeless masterpiece of storytelling:*

Second Day, Eighth Story
Fourth Day, First Story
Fifth Day, Ninth Story

SECOND DAY: EIGHTH STORY

The Count of Antwerp, labouring under a false accusation, goes into exile. He leaves his two children in different places in England, and takes service in Ireland. Returning to England an unknown man, he finds his sons pros- perous. He serves as a groom in the army of the King of France; his innocence is established, and he is restored to his former honours.

Vast indeed is the field that lies before us, wherein to roam at large; 'twould readily afford each of us not one course but ten, so richly has Fortune diversified it with episodes both strange and sombre; wherefore selecting one such from this infinite store, I say:—That, after the transference of the Roman Empire from the Franks to the Germans, the greatest enmity prevailed between the two nations, with warfare perpetual and relentless: wherefore, deeming that the offensive would be their best defence, the King of France and his son mustered all the forces they could raise from their own dominions and those of their kinsmen and allies, and arrayed a grand army for the subjugation of their enemies. Before they took the field, as they could not leave the realm without a governor, they chose for that office Gautier, Count of Antwerp, a true knight and sage counsellor, and their very loyal ally and vassal, choosing him the rather, because, albeit he was a thorough master of the art of war, yet they deemed him less apt to support its hardships than for the conduct of affairs of a delicate nature. Him, therefore, they set in their place as their vicar-general and regent of the whole realm of France, and having so done, they took the field.

Count Gautier ordered his administration wisely and in a regular course, discussing all matters with the queen and her daughter-in-law; whom, albeit they were left under his charge and jurisdiction, he nevertheless treated as his ladies paramount. The Count was about forty years of age, and the very mould of manly beauty; in bearing as courteous and chivalrous as ever a gentleman might be, and withal so debonair and dainty, so feat and trim of person that he had not his peer among the gallants of that day. His wife was dead, leaving him two children and no more, to wit, a boy and a girl, still quite young.

Now the King and his son being thus away at the war, and the Count frequenting the court of the two said ladies, and consulting with them upon affairs of state, it so befell that the Prince's lady regarded him with no small favour, being very sensible alike of the advantages of his person and the nobility of his bearing; whereby she conceived for him a passion which was all the more ardent because it was secret. And, as he was without a wife, and she was still in the freshness of her youth, she saw not why she should not readily be gratified; but supposing that nothing stood in the way but her own shamefastness, she resolved to be rid of that, and disclose her mind to him without any reserve. So one day, when she was alone, she seized her opportunity, and sent for him, as if she were desirous to converse with him on indifferent topics.

The Count, his mind entirely aloof from the lady's purpose, presented himself forthwith, and at her invitation sate down by her side on a settee. They were quite alone in the room; but the Count had twice asked her the reason why she had so honoured him, before, overcome by passion, she broke silence, and crimson from brow to neck with shame, half sobbing, trembling in every limb, and faltering at every word, she thus spoke:—

"Dearest friend and sweet my lord, sagacity such as yours cannot but be apt to perceive how great is the frailty of men and women, and how, for divers reasons, it varies in different persons in such a degree that no just judge would mete out the same measure to each indifferently, though the fault were apparently the same. Who would not acknowledge that a poor man or woman, fain to earn daily bread by the sweat of the brow, is far more reprehensible in yielding to the solicitations of love, than a rich lady, whose life is lapped in ease and unrestricted luxury? Not a soul, I am persuaded, but would so acknowledge!

"Wherefore I deem that the possession of these boons of fortune should go far indeed to acquit the possessor, if she, perchance, indulge an errant love; and, for the rest, that, if she have chosen a wise and worthy lover, she should be entirely exonerated. And as I think I may fairly claim the benefit of both these pleas, and of others beside, to wit, my youth and my husband's absence, which naturally incline me to love, 'tis meet that I now urge them in your presence in defence of my passion; and if they have the weight with you which they should have with the wise, I pray you to afford me your help and counsel in the matter wherein I shall demand it.

"I avow that in the absence of my husband I have been unable to withstand the promptings of the flesh and the power of love, forces of such potency that even the strongest men—not to speak of delicate women—have not seldom been, nay daily are, overcome by them; and so, living thus, as you see me, in ease and luxury, I have allowed the allurements of love to draw me on until at last I find myself a prey to passion. Wherein were I discovered, I were, I confess, dishonoured; but discovery being avoided, I count the dishonour all but nought. Moreover, love has been so gracious to me that not only has he spared to blind me in the choice of my lover, but he has even lent me his most effective aid, pointing me to one well worthy of the love of a lady such as I, even to yourself; whom, if I misread not my mind, I deem the most handsome and courteous and debonair, and therewithal the sagest cavalier that the realm of France may shew. And as you are without a wife, so may I say that I find myself without a husband. Wherefore in return for this great love I bear you, deny me not, I pray you, yours; but have pity on my youth, which wastes away for you like ice before the fire."

These words were followed by such a flood of tears, that, albeit she had intended yet further to press her suit, speech failed her; her eyes drooped, and, almost swooning with emotion, she let her head fall upon the Count's breast.

The Count, who was the most loyal of knights, began with all severity to chide her mad passion and to thrust her from him—for she was now making as if she would throw her arms around his neck—and to asseverate with oaths that he would rather be hewn in pieces than either commit, or abet another in committing such an offence against the honour of his lord; when the lady, catching his drift, and forgetting all her love in a sudden frenzy of rage, cried out:—"So! unknightly knight, is it thus you flout my love? Now Heaven forbid, but, as you would be the death of me, I either do you to death or drive you from the world!"

So saying, she dishevelled and tore her hair and rent her garments to shreds about her bosom. Which done, she began shrieking at the top of her voice:—"Help! help! The Count of Antwerp threatens to violate me!"

Whereupon the Count, who knew that a clear conscience was no protection against the envy of courtiers, and doubted that his innocence would prove scarce a match for the cunning of the lady, started to his feet, and hied him with all speed out of the room, out of the palace, and back to his own house. Counsel of none he sought; but forthwith set his children on horseback, and taking horse himself, departed post haste for Calais. The lady's cries brought not a few to her aid, who, observing her plight, not only gave entire credence to her story, but improved upon it, alleging that the debonair and accomplished Count had long employed all the arts of seduction to compass his end. So they rushed in hot haste to the Count's house, with intent to arrest him, and not finding him, sacked it and razed it to the ground. The news, as glosed and garbled, being carried to the King and Prince in the field, they were mightily incensed, and offered a great reward for the Count, dead or alive, and condemned him and his posterity to perpetual banishment.

Meanwhile the Count, sorely troubled that by his flight his innocence shewed as guilt, pursued his journey, and concealing his identity, and being recognised by none, arrived with his two children at Calais. Thence he forthwith crossed to England, and, meanly clad, fared on for London, taking care as he went to school his children in all that belonged to their new way of life, and especially in two main articles: to wit, that they should bear with resignation the poverty to which, by no fault of theirs, but solely by one of Fortune's caprices, they and he were reduced, and that they should be most sedulously on their guard to betray to none, as they valued their lives, whence they were, or who their father was. The son, Louis by name, was perhaps nine, and the daughter, Violante, perhaps seven years of age. For years so tender they proved apt pupils, and afterwards shewed by their conduct that they had well learned their father's lesson. He deemed it expedient to change their names, and accordingly called the boy Perrot and the girl Jeannette. So, meanly clad, the Count and his two children arrived at London, and there made shift to get a living by going about soliciting alms in the guise of French mendicants.

Now, as for this purpose they waited one morning outside a church, it so befell that a great lady, the wife of one of the marshals of the King of England, observed them, as she left the church, asking alms, and demanded of the Count whence he was, and whether the children were his. He answered that he was from Picardy, that the children were his, and that he had been fain to leave Picardy by reason of the misconduct of their reprobate elder brother. The lady looked at the girl, who being fair, and of gentle and winning mien and manners, found much favour in her eyes. So the kindhearted lady said to the Count:—"My good man, if thou art willing to leave thy little daughter with me, I like her looks so well that I will gladly take her; and if she grow up a good woman, I will see that she is suitably married when the right time comes." The Count was much gratified by the proposal, which he forthwith accepted, and parted with the girl, charging the lady with tears to take every care of her.

Having thus placed the girl with one in whom he felt sure that he might trust, he determined to tarry no longer in London; wherefore, taking Perrot with him and begging as he went, he made his way to Wales, not without great suffering, being unused to go afoot. Now in Wales another of the King's marshals had his court, maintaining great state and a large number of retainers; to which court the Count and his son frequently repaired, there to get food; and there Perrot, finding the marshal's son and other gentlemen's sons vying with one another in boyish exercises, as running and leaping, little by little joined their company, and shewed himself a match or more for them all in all their contests. The marshal's attention being thus drawn to him, he was well pleased with the boy's mien and bearing, and asked who he was. He was told that he was the son of a poor man who sometimes came there to solicit alms. Whereupon he asked the Count to let him have the boy, and the Count, to whom God could have granted no greater boon, readily consented, albeit he was very loath to part with Perrot.

Having thus provided for his son and daughter, the Count resolved to quit the island; and did so, making his way as best he could to Stamford, in Ireland, where he obtained a menial's place in the service of a knight, retainer to one of the earls of that country, and so abode there a long while, doing all the irksome and wearisome drudgery of a lackey or groom.

Meanwhile under the care of the gentle lady at London Violante or Jeannette increased, as in years and stature so also in beauty, and in such favour with the lady and her husband and every other member of the household and all who knew her that 'twas a wonder to see; nor was there any that, observing her bearing and manners, would not have said that estate or dignity there was none so high or honourable but she was worthy of it. So the lady, who, since she had received her from her father, had been unable to learn aught else about him than what he had himself told, was minded to marry her honourably according to what she deemed to be her rank. But God, who justly apportions reward according to merit, having regard to her noble birth, her innocence, and the load of suffering which the sin of another had laid upon her, ordered otherwise; and in His good providence, lest the young gentlewoman should be mated with a churl, permitted, we must believe, events to take the course they did.

The gentle lady with whom Jeannette lived had an only son, whom she and her husband loved most dearly, as well because he was a son as for his rare and noble qualities, for in truth there were few that could compare with him in courtesy and courage and personal beauty. Now the young man marked the extraordinary beauty and grace of Jeannette, who was about six years his junior, and fell so desperately in love with her that he had no eyes for any other maiden; but, deeming her to be of low degree, he not only hesitated to ask her of his parents in marriage, but, fearing to incur reproof for indulging a passion for an inferior, he did his utmost to conceal his love. Whereby it gave him far more disquietude than if he had avowed it; insomuch that—so extreme waxed his suffering—he fell ill, and that seriously. Divers physicians were called in, but, for all their scrutiny of his symptoms, they could not determine the nature of his malady, and one and all gave him up for lost. Nothing could exceed the sorrow and dejection of his father and mother, who again and again piteously implored him to discover to them the cause of his malady, and received no other answer than sighs or complaints that he seemed to be wasting away.

Now it so happened that one day, Jeannette, who from regard for his mother was sedulous in waiting upon him, for some reason or another came into the room where he lay, while a very young but skilful physician sate by him and held his pulse. The young man gave her not a word or other sign of recognition; but his passion waxed, his heart smote him, and the acceleration of his pulse at once betrayed his inward commotion to the physician, who, albeit surprised, remained quietly attentive to see how long it would last, and observing that it ceased when Jeannette left the room, conjectured that he was on the way to explain the young man's malady. So, after a while, still holding the young man's pulse, he sent for Jeannette, as if he had something to ask of her. She returned forthwith; the young man's pulse mounted as soon as she entered the room, and fell again as soon as she left it.

Wherefore the physician no longer hesitated, but rose, and taking the young man's father and mother aside, said to them:—"The restoration of your son's health rests not with medical skill, but solely with Jeannette, whom, as by unmistakable signs I have discovered, he ardently loves, though, so far I can see, she is not aware of it. So you know what you have to do, if you value his life."

The prospect thus afforded of their son's deliverance from death reassured the gentleman and his lady, albeit they were troubled, misdoubting it must be by his marriage with Jeannette.

So, when the physician was gone, they went to the sick lad, and the lady thus spoke:—"My son, never would I have believed that thou wouldst have concealed from me any desire of thine, least of all if such it were that privation should cause thee to languish; for well assured thou shouldst have been and shouldst be, that I hold thee dear as my very self, and that whatever may be for thy contentment, even though it were scarce seemly, I would do it for thee; but, for all thou hast so done, God has shewn Himself more merciful to theeward than thyself, and, lest thou die of this malady, has given me to know its cause, which is nothing else than the excessive love which thou bearest to a young woman, be she who she may. Which love in good sooth thou needest not have been ashamed to declare; for it is but natural at thy age; and hadst thou not loved, I should have deemed thee of very little worth. So, my son, be not shy of me, but frankly discover to me thy whole heart; and away with this gloom and melancholy whereof thy sickness is engendered, and be comforted, and assure thyself that there is nought that thou mayst require of me which I will not do to give thee ease, so far as my powers may reach, seeing that thou art dearer to me than my own life. Away with thy shamefastness and fears, and tell me if there is aught wherein I may be helpful to thee in the matter of thy love; and if I bestir not myself and bring it to pass, account me the most harsh mother that ever bore son."

The young man was at first somewhat shamefast to hear his mother thus speak, but, reflecting that none could do more for his happiness than she, he took courage, and thus spoke:—"Madam, my sole reason for concealing my love from you was that I have observed that old people for the most part forget that they once were young; but, as I see that no such unreasonableness is to be apprehended in you, I not only acknowledge the truth of what you say that you have discerned, but I will also disclose to you the object of my passion, on the understanding that your promise shall to the best of your power be performed, as it must be, if I am to be restored to you in sound health."

Whereupon the lady, making too sure of that which was destined to fall out otherwise than she expected, gave him every encouragement to discover all his heart, and promised to lose no time and spare no pains in endeavouring to compass his gratification. "Madam," said then the young man, "the rare beauty and exquisite manners of our Jeannette, my powerlessness to make her understand—I do not say commiserate—my love, and my reluctance to disclose it to any, have brought me to the condition in which you see me; and if your promise be not in one way or another performed, be sure that my life will be brief."

The lady, deeming that the occasion called rather for comfort than for admonition, replied with a smile:—"Ah! my son, was this then of all things the secret of thy suffering? Be of good cheer, and leave me to arrange the affair, when you are recovered."

So, animated by a cheerful hope, the young man speedily gave sign of a most marked improvement, which the lady observed with great satisfaction, and then began to cast about how she might keep her promise.

So one day she sent for Jeannette, and in a tone of gentle raillery asked her if she had a lover. Jeannette turned very red as she answered:—"Madam, 'twould scarce, nay, 'twould ill become a damsel such as I, poor, outcast from home, and in the service of another, to occupy herself with thoughts of love."

Whereto the lady answered:—"So you have none, we will give you one, who will brighten all your life and give you more joy of your beauty; for it is not right that so fair a damsel as you remain without a lover."

"Madam," rejoined Jeannette, "you found me living in poverty with my father, you adopted me, you have brought me up as your daughter; wherefore I should, if possible, comply with your every wish; but in this matter I will render you no compliance, nor do I doubt that I do well. So you will give me a husband, I will love him, but no other will I love; for, as patrimony I now have none save my honour, that I am minded to guard and preserve while my life shall last."

Serious though the obstacle was which these words opposed to the plan by which the lady had intended to keep her promise to her son, her sound judgment could not but secretly acknowledge that the spirit which they evinced was much to be commended in the damsel. Wherefore she said:—"Nay but, Jeannette; suppose that our Lord the King, who is a young knight as thou art a most fair damsel, craved some indulgence of thy love, wouldst thou deny him?"

"The King," returned Jeannette without the least hesitation, "might constrain me, but with my consent he should never have aught of me that was not honourable."

Whereto the lady made no answer, for she now understood the girl's temper; but, being minded to put her to the proof, she told her son that, as soon as he was recovered, she would arrange that he should be closeted with her in the same room, and be thus able to use all his arts to bring her to his will, saying that it ill became her to play the part of procuress and urge her son's suit upon her own maid. But as the young man, by no means approving this idea, suddenly grew worse, the lady at length opened her mind to Jeannette, whom she found in the same frame as before, and indeed even more resolute. Wherefore she told her husband all that she had done; and as both preferred that their son should marry beneath him, and live, than that he should remain single and die, they resolved, albeit much disconcerted, to give Jeannette to him to wife; and so after long debate they did. Whereat Jeannette was overjoyed, and with devout heart gave thanks to God that He had not forgotten her; nevertheless she still gave no other account of herself than that she was the daughter of a Picard. So the young man recovered, and blithe at heart as ne'er another, was married, and began to speed the time gaily with his bride.

Meanwhile Perrot, left in Wales with the marshal of the King of England, had likewise with increase of years increase of favour with his master, and grew up most shapely and well-favoured, and of such prowess that in all the island at tourney or joust or any other passage of arms he had not his peer; being everywhere known and renowned as Perrot the Picard. And as God had not forgotten Jeannette, so likewise He made manifest by what follows that He had not forgotten Perrot. Well-nigh half the population of those parts being swept off by a sudden visitation of deadly pestilence, most of the survivors fled therefrom in a panic, so that the country was, to all appearance, entirely deserted. Among those that died of the pest were the marshal, his lady, and his son, besides brothers and nephews and kinsfolk in great number; whereby of his entire household there were left only one of his daughters, now marriageable, and a few servants, among them Perrot. Now Perrot being a man of such notable prowess, the damsel, soon after the pestilence had spent itself, took him, with the approval and by the advice of the few folk that survived, to be her husband, and made him lord of all that fell to her by inheritance. Nor was it long before the King of England, learning that the marshal was dead, made Perrot the Picard, to whose merit he was no stranger, marshal in the dead man's room. Such, in brief, was the history of the two innocent children, with whom the Count of Antwerp had parted, never expecting to see them again.

'Twas now the eighteenth year since the Count of Antwerp had taken flight from Paris, when, being still in Ireland, where he had led a very sorry and suffering sort of life, and feeling that age was now come upon him, he felt a longing to learn, if possible, what was become of his children. The fashion of his outward man was now completely changed; for long hardship had (as he well knew) given to his age a vigour which his youth, lapped in ease, had lacked. So he hesitated not to take his leave of the knight with whom he had so long resided, and poor and in sorry trim he crossed to England, and made his way to the place where he had left Perrot—to find him a great lord and marshal of the King, and in good health, and withal a hardy man and very handsome. All which was very grateful to the old man; but yet he would not make himself known to his son, until he had learned the fate of Jeannette.

So forth he fared again, nor did he halt until he was come to London, where, cautiously questing about for news of the lady with whom he had left his daughter, and how it fared with her, he learned that Jeannette was married to the lady's son. Whereat, in the great gladness of his heart, he counted all his past adversity but a light matter, since he had found his children alive and prosperous. But sore he yearned to see Jeannette. Wherefore he took to loitering, as poor folk are wont, in the neighbourhood of the house. And so one day Jacques Lamiens—such was the name of Jeannette's husband— saw him and had pity on him, observing that he was poor and aged, and bade one of his servants take him indoors, and for God's sake give him something to eat; and nothing loath the servant did so.

Now Jeannette had borne Jacques several children, the finest and the most winsome children in the world, the eldest no more than eight years old; who gathered about the Count as he ate, and, as if by instinct divining that he was their grandfather, began to make friends with him. He, knowing them for his grandchildren, could not conceal his love, and repaid them with caresses; insomuch that they would not hearken to their governor when he called them, but remained with the Count. Which being reported to Jeannette, she came out of her room, crossed to where the Count was sitting with the children, and bade them do as their master told them, or she would certainly have them whipped. The children began to cry, and to say that they would rather stay with the worthy man, whom they liked much better than their master; whereat both the lady and the Count laughed in sympathy.

The Count had risen, with no other intention—for he was not minded to disclose his paternity—than to pay his daughter the respect due from his poverty to her rank, and the sight of her had thrilled his soul with a wondrous delight. By her he was and remained unrecognised; utterly changed as he was from his former self; aged, grey-haired, bearded, lean and tanned—in short to all appearance another man than the Count.

However, seeing that the children were unwilling to leave him, but wept when she made as if she would constrain them, she bade the master let them be for a time. So the children remained with the worthy man, until by chance Jacques' father came home, and learned from the master what had happened. Whereupon, having a grudge against Jeannette, he said:—"Let them be; and God give them the ill luck which He owes them: whence they sprang, thither they must needs return; they descend from a vagabond on the mother's side, and so 'tis no wonder that they consort readily with vagabonds."

The Count caught these words and was sorely pained, but, shrugging his shoulders, bore the affront silently as he had borne many another. Jacques, who had noted his children's fondness for the worthy man, to wit, the Count, was displeased; but nevertheless, such was the love he bore them, that, rather than see them weep, he gave order that, if the worthy man cared to stay there in his service, he should be received. The Count answered that he would gladly do so, but that he was fit for nothing except to look after horses, to which he had been used all his life. So a horse was assigned him, and when he had groomed him, he occupied himself in playing with the children.

While Fortune thus shaped the destinies of the Count of Antwerp and his children, it so befell that after a long series of truces made with the Germans the King of France died, and his crown passed to his son, whose wife had been the occasion of the Count's banishment. The new king, as soon as the last truce with the Germans was run out, renewed hostilities with extraordinary vigour, being aided by his brother of England with a large army under the command of his marshal, Perrot, and his other marshal's son, Jacques Lamiens. With them went the worthy man, that is to say, the Count, who, unrecognised by any, served for a long while in the army in the capacity of groom, and acquitted himself both in counsel and in arms with a wisdom and valour unwonted in one of his supposed rank. The war was still raging when the Queen of France fell seriously ill, and, as she felt her end approach, made a humble and contrite confession of all her sins to the Archbishop of Rouen, who was universally reputed a good and most holy man. Among her other sins she confessed the great wrong that she had done to the Count of Antwerp; nor was she satisfied to confide it to the Archbishop, but recounted the whole affair, as it had passed, to not a few other worthy men, whom she besought to use their influence with the King to procure the restitution of the Count, if he were still alive, and if not, of his children, to honour and estate. And so, dying shortly afterwards, she was honourably buried. The Queen's confession wrung from the King a sigh or two of compunction for a brave man cruelly wronged; after which he caused proclamation to be made throughout the army and in many other parts, that whoso should bring him tidings of the Count of Antwerp, or his children, should receive from him such a guerdon for each of them as should justly be matter of marvel; seeing that he held him acquitted, by confession of the Queen, of the crime for which he had been banished, and was therefore now minded to grant him not only restitution but increase of honour and estate.

Now the Count, being still with the army in his character of groom, heard the proclamation, which he did not doubt was made in good faith. Wherefore he hied him forthwith to Jacques, and begged a private interview with him and Perrot, that he might discover to them that whereof the King was in quest. So the meeting was had; and Perrot was on the point of declaring himself, when the Count anticipated him:—"Perrot," he said, "Jacques here has thy sister to wife, but never a dowry had he with her. Wherefore that thy sister be not dowerless, 'tis my will that he, and no other, have this great reward which the King offers for thee, son, as he shall certify, of the Count of Antwerp, and for his wife and thy sister, Violante, and for me, Count of Antwerp, thy father."

So hearing, Perrot scanned the Count closely, and forthwith recognising him, burst into tears, and throwing himself at his feet embraced him, saying:—"My father, welcome, welcome indeed art thou."

Whereupon, between what he had heard from the Count and what he had witnessed on the part of Perrot, Jacques was so overcome with wonder and delight, that at first he was at a loss to know how to act. However, giving entire credence to what he had heard, and recalling insulting language which he had used towards the quondam groom, the Count, he was sore stricken with shame, and wept, and fell at the Count's feet, and humbly craved his pardon for all past offences; which the Count, raising him to his feet, most graciously granted him. So with many a tear and many a hearty laugh the three men compared their several fortunes; which done, Perrot and Jacques would have arrayed the Count in manner befitting his rank, but he would by no means suffer it, being minded that Jacques, so soon as he was well assured that the guerdon was forthcoming, should present him to the King in his garb of groom, that thereby the King might be the more shamed. So Jacques, with the Count and Perrot, went presently to the King and offered to present to him the Count and his children, provided the guerdon were forthcoming according to the proclamation. Jacques wondered not a little as forthwith at a word from the King a guerdon was produced ample for all three, and he was bidden take it away with him, so only that he should in very truth produce, as he had promised, the Count and his children in the royal presence.

Then, withdrawing a little and causing his quondam groom, now Count, to come forward with Perrot, he said:—"Sire, father and son are before you; the daughter, my wife, is not here, but, God willing, you shall soon see her."

So hearing, the King surveyed the Count, whom, notwithstanding his greatly changed appearance, he at length recognised, and well-nigh moved to tears, he raised him from his knees to his feet, and kissed and embraced him. He also gave a kindly welcome to Perrot, and bade forthwith furnish the Count with apparel, servants and horses, suited to his rank; all which was no sooner said than done. Moreover the King shewed Jacques no little honour, and particularly questioned him of all his past adventures.

As Jacques was about to take the noble guerdons assigned him for the discovery of the Count and his children, the Count said to him:— "Take these tokens of the magnificence of our Lord the King, and forget not to tell thy father that that 'tis from no vagabond that thy children, his and my grandchildren, descend on the mother's side."

So Jacques took the guerdons, and sent for his wife and mother to join him at Paris. Thither also came Perrot's wife: and there with all magnificence they were entertained by the Count, to whom the King had not only restored all his former estates and honours, but added thereto others, whereby he was now become a greater man than he had ever been before. Then with the Count's leave they all returned to their several houses. The Count himself spent the rest of his days at Paris in greater glory than ever.

FOURTH DAY: FIRST STORY

Tancred, Prince of Salerno, slays his daughter's lover, and sends her his heart in a golden cup: she pours upon it a poisonous distillation, which she drinks and dies.

Tancred, Prince of Salerno, a lord most humane and kind of heart, but that in his old age he imbrued his hands in the blood of a lover, had in the whole course of his life but one daughter; and had he not had her, he had been more fortunate.

Never was daughter more tenderly beloved of father than she of the Prince, who, for that cause not knowing how to part with her, kept her unmarried for many a year after she had come of marriageable age: then at last he gave her to a son of the Duke of Capua, with whom she had lived but a short while, when he died and she returned to her father. Most lovely was she of form and feature (never woman more so), and young and light of heart, and more knowing, perchance, than beseemed a woman. Dwelling thus with her loving father, as a great lady, in no small luxury, nor failing to see that the Prince, for the great love he bore her, was at no pains to provide her with another husband, and deeming it unseemly on her part to ask one of him, she cast about how she might come by a gallant to be her secret lover. And seeing at her father's court not a few men, both gentle and simple, that resorted thither, as we know men use to frequent courts, and closely scanning their mien and manners, she preferred before all others the Prince's page, Guiscardo by name, a man of very humble origin, but preeminent for native worth and noble bearing; of whom, seeing him frequently, she became hotly enamoured, hourly extolling his qualities more and more highly.

The young man, who for all his youth by no means lacked shrewdness, read her heart, and gave her his own on such wise that his love for her engrossed his mind to the exclusion of almost everything else. While thus they burned in secret for one another, the lady, desiring of all things a meeting with Guiscardo, but being shy of making any her confidant, hit upon a novel expedient to concert the affair with him. She wrote him a letter containing her commands for the ensuing day, and thrust it into a cane in the space between two of the knots, which cane she gave to Guiscardo, saying:—"Thou canst let thy servant have it for a bellows to blow thy fire up to night."

Guiscardo took it, and feeling sure that 'twas not unadvisedly that she made him such a present, accompanied with such words, hied him straight home, where, carefully examining the cane, he observed that it was cleft, and, opening it, found the letter; which he had no sooner read, and learned what he was to do, than, pleased as ne'er another, he fell to devising how to set all in order that he might not fail to meet the lady on the following day, after the manner she had prescribed.

Now hard by the Prince's palace was a grotto, hewn in days of old in the solid rock, and now long disused, so that an artificial orifice, by which it received a little light, was all but choked with brambles and plants that grew about and overspread it. From one of the ground-floor rooms of the palace, which room was part of the lady's suite, a secret stair led to the grotto, though the entrance was barred by a very strong door. This stair, having been from time immemorial disused, had passed out of mind so completely that there was scarce any that remembered that it was there: but Love, whose eyes nothing, however secret, may escape, had brought it to the mind of the enamoured lady.

For many a day, using all secrecy, that none should discover her, she had wrought with her tools, until she had succeeded in opening the door; which done, she had gone down into the grotto alone, and having observed the orifice, had by her letter apprised Guiscardo of its apparent height above the floor of the grotto, and bidden him contrive some means of descending thereby. Eager to carry the affair through, Guiscardo lost no time in rigging up a ladder of ropes, whereby he might ascend and descend; and having put on a suit of leather to protect him from the brambles, he hied him the following night (keeping the affair close from all) to the orifice, made the ladder fast by one of its ends to a massive trunk that was rooted in the mouth of the orifice, climbed down the ladder, and awaited the lady.

On the morrow, making as if she would fain sleep, the lady dismissed her damsels, and locked herself into her room: she then opened the door of the grotto, hied her down, and met Guiscardo, to their marvellous mutual satisfaction. The lovers then repaired to her room, where in exceeding great joyance they spent no small part of the day. Nor were they neglectful of the precautions needful to prevent discovery of their amour; but in due time Guiscardo returned to the grotto; whereupon the lady locked the door and rejoined her damsels. At nightfall Guiscardo reascended his ladder, and, issuing forth of the orifice, hied him home; nor, knowing now the way, did he fail to revisit the grotto many a time thereafter.

But Fortune, noting with envious eye a happiness of such degree and duration, gave to events a dolorous turn, whereby the joy of the two lovers was converted into bitter lamentation. 'Twas Tancred's custom to come from time to time quite alone to his daughter's room, and tarry talking with her a while. Whereby it so befell that he came down there one day after breakfast, while Ghismonda—such was the lady's name—was in her garden with her damsels; so that none saw or heard him enter; nor would he call his daughter, for he was minded that she should not forgo her pleasure. But, finding the windows closed and the bed-curtains drawn down, he seated himself on a divan that stood at one of the corners of the bed, rested his head on the bed, drew the curtain over him, and thus, hidden as if of set purpose, fell asleep.

As he slept Ghismonda, who, as it happened, had caused Guiscardo to come that day, left her damsels in the garden, softly entered the room, and having locked herself in, unwitting that there was another in the room, opened the door to Guiscardo, who was in waiting. Straightway they got them to bed, as was their wont; and, while they were solaced and disported them together, it so befell that Tancred awoke, and heard and saw what they did: whereat he was troubled beyond measure, and at first was minded to upbraid them; but on second thoughts he deemed it best to hold his peace, and avoid discovery, if so he might with greater stealth and less dishonour carry out the design which was already in his mind.

The two lovers continued long together, as they were wont, all unwitting of Tancred; but at length they saw fit to get out of bed, when Guiscardo went back to the grotto, and the lady hied her forth of the room. Whereupon Tancred, old though he was, got out at one of the windows, clambered down into the garden, and, seen by none, returned sorely troubled to his room. By his command two men took Guiscardo early that same night, as he issued forth of the orifice accoutred in his suit of leather, and brought him privily to Tancred; who, as he saw him, all but wept, and said:—"Guiscardo, my kindness to thee is ill requited by the outrage and dishonour which thou hast done me in the person of my daughter, as to-day I have seen with my own eyes."

To whom Guiscardo could answer nought but:—"Love is more potent than either you or I."

Tancred then gave order to keep him privily under watch and ward in a room within the palace; and so 'twas done. Next day, while Ghismonda wotted nought of these matters, Tancred, after pondering divers novel expedients, hied him after breakfast, according to his wont, to his daughter's room, where, having called her to him and locked himself in with her, he began, not without tears, to speak on this wise:—

"Ghismonda, conceiving that I knew thy virtue and honour, never, though it had been reported to me, would I have credited, had I not seen with my own eyes, that thou wouldst so much as in idea, not to say fact, have ever yielded thyself to any man but thy husband: wherefore, for the brief residue of life that my age has in store for me, the memory of thy fall will ever be grievous to me. And would to God, as thou must needs demean thyself to such dishonour, thou hadst taken a man that matched thy nobility; but of all the men that frequent my court, thou must needs choose Guiscardo, a young man of the lowest condition, a fellow whom we brought up in charity from his tender years; for whose sake thou hast plunged me into the abyss of mental tribulation, insomuch that I know not what course to take in regard of thee. As to Guiscardo, whom I caused to be arrested last night as he issued from the orifice, and keep in durance, my course is already taken, but how I am to deal with thee, God knows, I know not. I am distraught between the love which I have ever borne thee, love such as no father ever bare to daughter, and the most just indignation evoked in me by thy signal folly; my love prompts me to pardon thee, my indignation bids me harden my heart against thee, though I do violence to my nature. But before I decide upon my course, I would fain hear what thou hast to say to this." So saying, he bent his head, and wept as bitterly as any child that had been soundly thrashed.

Her father's words, and the tidings they conveyed that not only was her secret passion discovered, but Guiscardo taken, caused Ghismonda immeasurable grief, which she was again and again on the point of evincing, as most women do, by cries and tears; but her high spirit triumphed over this weakness; by a prodigious effort she composed her countenance, and taking it for granted that her Guiscardo was no more, she inly devoted herself to death rather than a single prayer for herself should escape her lips. Wherefore, not as a woman stricken with grief or chidden for a fault, but unconcerned and unabashed, with tearless eyes, and frank and utterly dauntless mien, thus answered she her father:—

"Tancred, your accusation I shall not deny, neither will I cry you mercy, for nought should I gain by denial, nor aught would I gain by supplication: nay more; there is nought I will do to conciliate thy humanity and love; my only care is to confess the truth, to defend my honour by words of sound reason, and then by deeds most resolute to give effect to the promptings of my high soul. True it is that I have loved and love Guiscardo, and during the brief while I have yet to live shall love him, nor after death, so there be then love, shall I cease to love him; but that I love him, is not imputable to my womanly frailty so much as to the little zeal thou shewedst for my bestowal in marriage, and to Guiscardo's own worth. It should not have escaped thee, Tancred, creature of flesh and blood as thou art, that thy daughter was also a creature of flesh and blood, and not of stone or iron; it was, and is, thy duty to bear in mind (old though thou art) the nature and the might of the laws to which youth is subject; and, though thou hast spent part of thy best years in martial exercises, thou shouldst nevertheless have not been ignorant how potent is the influence even upon the aged—to say nothing of the young—of ease and luxury. And not only am I, as being thy daughter, a creature of flesh and blood, but my life is not so far spent but that I am still young, and thus doubly fraught with fleshly appetite, the vehemence whereof is marvellously enhanced by reason that, having been married, I have known the pleasure that ensues upon the satisfaction of such desire. Which forces being powerless to withstand, I did but act as was natural in a young woman, when I gave way to them, and yielded myself to love.

"Nor in sooth did I fail to the utmost of my power so to order the indulgence of my natural propensity that my sin should bring shame neither upon thee nor upon me. To which end Love in his pity, and Fortune in a friendly mood, found and discovered to me a secret way, whereby, none witting, I attained my desire: this, from whomsoever thou hast learned it, howsoever thou comest to know it, I deny not. 'Twas not at random, as many women do, that I loved Guiscardo; but by deliberate choice I preferred him before all other men, and of determinate forethought I lured him to my love, whereof, through his and my discretion and constancy, I have long had joyance. Wherein 'twould seem that thou, following rather the opinion of the vulgar than the dictates of truth, find cause to chide me more severely than in my sinful love, for, as if thou wouldst not have been vexed, had my choice fallen on a nobleman, thou complainest that I have forgathered with a man of low condition; and dost not see that therein thou censurest not my fault but that of Fortune, which not seldom raises the unworthy to high place and leaves the worthiest in low estate.

"But leave we this: consider a little the principles of things: thou seest that in regard of our flesh we are all moulded of the same substance, and that all souls are endowed by one and the same Creator with equal faculties, equal powers, equal virtues. 'Twas merit that made the first distinction between us, born as we were, nay, as we are, all equal, and those whose merits were and were approved in act the greatest were called noble, and the rest were not so denoted. Which law, albeit overlaid by the contrary usage of after times, is not yet abrogated, nor so impaired but that it is still traceable in nature and good manners; for which cause whoso with merit acts, does plainly shew himself a gentleman; and if any denote him otherwise, the default is his own and not his whom he so denotes. Pass in review all thy nobles, weigh their merits, their manners and bearing, and then compare Guiscardo's qualities with theirs: if thou wilt judge without prejudice, thou wilt pronounce him noble in the highest degree, and thy nobles one and all churls.

"As to Guiscardo's merits and worth I did but trust the verdict which thou thyself didst utter in words, and which mine own eyes confirmed. Of whom had he such commendation as of thee for all those excellences whereby a good man and true merits commendation? And in sooth thou didst him but justice; for, unless mine eyes have played me false, there was nought for which thou didst commend him but I had seen him practise it, and that more admirably than words of thine might express; and had I been at all deceived in this matter, 'twould have been by thee. Wilt thou say then that I have forgathered with a man of low condition? If so, thou wilt not say true. Didst thou say with a poor man, the impeachment might be allowed, to thy shame, that thou so ill hast known how to requite a good man and true that is thy servant; but poverty, though it take away all else, deprives no man of gentilesse. Many kings, many great princes, were once poor, and many a ditcher or herdsman has been and is very wealthy. As for thy last perpended doubt, to wit, how thou shouldst deal with me, banish it utterly from thy thoughts.

"If in thy extreme old age thou art minded to manifest a harshness unwonted in thy youth, wreak thy harshness on me, resolved as I am to cry thee no mercy, prime cause as I am that this sin, if sin it be, has been committed; for of this I warrant thee, that as thou mayst have done or shalt do to Guiscardo, if to me thou do not the like, I with my own hands will do it. Now get thee gone to shed thy tears with the women, and when thy melting mood is over, ruthlessly destroy Guiscardo and me, if such thou deem our merited doom, by one and the same blow."

The loftiness of his daughter's spirit was not unknown to the Prince; but still he did not credit her with a resolve quite as firmly fixed as her words implied, to carry their purport into effect. So, parting from her without the least intention of using harshness towards her in her own person, he determined to quench the heat of her love by wreaking his vengeance on her lover, and bade the two men that had charge of Guiscardo to strangle him noiselessly that same night, take the heart out of the body, and send it to him. The men did his bidding: and on the morrow the Prince had a large and beautiful cup of gold brought to him, and having put Guiscardo's heart therein, sent it by the hand of one of his most trusted servants to his daughter, charging the servant to say, as he gave it to her:—"Thy father sends thee this to give thee joy of that which thou lovest best, even as thou hast given him joy of that which he loved best."

Now when her father had left her, Ghismonda, wavering not a jot in her stern resolve, had sent for poisonous herbs and roots, and therefrom had distilled a water, to have it ready for use, if that which she apprehended should come to pass. And when the servant appeared with the Prince's present and message, she took the cup unblenchingly, and having lifted the lid, and seen the heart, and apprehended the meaning of the words, and that the heart was beyond a doubt Guiscardo's, she raised her head, and looking straight at the servant, said:—"Sepulture less honourable than of gold had ill befitted heart such as this: herein has my father done wisely."

Which said, she raised it to her lips, and kissed it saying:—"In all things and at all times, even to this last hour of my life, have I found my father most tender in his love, but now more so than ever before; wherefore I now render him the last thanks which will ever be due from me to him for this goodly present."

So she spoke, and straining the cup to her, bowed her head over it, and gazing at the heart, said:—"Ah! sojourn most sweet of all my joys, accursed be he by whose ruthless act I see thee with the bodily eye: 'twas enough that to the mind's eye thou wert hourly present. Thou has run thy course; thou hast closed the span that Fortune allotted thee; thou hast reached the goal of all; thou hast left behind thee the woes and weariness of the world; and thy enemy has himself granted thee sepulture accordant with thy deserts. No circumstance was wanting to duly celebrate thy obsequies, save the tears of her whom, while thou livedst, thou didst so dearly love; which that thou shouldst not lack, my remorseless father was prompted of God to send thee to me, and, albeit my resolve was fixed to die with eyes unmoistened and front all unperturbed by fear, yet will I accord thee my tears; which done, my care shall be forthwith by thy means to join my soul to that most precious soul which thou didst once enshrine. And is there other company than hers, in which with more of joy and peace I might fare to the abodes unknown? She is yet here within, I doubt not, contemplating the abodes of her and my delights, and— for sure I am that she loves me—awaiting my soul that loves her before all else."

Having thus spoken, she bowed herself low over the cup; and, while no womanish cry escaped her, 'twas as if a fountain of water were unloosed within her head, so wondrous a flood of tears gushed from her eyes, while times without number she kissed the dead heart. Her damsels that stood around her knew not whose the heart might be or what her words might mean, but melting in sympathy, they all wept, and compassionately, as vainly, enquired the cause of her lamentation, and in many other ways sought to comfort her to the best of their understanding and power.

When she had wept her fill, she raised her head, and dried her eyes. Then:—"O heart," said she, "much cherished heart, discharged is my every duty towards thee; nought now remains for me to do but to come and unite my soul with thine."

So saying, she sent for the vase that held the water which the day before she had distilled, and emptied it into the cup where lay the heart bathed in her tears; then, nowise afraid, she set her mouth to the cup, and drained it dry, and so with the cup in her hand she got her upon her bed, and having there disposed her person in guise as seemly as she might, laid her dead lover's heart upon her own, and silently awaited death. Meanwhile the damsels, seeing and hearing what passed, but knowing not what the water was that she had drunk, had sent word of each particular to Tancred; who, apprehensive of that which came to pass, came down with all haste to his daughter's room, where he arrived just as she got her upon her bed, and, now too late, addressed himself to comfort her with soft words, and seeing in what plight she was, burst into a flood of bitter tears. To whom the lady said:—

"Reserve thy tears, Tancred, till Fortune send thee hap less longed for than this: waste them not on me who care not for them. Whoever yet saw any but thee bewail the consummation of his desire? But, if of the love thou once didst bear me any spark still lives in thee, be it thy parting grace to me, that, as thou brookedst not that I should live with Guiscardo in privity and seclusion, so wherever thou mayst have caused Guiscardo's body to be cast, mine may be united with it in the common view of all."

The Prince replied not for excess of grief; and the lady, feeling that her end was come, strained the dead heart to her bosom, saying:— "Fare ye well; I take my leave of you"; and with eyelids drooped and every sense evanished departed this life of woe. Such was the lamentable end of the loves of Guiscardo and Ghismonda; whom Tancred, tardily repentant of his harshness, mourned not a little, as did also all the folk of Salerno, and had honourably interred side by side in the same tomb.

FIFTH DAY: NINTH STORY

Federigo degli Alberighi loves and is not loved in return: he wastes his substance by lavishness until nought is left but a single falcon, which, his lady being come to see him at his house, he gives her to eat: she, knowing his case, changes her mind, takes him to husband and makes him rich.

You are then to know, that Coppo di Borghese Domenichi, a man that in our day was, and perchance still is, had in respect and great reverence in our city, being not only by reason of his noble lineage, but, and yet more, for manners and merit most illustrious and worthy of eternal renown, was in his old age not seldom wont to amuse himself by discoursing of things past with his neighbours and other folk; wherein he had not his match for accuracy and compass of memory and concinnity of speech. Among other good stories, he would tell, how that there was of yore in Florence a gallant named Federigo di Messer Filippo Alberighi, who for feats of arms and courtesy had not his peer in Tuscany; who, as is the common lot of gentlemen, became enamoured of a lady named Monna Giovanna, who in her day held rank among the fairest and most elegant ladies of Florence; to gain whose love he jousted, tilted, gave entertainments, scattered largess, and in short set no bounds to his expenditure. However the lady, no less virtuous than fair, cared not a jot for what he did for her sake, nor yet for him.

Spending thus greatly beyond his means, and making nothing, Federigo could hardly fail to come to lack, and was at length reduced to such poverty that he had nothing left but a little estate, on the rents of which he lived very straitly, and a single falcon, the best in the world. The estate was at Campi, and thither, deeming it no longer possible for him to live in the city as he desired, he repaired, more in love than ever before; and there, in complete seclusion, diverting himself with hawking, he bore his poverty as patiently as he might.

Now, Federigo being thus reduced to extreme poverty, it so happened that one day Monna Giovanna's husband, who was very rich, fell ill, and, seeing that he was nearing his end, made his will, whereby he left his estate to his son, who was now growing up, and in the event of his death without lawful heir named Monna Giovanna, whom he dearly loved, heir in his stead; and having made these dispositions he died.

Monna Giovanna, being thus left a widow, did as our ladies are wont, and repaired in the summer to one of her estates in the country which lay very near to that of Federigo. And so it befell that the urchin began to make friends with Federigo, and to shew a fondness for hawks and dogs, and having seen Federigo's falcon fly not a few times, took a singular fancy to him, and greatly longed to have him for his own, but still did not dare to ask him of Federigo, knowing that Federigo prized him so much. So the matter stood when by chance the boy fell sick; whereby the mother was sore distressed, for he was her only son, and she loved him as much as might be, insomuch that all day long she was beside him, and ceased not to comfort him, and again and again asked him if there were aught that he wished for, imploring him to say the word, and, if it might by any means be had, she would assuredly do her utmost to procure it for him.

Thus repeatedly exhorted, the boy said:—"Mother mine, do but get me Federigo's falcon, and I doubt not I shall soon be well."

Whereupon the lady was silent a while, bethinking her what she should do. She knew that Federigo had long loved her, and had never had so much as a single kind look from her: wherefore she said to herself:—How can I send or go to beg of him this falcon, which by what I hear is the best that ever flew, and moreover is his sole comfort? And how could I be so unfeeling as to seek to deprive a gentleman of the one solace that is now left him? And so, albeit she very well knew that she might have the falcon for the asking, she was perplexed, and knew not what to say, and gave her son no answer. At length, however, the love she bore the boy carried the day, and she made up her mind, for his contentment, come what might, not to send, but to go herself and fetch him the falcon. So:—"Be of good cheer, my son," she said, "and doubt not thou wilt soon be well; for I promise thee that the very first thing that I shall do to-morrow morning will be to go and fetch thee the falcon." Whereat the child was so pleased that he began to mend that very day.

On the morrow the lady, as if for pleasure, hied her with another lady to Federigo's little house, and asked to see him. 'Twas still, as for some days past, no weather for hawking, and Federigo was in his garden, busy about some small matters which needed to be set right there. When he heard that Monna Giovanna was at the door, asking to see him, he was not a little surprised and pleased, and hied him to her with all speed.

As soon as she saw him, she came forward to meet him with womanly grace, and having received his respectful salutation, said to him:—"Good morrow, Federigo," and continued:—"I am come to requite thee for what thou hast lost by loving me more than thou shouldst: which compensation is this, that I and this lady that accompanies me will breakfast with thee without ceremony this morning."

"Madam," Federigo replied with all humility, "I mind not ever to have lost aught by loving you, but rather to have been so much profited that, if I ever deserved well in aught, 'twas to your merit that I owed it, and to the love that I bore you. And of a surety had I still as much to spend as I have spent in the past, I should not prize it so much as this visit you so frankly pay me, come as you are to one who can afford you but a sorry sort of hospitality."

Which said, with some confusion, he bade her welcome to his house, and then led her into his garden, where, having none else to present to her by way of companion, he said:—"Madam, as there is none other here, this good woman, wife of this husbandman, will bear you company, while I go to have the table set."

Now, albeit his poverty was extreme, yet he had not known as yet how sore was the need to which his extravagance had reduced him; but this morning 'twas brought home to him, for that he could find nought wherewith to do honour to the lady, for love of whom he had done the honours of his house to men without number: wherefore, distressed beyond measure, and inwardly cursing his evil fortune, he sped hither and thither like one beside himself, but never a coin found he, nor yet aught to pledge. Meanwhile it grew late, and sorely he longed that the lady might not leave his house altogether unhonoured, and yet to crave help of his own husbandman was more than his pride could brook.

In these desperate straits his glance happened to fall on his brave falcon on his perch in his little parlour. And so, as a last resource, he took him, and finding him plump, deemed that he would make a dish meet for such a lady. Wherefore, without thinking twice about it, he wrung the bird's neck, and caused his maid forthwith pluck him and set him on a spit, and roast him carefully; and having still some spotless table-linen, he had the table laid therewith, and with a cheerful countenance hied him back to his lady in the garden, and told her that such breakfast as he could give her was ready. So the lady and her companion rose and came to table, and there, with Federigo, who waited on them most faithfully, ate the brave falcon, knowing not what they ate.

When they were risen from table, and had dallied a while in gay converse with him, the lady deemed it time to tell the reason of her visit: wherefore, graciously addressing Federigo, thus began she:—

"Federigo, by what thou rememberest of thy past life and my virtue, which, perchance, thou hast deemed harshness and cruelty, I doubt not thou must marvel at my presumption, when thou hearest the main purpose of my visit; but if thou hadst sons, or hadst had them, so that thou mightest know the full force of the love that is borne them, I should make no doubt that thou wouldst hold me in part excused. Nor, having a son, may I, for that thou hast none, claim exemption from the laws to which all other mothers are subject, and, being thus bound to own their sway, I must, though fain were I not, and though 'tis neither meet nor right, crave of thee that which I know thou dost of all things and with justice prize most highly, see-ing that this extremity of thy adverse fortune has left thee nought else wherewith to delight, divert and console thee; which gift is no other than thy falcon, on which my boy has so set his heart that, if I bring him it not, I fear lest he grow so much worse of the malady that he has, that thereby it may come to pass that I lose him. And so, not for the love which thou dost bear me, and which may nowise bind thee, but for that nobleness of temper, whereof in courtesy more conspicuously than in aught else thou hast given proof, I implore thee that thou be pleased to give me the bird, that thereby I may say that I have kept my son alive, and thus made him for aye thy debtor."

No sooner had Federigo apprehended what the lady wanted, than, for grief that 'twas not in his power to serve her, because he had given her the falcon to eat, he fell a weeping in her presence, before he could so much as utter a word. At first the lady supposed that 'twas only because he was loath to part with the brave falcon that he wept, and as good as made up her mind that he would refuse her: however, she awaited with patience Federigo's answer, which was on this wise:—

"Madam, since it pleased God that I should set my affections upon you there have been matters not a few, in which to my sorrow I have deemed Fortune adverse to me; but they have all been trifles in comparison of the trick that she now plays me: the which I shall never forgive her, seeing that you are come here to my poor house, where, while I was rich, you deigned not to come, and ask a trifling favour of me, which she has put it out of my power to grant: how 'tis so, I will briefly tell you. When I learned that you, of your grace, were minded to breakfast with me, having respect to your high dignity and desert, I deemed it due and seemly that in your honour I should regale you, to the best of my power, with fare of a more excellent quality than is commonly set before others; and, calling to mind the falcon which you now ask of me, and his excellence, I judged him meet food for you, and so you have had him roasted on the trencher this morning; and well indeed I thought I had bestowed him; but, as now I see that you would fain have had him in another guise, so mortified am I that I am not able to serve you, that I doubt I shall never know peace of mind more."

In witness whereof he had the feathers and feet and beak of the bird brought in and laid before her.

The first thing the lady did, when she had heard Federigo's story, and seen the relics of the bird, was to chide him that he had killed so fine a falcon to furnish a woman with a breakfast; after which the magnanimity of her host, which poverty had been and was powerless to impair, elicited no small share of inward commendation. Then, frustrate of her hope of possessing the falcon, and doubting of her son's recovery, she took her leave with the heaviest of hearts, and hied her back to the boy: who, whether for fretting, that he might not have the falcon, or by the unaided energy of his disorder, departed this life not many days after, to the exceeding great grief of his mother.

For a while she would do nought but weep and bitterly bewail herself; but being still young, and left very wealthy, she was often urged by her brothers to marry again, and though she would rather have not done so, yet being importuned, and remembering Federigo's high desert, and the magnificent generosity with which he had finally killed his falcon to do her honour, she said to her brothers:—"Gladly, with your consent, would I remain a widow, but if you will not be satisfied except I take a husband, rest assured that none other will I ever take save Federigo degli Alberighi."

Whereupon her brothers derided her, saying:—"Foolish woman, what is't thou sayst? How shouldst thou want Federigo, who has not a thing in the world?"

To whom she answered:—"My brothers, well wot I that 'tis as you say; but I had rather have a man without wealth than wealth without a man."

The brothers, perceiving that her mind was made up, and knowing Federigo for a good man and true, poor though he was, gave her to him with all her wealth. And so Federigo, being mated with such a wife, and one that he had so much loved, and being very wealthy to boot, lived happily, keeping more exact accounts, to the end of his days.

THE CANTERBURY TALES

Geoffrey Chaucer

Geoffrey Chaucer (c. 1340–1400) wrote The Canterbury Tales *in Middle English at the end of the fourteenth century, a collection of twenty-four stories told by pilgrims to entertain themselves and each other on their way to visit the shrine of Thomas à Becket at Canterbury. The tales, one of the unique masterpieces of Western literature, provide a rich, amusing, and varied portrait of English life at that time. This selection includes three of the original Canterbury tales translated into modern English verse by J. U. Nicolson: "The Reeve's[1] Tale," "The Cook's Tale," and "The Lawyer's Tale," and each of their Prologues.*

THE REEVE'S PROLOGUE

When folk had laughed their fill at this nice pass
Of Absalom and clever Nicholas,
Then divers folk diversely had their say;
And most of them were well amused and gay,
Nor at this tale did I see one man grieve,
Save it were only old Oswald the reeve,
Because he was a carpenter by craft.
A little anger in his heart was left,
And he began to grouse and blame a bit.
   "S' help me," said he, "full well could I be quit
With blearing of a haughty miller's eye,
If I but chose to speak of ribaldry.
But I am old; I will not play, for age;
Grass time is done, my fodder is rummage,

---

[1] A reeve was a manager of an estate or farm.

This white top advertises my old years,
My heart, too, is as mouldy as my hairs,
Unless I fare like medlar, all perverse.
For that fruit's never ripe until it's worse,
And falls among the refuse or in straw.
We ancient men, I fear, obey this law:
Until we're rotten, we cannot be ripe;
We dance, indeed, the while the world will pipe.
Desire sticks in our nature like a nail
To have, if hoary head, a verdant tail,
As has the leek; for though our strength be gone,
Our wish is yet for folly till life's done.
For when we may not act, then will we speak;
Yet in our ashes is there fire to reek
     "Four embers have we, which I shall confess:
Boasting and lying, anger, covetousness;
These four remaining sparks belong to eld.
Our ancient limbs may well be hard to wield,
But lust will never fail us, that is truth.
And yet I have had always a colt's tooth,
As many years as now are past and done
Since first my tap of life began to run.
For certainly, when I was born, I know
Death turned my tap of life and let it flow;
And ever since that day the tap has run
Till nearly empty now is all the tun.
The stream of life now drips upon the chime;[2]
The silly tongue may well ring out the time
Of wretchedness that passed so long before;
For oldsters, save for dotage, there's no more."
     Now when our host had heard this sermoning,
Then did he speak as lordly as a king;
He said: "To what amounts, now, all this wit?
Why should we talk all day of holy writ?
The devil makes a steward for to preach,
And of a cobbler, a sailor or a leech.
Tell forth your tale, and do not waste the time.
Here's Deptford! And it is half way to prime.

---

[2] Chime (or chimb): the edge or rim of a cask, formed by the projecting ends of
the staves.

There's Greenwich town that many a scoundrel's in;
It is high time your story should begin."

   "Now, sirs," then said this Oswald called the reeve,
"I pray you all, now, that you will not grieve
Though I reply and somewhat twitch his cap;
It's lawful to meet force with force, mayhap.

   "This drunken miller has related here
How was beguiled and fooled a carpenter—
Perchance in scorn of me, for I am one.
So, by your leave, I'll him requite anon;
All in his own boor's language will I speak.
I only pray to God his neck may break.
For in my eye he well can see the mote,
But sees not in his own the beam, you'll note."

THE REEVE'S TALE

At Trumpington, not far from Cambridge town,
There is a bridge wherethrough a brook runs down,
Upon the side of which brook stands a mill;
And this is very truth that now I tell.
A miller dwelt there, many and many a day;
As any peacock he was proud and gay.
He could mend nets, and he could fish, and flute,
Drink and turn cups, and wrestle well, and shoot;
And in his leathern belt he did parade
A cutlass with a long and trenchant blade.
A pretty dagger had he in his pouch;
There was no man who durst this man to touch.
A Sheffield whittler bore he in his hose;
Round was his face and turned-up was his nose.
As bald as any ape's head was his skull;
He was a market-swaggerer to the full.
There durst no man a hand on him to lay,
Because he swore he'd make the beggar pay.
A thief he was, forsooth, of corn and meal,
And sly at that, accustomed well to steal.
His name was known as arrogant Simpkin.
A wife he had who came of gentle kin;
The parson of the town her father was.

With her he gave full many a pan of brass,[3]
To insure that Simpkin with his blood ally.
She had been bred up in a nunnery;
For Simpkin would not have a wife, he said,
Save she were educated and a maid
To keep up his estate of yeomanry.
And she was proud and bold as is a pie.
A handsome sight it was to see those two;
On holy days before her he would go
With a broad tippet bound about his head;
And she came after in a skirt of red,
While Simpkin's hose were dyed to match that same.
There durst no man to call her aught but dame;
Nor was there one so hardy, in the way,
As durst flirt with her or attempt to play,
Unless he would be slain by this Simpkin
With cutlass or with knife or with bodkin.
For jealous folk are dangerous, you know,
At least they'd have their wives to think them so.
Besides, because she was a dirty bitch,
She was as high as water in a ditch;
And full of scorn and full of back-biting.
She thought a lady should be quite willing
To greet her for her kin and culture, she
Having been brought up in that nunnery.

A daughter had they got between the two,
Of twenty years, and no more children, no,
Save a boy baby that was six months old;
It lay in cradle and was strong and bold.
This girl right stout and well developed was,
With nose tip-tilted and eyes blue as glass,
With buttocks broad, and round breasts full and high,
But golden was her hair, I will not lie.

The parson of the town, since she was fair,
Was purposeful to make of her his heir,
Both of his chattels and of his estate,
But all this hinged upon a proper mate.
He was resolved that he'd bestow her high

---

[3] Brass: money of brass, bronze or copper.

Into some blood of worthy ancestry;
For Holy Church's goods must be expended
On Holy Church's blood, as it's descended.
Therefore he'd honour thus his holy blood,
Though Holy Church itself became his food.

Large tolls this miller took, beyond a doubt,
With wheat and malt from all the lands about;
Of which I'd specify among them all
A Cambridge college known as Soler Hall;
He ground their wheat and all their malt he ground.

And on a day it happened, as they found,
The manciple got such a malady
That all men surely thought that he should die.
Whereon this miller stole both flour and wheat
A hundredfold more than he used to cheat;
For theretofore he stole but cautiously,
But now he was a thief outrageously,
At which the warden scolded and raised hell;
The miller snapped his fingers, truth to tell,
And cracked his brags and swore it wasn't so.

There were two poor young clerks, whose names I know,
That dwelt within this Hall whereof I say.
Willful they were and lusty, full of play,
And (all for mirth and to make revelry)
After the warden eagerly did they cry
To give them leave, at least for this one round,
To go to mill and see their produce ground;
And stoutly they proclaimed they'd bet their neck
The miller should not steal one half a peck
Of grain, by trick, nor yet by force should thieve;
And at the last the warden gave them leave.
John was the one and Alain was that other;
In one town were they born, and that called Strother,
Far in the north, I cannot tell you where.

This Alain, he made ready all his gear,
And on a horse loaded the sack anon.
Forth went Alain the clerk, and also John,
With good sword and with buckler at their side.
John knew the way and didn't need a guide,
And at the mill he dropped the sack of grain.
"Ah, Simon, hail, good morn," first spoke Alain.

"How fares it with your fair daughter and wife?"

"Alain! Welcome," said Simpkin, "by my life,
And John also. How now? What do you here?"

"Simon," said John, "by God, need makes no peer;
He must himself serve who's no servant, eh?
Or else he's but a fool, as all clerks say.
Our manciple—I hope he'll soon be dead,
So aching are the grinders in his head—
And therefore am I come here with Alain
To grind our corn and carry it home again;
I pray you speed us thither, as you may."

"It shall be done," said Simpkin, "by my fay.
What will you do the while it is in hand?"

"By God, right by the hopper will I stand,"
Said John, "and see just how the corn goes in;
I never have seen, by my father's kin,
Just how the hopper waggles to and fro."

Alain replied: "Well, John, and will you so?
Then will I get beneath it, by my crown,
To see there how the meal comes sifting down
Into the trough; and that shall be my sport.
For, John, in faith, I must be of your sort;
I am as bad a miller as you be."

The miller smiled at this, their delicacy,
And thought: "All this is done but for a wile;
They think there is no man may them beguile;
But, by my thrift, I will yet blear their eyes,
For all the tricks in their philosophies.
The more odd tricks and stratagems they make,
The more I'll steal when I begin to take.
In place of flour I'll give them only bran.
'The greatest clerk is not the wisest man,'
As once unto the grey wolf said the mare.
But all their arts—I rate them not a tare."

Out of the door he went, then, secretly,
When he had seen his chance, and quietly;
He looked up and looked down, until he found
The clerks' horse where it stood, securely bound.
Behind the mill, under an arbour green;
And to the horse he went, then, all unseen;
He took the bridle off him and anon,

When the said horse was free, why he was gone
Toward the fen, for wild mares ran therein,
And with a neigh he went, through thick and thin.

This miller straight went back and no word said,
But did his business and with these clerks played,
Until their corn was fairly, fully ground.
But when the flour was sacked and the ears bound,
This John went out, to find his horse away,
And so he cried: "Hello!" and "Weladay!
Our horse is lost! Alain, for Jesus' bones
Get to your feet, come out, man, now, at once!
Alas, our warden's palfrey's lost and lorn!"

This Alain forgot all, both flour and corn,
Clean out of mind was all his husbandry,
"What? Which way did he go?" began to cry.

The wife came bounding from the house, and then
She said: "Alas! Your horse went to the fen,
With the wild mares, as fast as he could go.
A curse light on the hand that tied him so,
And him that better should have knotted rein!"

"Alas!" quoth John, "Alain, for Jesus' pain,
Lay off your sword, and I will mine also;
I am as fleet, God knows, as is a roe;
By God's heart, he shall not escape us both!
Why didn't you put him in the barn? My oath!
Bad luck, by God, Alain, you are a fool!"

These foolish clerks began to run and roll
Toward the marshes, both Alain and John.

And when the miller saw that they were gone,
He half a bushel of their flour did take
And bade his wife go knead it and bread make.
He said: "I think those clerks some trickery feared;
Yet can a miller match a clerkling's beard,
For all his learning; let them go their way.
Look where they go, yea, let the children play,
They'll catch him not so readily, by my crown!"

Those simple clerks went running up and down
With "Look out! Halt! Halt! Down here! 'Ware the rear!
Go whistle, you, and I will watch him here!"
But briefly, till it came to utter night,
They could not, though they put forth all their might,

That stallion catch, he always ran so fast,
Till in a ditch they trapped him at the last.

Weary and wet, as beast is in the rain,
Came foolish John and with him came Alain.
"Alas," said John, "the day that I was born!
Now are we bound toward mockery and scorn.
Our corn is stolen, folk will call us fools,
The warden and the fellows at the schools,
And specially this miller. Weladay!"

Thus John complained as he went on his way
Toward the mill, with Bayard[4] once more bound.
The miller sitting by the fire he found,
For it was night, and farther could they not;
But, for the love of God, they him besought
For shelter and for supper, for their penny.

The miller said to them: "If there be any,
Such as it is, why you shall have your part.
My house is small, but you have learned your art;
You can, by metaphysics, make a place
A full mile wide in twenty feet of space.
Let us see now if this place will suffice,
Or make more room with speech, by some device."

"Now, Simon," said John, "by Saint Cuthbert's beard,
You're always merry and have well answered.
As I've heard, man shall take one of two things:
Such as he finds, or take such as he brings.
But specially, I pray you, mine host dear,
Give us some meat and drink and some good cheer,
And we will pay you, truly, to the full.
With empty hand no man takes hawk or gull;
Well, here's our silver, ready to be spent."

This miller to the town his daughter sent
For ale and bread, and roasted them a goose,
And tied their horse, that it might not go loose;
And then in his own chamber made a bed,
With sheets and with good blankets fairly spread,
Not from his bed more than twelve feet, or ten.
The daughter made her lone bed near the men,
In the same chamber with them, by and by;

---

[4] Bayard: the horse, any horse.

It could not well be bettered, and for why?
There was no larger room in all the place.
They supped and talked, and gained some small solace,
And drank strong ale, that evening, of the best.
Then about midnight all they went to rest.
    Well had this miller varnished his bald head,
For pale he was with drinking, and not red.
He hiccoughed and he mumbled through his nose,
As he were chilled, with humours lachrymose.
To bed he went, and with him went his wife.
As any jay she was with laughter rife,
So copiously was her gay whistle wet.
The cradle near her bed's foot-board was set,
Handy for rocking and for giving suck.
And when they'd drunk up all there was in crock,
To bed went miller's daughter, and anon
To bed went Alain and to bed went John.
There was no more; they did not need a dwale.[5]
This miller had so roundly bibbed his ale
That, like a horse, he snorted in his sleep,
While of his tail behind he kept no keep.
His wife joined in his chorus, and so strong,
Men might have heard her snores a full furlong;
And the girl snored, as well, for company.
    Alain the clerk, who heard this melody,
He poked at John and said: "Asleep? But how?
Did you hear ever such a song ere now?
Lo, what a compline is among them all!
Now may the wild-fire on their bodies fall!
Who ever heard so outlandish a thing?
But they shall have the flour of ill ending.
Through this long night there'll be for me no rest;
But never mind, 'twill all be for the best.
For, John," said he, "so may I ever thrive,
As, if I can, that very wench I'll swive.
Some recompense the law allows to us;
For, John, there is a statute which says thus,
That if a man in one point be aggrieved,
Yet in another shall he be relieved.

---

[5] Dwale: an opiate, a sleeping potion.

Our corn is stolen, to that there's no nay,
And we have had an evil time this day.
But since I may not have amending, now,
Against my loss I'll set some fun—and how!
By God's great soul it shan't be otherwise!"

This John replied: "Alain, let me advise.
The miller is a dangerous man," he said,
"And if he be awakened, I'm afraid
He may well do us both an injury."

But Alain said: "I count him not a fly."
And up he rose and to the girl he crept.
This wench lay on her back and soundly slept,
Until he'd come so near, ere she might spy,
It was too late to struggle, then, or cry;
And, to be brief, these two were soon as one.
Now play, Alain! For I will speak of John.

This John lay still a quarter-hour, or so,
Pitied himself and wept for all his woe.
"Alas," said he, "this is a wicked jape!
Now may I say that I am but an ape.
Yet has my friend, there, something for his harm;
He has the miller's daughter on his arm.
He ventured, and his pains are now all fled,
While I lie like a sack of chaff in bed;
And when this jape is told, another day,
I shall be held an ass, a milksop, yea!
I will arise and chance it, by my fay!
'Unhardy is unhappy,' as they say."

And up he rose, and softly then he went
To find the cradle for expedient,
And bore it over to his own foot-board.

Soon after this the wife no longer snored,
But woke and rose and went outside to piss,
And came again and did the cradle miss,
And groped round, here and there, but found it not.
"Alas!" thought she, "my way I have forgot.
I nearly found myself in the clerks' bed.
Eh, *ben'cite,* but that were wrong!" she said.
And on, until by cradle she did stand.
And, groping a bit farther with her hand,
She found the bed, and thought of naught but good,

Because her baby's cradle by it stood,
And knew not where she was, for it was dark;
But calmly then she crept in by the clerk,
And lay right still, and would have gone to sleep.
But presently this John the clerk did leap,
And over on this goodwife did he lie.
No such gay time she'd known in years gone by.
He pricked her hard and deep, like one gone mad.
And so a jolly life these two clerks had
Till the third cock began to crow and sing.

    Alain grew weary in the grey dawning,
For he had laboured hard through all the night;
And said: "Farewell, now, Maudy, sweet delight!
The day is come, I may no longer bide;
But evermore, whether I walk or ride,
I am your own clerk, so may I have weal."

    "Now, sweetheart," said she, "go and fare you well!
But ere you go, there's one thing I must tell.
When you go walking homeward past the mill,
Right at the entrance, just the door behind,
You shall a loaf of half a bushel find
That was baked up of your own flour, a deal
Of which I helped my father for to steal.
And, darling, may God save you now and keep!"
And with that word she almost had to weep.

    Alain arose and thought: "Ere it be dawn,
I will go creep in softly by friend John."
And found the cradle with his hand, anon.
"By God!" thought he, "all wrong I must have gone;
My head is dizzy from my work tonight,
And that's why I have failed to go aright.
I know well, by this cradle, I am wrong,
For here the miller and his wife belong."
And on he went, and on the devil's way,
Unto the bed wherein the miller lay.
He thought to have crept in by comrade John,
So, to the miller, in he got anon,
And caught him round the neck, and softly spake,
Saying: "You, John, you old swine's head, awake,
For Christ's own soul, and hear a noble work,
For by Saint James, and as I am a clerk,

I have, three times in this short night, no lack,
Swived that old miller's daughter on her back,
While you, like any coward, were aghast."
    "You scoundrel," cried the miller, "you trespassed?
Ah, traitor false and treacherous clerk!" cried he,
"You shall be killed, by God's own dignity!
Who dares be bold enough to bring to shame
My daughter, who is born of such a name?"
    And by the gullet, then, he caught Alain.
And pitilessly he handled him amain,
And on the nose he smote him with his fist.
Down ran the bloody stream upon his breast;
And on the floor, with nose and mouth a-soak,
They wallowed as two pigs do in a poke.
And up they came, and down they both went, prone,
Until the miller stumbled on a stone,
And reeled and fell down backwards on his wife,
Who nothing knew of all this silly strife;
For she had fallen into slumber tight
With John the clerk, who'd been awake all night.
But at the fall, from sleep she started out.
"Help, holy Cross of Bromholm!" did she shout,
"In *manus tuas*, Lord, to Thee I call!
Simon, awake, the Fiend is on us all
My heart is broken, help, I am but dead!
There lies one on my womb, one on my head!
Help, Simpkin, for these treacherous clerks do fight!"
    John started up, as fast as well he might,
And searched along the wall, and to and fro,
To find a staff; and she arose also,
And knowing the room better than did John,
She found a staff against the wall, anon;
And then she saw a little ray of light,
For through a hole the moon was shining bright;
And by that light she saw the struggling two,
But certainly she knew not who was who,
Except she saw a white thing with her eye.
And when she did this same white thing espy,
She thought the clerk had worn a nightcap here.
And with the staff she nearer drew, and near,
And, thinking to hit Alain on his poll,
She fetched the miller on his bald white skull,

And down he went, crying out, "Help, help, I die!"
The two clerks beat him well and let him lie;
And clothed themselves, and took their horse anon.
And got their flour, and on their way were gone.
And at the mill they found the well-made cake
Which of their meal the miller's wife did bake.
    Thus is the haughty miller soundly beat,
And thus he's lost his pay for grinding wheat,
And paid for the two suppers, let me tell,
Of Alain and of John, who've tricked him well.
His wife is taken, also his daughter sweet;
Thus it befalls a miller who's a cheat.
And therefore is this proverb said with truth,
"An evil end to evil man, forsooth."
The cheater shall himself well cheated be.
And God, Who sits on high in majesty,
Save all this company, both strong and frail!
Thus have I paid this miller with my tale.

HERE IS ENDED THE REEVE'S TALE

THE COOK'S PROLOGUE

The cook from London, while the reeve yet spoke,
Patted his back with pleasure at the joke.
"Ha, ha!" laughed he, "by Christ's great suffering,
This miller had a mighty sharp ending
Upon his argument of harbourage!
For well says Solomon, in his language,
'Bring thou not every man into thine house;'
For harbouring by night is dangerous.
Well ought a man to know the man that he
Has brought into his own security.
I pray God give me sorrow and much care
If ever, since I have been Hodge[6] of Ware,
Heard I of miller better brought to mark.
A wicked jest was played him in the dark.
But God forbid that we should leave off here;
And therefore, if you'll lend me now an ear,
From what I know, who am but a poor man,

---

[6] Hodge: a nickname for Roger.

I will relate, as well as ever I can,
A little trick was played in our city."
     Our host replied: "I grant it readily.
Now tell on, Roger; see that it be good;
For many a pasty have you robbed of blood,
And many a Jack of Dover[7] have you sold
That has been heated twice and twice grown cold.
From many a pilgrim have you had Christ's curse,
For of your parsley they yet fare the worse,
Which they have eaten with your stubble goose;[8]
For in your shop full many a fly is loose.
Now tell on, gentle Roger, by your name.
But yet, I pray, don't mind if I make game,
A man may tell the truth when it's in play."
     "You say the truth," quoth Roger, "by my fay!
But 'true jest, bad jest' as the Fleming saith.
And therefore, Harry Bailey, on your faith,
Be you not angry ere we finish here,
If my tale should concern an inn-keeper.
Nevertheless, I'll tell not that one yet,
But ere we part your jokes will I upset."
     And thereon did he laugh, in great good cheer,
And told his tale, as you shall straightway hear.

THUS ENDS THE PROLOGUE OF THE COOK'S TALE

THE COOK'S TALE

There lived a 'prentice, once, in our city,
And of the craft of victuallers was he;
Happy he was as goldfinch in the glade,
Brown as a berry, short, and thickly made,
With black hair that he combed right prettily.
He could dance well, and that so jollily,
That he was nicknamed Perkin Reveller.
He was as full of love, I may aver,
As is a beehive full of honey sweet;

---

[7] Jack of Dover: a slang term for a meat pie which, not being sold the day it was cooked, the gravy was drawn off.
[8] Stubble goose: an old goose fed on stubble, not on grain.

Well for the wench that with him chanced to meet.
At every bridal would he sing and hop,
Loving the tavern better than the shop.
  When there was any festival in Cheap,
Out of the shop and thither would he leap,
And, till the whole procession he had seen,
And danced his fill, he'd not return again.
He gathered many fellows of his sort
To dance and sing and make all kinds of sport.
And they would have appointments for to meet
And play at dice in such, or such, a street.
For in the whole town was no apprentice
Who better knew the way to throw the dice
Than Perkin; and therefore he was right free
With money, when in chosen company.
His master found this out in business there;
For often-times he found the till was bare.
For certainly a revelling bond-boy
Who loves dice, wine, dancing, and girls of joy—
His master, in his shop, shall feel the effect,
Though no part have he in this said respect;
For theft and riot always comrades are,
And each alike he played on gay guitar.
Revels and truth, in one of low degree,
Do battle always, as all men may see.
  This 'prentice shared his master's fair abode
Till he was nigh out of his 'prenticehood,
Though he was checked and scolded early and late,
And sometimes led, for drinking, to Newgate;
But at the last his master did take thought,
Upon a day, when he his ledger sought,
On an old proverb wherein is found this word:
"Better take rotten apple from the hoard
Than let it lie to spoil the good ones there."
So with a drunken servant should it fare;
It is less ill to let him go, apace,
Than ruin all the others in the place.
Therefore he freed and cast him loose to go
His own road unto future care and woe;
And thus this jolly 'prentice had his leave.
Now let him riot all night long, or thieve.

But since there's never thief without a buck
To help him waste his money and to suck
All he can steal or borrow by the way,
Anon he sent his bed and his array
To one he knew, a fellow of his sort,
Who loved the dice and revels and all sport,
And had a wife that kept, for countenance,
A shop, and whored to gain her sustenance.

OF THIS COOK'S TALE CHAUCER MADE NO MORE

INTRODUCTION
TO THE LAWYER'S PROLOGUE

The Words of the Host to the Company

Our good host saw well that the shining sun
The arc of artificial day[9] had run
A quarter part, plus half an hour or more;
And though not deeply expert in such lore,
He reckoned that it was the eighteenth day
Of April, which is harbinger to May;
And saw well that the shadow of each tree
Was, as to length, of even quantity
As was the body upright causing it.
And therefore by the shade he had the wit
To know that Phoebus, shining there so bright,
Had climbed degrees full forty-five in height;
And that, that day, and in that latitude,
It was ten of the clock, he did conclude,
And suddenly he put his horse about.

"Masters," quoth he, "I warn all of this rout,
A quarter of this present day is gone;
Now for the love of God and of Saint John,
Lose no more time, or little as you may;
Masters, the time is wasting night and day,
And steals away from us, what with our sleeping
And with our sloth, when we awake are keeping,
As does the stream, that never turns again,

---

[9] From sunrise to sunset.

Descending from the mountain to the plain.
And well may Seneca, and many more,
Bewail lost time far more than gold in store.
'For chattels lost may yet recovered be,
But time lost ruins us for aye,' says he.
It will not come again, once it has fled,
Not any more than will Mag's maidenhead
When she has lost it in her wantonness;
Let's not grow mouldy thus in idleness.
"Sir Lawyer," said he, "as you have hope of bliss,
Tell us a tale, as our agreement is;
You have submitted, by your free assent,
To stand, in this case, to my sole judgment;
Acquit yourself, keep promise with the rest,
And you'll have done your duty, at the least."

    "Mine host," said he, "by the gods, I consent;
To break a promise is not my intent.
A promise is a debt, and by my fay
I keep all mine; I can no better say.
For such law as man gives to other wight,
He should himself submit to it, by right;
Thus says our text; nevertheless, 'tis true
I can relate no useful tale to you,
But Chaucer, though he speaks but vulgarly
In metre and in rhyming dextrously,
Has told them in such English as he can,
In former years, as knows full many a man.
For if he has not told them, my dear brother,
In one book, why he's done so in another.
For he has told of lovers, up and down,
More than old Ovid mentions, of renown,
In his *Epistles,* that are now so old.
Why should I then re-tell what has been told?
In youth he told of Ceyx and Alcyon,
And has since then spoken of everyone—
Of noble wives and lovers did he speak.
And whoso will that weighty volume seek
Called *Legend of Good Women,* need not chide;
There may be ever seen the large wounds wide
Of Lucrece, Babylonian Thisbe;
Dido's for false Aeneas when fled he;

Demophoon and Phyllis and her tree;
The plaint of Deianira and Hermione;
Of Ariadne and Hypsipyle;
The barren island standing in the sea;
The drowned Leander and his fair Hero;
The tears of Helen and the bitter woe
Of Briseis and that of Laodomea;
The cruelty of that fair Queen Medea,
Her little children hanging by the neck
When all her love for Jason came to wreck!
O Hypermnestra, Penelope, Alcestis,
Your wifehood does he honour, since it best is!
    "But certainly no word has written he
Of that so wicked woman, Canace,
Who loved her own blood brother sinfully.
Of suchlike cursed tales, I say 'Let be!'
Nor yet of Tyrian Apollonius;
Nor how the wicked King Antiochus
Bereft his daughter of her maidenhead
(Which is so horrible a tale to read),
When down he flung her on the paving stones.
And therefore he, advisedly, truth owns,
Would never write, in one of his creations,
Of such unnatural abominations.
And I'll refuse to tell them, if I may.
    "But for my tale, what shall I do this day?
Any comparison would me displease
To Muses whom men call Pierides
(The *Metamorphoses* show what I mean).
Nevertheless, I do not care a bean
Though I come after him with my plain fare.
I'll stick to prose. Let him his rhymes prepare."
    And thereupon, with sober face and cheer,
He told his tale, as you shall read it here.

THE LAWYER'S PROLOGUE

O Hateful evil! State of Poverty!
With thirst, with cold, with hunger so confounded!
To ask help shameth thy heart's delicacy;

If none thou ask, by need thou art so wounded
That need itself uncovereth all the wound hid!
Spite of thy will thou must, for indigence,
Go steal, or beg, or borrow thine expense.

Thou blamest Christ, and thou say'st bitterly,
He misdistributes riches temporal;
Thy neighbour dost thou censure, sinfully,
Saying thou hast too little and he hath all.
"My faith," sayest thou, "sometime the reckoning shall
Come on him, when his tail shall burn for greed,
Not having helped the needy in their need."

Hear now what is the judgment of the wise:
"Better to die than live in indigence;"
"Thy very pauper neighbours thee despise."
If thou be poor, farewell thy reverence!
Still of the wise man take this full sentence:
"The days of the afflicted are all sin."
Beware, therefore, that thou come not therein!

"If thou be poor, thy brother hateth thee,
And all thy friends will flee from thee, alas!"
O wealthy merchants, full of weal ye be,
O noble, prudent folk in happier case!
Your dice-box doth not tumble out ambsace,[10]
But with *six-cinq*[11] ye throw against your chance;[12]
And so, at Christmas, merrily may ye dance!

Ye search all land and sea for your winnings,
And, as wise folk, ye know well the estate
Of all realms; ye are sires of happenings
And tales of peace and tales of war's debate.
But I were now of tales all desolate,
Were 't not a merchant, gone this many a year,
Taught me the story which you now shall hear.

---

[10] Double-ace.
[11] Six and five.
[12] Chance: similar to the "point" in the modern game of craps.

THE LAWYER'S TALE

In Syria, once, there dwelt a company
Of traders rich, all sober men and true,
That far abroad did send their spicery,
And cloth of gold, and satins rich in hue;
Their wares were all so excellent and new
That everyone was eager to exchange
With them, and sell them divers things and strange.

It came to pass, the masters of this sort
Decided that to Rome they all would wend,
Were it for business or for only sport;
No other message would they thither send,
But went themselves to Rome; this is the end.
And there they found an inn and took their rest
As seemed to their advantage suited best.

Sojourned have now these merchants in that town
A certain time, as fell to their pleasance.
And so it happened that the high renown
Of th' emperor's daughter, called the fair Constance,
Reported was, with every circumstance,
Unto these Syrian merchants, in such wise,
From day to day, as I will now apprise.

This was the common voice of every man:
"Our emperor of Rome, God save and see,
A daughter has that since the world began,
To reckon as well her goodness as beauty,
Was never such another as is she;
I pray that God her fame will keep, serene,
And would she were of all Europe the queen.

"In her is beauty high, and without pride;
Youth, without crudity or levity;
In all endeavours, virtue is her guide;
Meekness in her has humbled tyranny;
She is the mirror of all courtesy;
Her heart's a very shrine of holiness;
Her hand is freedom's agent for largess."

And all this voice said truth, as God is true.
But to our story let us turn again.
These merchants all have freighted ships anew,
And when they'd seen the lovely maid, they fain
Would seek their Syrian homes with all their train,
To do their business as they'd done of yore,
And live in weal; I cannot tell you more.

Now so it was, these merchants stood in grace
Of Syria's sultan; and so wise was he
That when they came from any foreign place
He would, of his benignant courtesy,
Make them good cheer, inquiring earnestly
For news of sundry realms, to learn, by word,
The wonders that they might have seen and heard.

Among some other things, especially
These merchants told him tales of fair Constance;
From such nobility, told of earnestly,
This sultan caught a dream of great pleasance,
And she so figured in his remembrance
That all his wish and all his busy care
Were, throughout life, to love that lady fair.

Now peradventure, in that mighty book
Which men call heaven, it had come to pass,
In stars, when first a living breath he took,
That he for love should get his death, alas!
For in the stars, far clearer than is glass,
Is written, God knows, read it he who can,—
And truth it is—the death of every man.

In stars, full many a winter over-worn,
Was written the death of Hector, Achilles,
Of Pompey, Julius, long ere they were born;
The strife at Thebes; and of great Hercules,
Of Samson, of Turnus, of Socrates,
The death to each; but men's wits are so dull
There is no man may read this to the full.

This sultan for his privy-council sent,

And, but to tell it briefly in this place,
He did to them declare his whole intent,
And said that, surely, save he might have grace
To gain Constance within a little space,
He was but dead; and charged them, speedily
To find out, for his life, some remedy.

By divers men, then, divers things were said;
They reasoned, and they argued up and down;
Full much with subtle logic there they sped;
They spoke of spells, of treachery in Rome town;
But finally, as to an end foreknown,
They were agreed that nothing should gainsay
A marriage, for there was no other way.

Then saw they therein so much difficulty,
When reasoning of it (to make all plain,
Because such conflict and diversity
Between the laws of both lands long had lain)
They held: "No Christian emperor were fain
To have his child wed under our sweet laws,
Given us by Mahomet for God's cause."

But he replied: "Nay, rather then than lose
The Lady Constance, I'll be christened, yes!
I must be hers, I can no other choose.
I pray you let be no rebelliousness;
Save me my life, and do not be careless
In getting her who thus alone may cure
The woe whereof I cannot long endure."

What needs a copious dilation now?
I say: By treaties and by embassy,
And the pope's mediation, high and low,
And all the Church and all the chivalry,
That, to destruction of Manometry
And to augmenting Christian faith so dear,
They were agreed, at last, as you shall hear.

The sultan and his entire baronage
And all his vassals, they must christened be,

And he shall have Constance in true marriage,
And gold (I know not in what quantity),
For which was found enough security;
This, being agreed, was sworn by either side.
Now, Constance fair, may great God be your guide!

Now would some men expect, as I may guess,
That I should tell of all the purveyance
The emperor, of his great nobleness,
Has destined for his daughter, fair Constance.
But men must know that so great ordinance
May no one tell within a little clause
As was arrayed there for so high a cause.

Bishops were named who were with her to wend,
Ladies and lords and knights of high renown,
And other folk—but I will make an end,
Except that it was ordered through the town
That everyone, with great devotion shown,
Should pray to Christ that He this marriage lead
To happy end, and the long voyage speed.

The day is come, at last, for leave-taking,
I say, the woeful, fatal day is come,
When there may be no longer tarrying,
But to go forth make ready all and some;
Constance, who was with sorrow overcome,
Rose, sad and pale, and dressed herself to wend;
For well she saw there was no other end.

Alas! What wonder is it that she wept?
She shall be sent to a strange country, far
From friends that her so tenderly have kept,
And bound to one her joy to make or mar
Whom she knows not, nor what his people are.
Husbands are all good, and have been of yore,
That know their wives, but I dare say no more.

"Father," she said, "your wretched child, Constance,
Your daughter reared in luxury so soft,
And you, my mother, and my chief pleasance,

Above all things, save Christ Who rules aloft,
Constance your child would be remembered oft
Within your prayers, for I to Syria go,
Nor shall I ever see you more, ah no!

"Unto the land of Barbary[13] my fate
Compels me now, because it is your will;
But Christ, Who died to save our sad estate,
So give me grace, His mandates I'll fulfill;
I, wretched woman, though I die, 'tis nil.
Women are born to slave and to repent,
And to be subject to man's government."

I think, at Troy, when Pyrrhus broke the wall;
When Ilium burned; when Thebes fell, that city;
At Rome, for all the harm from Hannibal,
Who vanquished Roman arms in campaigns three—
I think was heard no weeping for pity
As in the chamber at her leave-taking;
Yet go she must, whether she weep or sing.

O primal-moving, cruel Firmament,
With thy diurnal pressure, that doth sway
And hurl all things from East to Occident,
Which otherwise would hold another way,
Thy pressure set the heavens in such array,
At the beginning of this wild voyage,
That cruel Mars hath murdered this marriage.

Unfortunate ascendant tortuous,
Of which the lord has helpless fall'n, alas,
Out of his angle to the darkest house!
O Mars! O Atazir in present case![14]
O feeble Moon, unhappy is thy pace!
Thou'rt in conjunction where thou'rt not received,
And where thou should'st go, thou hast not achieved.

---

[13] Barbary: (Barbre, in original); from F. *barbarie,* barbarous, but with especial reference to Saracens or pagans. Hence confused with Ar. *Barbar,* the people of Barbary.

[14] Atazir: the influence of a star on other stars or on men.

Imprudent emperor of Rome, alas!
Was no philosopher[15] in all thy town?
Is one time like another in such case?
Indeed, can there be no election shown,
Especially to folk of high renown,
And when their dates of birth may all men know?
Alas! We are too ignorant or too slow.

To ship is brought this fair and woeful maid,
Full decorously, with every circumstance.
"Now Jesus Christ be with you all," she said;
And there's no more, save "Farewell, fair Constance!"
She strove to keep a cheerful countenance,
And forth I let her sail in this manner,
And turn again to matters far from her.

The mother of the sultan, well of vices,
Has heard the news of her son's full intent,
How he will leave the ancient sacrifices;
And she at once for her own council sent;
And so they came to learn what thing she meant.
And when they were assembled, each compeer,
She took her seat and spoke as you shall hear.

"My lords," said she, "you know well, every man,
My son intends to forgo and forget
The holy precepts of our Alkoran,
Given by God's own prophet, Mahomet.
But I will make one vow to great God yet:
The life shall rather from my body start
Than Islam's laws out of my faithful heart!

"What should we get from taking this new creed
But thralldom for our bodies and penance?
And afterward, be drawn to Hell, indeed,
For thus denying our faith's inheritance?
But, lords, if you will give your sustenance,
And join me for the wisdom I've in store,
I swear to save us all for evermore."

---

[15] Philosopher: astrologer in the present instance.

They swore and they assented, every man,
To live by her and die, and by her stand;
And each of them, in what best wise he can,
Shall gather friends and followers into band;
And she shall take the enterprise in hand,
The form of which I soon will you apprise,
And to them all she spoke, then, in this wise.

"We will first feign the Christian faith to take;
Cold water will not harm us from the rite;
And I will such a feast and revel make
As will, I trust, to lull be requisite.
For though his wife be christened ever so white,
She shall have need to wash away the red,
Though a full font of water be there sped."

O sultana, root of iniquity!
Virago, you Semiramis second!
O serpent hid in femininity,
Just as the Serpent deep in Hell is bound!
O pseudo-woman, all that may confound
Virtue and innocence, through your malice,
Is bred in you, the nest of every vice!

O Satan, envious since that same day
When thou wert banished from our heritage,
Well know'st thou unto woman thine old way!
Thou made'st Eve bring us into long bondage.
Thou wilt destroy this Christian marriage.
Thine instrument—ah welaway the while!—
Make'st thou of woman when thou wilt beguile!

Now this sultana whom I blame and harry,
Let, secretly, her council go their way.
Why should I longer in my story tarry?
She rode unto the sultan, on a day,
And told him she'd renounce her old faith, yea,
Be christened at priests' hands, with all the throng,
Repentant she'd been heathen for so long.

Beseeching him to do her the honour

To let her have the Christian men to feast:
"To entertain them will be my labour."
The sultan said: "I'll be at your behest."
And, kneeling, thanked her for that fair request,
So glad he was he knew not what to say;
She kissed her son, and homeward went her way.

Explicit prima pars.
Sequitur pars secunda.

Arrived now are these Christian folk at land,
In Syria, with a great stately rout,
And hastily this sultan gave command,
First to his mother and all the realm about,
Saying his wife was come, beyond a doubt,
And prayed her that she ride to meet the queen,
That all due honour might be shown and seen.

Great was the crush and rich was the array
Of Syrians and Romans, meeting here;
The mother of the sultan, rich and gay,
Received her open-armed, with smiling cheer,
As any mother might a daughter dear;
And to the nearest city, with the bride,
At gentle pace, right festively they ride.

I think the triumph of great Julius,
Whereof old Lucan make so long a boast,
Was not more royal nor more curious
Than was the assembling of this happy host.
But this same Scorpion, this wicked ghost—
The old sultana, for all her flattering,
Chose in that sign full mortally to sting.

The sultan came himself, soon after this,
So regally 'twere wonderful to tell,
And welcomed her into all joy and bliss.
And thus in such delight I let them dwell.
The fruit of all is what I now shall tell.
When came the time, men thought it for the best
Their revels cease, and got them home to rest.

The time came when this old sultana there
Has ordered up the feast of which I told,
Whereto the Christian folk did them prepare,
The company together, young and old.
There men might feast and royalty behold,
With dainties more than I can e'en surmise;
But all too dear they've bought it, ere they rise.

O sudden woe! that ever will succeed
On worldly bliss, infused with bitterness;
That ends the joy of earthly toil, indeed;
Woe holds at last the place of our gladness.
Hear, now, this counsel for your certainness:
Upon your most glad day, bear then in mind
The unknown harm and woe that come behind.

For, but to tell you briefly, in one word—
The sultan and the Christians, every one,
Were all hewed down and thrust through at the board,
Save the fair Lady Constance, she alone.
This old sultana, aye, this cursed crone
Has, with her followers, done this wicked deed,
For she herself would all the nation lead.

There was no Syrian that had been converted,
Being of the sultan's council resolute,
But was struck down, ere from the board he'd started.
And Constance have they taken now, hot-foot,
And on a ship, of rudder destitute,
They her have placed, bidding her learn to sail
From Syria to Italy—or fail.

A certain treasure that she'd brought, they add,
And, truth to tell, of food great quantity
They have her given, and clothing too she had;
And forth she sails upon the wide salt sea.
O Constance mine, full of benignity,
O emperor's young daughter, from afar
He that is Lord of fortune be your star!

She crossed herself, and in a pious voice

Unto the Cross of Jesus thus said she:
O bright, O blessed Altar of my choice,
Red with the Lamb's blood full of all pity,
That washed the world from old iniquity,
Me from the Fiend and from his claws, oh keep
That day when I shall drown within the deep!

"Victorious Tree, Protection of the true,
The only thing that worthy was to bear
The King of Heaven with His wounds so new,
The White Lamb Who was pierced through with the spear,
Driver of devils out of him and her
Who on Thine arms do lay themselves in faith,
Keep me and give me grace before my death!"

For years and days drifted this maiden pure,
Through all the seas of Greece and to the strait
Of dark Gibraltar did she adventure;
On many a sorry meal now may she bait;
Upon her death full often may she wait
Before the wild waves and the winds shall drive
Her vessel where it shall some day arrive.

Men might well ask: But why was she not slain?
And at that feast who could her body save?
And I reply to that demand, again:
Who saved young Daniel in the dreadful cave
Where every other man, master and knave,
Was killed by lions ere he might up-start?
No one, save God, Whom he bore in his heart.

God willed to show this wondrous miracle
Through her, that we should see His mighty works;
And Christ Who every evil can dispel,
By certain means does oft, as know all clerks,
Do that whereof the end in darkness lurks
For man's poor wit, which of its ignorance
Cannot conceive His careful purveyance.

Now, since she was not slain at feast we saw,
Who kept her that she drowned not in the sea?

But who kept Jonah in the fish's maw
Till he was spewed forth there at Nineveh?
Well may men know it was no one but He
Who saved the Hebrew people from drowning
When, dry-shod, through the sea they went walking.

Who bade the four great spirits of tempest,
That power have to harry land and sea,
"Not north, nor south, nor yet to east, nor west
Shall ye molest the ocean, land, or tree"?
Truly, the Captain of all this was He
Who from the storm has aye this woman kept,
As well when waking as in hours she slept.

Where might this woman get her drink and meat?
Three years and more, how lasted her supply?
Who gave Egyptian Mary food to eat
In cave or desert? None but Christ, say I.
Five thousand folk, the gospels testify,
On five loaves and two fishes once did feed.
And thus God sent abundance for her need.

Forth into our own ocean then she came,
Through all our wild white seas, until at last,
Under a keep, whose name I cannot name,
Far up Northumberland, her ship was cast,
And on the sands drove hard and stuck so fast
That thence it moved not, no, for all the tide,
It being Christ's will that she should there abide.

The warden of the castle down did fare
To view this wreck, and through the ship he sought
And found this weary woman, full of care;
He found, also, the treasure she had brought.
In her own language mercy she besought
That he would help her soul from body win
To free her from the plight that she was in.

A kind of bastard Latin did she speak,
But, nevertheless, these folk could understand;
The constable no longer thought to seek,

But led the sorrowing woman to the land;
There she knelt down and thanked God, on the sand,
But who or what she was, she would not say,
For threat or promise, though she died that day.

She said she'd been bewildered by the sea,
And had lost recollection, by her truth;
The warden had for her so great pity,
As had his wife, that both they wept for ruth.
She was so diligent to toil, in sooth,
To serve and please all folk within that place,
That all loved her who looked upon her face.

This warden and Dame Hermengild, his wife,
Were pagans, and that country, everywhere;
But Hermengild now loved her as her life,
And Constance has so long abided there,
And prayed so oft, with many a tearful prayer,
That Jesus has converted, through His grace,
Dame Hermengild, the lady of that place.

In all that land no Christian dared speak out
All Christians having fled from that country,
For pagan men had conquered all about
The regions of the north, by land and sea;
To Wales was fled the Christianity
Of the old Britons dwelling in this isle;
That was their refuge in the wild meanwhile.

Yet ne'er were Christian Britons so exiled
But some of them assembled, privately,
To honour Christ, and heathen folk beguiled;
And near the castle dwelt of such men three.
But one of them was blind and could not see,
Save with the inner optics of his mind,
Wherewith all men see after they go blind.

Bright was the sun upon that summer's day
When went the warden and his wife also,
And Constance, down the hill, along the way
Toward the sea, a furlong off, or so,

To frolic and to wander to and fro;
And in their walk on this blind man they came,
With eyes fast shut, a creature old and lame.

"In name of Christ!" this blind old Briton cried,
"Dame Hermengild, give me my sight again."
But she was frightened of the words, and sighed,
Lest that her husband, briefly to be plain,
Should have her, for her love of Jesus, slain;
Till Constance strengthened her and bade her work
The will of God, as daughter of His kirk.

The warden was confounded by that sight,
And asked: "What mean these words and this affair?"
Constance replied: "Sir, it is Jesus' might
That helps all poor folk from the foul Fiend's snare."
And so far did she our sweet faith declare
That she the constable, before 'twas eve,
Converted, and in Christ made him believe.

This constable, though not lord of that place
Where he'd found Constance, wrecked upon the sand,
Had held it well for many a winter's space,
For Alla, king of all Northumberland,
Who was full wise and hardy of his hand
Against the Scots, as men may read and hear,
But I will to my tale again—give ear.

Satan, that ever waits, men to beguile,
Saw now, in Constance, all perfection grown,
And wondering how to be revenged the while,
He made a young knight, living in the town,
Love her so madly, with foul passion flown,
That verily he thought his life should spill,
Save that, of her, he once might have his will.

He wooed her, but it all availed him naught;
She would not sin in any wise or way;
And, for despite, he plotted in his thought
To make her die a death of shame some day.
He waited till the warden was away,

And, stealthily by night, he went and crept
To Hermengild's bed-chamber, while she slept.

Weary with waking for her orisons,
Slept Constance, and Dame Hermengild also.
This knight, by Satan's tempting, came at once
And softly to the bedside he did go.
And cut the throat of Hermengild, and so
Laid the hot reeking knife by fair Constance,
And went his way—where God give him mischance!

Soon after came the warden home again,
And with him Alla, king of all that land,
And saw his wife so pitilessly slain,
For which he wept and cried and wrung his hand;
And in the bed the bloody dagger, and
The Lady Constance. Ah! What could she say?
For very woe her wits went all away.

King Alla was apprised of this sad chance,
And told the time, and where, and in what wise
Was found in a wrecked ship the fair Constance,
As heretofore you've heard my tale apprise.
But in the king's heart pity did arise
When he saw so benignant a creature
Fallen in distress of such misadventure.

For as the lamb unto his death is brought,
So stood this innocent before the king;
And the false knight that had this treason wrought,
He swore that it was she had done this thing.
Nevertheless, there was much sorrowing
Among the people, saying, "We cannot guess
That she has done so great a wickedness.

"For we have seen her always virtuous,
And loving Hermengild as she loved life."
To this bore witness each one in that house,
Save he that slew the victim with his knife.
The gentle king suspected motive rife
In that man's heart; and thought he would inquire

Deeper therein, the truth to learn entire.

Alas, Constance! You have no champion,
And since you cannot fight, it's welaway!
But He Who died for us the cross upon,
And Satan bound (who lies yet where he lay),
So be your doughty Champion this day!
For, except Christ a miracle make known,
You shall be slain, though guiltless, and right soon.

She dropped upon her knees and thus she prayed:
"Immortal God, Who saved the fair Susanna
From lying blame, and Thou, O gracious Maid
(Mary, I mean, the daughter of Saint Anna),
Before whose Child the angels sing hosanna,
If I be guiltless of this felony,
My succour be, for otherwise I die!"

Have you not sometime seen a pallid face
Among the crowd, of one that's being led
Toward his death—one who had got no grace?
And such a pallor on his face was spread
All men must mark it, full of horrid dread,
Among the other faces in the rout.
So stood fair Constance there and looked about.

O queens that live in all prosperity,
Duchesses, and you ladies, every one,
Have pity, now, on her adversity;
An emperor's young daughter stands alone;
She has no one to whom to make her moan.
O royal blood that stands there in such dread,
Far are your friends away in your great need!

This King Alla has such compassion shown
(Since gentle heart is full of all pity),
That from his two eyes ran the tears right down.
"Now hastily go fetch a book," quoth he,
"And if this knight will swear that it was she
Who slew the woman, then will we make clear
The judge we shall appoint the case to hear."

A book of Gospels writ in British tongue
Was brought, and on this Book he swore anon
Her guilt; but then the people all among
A clenched hand smote him on the shoulder-bone,
And down he fell, as stunned as by a stone,
And both his eyes burst forth out of his face
In sight of everybody in that place.

A voice was heard by all that audience,
Saying: "You have here slandered the guiltless
Daughter of Holy Church, in high Presence;
Thus have you done, and further I'll not press."
Whereat were all the folk aghast, no less;
As men amazed they stand there, every one,
For dread of vengeance, save Constance alone.

Great was the fear and, too, the repentance
Of those that held a wrong suspicion there
Against this simple innocent Constance;
And by this miracle so wondrous fair,
And by her mediation and her prayer,
The king, with many another in that place,
Was there converted, thanks to Christ His grace!

This lying knight was slain for his untruth,
By sentence of King Alla, hastily;
Yet Constance had upon his death great ruth.
And after this, Jesus, of His mercy,
Caused Alla take in marriage, solemnly,
This holy maiden, so bright and serene,
And thus has Christ made fair Constance a queen.

But who was sad, if I am not to lie,
At this but Lady Donegild, she who
Was the king's mother, full of tyranny?
She thought her wicked heart must burst in two;
She would he'd never thought this thing to do;
And so she hugged her anger that he'd take
So strange a wife as this creature must make.

Neither with chaff nor straw it pleases me

To make a long tale, here, but with the corn.
Why should I tell of all the royalty
At that wedding, or who went first, well-born,
Or who blew out a trumpet or a horn?
The fruit of every tale is but to say,
They eat and drink and dance and sing and play.

They went to bed, as was but just and right,
For though some wives are pure and saintly things,
They must endure, in patience, in the night,
Such necessaries as make pleasurings
To men whom they have wedded well with rings,
And lay their holiness a while aside;
There may no better destiny betide.

On her he got a man-child right anon;
And to a bishop and the warden eke
He gave his wife to guard, while he was gone
To Scotland, there his enemies to seek;
Now Constance, who so humble is, and meek,
So long is gone with child that, hushed and still,
She keeps her chamber, waiting on Christ's will.

The time was come, a baby boy she bore;
Mauritius they did name him at the font;
This constable sent forth a messenger
And wrote unto King Alla at the front
Of all this glad event, a full account,
And other pressing matters did he say.
He took the letter and went on his way.

This messenger, to forward his own ends,
To the king's mother rode with swiftest speed,
Humbly saluting her as down he bends:
"Madam," quoth he, "be joyful now indeed!
To God a hundred thousand thanks proceed.
The queen has borne a child, beyond all doubt,
To joy and bliss of all this land about.

"Lo, here are letters sealed that say this thing,
Which I must bear with all the speed I may;

If you will send aught to your son, the king,
I am your humble servant, night and day."
Donegild answered: "As for this time, nay;
But here tonight I'd have you take your rest;
Tomorrow I will say what I think best."

This messenger drank deep of ale and wine,
And stolen were his letters, stealthily,
Out of his box, while slept he like a swine;
And counterfeited was, right cleverly,
Another letter, wrought full sinfully,
Unto the king, of this event so near,
All from the constable, as you shall hear.

The letter said, the queen delivered was
Of such a fiendish, horrible creature,
That in the castle none so hardy as
Durst, for a lengthy time, there to endure.
The mother was an elf or fairy, sure,
Come there by chance of charm, or sorcery,
And all good men hated her company.

Sad was the king when this letter he'd seen;
But to no man he told his sorrows sore,
But with his own hand he wrote back again:
"Welcome what's sent from Christ, for evermore,
To me, who now am learned in His lore;
Lord, welcome be Thy wish, though hidden still,
My own desire is but to do Thy will.

"Guard well this child, though foul it be or fair,
And guard my wife until my home-coming;
Christ, when He wills it, may send me an heir
More consonant than this with my liking."
This letter sealed, and inwardly weeping,
To the same messenger 'twas taken soon,
And forth he went; there's no more to be done.

O messenger, possessed of drunkenness,
Strong is your breath, your limbs do falter aye,
And you betray all secrets, great and less;

Your mind is gone, you jangle like a jay;
Your face is mottled in a new array!
Where drunkenness can rèign, in any rout,
There is no counsel kept, beyond a doubt.

O Donegild, there is no English mine
Fit for your malice and your tyranny!
Therefore you to the Fiend I do resign,
Let him go write of your foul treachery!
Fie, mannish women! Nay, by God, I lie!
Fie, *fiendish spirit,* for I dare well tell,
Though you walk here, your spirit is in Hell!

This messenger came from the king again,
And at the king's old mother's court did light,
And she was of this messenger full fain
To please him in whatever way she might.
He drank until his girdle was too tight,
He slept and snored and mumbled, drunken-wise,
All night, until the sun began to rise.

Again were his letters stolen, every one,
And others counterfeited, in this wise:
"The king commands his constable, anon,
On pain of hanging by the high justice,
That he shall suffer not, in any guise,
Constance within the kingdom to abide
Beyond three days and quarter of a tide.

"But in the ship wherein she came to strand
She and her infant son and all her gear
Shall be embarked and pushed out from the land,
And charge her that she never again come here."
O Constance mine, well might your spirit fear,
And, sleeping, in your dream have great grievance
When Donegild arranged this ordinance.

This messenger, the morrow, when he woke,
Unto the castle held the nearest way,
And to the constable the letter took;
And when he'd read and learned what it did say,

Often he cried "Alas!" and "Welaway!
Lord Christ," quoth he, "how may this world endure?
So full of sin is many a bad creature.

O mighty God, and is it then Thy will?
Since Thou art righteous judge, how can it be
That innocence may suffer so much ill
And wicked folk reign in prosperity?
O good Constance, alas! Ah, woe is me
That I must be your torturer, or die
A shameful death! There is no other way."

Wept both the young and old of all that place
Because the king this cursed letter sent,
And Constance, with a deathly pallid face,
Upon the fourth day to the ship she went.
Nevertheless, she took as good intent
The will of Christ, and kneeling on the strand,
She said: "Lord, always welcome Thy command!

"He that did keep me from all lying blame
The while I lived among you, sun and snow,
He can still guard me from all harm and shame
Upon salt seas, albeit I see not how.
As strong as ever He was, so is He now.
In Him I trust and in His Mother dear,
He is my sail, the star by which I steer."

Her little child lay crying in her arm,
And kneeling, piteously to him she said:
"Peace, little son, I will do you no harm."
With that the kerchief took she from her braid,
And binding it across his eyes, she laid
Again her arm about and lulled him fast
Asleep, and then to Heaven her eyes up-cast.

"Mother," she said, "O Thou bright Maid, Mary,
True is it that through woman's incitement
Mankind was banished and is doomed to die,
For which Thy Son upon the cross was rent;
Thy blessed eyes saw all of His torment;

Wherefore there's no comparison between
Thy woe and any woe of man, though keen.

"Thou sawest them slay Thy Son before Thine eyes;
And yet lives now my little child, I say!
O Lady bright, to Whom affliction cries,
Thou glory of womanhood, O Thou fair May,
Haven of refuge, bright star of the day,
Pity my child, Who of Thy gentleness
Hast pity on mankind in all distress!

"O little child, alas! What is your guilt,
Who never wrought the smallest sin? Ah me,
Why will your too hard father have you killed?
Have mercy, O dear constable!" cried she,
"And let my little child bide, safe from sea;
And if you dare not save him, lest they blame,
Then kiss him once in his dear father's name!"

Therewith she gazed long backward at the land,
And said: "Farewell, my husband merciless!"
And up she rose and walked right down the strand
Toward the ship; followed her all the press;
And ever she prayed her child to cry the less;
And took her leave; and with a high intent
She crossed herself; and aboard ship she went.

Victualled had been the ship, 'tis true—indeed
Abundantly—for her, and for long space;
Of many other things that she should need
She had great plenty, thanks be to God's grace!
Through wind and weather may God find her place
And bring her home! I can no better say;
But out to sea she stood upon her way.

Explicit secunda pars.
Sequitur pars tercia.

Alla the king came home soon after this
Unto his castle, of the which I've told,
And asked for wife and child, whom he did miss.

The constable about his heart grew cold,
And plainly all the story he then told,
As you have heard, I cannot tell it better,
And showed the king his seal and the false letter.

And said: "My lord, as you commanded me,
On pain of death, so have I done—in vain!"
The messenger was tortured until he
Made known the facts to all men, full and plain,
From night to night, in what beds he had lain.
And thus, by dint of subtle questioning,
'Twas reasoned out from whom this harm did spring.

The hand was known, now, that the letter wrote,
And all the venom of this cursed deed,
But in what wise I certainly know not,
The effect is this, that Alla, for her meed,
His mother slew, as men may plainly read,
She being false to her sworn allegiance,
And thus old Donegild ended with mischance.

The sorrow that this Alla, night and day,
Felt for his wife, and for his child also,
There is no human tongue on earth to say.
But now will I back to fair Constance go,
Who drifted on the seas, in pain and woe,
Five years and more, as was Lord Christ's command,
Before her ship approached to any land.

Under a heathen castle, at the last,
Whereof the name not in my text I find,
Constance and her young son the sea did cast.
Almighty God, Redeemer of mankind,
Have Constance and her little child in mind!
Who must fall into heathen hands and soon
Be near to death, as I shall tell anon.

Down from the castle came full many a wight
To stare upon the ship and on Constance.
But briefly, from the castle, on a night,
The warden's steward—God give him mischance!—

A thief who had renounced allegiance
To Christ, came to the ship and said he should
Possess her body, whether or not she would.

Woe for this wretched woman then began,
Her child cried out and she cried, piteously;
But blessed Mary helped her soon; the man
With whom she struggled well and mightily,
This thief fell overboard all suddenly,
And in the sea was drowned by God's vengeance;
And thus has Christ unsullied kept Constance.

O foul desire of lechery, lo thine end!
Not only dost thou cripple a man's mind,
But verily dost thou his body rend;
The end of all thy work and thy lusts blind
Is bitterness; how many may we find
That not for actions but for mere intent
To do this sin, to shame or death are sent.

How could this poor weak woman have the strength
To keep herself against that renegade?
Goliath of immeasurable length,
How could young David such a death have made,
So slight and without armour? How arrayed
Himself to look upon that dreadful face?
Men may well see, it was but God's own grace!

Who gave to Judith courage all reckless
To slay him, Holofernes, in his tent,
And to deliver out of wretchedness
The folk of God? I say, for this intent
That just as God a soul of vigour sent
To them, and saved them out of their mischance,
So sent He might and vigour to Constance.

Forth went her ship and through the narrow mouth
Of Ceuta and Gibraltar, on its way,
Sometimes to west, and sometimes north or south,
Aye and sometimes east, many a weary day,
Until Christ's Mother (blest be She for aye!)

Did destine, out of good that is endless,
To make an end of Constance' heaviness.

But let us leave this Constance now, and turn
To speak of that same Roman emperor
Who does, from Syria, by letters, learn
The slaughter of Christians and the dishonour
Done to his daughter by a vile traitor—
I mean that old sultana, years ago,
Who, at the feast, slew all men, high and low.

For which this emperor did send anon
A senator, with royal ordinance,
And other lords, God knows, and many a one,
On Syrians to take full high vengeance.
They burn, they slay, they give them all mischance
Through many a day; but, briefly to make end,
Homeward to Rome, at last, the victors wend.

This senator returned with victory
To Rome again, sailing right royally,
And spoke the ship (so goes the old story)
In which our Constance sat so piteously,
Nothing he knew of who she was, or why
She was in such a plight; nor would she say
Aught of herself, though she might die that day.

He took her into Rome, and to his wife
Gave her in charge, and her young son also;
And in his house she lived awhile her life.
Thus can Our Lady bring from deepest woe
Most woeful Constance, aye and more, we know.
And for a long time dwelt she in that place,
Engaged in God's good works, such was her grace.

The senator's good wife her own aunt was,
Yet for all that she knew her never the more;
I will no longer tarry in this case,
But to King Alla, whom we left, of yore,
Weeping for his lost wife and sighing sore.
I will return, and I will leave Constance

Under the senator's roof and governance.

King Alla, who had had his mother slain,
Upon a day fell to such repentance,
That, but to tell it briefly and be plain,
To Rome he came to pay his just penance
And put himself in the pope's ordinance,
In high and low; and Jesus Christ he sought
To pardon all the wicked deeds he'd wrought.

The news anon through all Rome town was borne,
How King Alla would come on pilgrimage,
By harbingers that unto him were sworn;
Whereat the senator, as was usage,
Rode out to him, with many of his lineage,
As well to show his own magnificence
As do to any king a reverence.

Great welcome gave this noble senator
To King Alla, and he to him also;
Each of them showed the other much honour;
And so befell that, in a day or so,
This senator to King Alla did go
To feast, and briefly, if I may not lie,
Constance' young son went in his company.

Some men would say, 'twas instance of Constance
That sent him with the senator to feast;
I cannot tell you every circumstance,
Be it as may be, he was there, at least.
But truth is that, at his mother's behest,
Before the king, during the banquet's space,
The child stood, looking in King Alla's face.

This child aroused within the king great wonder,
And to the senator he said, anon:
"Whose is the fair child that is standing yonder?"
"I know not," quoth he, "by God and Saint John!
A mother he has, but father has he none
That I know of"—and briefly, at a bound,
He told King Alla how this child was found.

"But God knows," said this senator, as well,
"So virtuous a liver, in my life
1 never saw, as she is, nor heard tell
Of earthly woman, maiden, no nor wife.
I dare say, she would rather have a knife
Thrust through her breast than play a female trick;
There is no man could bring her to the prick."

Now this boy was as like unto Constance
As it was possible for one to be.
Alla had kept the face in remembrance
Of Dame Constance, and thereon now mused he:
Mayhap the mother of the child was she
Who was his wife. And inwardly he sighed,
And left the table with a hasty stride.

"In faith," thought he, "a phantom's in my head!
I ought to hold, by any right judgment,
That in the wide salt sea my wife is dead."
And afterward he made this argument:
"How know I but that Christ has hither sent
My wife by sea, as surely as she went
To my own land, the which was evident?"

And, after noon, home with the senator
Went Alla, all to test this wondrous chance.
The senator did Alla great honour,
And hastily he sent for fair Constance.
But, trust me, she was little fain to dance
When she had heard the cause of that command.
Scarcely upon her two feet could she stand.

When Alla saw his wife, he greeted her,
Then wept till it was a sad thing to see.
For, at the first glance, when she entered there,
He knew full verily that it was she.
And she for grief stood dumb as ever tree;
So was her heart shut up in her distress
When she remembered his unkindliness.

Twice did she swoon away there, in his sight;

He wept and he protested piteously.
"Now God," quoth he, "and all His angels bright
So truly on my spirit have mercy
As of your ills all innocent am I,
As is Maurice, my son, so like your face,
Or may the foul Fiend take me from this place!"

Long was the sobbing and the bitter pain
Before their woeful hearts could find surcease;
Great was the pity to hear them complain,
Whereof their sorrows surely did increase.
I pray you all my labour to release;
1 cannot tell their grief until tomorrow,
I am so weary, speaking long of sorrow.

But, truth being known and all doubt now dismissed,
And Alla proven guiltless of her woe,
I think a hundred times they must have kissed,
And such great bliss there was between the two
That, save the joy that nevermore shall go,
There was naught like it, present time or past,
Nor shall be, ever, while the world shall last.

Then prayed she of her husband, all meekly,
As for her pain a splendid anodyne,
That he would pray her father, specially,
That, of his majesty, he would incline
And that, some day, would come with him to dine;
She prayed him, also, he should in no way
Unto her father one word of her say.

Some men would say, it was the child Maurice
Did bear this message to the emperor;
But, as I guess, King Alla was too nice
In etiquette to one of such honour
As he that was of Christendom the flower,
To send a child; and it is best to deem
He went himself, and so it well may seem.

This emperor has granted, graciously,
To come to dinner, as he's been besought,

And, well I think, he pondered busily
Upon the child, and on his daughter thought.
Alla went to his inn, and, as he ought,
Made ready for the feast in every wise
As far as his experience could devise.

The morrow came, and Alla rose to dress,
And, too, his wife, the emperor to meet;
And forth they rode in joy and happiness.
And when she saw her father in the street,
She lighted down, and falling at his feet,
"Father," quoth she, "your young child, your Constance,
Is now gone clean out of your remembrance.

"I am your daughter Constance," then said she,
"That once you sent to Syria. 'Tis I.
It is I, father, who, on the salt sea,
Was sent, alone to drift and doomed to die.
But now, good father, mercy must I cry:
Send me no more to heathendom, godless,
But thank my lord, here, for his kindliness."

But all the tender joy, who'll tell it all
That was between the three who thus are met?
But of my tale, now, make an end I shall;
The day goes fast, I will no longer fret.
These happy folk at dinner are all set,
And there, in joy and bliss, I let them dwell;
Happier a thousand fold than I can tell.

This child Maurice was, since then, emperor
Made by the pope, and lived right christianly.
Unto Christ's Church he did a great honour;
But I let all his story pass me by.
Of Constance is my tale, especially.
In ancient Roman histories men may find
The life of Maurice; I've it not in mind.

This King Alla, when came the proper day,
With his Constance, his saintly wife so sweet,
To England went again, by the straight way,

Where they did live in joy and quiet meet.
But little while it lasts us, thus complete.
Joy of this world, for time will not abide;
From day to day it changes as the tide.

Who ever lived in such delight one day
That was not stirred therefrom by his conscience,
Desire, or anger, or some kindred fray,
Envy, or pride, or passion, or offense?
I say but to one ending this sentence:
That but a little while in joy's pleasance
Lasted the bliss of Alla and Constance.

For death, that takes from high and low his rent,
When but a year had passed, as I should guess,
Out of the world King Alla quickly sent,
For whom Constance felt heavy wretchedness.
Now let us pray that God his soul will bless!
And of Dame Constance, finally to say,
Towards the town of Rome she took her way.

To Rome is come this holy one and pure,
And finds that all her friends are safe and sound;
For now she's done with all her adventure;
And when she'd come there, and her father found,
Down on her two knees fell she to the ground,
Weeping but joyful gave she God her praise
A hundred thousand times for all His ways.

In virtue, and with alms and holy deed,
They all live there, nor ever asunder wend;
Till death does part them, such a life they lead.
And fare now well, my tale is at an end.
And Jesus Christ, Who of His might may send
Joy after woe, govern us by His grace
And keep us all that now are in this place! Amen.

HERE ENDS THE LAWYER'S TALE

THE IMITATION OF CHRIST

Thomas à Kempis

Often described as, after the Bible, the most widely read devotional book in the history of Western civilization, The Imitation of Christ *was written in Latin in the first half of the fifteenth century by Thomas à Kempis (c. 1380–1471), a member of the Dutch religious community Brethren of the Common Life. It circulated widely in manuscript form and was first published at Augsburg, Germany in 1471–1472, not long after the invention of printing by moveable type. Many other editions were printed before the end of the fifteenth century. Divided into four Books, the title of this short work of meditations on the life and teachings of Christ derives from the title of the first chapter of the first Book, "The imitation of Christ and contempt for the vanities of the world." Reprinted here is the complete Book One, "Thoughts Helpful in the Life of the Soul."*

BOOK ONE

THOUGHTS HELPFUL IN THE LIFE OF THE SOUL

THE FIRST CHAPTER

Imitating Christ and Despising All Vanities on Earth

"He who follows Me, walks not in darkness," says the Lord.[1] By these words of Christ we are advised to imitate His life and habits, if we wish to be truly enlightened and free from all blindness of heart. Let our chief effort, therefore, be to study the life of Jesus Christ.

---

[1] John 8:12.

The teaching of Christ is more excellent than all the advice of the saints, and he who has His spirit will find in it a hidden strength. Now, there are many who hear the Gospel often but care little for it because they have not the spirit of Christ. Yet whoever wishes to understand fully the words of Christ must try to pattern his whole life on that of Christ.

What good does it do to speak learnedly about the Trinity if, lacking humility, you displease the Trinity? Indeed it is not learning that makes a man holy and just, but a virtuous life makes him pleasing to God. I would rather feel contrition than know how to define it. For what would it profit us to know the whole Bible by heart and the principles of all the philosophers if we live without grace and the love of God? Vanity of vanities and all is vanity, except to love God and serve Him alone.

This is the greatest wisdom—to seek the kingdom of heaven through contempt of the world. It is vanity, therefore, to seek and trust in riches that perish. It is vanity also to court honor and to be puffed up with pride. It is vanity to follow the lusts of the body and to desire things for which severe punishment later must come. It is vanity to wish for long life and to care little about a well-spent life. It is vanity to be concerned with the present only and not to make provision for things to come. It is vanity to love what passes quickly and not to look ahead where eternal joy abides.

Often recall the proverb: "The eye is not satisfied with seeing nor the ear filled with hearing."[2] Try, moreover, to turn your heart from the love of things visible and bring yourself to things invisible. For they who follow their own evil passions stain their consciences and lose the grace of God.

THE SECOND CHAPTER

Having a Humble Opinion of Self

Every man naturally desires knowledge; but what good is knowledge without fear of God? Indeed a humble rustic who serves God is better than a proud intellectual who neglects his soul to study the course of the stars. He who knows himself well becomes mean in his own eyes and is not happy when praised by men.

---

[2] Eccles. 1:8.

If I knew all things in the world and had not charity, what would it profit me before God Who will judge me by my deeds?

Shun too great a desire for knowledge, for in it there is much fretting and delusion. Intellectuals like to appear learned and to be called wise. Yet there are many things the knowledge of which does little or no good to the soul, and he who concerns himself about other things than those which lead to salvation is very unwise.

Many words do not satisfy the soul; but a good life eases the mind and a clean conscience inspires great trust in God.

The more you know and the better you understand, the more severely will you be judged, unless your life is also the more holy. Do not be proud, therefore, because of your learning or skill. Rather, fear because of the talent given you. If you think you know many things and understand them well enough, realize at the same time that there is much you do not know. Hence, do not affect wisdom, but admit your ignorance. Why prefer yourself to anyone else when many are more learned, more cultured than you?

If you wish to learn and appreciate something worth while, then love to be unknown and considered as nothing. Truly to know and despise self is the best and most perfect counsel. To think of oneself as nothing, and always to think well and highly of others is the best and most perfect wisdom. Wherefore, if you see another sin openly or commit a serious crime, do not consider yourself better, for you do not know how long you can remain good. All men are frail, but you must admit that none is more frail than yourself.

THE THIRD CHAPTER

The Doctrine of Truth

Happy is he to whom truth manifests itself, not in signs and words that fade, but as it actually is. Our opinions, our senses often deceive us and we discern very little.

What good is much discussion of involved and obscure matters when our ignorance of them will not be held against us on Judgment Day? Neglect of things which are profitable and necessary and undue concern with those which are irrelevant and harmful, are great folly.

We have eyes and do not see.

What, therefore, have we to do with questions of philosophy? He to whom the Eternal Word speaks is free from theorizing. For from this Word are all things and of Him all things speak—the Beginning

Who also speaks to us. Without this Word no man understands or judges aright. He to whom it becomes everything, who traces all things to it and who sees all things in it, may ease his heart and remain at peace with God.

O God, You Who are the truth, make me one with You in love everlasting. I am often wearied by the many things I hear and read, but in You is all that I long for. Let the learned be still, let all creatures be silent before You; do You alone speak to me.

The more recollected a man is, and the more simple of heart he becomes, the easier he understands sublime things, for he receives the light of knowledge from above. The pure, simple, and steadfast spirit is not distracted by many labors, for he does them all for the honor of God. And since he enjoys interior peace he seeks no selfish end in anything. What, indeed, gives more trouble and affliction than uncontrolled desires of the heart?

A good and devout man arranges in his mind the things he has to do, not according to the whims of evil inclination but according to the dictates of right reason. Who is forced to struggle more than he who tries to master himself? This ought to be our purpose, then: to conquer self, to become stronger each day, to advance in virtue.

Every perfection in this life has some imperfection mixed with it and no learning of ours is without some darkness. Humble knowledge of self is a surer path to God than the ardent pursuit of learning. Not that learning is to be considered evil, or knowledge, which is good in itself and so ordained by God; but a clean conscience and virtuous life ought always to be preferred. Many often err and accomplish little or nothing because they try to become learned rather than to live well.

If men used as much care in uprooting vices and implanting virtues as they do in discussing problems, there would not be so much evil and scandal in the world, or such laxity in religious organizations. On the day of judgment, surely, we shall not be asked what we have read but what we have done; not how well we have spoken but how well we have lived.

Tell me, where now are all the masters and teachers whom you knew so well in life and who were famous for their learning? Others have already taken their places and I know not whether they ever think of their predecessors. During life they seemed to be something; now they are seldom remembered. How quickly the glory of the world passes away! If only their lives had kept pace with their learning, then their study and reading would have been worth while.

How many there are who perish because of vain worldly knowledge and too little care for serving God. They became vain in their own conceits because they chose to be great rather than humble.

He is truly great who has great charity. He is truly great who is little in his own eyes and makes nothing of the highest honor. He is truly wise who looks upon all earthly things as folly that he may gain Christ. He who does God's will and renounces his own is truly very learned.

THE FOURTH CHAPTER

Prudence in Action

Do not yield to every impulse and suggestion but consider things carefully and patiently in the light of God's will. For very often, sad to say, we are so weak that we believe and speak evil of others rather than good. Perfect men, however, do not readily believe every talebearer, because they know that human frailty is prone to evil and is likely to appear in speech.

Not to act rashly or to cling obstinately to one's opinion, not to believe everything people say or to spread abroad the gossip one has heard, is great wisdom.

Take counsel with a wise and conscientious man. Seek the advice of your betters in preference to following your own inclinations.

A good life makes a man wise according to God and gives him experience in many things, for the more humble he is and the more subject to God, the wiser and the more at peace he will be in all things.

THE FIFTH CHAPTER

Reading the Holy Scripture

Truth, not eloquence, is to be sought in reading the Holy Scriptures; and every part must be read in the spirit in which it was written. For in the Scriptures we ought to seek profit rather than polished diction.

Likewise we ought to read simple and devout books as willingly as learned and profound ones. We ought not to be swayed by the authority of the writer, whether he be a great literary light or an insignificant person, but by the love of simple truth. We ought not to ask who is speaking, but mark what is said. Men pass away, but the truth of the Lord remains forever. God speaks to us in many ways without regard for persons.

Our curiosity often impedes our reading of the Scriptures, when we wish to understand and mull over what we ought simply to read and pass by.

If you would profit from it, therefore, read with humility, simplicity, and faith, and never seek a reputation for being learned. Seek willingly and listen attentively to the words of the saints; do not be displeased with the sayings of the ancients, for they were not made without purpose.

THE SIXTH CHAPTER

Unbridled Affections

When a man desires a thing too much, he at once becomes ill at ease. A proud and avaricious man never rests, whereas he who is poor and humble of heart lives in a world of peace. An unmortified man is quickly tempted and overcome in small, trifling evils; his spirit is weak, in a measure carnal and inclined to sensual things; he can hardly abstain from earthly desires. Hence it makes him sad to forego them; he is quick to anger if reproved. Yet if he satisfies his desires, remorse of conscience overwhelms him because he followed his passions and they did not lead to the peace he sought.

True peace of heart, then, is found in resisting passions, not in satisfying them. There is no peace in the carnal man, in the man given to vain attractions, but there is peace in the fervent and spiritual man.

THE SEVENTH CHAPTER

Avoiding False Hope and Pride

Vain is the man who puts his trust in men, in created things.

Do not be ashamed to serve others for the love of Jesus Christ and to seem poor in this world. Do not be self-sufficient but place your trust in God. Do what lies in your power and God will aid your good will. Put no trust in your own learning nor in the cunning of any man, but rather in the grace of God Who helps the humble and humbles the proud.

If you have wealth, do not glory in it, nor in friends because they are powerful, but in God Who gives all things and Who desires above all to give Himself. Do not boast of personal stature or of physical beauty, qualities which are marred and destroyed by a little sickness. Do not take pride in your talent or ability, lest you displease God to Whom belongs all the natural gifts that you have.

Do not think yourself better than others lest, perhaps, you be accounted worse before God Who knows what is in man. Do not take pride in your good deeds, for God's judgments differ from those of men and what pleases them often displeases Him. If there is good in you, see more good in others, so that you may remain humble. It does no harm to esteem yourself less than anyone else, but it is very harmful to think yourself better than even one. The humble live in continuous peace, while in the hearts of the proud are envy and frequent anger.

THE EIGHTH CHAPTER

Shunning Over-Familiarity

Do not open your heart to every man, but discuss your affairs with one who is wise and who fears God. Do not keep company with young people and strangers. Do not fawn upon the rich, and do not be fond of mingling with the great. Associate with the humble and the simple, with the devout and virtuous, and with them speak of edifying things. Be not intimate with any woman, but generally commend all good women to God. Seek only the intimacy of God and of His angels, and avoid the notice of men.

We ought to have charity for all men but familiarity with all is not expedient. Sometimes it happens that a person enjoys a good reputation among those who do not know him, but at the same time is held in slight regard by those who do. Frequently we think we are pleasing others by our presence and we begin rather to displease them by the faults they find in us.

THE NINTH CHAPTER

Obedience and Subjection

It is a very great thing to obey, to live under a superior and not to be one's own master, for it is much safer to be subject than it is to command. Many live in obedience more from necessity than from love. Such become discontented and dejected on the slightest pretext; they will never gain peace of mind unless they subject themselves wholeheartedly for the love of God.

Go where you may, you will find no rest except in humble obedience to the rule of authority. Dreams of happiness expected from change and different places have deceived many.

Everyone, it is true, wishes to do as he pleases and is attracted to those who agree with him. But if God be among us, we must at times give up our opinions for the blessings of peace.

Furthermore, who is so wise that he can have full knowledge of everything? Do not trust too much in your own opinions, but be willing to listen to those of others. If, though your own be good, you accept another's opinion for love of God, you will gain much more merit; for I have often heard that it is safer to listen to advice and take it than to give it. It may happen, too, that while one's own opinion may be good, refusal to agree with others when reason and occasion demand it, is a sign of pride and obstinacy.

THE TENTH CHAPTER

Avoiding Idle Talk

Shun the gossip of men as much as possible, for discussion of worldly affairs, even though sincere, is a great distraction inasmuch as we are quickly ensnared and captivated by vanity.

Many a time I wish that I had held my peace and had not associated with men. Why, indeed, do we converse and gossip among ourselves when we so seldom part without a troubled conscience? We do so because we seek comfort from one another's conversation and wish to ease the mind wearied by diverse thoughts. Hence, we talk and think quite fondly of things we like very much or of things we dislike intensely. But, sad to say, we often talk vainly and to no purpose; for this external pleasure effectively bars inward and divine consolation. Therefore we must watch and pray lest time pass idly.

When the right and opportune moment comes for speaking, say something that will edify.

Bad habits and indifference to spiritual progress do much to remove the guard from the tongue. Devout conversation on spiritual matters, on the contrary, is a great aid to spiritual progress, especially when persons of the same mind and spirit associate together in God.

THE ELEVENTH CHAPTER

Acquiring Peace and Zeal for Perfection

We should enjoy much peace if we did not concern ourselves with what others say and do, for these are no concern of ours. How can a man who meddles in affairs not his own, who seeks strange distractions, and who is little or seldom inwardly recollected, live long in peace?

Blessed are the simple of heart for they shall enjoy peace in abundance.

Why were some of the saints so perfect and so given to contemplation? Because they tried to mortify entirely in themselves all earthly desires, and thus they were able to attach themselves to God with all their heart and freely to concentrate their innermost thoughts.

We are too occupied with our own whims and fancies, too taken up with passing things. Rarely do we completely conquer even one vice, and we are not inflamed with the desire to improve ourselves day by day; hence, we remain cold and indifferent. If we mortified our bodies perfectly and allowed no distractions to enter our minds, we could appreciate divine things and experience something of heavenly contemplation.

The greatest obstacle, indeed, the only obstacle, is that we are not free from passions and lusts, that we do not try to follow the perfect way of the saints. Thus when we encounter some slight difficulty, we are too easily dejected and turn to human consolations. If we tried, however, to stand as brave men in battle, the help of the Lord from heaven would surely sustain us. For He Who gives us the opportunity of fighting for victory, is ready to help those who carry on and trust in His grace.

If we let our progress in religious life depend on the observance of its externals alone, our devotion will quickly come to an end. Let us, then, lay the ax to the root that we may be freed from our passions and thus have peace of mind.

If we were to uproot only one vice each year, we should soon become perfect. The contrary, however, is often the case—we feel that we were better and purer in the first fervor of our conversion than we are after many years in the practice of our faith. Our fervor and progress ought to increase day by day; yet it is now considered noteworthy if a man can retain even a part of his first fervor.

If we did a little violence to ourselves at the start, we should afterwards be able to do all things with ease and joy. It is hard to break old habits, but harder still to go against our will.

If you do not overcome small, trifling things, how will you overcome the more difficult? Resist temptations in the beginning, and unlearn the evil habit lest perhaps, little by little, it lead to a more evil one.

If you but consider what peace a good life will bring to yourself and what joy it will give to others, I think you will be more concerned about your spiritual progress.

THE TWELFTH CHAPTER

The Value of Adversity

It is good for us to have trials and troubles at times, for they often remind us that we are on probation and ought not to hope in any worldly thing. It is good for us sometimes to suffer contradiction, to be misjudged by men even though we do well and mean well. These things help us to be humble and shield us from vainglory. When to all outward appearances men give us no credit, when they do not think well of us, then we are more inclined to seek God Who sees our hearts. Therefore, a man ought to root himself so firmly in God that he will not need the consolations of men.

When a man of good will is afflicted, tempted, and tormented by evil thoughts, he realizes clearly that his greatest need is God, without Whom he can do no good. Saddened by his miseries and sufferings, he laments and prays. He wearies of living longer and wishes for death that he might be dissolved and be with Christ. Then he understands fully that perfect security and complete peace cannot be found on earth.

THE THIRTEENTH CHAPTER

Resisting Temptation

So long as we live in this world we cannot escape suffering and temptation. Whence it is written in Job: "The life of man upon earth is a warfare."[3] Everyone, therefore, must guard against temptation and must watch in prayer lest the devil, who never sleeps but goes about seeking whom he may devour, find occasion to deceive him. No one is so perfect or so holy but he is sometimes tempted; man cannot be altogether free from temptation.

Yet temptations, though troublesome and severe, are often useful to a man, for in them he is humbled, purified, and instructed. The saints all passed through many temptations and trials to profit by them, while those who could not resist became reprobate and fell away. There is no state so holy, no place so secret that temptations and trials will not come. Man is never safe from them as long as he lives, for they come from within us—in sin we were born. When one temptation or trial passes, another comes; we shall always have something to suffer because we have lost the state of original blessedness.

Many people try to escape temptations, only to fall more deeply. We cannot conquer simply by fleeing, but by patience and true humility we become stronger than all our enemies. The man who only shuns temptations outwardly and does not uproot them will make little progress; indeed they will quickly return, more violent than before.

Little by little, in patience and long-suffering you will overcome them, by the help of God rather than by severity and your own rash ways. Often take counsel when tempted; and do not be harsh with others who are tempted, but console them as you yourself would wish to be consoled.

The beginning of all temptation lies in a wavering mind and little trust in God, for as a rudderless ship is driven hither and yon by waves, so a careless and irresolute man is tempted in many ways.

Fire tempers iron and temptation steels the just.

Often we do not know what we can stand, but temptation shows us what we are.

Above all, we must be especially alert against the beginnings of temptation, for the enemy is more easily conquered if he is refused admittance to the mind and is met beyond the threshold when he knocks.

Someone has said very aptly: "Resist the beginnings; remedies come too late, when by long delay the evil has gained strength." First, a mere thought comes to mind, then strong imagination, followed by

---

[3] Job 7:1.

pleasure, evil delight, and consent. Thus, because he is not resisted in the beginning, Satan gains full entry. And the longer a man delays in resisting, so much the weaker does he become each day, while the strength of the enemy grows against him.

Some suffer great temptations in the beginning of their conversion, others toward the end, while some are troubled almost constantly throughout their life. Others, again, are tempted but lightly according to the wisdom and justice of Divine Providence Who weighs the status and merit of each and prepares all for the salvation of His elect.

We should not despair, therefore, when we are tempted, but pray to God the more fervently that He may see fit to help us, for according to the word of Paul, He will make issue with temptation that we may be able to bear it. Let us humble our souls under the hand of God in every trial and temptation for He will save and exalt the humble in spirit.

In temptations and trials the progress of a man is measured; in them opportunity for merit and virtue is made more manifest.

When a man is not troubled it is not hard for him to be fervent and devout, but if he bears up patiently in time of adversity, there is hope for great progress.

Some, guarded against great temptations, are frequently overcome by small ones in order that, humbled by their weakness in small trials, they may not presume on their own strength in great ones.

THE FOURTEENTH CHAPTER

Avoiding Rash Judgment

Turn your attention upon yourself and beware of judging the deeds of other men, for in judging others a man labors vainly, often makes mistakes, and easily sins; whereas, in judging and taking stock of himself he does something that is always profitable.

We frequently judge that things are as we wish them to be, for through personal feeling true perspective is easily lost.

If God were the sole object of our desire, we should not be disturbed so easily by opposition to our opinions. But often something lurks within or happens from without to draw us along with it.

Many, unawares, seek themselves in the things they do. They seem even to enjoy peace of mind when things happen according to their wish and liking, but if otherwise than they desire, they are soon disturbed and saddened. Differences of feeling and opinion often divide friends and acquaintances, even those who are religious and devout.

An old habit is hard to break, and no one is willing to be led farther than he can see.

If you rely more upon your intelligence or industry than upon the virtue of submission to Jesus Christ, you will hardly, and in any case slowly, become an enlightened man. God wants us to be completely subject to Him and, through ardent love, to rise above all human wisdom.

THE FIFTEENTH CHAPTER

Works Done in Charity

Never do evil for anything in the world, or for the love of any man. For one who is in need, however, a good work may at times be purposely left undone or changed for a better one. This is not the omission of a good deed but rather its improvement.

Without charity external work is of no value, but anything done in charity, be it ever so small and trivial, is entirely fruitful inasmuch as God weighs the love with which a man acts rather than the deed itself.

He does much who loves much. He does much who does a thing well. He does well who serves the common good rather than his own interests.

Now, that which seems to be charity is oftentimes really sensuality, for man's own inclination, his own will, his hope of reward, and his self-interest, are motives seldom absent. On the contrary, he who has true and perfect charity seeks self in nothing, but searches all things for the glory of God. Moreover, he envies no man, because he desires no personal pleasure nor does he wish to rejoice in himself; rather he desires the greater glory of God above all things. He ascribes to man nothing that is good but attributes it wholly to God from Whom all things proceed as from a fountain, and in Whom all the blessed shall rest as their last end and fruition.

If man had but a spark of true charity he would surely sense that all the things of earth are full of vanity!

THE SIXTEENTH CHAPTER

Bearing with the Faults of Others

Until God ordains otherwise, a man ought to bear patiently whatever he cannot correct in himself and in others. Consider it better thus—perhaps to try your patience and to test you, for without such patience and trial your merits are of little account. Nevertheless, under such difficulties you should pray that God will consent to help you bear them calmly.

If, after being admonished once or twice, a person does not amend, do not argue with him but commit the whole matter to God that His will and honor may be furthered in all His servants, for God knows well how to turn evil to good. Try to bear patiently with the defects and infirmities of others, whatever they may be, because you also have many a fault which others must endure.

If you cannot make yourself what you would wish to be, how can you bend others to your will? We want them to be perfect, yet we do not correct our own faults. We wish them to be severely corrected, yet we will not correct ourselves. Their great liberty displeases us, yet we would not be denied what we ask. We would have them bound by laws, yet we will allow ourselves to be restrained in nothing. Hence, it is clear how seldom we think of others as we do of ourselves.

If all were perfect, what should we have to suffer from others for God's sake? But God has so ordained, that we may learn to bear with one another's burdens, for there is no man without fault, no man without burden, no man sufficient to himself nor wise enough. Hence we must support one another, console one another, mutually help, counsel, and advise, for the measure of every man's virtue is best revealed in time of adversity—adversity that does not weaken a man but rather shows what he is.

THE SEVENTEENTH CHAPTER

Monastic Life

If you wish peace and concord with others, you must learn to break your will in many things. To live in monasteries or religious communities, to remain there without complaint, and to persevere faithfully till death is no small matter. Blessed indeed is he who there lives a good life and there ends his days in happiness.

If you would persevere in seeking perfection, you must consider yourself a pilgrim, an exile on earth. If you would become a religious, you must be content to seem a fool for the sake of Christ. Habit and tonsure change a man but little; it is the change of life, the complete mortification of passions that endow a true religious.

He who seeks anything but God alone and the salvation of his soul will find only trouble and grief, and he who does not try to become the least, the servant of all, cannot remain at peace for long.

You have come to serve, not to rule. You must understand, too, that you have been called to suffer and to work, not to idle and gossip away your time. Here men are tried as gold in a furnace. Here no man can remain unless he desires with all his heart to humble himself before God.

THE EIGHTEENTH CHAPTER

The Example Set Us by the Holy Fathers

Consider the lively examples set us by the saints, who possessed the light of true perfection and religion, and you will see how little, how nearly nothing, we do. What, alas, is our life, compared with theirs? The saints and friends of Christ served the Lord in hunger and thirst, in cold and nakedness, in work and fatigue, in vigils and fasts, in prayers and holy meditations, in persecutions and many afflictions. How many and severe were the trials they suffered—the Apostles, martyrs, confessors, virgins, and all the rest who willed to follow in the footsteps of Christ! They hated their lives on earth that they might have life in eternity.

How strict and detached were the lives the holy hermits led in the desert! What long and grave temptations they suffered! How often were they beset by the enemy! What frequent and ardent prayers they offered to God! What rigorous fasts they observed! How great their zeal and their love for spiritual perfection! How brave the fight they waged to master their evil habits! What pure and straightforward purpose they showed toward God! By day they labored and by night they spent themselves in long prayers. Even at work they did not cease from mental prayer. They used all their time profitably; every hour seemed too short for serving God, and in the great sweetness of contemplation, they forgot even their bodily needs.

They renounced all riches, dignities, honors, friends, and associates. They desired nothing of the world. They scarcely allowed themselves the necessities of life, and the service of the body, even when necessary, was irksome to them. They were poor in earthly things but rich in grace and virtue. Outwardly destitute, inwardly they were full of grace and divine consolation. Strangers to the world, they were close and intimate friends of God. To themselves they seemed as nothing, and they were despised by the world, but in the eyes of God they were precious and beloved. They lived in true humility and simple obedience; they walked in charity and patience, making progress daily on the pathway of spiritual life and obtaining great favor with God.

They were given as an example for all religious, and their power to stimulate us to perfection ought to be greater than that of the lukewarm to tempt us to laxity.

How great was the fervor of all religious in the beginning of their holy institution! How great their devotion in prayer and their rivalry for virtue! What splendid discipline flourished among them! What great reverence and obedience in all things under the rule of a superior! The footsteps they left behind still bear witness that they indeed were holy and perfect men who fought bravely and conquered the world.

Today, he who is not a transgressor and who can bear patiently the duties which he has taken upon himself is considered great. How lukewarm and negligent we are! We lose our original fervor very quickly and we even become weary of life from laziness! Do not you, who have seen so many examples of the devout, fall asleep in the pursuit of virtue!

THE NINETEENTH CHAPTER

The Practices of a Good Religious

The life of a good religious ought to abound in every virtue so that he is interiorly what to others he appears to be. With good reason there ought to be much more within than appears on the outside, for He who sees within is God, Whom we ought to reverence most highly wherever we are and in Whose sight we ought to walk pure as the angels.

Each day we ought to renew our resolutions and arouse ourselves to fervor as though it were the first day of our religious life. We ought to say: "Help me, O Lord God, in my good resolution and in

Your holy service. Grant me now, this very day, to begin perfectly, for thus far I have done nothing."

As our intention is, so will be our progress; and he who desires perfection must be very diligent. If the strong-willed man fails frequently, what of the man who makes up his mind seldom or half-heartedly? Many are the ways of failing in our resolutions; even a slight omission of religious practice entails a loss of some kind.

Just men depend on the grace of God rather than on their own wisdom in keeping their resolutions. In Him they confide every undertaking, for man, indeed, proposes but God disposes, and God's way is not man's. If an habitual exercise is sometimes omitted out of piety or in the interests of another, it can easily be resumed later. But if it be abandoned carelessly, through weariness or neglect, then the fault is great and will prove hurtful. Much as we try, we still fail too easily in many things. Yet we must always have some fixed purpose, especially against things which beset us the most. Our outward and inward lives alike must be closely watched and well ordered, for both are important to perfection.

If you cannot recollect yourself continuously, do so once a day at least, in the morning or in the evening. In the morning make a resolution and in the evening examine yourself on what you have said this day, what you have done and thought, for in these things perhaps you have often offended God and those about you.

Arm yourself like a man against the devil's assaults. Curb your appetite and you will more easily curb every inclination of the flesh. Never be completely unoccupied, but read or write or pray or meditate or do something for the common good. Bodily discipline, however, must be undertaken with discretion and is not to be practiced indiscriminately by everyone.

Devotions not common to all are not to be displayed in public, for such personal things are better performed in private. Furthermore, beware of indifference to community prayer through love of your own devotions. If, however, after doing completely and faithfully all you are bound and commanded to do, you then have leisure, use it as personal piety suggests.

Not everyone can have the same devotion. One exactly suits this person, another that. Different exercises, likewise, are suitable for different times, some for feast days and some again for weekdays. In time of temptation we need certain devotions. For days of rest and peace we need others. Some are suitable when we are sad, others when we are joyful in the Lord.

About the time of the principal feasts good devotions ought to be renewed and the intercession of the saints more fervently implored. From one feast day to the next we ought to fix our purpose as though we were then to pass from this world and come to the eternal holyday.

During holy seasons, finally, we ought to prepare ourselves carefully, to live holier lives, and to observe each rule more strictly, as though we were soon to receive from God the reward of our labors. If this end be deferred, let us believe that we are not well prepared and that we are not yet worthy of the great glory that shall in due time be revealed to us. Let us try, meanwhile, to prepare ourselves better for death.

"Blessed is the servant," says Christ, "whom his master, when he cometh, shall find watching. Amen I say to you: he shall make him ruler over all his goods."[4]

THE TWENTIETH CHAPTER

The Love of Solitude and Silence

Seek a suitable time for leisure and meditate often on the favors of God. Leave curiosities alone. Read such matters as bring sorrow to the heart rather than occupation to the mind. If you withdraw yourself from unnecessary talking and idle running about, from listening to gossip and rumors, you will find enough time that is suitable for holy meditation.

Very many great saints avoided the company of men wherever possible and chose to serve God in retirement. "As often as I have been among men," said one writer, "I have returned less a man." We often find this to be true when we take part in long conversations. It is easier to be silent altogether than not to speak too much. To stay at home is easier than to be sufficiently on guard while away. Anyone, then, who aims to live the inner and spiritual life must go apart, with Jesus, from the crowd.

No man appears in safety before the public eye unless he first relishes obscurity. No man is safe in speaking unless he loves to be silent. No man rules safely unless he is willing to be ruled. No man commands safely unless he has learned well how to obey. No man

---

[4] Luke 12:43, 44.

rejoices safely unless he has within him the testimony of a good conscience.

More than this, the security of the saints was always enveloped in the fear of God, nor were they less cautious and humble because they were conspicuous for great virtues and graces. The security of the wicked, on the contrary, springs from pride and presumption, and will end in their own deception.

Never promise yourself security in this life, even though you seem to be a good religious, or a devout hermit. It happens very often that those whom men esteem highly are more seriously endangered by their own excessive confidence. Hence, for many it is better not to be too free from temptations, but often to be tried lest they become too secure, too filled with pride, or even too eager to fall back upon external comforts.

If only a man would never seek passing joys or entangle himself with worldly affairs, what a good conscience he would have. What great peace and tranquillity would be his, if he cut himself off from all empty care and thought only of things divine, things helpful to his soul, and put all his trust in God.

No man deserves the consolation of heaven unless he persistently arouses himself to holy contrition. If you desire true sorrow of heart, seek the privacy of your cell and shut out the uproar of the world, as it is written: "In your chamber bewail your sins." There you will find what too often you lose abroad.

Your cell will become dear to you if you remain in it, but if you do not, it will become wearisome. If in the beginning of your religious life, you live within your cell and keep to it, it will soon become a special friend and a very great comfort.

In silence and quiet the devout soul advances in virtue and learns the hidden truths of Scripture. There she finds a flood of tears with which to bathe and cleanse herself nightly, that she may become the more intimate with her Creator the farther she withdraws from all the tumult of the world. For God and His holy angels will draw near to him who withdraws from friends and acquaintances.

It is better for a man to be obscure and to attend to his salvation than to neglect it and work miracles. It is praiseworthy for a religious seldom to go abroad, to flee the sight of men and have no wish to see them.

Why wish to see what you are not permitted to have? "The world passes away and the concupiscence thereof." Sensual craving sometimes entices you to wander around, but when the moment is past, what do you bring back with you save a disturbed conscience and heavy heart? A happy going often leads to a sad return, a merry evening to a mournful dawn. Thus, all carnal joy begins sweetly but in the end brings remorse and death.

What can you find elsewhere that you cannot find here in your cell? Behold heaven and earth and all the elements, for of these all things are made. What can you see anywhere under the sun that will remain long? Perhaps you think you will completely satisfy yourself, but you cannot do so, for if you should see all existing things, what would they be but an empty vision?

Raise your eyes to God in heaven and pray because of your sins and shortcomings. Leave vanity to the vain. Set yourself to the things which God has commanded you to do. Close the door upon yourself and call to you Jesus, your Beloved. Remain with Him in your cell, for nowhere else will you find such peace. If you had not left it, and had not listened to idle gossip, you would have remained in greater peace. But since you love, sometimes, to hear news, it is only right that you should suffer sorrow of heart from it.

THE TWENTY-FIRST CHAPTER

Sorrow of Heart

If you wish to make progress in virtue, live in the fear of the Lord, do not look for too much freedom, discipline your senses, and shun inane silliness. Sorrow opens the door to many a blessing which dissoluteness usually destroys.

It is a wonder that any man who considers and meditates on his exiled state and the many dangers to his soul, can ever be perfectly happy in this life. Lighthearted and heedless of our defects, we do not feel the real sorrows of our souls, but often indulge in empty laughter when we have good reason to weep. No liberty is true and no joy is genuine unless it is founded in the fear of the Lord and a good conscience.

Happy is the man who can throw off the weight of every care and recollect himself in holy contrition. Happy is the man who casts from him all that can stain or burden his conscience.

Fight like a man. Habit is overcome by habit.

If you leave men alone, they will leave you alone to do what you have to do. Do not busy yourself about the affairs of others and do not become entangled in the business of your superiors. Keep an eye primarily on yourself and admonish yourself instead of your friends.

If you do not enjoy the favor of men, do not let it sadden you; but consider it a serious matter if you do not conduct yourself as well or as carefully as is becoming for a servant of God and a devout religious.

It is often better and safer for us to have few consolations in this life, especially comforts of the body. Yet if we do not have divine consolation or experience it rarely, it is our own fault because we seek no sorrow of heart and do not forsake vain outward satisfaction.

Consider yourself unworthy of divine solace and deserving rather of much tribulation. When a man is perfectly contrite, the whole world is bitter and wearisome to him.

A good man always finds enough over which to mourn and weep; whether he thinks of himself or of his neighbor he knows that no one lives here without suffering, and the closer he examines himself the more he grieves.

The sins and vices in which we are so entangled that we can rarely apply ourselves to the contemplation of heaven are matters for just sorrow and inner remorse.

I do not doubt that you would correct yourself more earnestly if you would think more of an early death than of a long life. And if you pondered in your heart the future pains of hell or of purgatory, I believe you would willingly endure labor and trouble and would fear no hardship. But since these thoughts never pierce the heart and since we are enamored of flattering pleasure, we remain very cold and indifferent. Our wretched body complains so easily because our soul is altogether too lifeless.

Pray humbly to the Lord, therefore, that He may give you the spirit of contrition and say with the Prophet: "Feed me, Lord, with the bread of mourning and give me to drink of tears in full measure."[5]

THE TWENTY-SECOND CHAPTER

Thoughts on the Misery of Man

Wherever you are, wherever you go, you are miserable unless you turn to God. So why be dismayed when things do not happen as

---

[5] Ps. 79:6.

you wish and desire? Is there anyone who has everything as he wishes? No—neither I, nor you, nor any man on earth. There is no one in the world, be he Pope or king, who does not suffer trial and anguish.

Who is the better off then? Surely, it is the man who will suffer something for God. Many unstable and weak-minded people say: "See how well that man lives, how rich, how great he is, how powerful and mighty." But you must lift up your eyes to the riches of heaven and realize that the material goods of which they speak are nothing. These things are uncertain and very burdensome because they are never possessed without anxiety and fear. Man's happiness does not consist in the possession of abundant goods; a very little is enough.

Living on earth is truly a misery. The more a man desires spiritual life, the more bitter the present becomes to him, because he understands better and sees more clearly the defects, the corruption of human nature. To eat and drink, to watch and sleep, to rest, to labor, and to be bound by other human necessities is certainly a great misery and affliction to the devout man who would gladly be released from them and be free from all sin. Truly, the inner man is greatly burdened in this world by the necessities of the body, and for this reason the Prophet prayed that he might be as free from them as possible, when he said: "From my necessities, O Lord, deliver me."[6]

But woe to those who know not their own misery, and greater woe to those who love this miserable and corruptible life. Some, indeed, can scarcely procure its necessities either by work or by begging; yet they love it so much that, if they could live here always, they would care nothing for the kingdom of God.

How foolish and faithless of heart are those who are so engrossed in earthly things as to relish nothing but what is carnal! Miserable men indeed, for in the end they will see to their sorrow how cheap and worthless was the thing they loved.

The saints of God and all devout friends of Christ did not look to what pleases the body nor to the things that are popular from time to time. Their whole hope and aim centered on the everlasting good. Their whole desire pointed upward to the lasting and invisible realm, lest the love of what is visible drag them down to lower things.

Do not lose heart, then, my brother, in pursuing your spiritual life. There is yet time, and your hour is not past. Why delay your

---

[6] Ps. 24:17.

purpose? Arise! Begin at once and say: "Now is the time to act, now is the time to fight, now is the proper time to amend."

When you are troubled and afflicted, that is the time to gain merit. You must pass through water and fire before coming to rest. Unless you do violence to yourself you will not overcome vice.

So long as we live in this fragile body, we can neither be free from sin nor live without weariness and sorrow. Gladly would we rest from all misery, but in losing innocence through sin we also lost true blessedness. Therefore, we must have patience and await the mercy of God until this iniquity passes, until mortality is swallowed up in life.

How great is the frailty of human nature which is ever prone to evil! Today you confess your sins and tomorrow you again commit the sins which you confessed. One moment you resolve to be careful, and yet after an hour you act as though you had made no resolution.

We have cause, therefore, because of our frailty and feebleness, to humble ourselves and never think anything great of ourselves. Through neglect we may quickly lose that which by God's grace we have acquired only through long, hard labor. What, eventually, will become of us who so quickly grow lukewarm? Woe to us if we presume to rest in peace and security when actually there is no true holiness in our lives. It would be beneficial for us, like good novices, to be instructed once more in the principles of a good life, to see if there be hope of amendment and greater spiritual progress in the future.

THE TWENTY-THIRD CHAPTER

Thoughts on Death

Very soon your life here will end; consider, then, what may be in store for you elsewhere. Today we live; tomorrow we die and are quickly forgotten. Oh, the dullness and hardness of a heart which looks only to the present instead of preparing for that which is to come!

Therefore, in every deed and every thought, act as though you were to die this very day. If you had a good conscience you would not fear death very much. It is better to avoid sin than to fear death. If you are not prepared today, how will you be prepared tomorrow? Tomorrow is an uncertain day; how do you know you will have a tomorrow?

What good is it to live a long life when we amend that life so little? Indeed, a long life does not always benefit us, but on the contrary, frequently adds to our guilt. Would that in this world we had lived well throughout one single day. Many count up the years they have spent in religion but find their lives made little holier. If it is so terrifying to die, it is nevertheless possible that to live longer is more dangerous. Blessed is he who keeps the moment of death ever before his eyes and prepares for it every day.

If you have ever seen a man die, remember that you, too, must go the same way. In the morning consider that you may not live till evening, and when evening comes do not dare to promise yourself the dawn. Be always ready, therefore, and so live that death will never take you unprepared. Many die suddenly and unexpectedly, for in the unexpected hour the Son of God will come. When that last moment arrives you will begin to have a quite different opinion of the life that is now entirely past and you will regret very much that you were so careless and remiss.

How happy and prudent is he who tries now in life to be what he wants to be found in death. Perfect contempt of the world, a lively desire to advance in virtue, a love for discipline, the works of penance, readiness to obey, self-denial, and the endurance of every hardship for the love of Christ, these will give a man great expectations of a happy death.

You can do many good works when in good health; what can you do when you are ill? Few are made better by sickness. Likewise they who undertake many pilgrimages seldom become holy.

Do not put your trust in friends and relatives, and do not put off the care of your soul till later, for men will forget you more quickly than you think. It is better to provide now, in time, and send some good account ahead of you than to rely on the help of others. If you do not care for your own welfare now, who will care when you are gone?

The present is very precious; these are the days of salvation; now is the acceptable time. How sad that you do not spend the time in which you might purchase everlasting life in a better way. The time will come when you will want just one day, just one hour in which to make amends, and do you know whether you will obtain it?

See, then, dearly beloved, the great danger from which you can free yourself and the great fear from which you can be saved, if only you will always be wary and mindful of death. Try to live now in such a manner that at the moment of death you may be glad rather than fearful. Learn to die to the world now, that then you may begin to live with Christ. Learn to spurn all things now, that then you may freely go to Him. Chastise your body in penance now, that then you may have the confidence born of certainty.

Ah, foolish man, why do you plan to live long when you are not sure of living even a day? How many have been deceived and suddenly snatched away! How often have you heard of persons being killed by drownings, by fatal falls from high places, of persons dying at meals, at play, in fires, by the sword, in pestilence, or at the hands of robbers! Death is the end of everyone and the life of man quickly passes away like a shadow.

Who will remember you when you are dead? Who will pray for you? Do now, beloved, what you can, because you do not know when you will die, nor what your fate will be after death. Gather for yourself the riches of immortality while you have time. Think of nothing but your salvation. Care only for the things of God. Make friends for yourself now by honoring the saints of God, by imitating their actions, so that when you depart this life they may receive you into everlasting dwellings.

Keep yourself as a stranger here on earth, a pilgrim whom its affairs do not concern at all. Keep your heart free and raise it up to God, for you have not here a lasting home. To Him direct your daily prayers, your sighs and tears, that your soul may merit after death to pass in happiness to the Lord.

THE TWENTY-FOURTH CHAPTER

Judgment and the Punishment of Sin

In all things consider the end; how you shall stand before the strict Judge from Whom nothing is hidden and Who will pronounce judgment in all justice, accepting neither bribes nor excuses. And you, miserable and wretched sinner, who fear even the countenance of an angry man, what answer will you make to the God Who knows all your sins? Why do you not provide for yourself against the day of judgment when no man can be excused or defended by another because each will have enough to do to answer for himself? In this life your work is profitable, your tears acceptable, your sighs audible, your sorrow satisfying and purifying.

The patient man goes through a great and salutary purgatory when he grieves more over the malice of one who harms him than for his own injury; when he prays readily for his enemies and forgives offenses from his heart; when he does not hesitate to ask pardon of others; when he is more easily moved to pity than to anger; when he does frequent violence to himself and tries to bring the body into complete subjection to the spirit.

It is better to atone for sin now and to cut away vices than to keep them for purgation in the hereafter. In truth, we deceive ourselves by our ill-advised love of the flesh. What will that fire feed upon but our sins? The more we spare ourselves now and the more we satisfy the flesh, the harder will the reckoning be and the more we keep for the burning.

For a man will be more grievously punished in the things in which he has sinned. There the lazy will be driven with burning prongs, and gluttons tormented with unspeakable hunger and thirst; the wanton and lust-loving will be bathed in burning pitch and foul brimstone; the envious will howl in their grief like mad dogs.

Every vice will have its own proper punishment. The proud will be faced with every confusion and the avaricious pinched with the most abject want. One hour of suffering there will be more bitter than a hundred years of the most severe penance here. In this life men sometimes rest from work and enjoy the comfort of friends, but the damned have no rest or consolation.

You must, therefore, take care and repent of your sins now so that on the day of judgment you may rest secure with the blessed. For on that day the just will stand firm against those who tortured and oppressed them, and he who now submits humbly to the judgment of men will arise to pass judgment upon them. The poor and humble will have great confidence, while the proud will be struck with fear. He who learned to be a fool in this world and to be scorned for Christ will then appear to have been wise.

In that day every trial borne in patience will be pleasing and the voice of iniquity will be stilled; the devout will be glad; the irreligious will mourn; and the mortified body will rejoice far more than if it had been pampered with every pleasure. Then the cheap garment will shine with splendor and the rich one become faded and worn; the poor cottage will be more praised than the gilded palace. In that day persevering patience will count more than all the power in this world; simple obedience will be exalted above all worldly cleverness; a good and clean conscience will gladden the heart of man far more than the philosophy of the learned; and contempt for riches will be of more weight than every treasure on earth.

Then you will find more consolation in having prayed devoutly than in having fared daintily; you will be happy that you preferred silence to prolonged gossip.

Then holy works will be of greater value than many fair words; strictness of life and hard penances will be more pleasing than all earthly delights.

Learn, then, to suffer little things now that you may not have to suffer greater ones in eternity. Prove here what you can bear hereafter. If you can suffer only a little now, how will you be able to endure eternal torment? If a little suffering makes you impatient now, what will hell fire do? In truth, you cannot have two joys: you cannot taste the pleasures of this world and afterward reign with Christ.

If your life to this moment had been full of honors and pleasures, what good would it do if at this instant you should die? All is vanity, therefore, except to love God and to serve Him alone.

He who loves God with all his heart does not fear death or punishment or judgment or hell, because perfect love assures access to God.

It is no wonder that he who still delights in sin fears death and judgment.

It is good, however, that even if love does not as yet restrain you from evil, at least the fear of hell does. The man who casts aside the fear of God cannot continue long in goodness but will quickly fall into the snares of the devil.

THE TWENTY-FIFTH CHAPTER

Zeal in Amending Our Lives

Be watchful and diligent in God's service and often think of why you left the world and came here. Was it not that you might live for God and become a spiritual man? Strive earnestly for perfection, then, because in a short time you will receive the reward of your labor, and neither fear nor sorrow shall come upon you at the hour of death.

Labor a little now, and soon you shall find great rest, in truth, eternal joy; for if you continue faithful and diligent in doing, God will undoubtedly be faithful and generous in rewarding. Continue to have reasonable hope of gaining salvation, but do not act as though you were certain of it lest you grow indolent and proud.

One day when a certain man who wavered often and anxiously between hope and fear was struck with sadness, he knelt in humble prayer before the altar of a church. While meditating on these things, he said: "Oh if I but knew whether I should persevere to the end!" Instantly he heard within the divine answer: "If you knew this, what would you do? Do now what you would do then and you will be quite secure." Immediately consoled and comforted, he resigned himself to the divine will and the anxious uncertainty ceased. His curiosity no longer sought to know what the future held for him, and he tried instead to find the perfect, the acceptable will of God in the beginning and end of every good work.

"Trust thou in the Lord and do good," says the Prophet; "dwell in the land and thou shalt feed on its riches."[7]

There is one thing that keeps many from zealously improving their lives, that is, dread of the difficulty, the toil of battle. Certainly they who try manfully to overcome the most difficult and unpleasant obstacles far outstrip others in the pursuit of virtue. A man makes the most progress and merits the most grace precisely in those matters wherein he gains the greatest victories over self and most mortifies his will. True, each one has his own difficulties to meet and conquer, but a diligent and sincere man will make greater progress even though he have more passions than one who is more even-tempered but less concerned about virtue.

Two things particularly further improvement—to withdraw oneself forcibly from those vices to which nature is viciously inclined, and to work fervently for those graces which are most needed.

Study also to guard against and to overcome the faults which in others very frequently displease you. Make the best of every opportunity, so that if you see or hear good example you may be moved to imitate it. On the other hand, take care lest you be guilty of those things which you consider reprehensible, or if you have ever been guilty of them, try to correct yourself as soon as possible. As you see others, so they see you.

How pleasant and sweet to behold brethren fervent and devout, well mannered and disciplined! How sad and painful to see them wandering in dissolution, not practicing the things to which they are

---

[7] Ps. 36:3.

called! How hurtful it is to neglect the purpose of their vocation and to attend to what is not their business!

Remember the purpose you have undertaken, and keep in mind the image of the Crucified. Even though you may have walked for many years on the pathway to God, you may well be ashamed if, with the image of Christ before you, you do not try to make yourself still more like Him.

The religious who concerns himself intently and devoutly with our Lord's most holy life and passion will find there an abundance of all things useful and necessary for him. He need not seek for anything better than Jesus.

If the Crucified should come to our hearts, how quickly and abundantly we would learn!

A fervent religious accepts all the things that are commanded him and does them well, but a negligent and lukewarm religious has trial upon trial, and suffers anguish from every side because he has no consolation within and is forbidden to seek it from without. The religious who does not live up to his rule exposes himself to dreadful ruin, and he who wishes to be more free and untrammeled will always be in trouble, for something or other will always displease him.

How do so many other religious who are confined in cloistered discipline get along? They seldom go out, they live in contemplation, their food is poor, their clothing coarse, they work hard, they speak but little, keep long vigils, rise early, pray much, read frequently, and subject themselves to all sorts of discipline. Think of the Carthusians and the Cistercians, the monks and nuns of different orders, how every night they rise to sing praise to the Lord. It were a shame that you should grow lazy in such holy service when so many religious have already begun to rejoice in God.

If there were nothing else to do but praise the Lord God with all your heart and voice, if you had never to eat, or drink, or sleep, but could praise God always and occupy yourself solely with spiritual pursuits, how much happier you would be than you are now, a slave to every necessity of the body! Would that there were no such needs, but only the spiritual refreshments of the soul which, sad to say, we taste too seldom!

When a man reaches a point where he seeks no solace from any creature, then he begins to relish God perfectly. Then also he will be content no matter what may happen to him. He will neither rejoice over great things nor grieve over small ones, but will place himself entirely and confidently in the hands of God, Who for him is all in all, to Whom nothing ever perishes or dies, for Whom all things live, and Whom they serve as He desires.

Always remember your end and do not forget that lost time never returns. Without care and diligence you will never acquire virtue. When you begin to grow lukewarm, you are falling into the beginning of evil; but if you give yourself to fervor, you will find peace and will experience less hardship because of God's grace and the love of virtue.

A fervent and diligent man is ready for all things. It is greater work to resist vices and passions than to sweat in physical toil. He who does not overcome small faults, shall fall little by little into greater ones.

If you have spent the day profitably, you will always be happy at eventide. Watch over yourself, arouse yourself, warn yourself, and regardless of what becomes of others, do not neglect yourself. The more violence you do to yourself, the more progress you will make.

EVERYMAN

Anonymous

In the Medieval period, miracle and morality plays were performed on holidays and at festivals, often by guild craftsmen, sometimes by professional actors, and were designed to provide moral instruction, with their principal characters often vivid personifications of virtue and vice. Perhaps the best known morality play was the anonymous Everyman, *which was originally written in Middle English and which dates from the late fifteenth-century Tudor period. The central character of* Everyman, *who represents all mankind, is summoned by Death, and must face final judgment on the strength of his good deeds. Reprinted here is the complete brief text of* Everyman.

CHARACTERS

EVERYMAN	STRENGTH
GOD: ADONAI	DISCRETION
DEATH	FIVE-WITS
MESSENGER	BEAUTY
FELLOWSHIP	KNOWLEDGE
COUSIN	CONFESSION
KINDRED	ANGEL
GOODS	DOCTOR
GOOD-DEEDS	

HERE BEGINNETH A TREATISE HOW THE HIGH FATHER OF HEAVEN
    SENDETH DEATH TO SUMMON EVERY CREATURE TO COME AND
    GIVE ACCOUNT OF THEIR LIVES IN THIS WORLD AND IS IN
    MANNER OF A MORAL PLAY.

Messenger.   I pray you all give your audience,
                And hear this matter with reverence,
                By figure a moral play—
                The *Summoning of Everyman* called it is,
                That of our lives and ending shows
                How transitory we be all day.
                This matter is wondrous precious,
                But the intent of it is more gracious,
                And sweet to bear away.
                The story saith,—Man, in the beginning,
                Look well, and take good heed to the ending,
                Be you never so gay!
                Ye think sin in the beginning full sweet,
                Which in the end causeth thy soul to weep,
                When the body lieth in clay.
                Here shall you see how *Fellowship* and *Jollity,*
                Both *Strength, Pleasure,* and *Beauty,*
                Will fade from thee as flower in May.
                For ye shall hear, how our heaven king
                Calleth *Everyman* to a general reckoning:
                Give audience, and hear what he doth say.
God.   I perceive here in my majesty,
                How that all creatures be to me unkind,
                Living without dread in worldly prosperity:
                Of ghostly sight the people be so blind,
                Drowned in sin, they know me not for their God;
                In worldly riches is all their mind,
                They fear not my rightwiseness, the sharp rod;
                My law that I shewed, when I for them died,
                They forget clean, and shedding of my blood red;
                I hanged between two, it cannot be denied;
                To get them life I suffered to be dead;
                I healed their feet, with thorns hurt was my head:
                I could do no more than I did truly,
                And now I see the people do clean forsake me.
                They use the seven deadly sins damnable;

As pride, covetise, wrath, and lechery,
Now in the world be made commendable;
And thus they leave of angels the heavenly company;
Everyman liveth so after his own pleasure,
And yet of their life they be nothing sure:
I see the more that I them forbear
The worse they be from year to year;
All that liveth appaireth[1] fast,
Therefore I will in all the haste
Have a reckoning of Everyman's person
For and[2] I leave the people thus alone
In their life and wicked tempests,
Verily they will become much worse than beasts;
For now one would by envy another up eat;
Charity they all do clean forget.
I hoped well that Everyman
In my glory should make his mansion,
And thereto I had them all elect;
But now I see, like traitors deject,
They thank me not for the pleasure that I to them meant,
Nor yet for their being that I them have lent;
I proffered the people great multitude of mercy,
And few there be that asketh it heartily;
They be so cumbered with worldly riches,
That needs on them I must do justice,
On Everyman living without fear.
Where art thou, *Death,* thou mighty messenger?

Death. Almighty God, I am here at your will,
Your commandment to fulfil.

God. Go thou to *Everyman,*
And show him in my name
A pilgrimage he must on him take,
Which he in no wise may escape;
And that he bring with him a sure reckoning
Without delay or any tarrying.

Death. Lord, I will in the world go run over all,
And cruelly outsearch both great and small;
Every man will I beset that liveth beastly

---

[1] *appaireth*] is impaired, degenerates.
[2] *and*] if.

Out of God's laws, and dreadeth not folly:
He that loveth riches I will strike with my dart,
His sight to blind, and from heaven to depart,
Except that alms be his good friend,
In hell for to dwell, world without end.
Lo, yonder I see *Everyman* walking;
Full little he thinketh on my coming;
His mind is on fleshly lusts and his treasure,
And great pain it shall cause him to endure
Before the Lord Heaven King.
Everyman, stand still; whither art thou going
Thus gaily? Hast thou thy Maker forget?

Everyman.   Why askst thou?
Wouldest thou wete?[3]

Death.   Yea, sir, I will show you;
In great haste I am sent to thee
From God out of his majesty.

Everyman.   What, sent to me?

Death.   Yea, certainly.
Though thou have forget him here,
He thinketh on thee in the heavenly sphere,
As, or[4] we depart, thou shalt know.

Everyman.   What desireth God of me?

Death.   That shall I show thee;
A reckoning he will needs have
Without any longer respite.

Everyman.   To give a reckoning longer leisure I crave;
This blind[5] matter troubleth my wit.

Death.   On thee thou must take a long journey:
Therefore thy book of count with thee thou bring;
For turn again thou can not by no way,
And look thou be sure of thy reckoning:
For before God thou shalt answer, and show
Thy many bad deeds and good but a few;
How thou hast spent thy life, and in what wise,
Before the chief lord of paradise.

---

[3] *wete*] wit, i.e., know.

[4] *or*] ere, before.

[5] *blind*] dark, obscure.

Have ado that we were in that way,[6]
For, wete thou well, thou shalt make none attournay.[7]

Everyman.   Full unready I am such reckoning to give.
I know thee not: what messenger art thou?

Death.   I am *Death,* that no man dreadeth.
For every man I rest and no man spareth;
For it is God's commandment
That all to me should be obedient.

Everyman.   O *Death,* thou comest when I had thee least in mind;
In thy power it lieth me to save,
Yet of my good will I give thee, if ye will be kind,
Yea, a thousand pound shalt thou have,
And defer this matter till another day.

Death.   *Everyman,* it may not be by no way;
I set not by gold, silver, nor riches,
Ne[8] by pope, emperor, king, duke, ne princes.
For and I would receive gifts great,
All the world I might get;
But my custom is clean contrary.
I give thee no respite: come hence, and not tarry.

Everyman.   Alas, shall I have no longer respite?
I may say *Death* giveth no warning:
To think on thee, it maketh my heart sick,
For all unready is my book of reckoning.
But twelve year and I might have abiding,
My counting book I would make so clear,
That my reckoning I should not need to fear.
Wherefore, *Death,* I pray thee, for God's mercy,
Spare me till I be provided of remedy.

Death.   Thee availeth not to cry, weep, and pray:
But haste thee lightly that you were gone the journey,
And prove thy friends if thou can.
For, wete thou well, the tide abideth no man,
And in the world each living creature
For *Adam's* sin must die of nature.

Everyman.   *Death,* if I should this pilgrimage take,
And my reckoning surely make,

---

[6] *Have ado . . . way*] [Let's] get to the business of proceeding on our way.
[7] *thou shalt . . . attournay*] you cannot make anyone your mediator.
[8] *Ne*] Nor.

Show me, for saint *charity*,
Should I not come again shortly?

Death.   No, *Everyman*; and thou be once there,
Thou mayst never more come here,
Trust me verily.

Everyman.   O gracious God, in the high seat celestial,
Have mercy on me in this most need;
Shall I have no company from this vale terrestrial
Of mine acquaintance that way me to lead?

Death.   Yea, if any be so hardy,
That would go with thee and bear thee company.
Hie[9] thee that you were gone to God's magnificence,
Thy reckoning to give before his presence.
What, weenest[10] thou thy life is given thee,
And thy worldly goods also?

Everyman.   I had wend so, verily.

Death.   Nay, nay; it was but lent thee;
For as soon as thou art go,
Another awhile shall have it, and then go therefro
Even as thou hast done.
Everyman, thou art mad; thou hast thy wits five,[11]
And here on earth will not amend thy life,
For suddenly I do come.

Everyman.   O wretched caitiff, whither shall I flee,
That I might scape this endless sorrow!
Now, gentle *Death,* spare me till to-morrow,
That I may amend me
With good advisement.

Death.   Nay, thereto I will not consent,
Nor no man will I respite,
But to the heart suddenly I shall smite
Without any advisement.
And now out of thy sight I will me hie;
See thou make thee ready shortly,
For thou mayst say this is the day
That no man living may scape away.

---

[9] *Hie*] Hurry, make haste.
[10] *weenest*] think, suppose.
[11] *thy wits five*] The five wits were commonly defined as common wit (sense), imagination, fantasy, estimation and memory.

Everyman.   Alas, I may well weep with sighs deep;
    Now have I no manner of company
    To help me in my journey, and me to keep;
    And also my writing is full unready.
    How shall I do now for to excuse me?
    I would to God I had never be gete![12]
    To my soul a full great profit it had be;
    For now I fear pains huge and great.
    The time passeth; Lord, help that all wrought;
    For though I mourn it availeth nought.
    The day passeth, and is almost a-go;[13]
    I wot not well what for to do.
    To whom were I best my complaint to make?
    What, and I to *Fellowship* thereof spake,
    And showed him of this sudden chance?
    For in him is all mine affiance;
    We have in the world so many a day
    Be on good friends in sport and play.
    I see him yonder, certainly;
    I trust that he will bear me company;
    Therefore to him will I speak to ease my sorrow.
    Well met, good *Fellowship,* and good morrow!
Fellowship speaketh.   Everyman, good morrow by this day.
    Sir, why lookest thou so piteously?
    If any thing be amiss, I pray thee, me say,
    That I may help to remedy.
Everyman.   Yea, good *Fellowship,* yea,
    I am in great jeopardy.
Fellowship.   My true friend, show to me your mind;
    I will not forsake thee, unto my life's end,
    In the way of good company.
Everyman.   That was well spoken, and lovingly.
Fellowship.   Sir, I must needs know your heaviness;
    I have pity to see you in any distress;
    If any have you wronged ye shall revenged be,
    Though I on the ground be slain for thee,—
    Though that I know before that I should die.

---

[12] *be gete*] been gotten, been born.
[13] *a-go*] gone.

Everyman.   Verily, *Fellowship,* gramercy.[14]
Fellowship.   Tush! by thy thanks I set not a straw.
Show me your grief, and say no more.
Everyman.   If I my heart should to you break,[15]
And then you to turn your mind from me,
And would not me comfort, when you hear me speak,
Then should I ten times sorrier be.
Fellowship.   Sir, I say as I will do in deed.
Everyman.   Then be you a good friend at need:
I have found you true here before.
Fellowship.   And so ye shall evermore;
For, in faith, and thou go to Hell,
I will not forsake thee by the way!
Everyman.   Ye speak like a good friend; I believe you well;
I shall deserve it, and I may.
Fellowship.   I speak of no deserving, by this day.
For he that will say and nothing do
Is not worthy with good company to go;
Therefore show me the grief of your mind,
As to your friend most loving and kind.
Everyman.   I shall show you how it is;
Commanded I am to go a journey,
A long way, hard and dangerous,
And give a strait count without delay
Before the high judge Adonai.[16]
Wherefore I pray you, bear me company,
As ye have promised, in this journey.
Fellowship.   That is matter indeed! Promise is duty,
But, and I should take such a voyage on me,
I know it well, it should be to my pain:
Also it make me afeard, certain.
But let us take counsel here as well as we can,
For your words would fear a strong man.
Everyman.   Why, ye said, If I had need,
Ye would me never forsake, quick[17] nor dead,
Though it were to hell truly.

---

[14] *gramercy*] great thanks.
[15] *break*] open.
[16] *Adonai*] God.
[17] *quick*] living.

Fellowship.   So I said, certainly,
    But such pleasures be set aside, thee sooth to say:
    And also, if we took such a journey,
    When should we come again?
Everyman.   Nay, never again till the day of doom.
Fellowship.   In faith, then will not I come there!
    Who hath you these tidings brought?
Everyman.   Indeed, *Death* was with me here.
Fellowship.   Now, by God that all hath bought,
    If *Death* were the messenger,
    For no man that is living to-day
    I will not go that loath journey—
    Not for the father that begat me!
Everyman.   Ye promised other wise, pardie.[18]
Fellowship.   I wot well I say so truly;
    And yet if thou wilt eat, and drink, and make good cheer,
    Or haunt to women, the lusty company,
    I would not forsake you, while the day is clear,
    Trust me verily!
Everyman.   Yea, thereto ye would be ready;
    To go to mirth, solace, and play,
    Your mind will sooner apply
    Than to bear me company in my long journey.
Fellowship.   Now, in good faith, I will not that way.
    But and thou wilt murder, or any man kill,
    In that I will help thee with a good will!
Everyman.   O that is a simple advice indeed!
    Gentle *fellow,* help me in my necessity;
    We have loved long, and now I need,
    And now, gentle *Fellowship,* remember me.
Fellowship.   Whether ye have loved me or no,
    By Saint John, I will not with thee go.
Everyman.   Yet I pray thee, take the labour, and do so much for me
    To bring me forward, for saint charity,
    And comfort me till I come without the town.
Fellowship.   Nay, and thou would give me a new gown,
    I will not a foot with thee go;
    But and you had tarried I would not have left thee so.

---

[18] *pardie*] par Dieu, by God.

And as now, God speed thee in thy journey,
For from thee I will depart as fast as I may.

Everyman. Whither away, *Fellowship?* will you forsake me?

Fellowship. Yea, by my fay,[19] to God I betake thee.

Everyman. Farewell, good *Fellowship*; for this my heart is sore;
Adieu for ever, I shall see thee no more.

Fellowship. In faith, *Everyman*, farewell now at the end;
For you I will remember that parting is mourning.

Everyman. Alack! shall we thus depart indeed?
Our Lady, help, without any more comfort,
Lo, *Fellowship* forsaketh me in my most need:
For help in this world whither shall I resort?
Fellowship herebefore with me would merry make;
And now little sorrow for me doth he take.
It is said, in prosperity men friends may find,
Which in adversity be full unkind.
Now whither for succour shall I flee,
Sith that[20] *Fellowship* hath forsaken me?
To my kinsmen I will truly,
Praying them to help me in my necessity;
I believe that they will do so,
For kind will creep where it may not go.
I will go say, for yonder I see them go.
Where be ye now, my friends and kinsmen?

Kindred. Here be we now at your commandment.
Cousin, I pray you show us your intent
In any wise, and not spare.

Cousin. Yea, *Everyman,* and to us declare
If ye be disposed to go any whither,
For wete you well, we will live and die together.

Kindred. In wealth and woe we will with you hold,
For over his kin a man may be bold.

Everyman. Gramercy, my friends and kinsmen kind.
Now shall I show you the grief of my mind:
I was commanded by a messenger,
That is an high king's chief officer;
He bade me go a pilgrimage to my pain,
And I know well I shall never come again;

---

[19] *fay*] faith.
[20] *Sith that*] Since, now that.

Also I must give a reckoning straight,
For I have a great enemy, that hath me in wait,
Which intendeth me for to hinder.
Kindred. What account is that which ye must render?
That would I know.
Everyman. Of all my works I must show
How I have lived and my days spent;
Also of ill deeds, that I have used
In my time, sith life was me lent;
And of all virtues that I have refused.
Therefore I pray you go thither with me,
To help to make mine account, for saint *charity*.
Cousin. What, to go thither? Is that the matter?
Nay, *Everyman,* I had liefer[21] fast bread and water
All this five year and more.
Everyman. Alas, that ever I was bore![22]
For now shall I never be merry
If that you forsake me.
Kindred. Ah, sir; what, ye be a merry man!
Take good heart to you, and make no moan.
But one thing I warn you, by Saint Anne,
As for me, ye shall go alone.
Everyman. My *Cousin,* will you not with me go?
Cousin. No, by our Lady; I have the cramp in my toe.
Trust not to me, for, so God me speed,
I will deceive you in your most need.
Kindred. It availeth not us to tice.[23]
Ye shall have my maid with all my heart;
She loveth to go to feasts, there to be nice,
And to dance, and abroad to start:
I will give her leave to help you in that journey,
If that you and she may agree.
Everyman. Now show me the very effect of your mind.
Will you go with me, or abide behind?
Kindred. Abide behind? yea, that I will and I may!
Therefore farewell until another day.

---

[21] *had liefer*] would rather.
[22] *bore*] born.
[23] *tice*] entice.

Everyman.   How should I be merry or glad?
    For fair promises to me make,
    But when I have most need, they me forsake.
    I am deceived; that maketh me sad.
Cousin.   Cousin *Everyman,* farewell now,
    For verily I will not go with you;
    Also of mine own an unready reckoning
    I have to account; therefore I make tarrying.
    Now, God keep thee, for now I go.
Everyman.   Ah, *Jesus,* is all come hereto?
    Lo, fair words maketh fools feign;
    They promise and nothing will do certain.
    My kinsmen promised me faithfully
    For to abide with me steadfastly,
    And now fast away do they flee:
    Even so *Fellowship* promised me.
    What friend were best me of to provide?
    I lose my time here longer to abide.
    Yet in my mind a thing there is;—
    All my life I have loved riches;
    If that my good now help me might,
    He would make my heart full light.
    I will speak to him in this distress.—
    Where art thou, my *Goods* and riches?
Goods.   Who calleth me? *Everyman?* what haste thou hast!
    I lie here in corners, trussed and piled so high,
    And in chests I am locked so fast,
    Also sacked in bags, thou mayst see with thine eye,
    I cannot stir; in packs low I lie.
    What would ye have, lightly[24] me say.
Everyman.   Come hither, *Good,* in all the haste thou may,
    For of counsel I must desire thee.
Goods.   Sir, and ye in the world have trouble or adversity,
    That can I help you to remedy shortly.
Everyman.   It is another disease that grieveth me;
    In this world it is not, I tell thee so.
    I am sent for another way to go,
    To give a straight account general
    Before the highest *Jupiter* of all;

---

[24] *lightly*] quickly.

And all my life I have had joy and pleasure in thee.
Therefore I pray thee go with me,
For, peradventure, thou mayst before God Almighty
My reckoning help to clean and purify;
For it is said ever among,
That money maketh all right that is wrong.

Goods. Nay, *Everyman,* I sing another song,
I follow no man in such voyages;
For and I went with thee
Thou shouldst fare much the worse for me;
For because on me thou did set thy mind,
Thy reckoning I have made blotted and blind,
That thine account thou cannot make truly;
And that hast thou for the love of me.

Everyman. That would grieve me full sore,
When I should come to that fearful answer.
Up, let us go thither together.

Goods. Nay, not so, I am too brittle, I may not endure;
I will follow no man one foot, be ye sure.

Everyman. Alas, I have thee loved, and had great pleasure
All my life-days on good and treasure.

Goods. That is to thy damnation without lesing,[25]
For my love is contrary to the love everlasting.
But if thou had me loved moderately during,
As, to the poor give part of me,
Then shouldst thou not in this dolour be,
Nor in this great sorrow and care.

Everyman. Lo, now was I deceived or[26] I was ware,
And all I may wyte[27] my spending of time.

Goods. What, weenest thou that I am thine?

Everyman. I had wend so.

Goods. Nay, *Everyman,* I say no;
As for a while I was lent thee,
A season thou hast had me in prosperity;
My condition is man's soul to kill;
If I save one, a thousand I do spill;

---

[25] *without lesing*] without lying, i.e. truly.
[26] *or*] ere, before.
[27] *wyte*] blame.

Weenest thou that I will follow thee?
Nay, from this world, not verily.

Everyman.   I had wend otherwise.

Goods.   Therefore to thy soul *Good* is a thief;
For when thou art dead, this is my guise[28]
Another to deceive in the same wise
As I have done thee, and all to his soul's reprief.[29]

Everyman.   O false *Good,* cursed thou be!
Thou traitor to God, that hast deceived me,
And caught me in thy snare.

Goods.   Marry, thou brought thyself in care,
Whereof I am glad,
I must needs laugh, I cannot be sad.

Everyman.   Ah, *Good,* thou hast had long my heartly love;
I gave thee that which should be the Lord's above.
But wilt thou not go with me in deed?
I pray thee truth to say.

Goods.   No, so God me speed,
Therefore farewell, and have good day.

Everyman.   O, to whom shall I make my moan
For to go with me in that heavy journey?
First *Fellowship* said he would with me gone;
His words were very pleasant and gay,
But afterward he left me alone.
Then spake I to my kinsmen all in despair,
And also they gave me words fair,
They lacked no fair speaking,
But all forsake me in the ending.
Then went I to my *Goods* that I loved best,
In hope to have comfort, but there had I least;
For my *Goods* sharply did me tell
That he bringeth many into hell.
Then of myself I was ashamed,
And so I am worthy to be blamed;
Thus may I well myself hate.
Of whom shall I now counsel take?
I think that I shall never speed
Till that I go to my *Good-Deed,*

---

[28] *guise*] custom, practice.
[29] *reprief*] reproach, blame.

But alas, she is so weak,
That she can neither go nor speak;
Yet will I venture on her now.—
My *Good-Deeds,* where be you?

Good-Deeds.   Here I lie cold in the ground;
Thy sins hath me sore bound,
That I cannot stir.

Everyman.   O, *Good-Deeds,* I stand in fear;
I must you pray of counsel,
For help now should come right well.

Good-Deeds.   *Everyman,* I have understanding
That ye be summoned account to make
Before *Messias,* of Jerusalem King;
And you do by me that journey what you will I take.[30]

Everyman.   Therefore I come to you, my moan to make;
I pray you, that ye will go with me.

Good-Deeds.   I would full fain, but I cannot stand verily.

Everyman.   Why, is there anything on you fall?[31]

Good-Deeds.   Yea, sir, I may thank you of[32] all;
If ye had perfectly cheered me,
Your book of account now full ready had be.
Look, the books of your works and deeds eke;[33]
Oh, see how they lie under the feet,
To your soul's heaviness.

Everyman.   Our Lord *Jesus,* help me!
For one letter here I can not see.

Good-Deeds.   There is a blind reckoning in time of distress!

Everyman.   *Good-Deeds,* I pray you, help me in this need,
Or else I am for ever damned indeed;
Therefore help me to make reckoning
Before the redeemer of all thing,
That king is, and was, and ever shall.

Good-Deeds.   *Everyman,* I am sorry of your fall,
And fain would I help you, and I were able.

Everyman.   *Good-Deeds,* your counsel I pray you give me.

---

[30] *And you . . . I take.*] If you do as I say, I will take that journey with you.
[31] *fall*] befallen.
[32] *of*] for.
[33] *eke*] also.

Good-Deeds.   That shall I do verily;
    Though that on my feet I may not go,
    I have a sister, that shall with you also,
    Called *Knowledge,* which shall with you abide,
    To help you to make that dreadful reckoning.
Knowledge.   *Everyman,* I will go with thee, and be thy guide,
    In thy most need to go by thy side.
Everyman.   In good condition I am now in every thing,
    And am wholly content with this good thing;
    Thanked be God my Creator.
Good-Deeds.   And when he hath brought thee there,
    Where thou shalt heal thee of thy smart,
    Then go you with your reckoning and your *Good-Deeds* together
    For to make you joyful at heart
    Before the blessed Trinity.
Everyman.   My *Good-Deeds,* gramercy;
    I am well content, certainly,
    With your words sweet.
Knowledge.   Now go we together lovingly,
    To *Confession,* that cleansing river.
Everyman.   For joy I weep; I would we were there;
    But, I pray you, give me cognition
    Where dwelleth that holy man, *Confession.*
Knowledge.   In the house of salvation:
    We shall find him in that place,
    That shall us comfort by God's grace.
    Lo, this is *Confession;* kneel down and ask mercy,
    For he is in good conceit[34] with God almighty.
Everyman.   O glorious fountain that all uncleanness doth clarify,
    Wash from me the spots of vices unclean,
    That on me no sin may be seen;
    I come with *Knowledge* for my redemption,
    Repent with hearty and full contrition;
    For I am commanded a pilgrimage to take,
    And great accounts before God to make.
    Now, I pray you, *Shrift,* mother of salvation,
    Help my good deeds for my piteous exclamation.
Confession.   I know your sorrow well, *Everyman;*
    Because with *Knowledge* ye come to me,

---

[34] *good conceit*] favorable opinion, i.e., highly esteemed by.

I will you comfort as well as I can,
And a precious jewel I will give thee,
Called penance, wise voider of adversity;
Therewith shall your body chastised be,
With abstinence and perseverance in God's service:
Here shall you receive that scourge of me,
Which is penance strong, that ye must endure,
To remember thy Saviour was scourged for thee
With sharp scourges, and suffered it patiently;
So must thou, or thou scape that painful pilgrimage;
Knowledge, keep him in this voyage,
And by that time *Good-Deeds* will be with thee.
But in any wise, be sure of mercy,
For your time draweth fast, and ye will saved be;
Ask God mercy, and He will grant truly,
When with the scourge of penance man doth him bind,
The oil of forgiveness then shall he find.

Everyman. Thanked be God for his gracious work!
For now I will my penance begin;
This hath rejoiced and lighted my heart,
Though the knots be painful and hard within.

Knowledge. *Everyman,* look your penance that ye fulfil,
What pain that ever it to you be,
And *Knowledge* shall give you counsel at will,
How your accounts ye shall make clearly.

Everyman. O eternal God, O heavenly figure,
O way of rightwiseness, O goodly vision,
Which descended down in a virgin pure
Because he would *Everyman* redeem,
Which *Adam* forfeited by his disobedience:
O blessed Godhead, elect and high-divine,
Forgive my grievous offence;
Here I cry thee mercy in this presence.
O ghostly treasure, O ransomer and redeemer
Of all the world, hope and conductor,
Mirror of joy, and founder of mercy,
Which illumineth heaven and earth thereby,
Hear my clamorous complaint, though it late be;
Receive my prayers; unworthy in this heavy life,
Though I be, a sinner most abominable,
Yet let my name be written in *Moses'* table;

O *Mary,* pray to the Maker of all thing,
Me for to help at my ending,
And save me from the power of my enemy,
For *Death* assaileth me strongly;
And, Lady, that I may by means of thy prayer
Of your Son's glory to be partaker,
By the means of his passion I it crave,
I beseech you, help my soul to save.—
Knowledge, give me the scourge of penance;
My flesh therewith shall give a quittance:
I will now begin, if God give me grace.

Knowledge.   *Everyman,* God give you time and space:
Thus I bequeath you in the hands of our Saviour,
Thus may you make your reckoning sure.

Everyman.   In the name of the Holy Trinity,
My body sore[35] punished shall be:
Take this body for the sin of the flesh;
Also thou delightest to go gay and fresh,
And in the way of damnation thou did me bring;
Therefore suffer now strokes and punishing.
Now of penance I will wade the water clear,
To save me from purgatory, that sharp fire.

Good-Deeds.   I thank God, now I can walk and go;
And am delivered of my sickness and woe.
Therefore with *Everyman* I will go, and not spare;
His good works I will help him to declare.

Knowledge.   Now, *Everyman,* be merry and glad;
Your *Good-Deeds* cometh now; ye may not be sad;
Now is your *Good-Deeds* whole and sound,
Going upright upon the ground.

Everyman.   My heart is light, and shall be evermore;
Now will I smite faster than I did before.

Good-Deeds.   *Everyman,* pilgrim, my special friend,
Blessed be thou without end;
For thee is prepared the eternal glory.
Ye have me made whole and sound,
Therefore I will bide by thee in every stound.[36]

---

[35] *sore*] grievously.
[36] *stound*] season.

Everyman. Welcome, my *Good-Deeds*; now I hear thy voice,
    I weep for very sweetness of love.
Knowledge. Be no more sad, but ever rejoice,
    God seeth thy living in his throne above;
    Put on this garment to thy behove,[37]
    Which is wet with your tears,
    Or else before God you may it miss,
    When you to your journey's end come shall.
Everyman. Gentle *Knowledge,* what do you it call?
Knowledge. It is a garment of sorrow:
    From pain it will you borrow;
    Contrition it is,
    That getteth forgiveness;
    It pleaseth God passing well.
Good-Deeds. *Everyman,* will you wear it for your heal?
Everyman. Now blessed be *Jesu, Mary's* Son!
    For now have I on true contrition.
    And let us go now without tarrying;
    Good-Deeds, have we clear our reckoning?
Good-Deeds. Yea, indeed I have it here.
Everyman. Then I trust we need not fear;
    Now, friends, let us not part in twain.[38]
Knowledge. Nay, Everyman, that will we not, certain.
Good-Deeds. Yet must thou lead with thee
    Three persons of great might.
Everyman. Who should they be?
Good-Deeds. *Discretion* and *Strength* they hight,[39]
    And thy *Beauty* may not abide behind.
Knowledge. Also ye must call to mind
    Your *Five-wits* as for your counsellors.
Good-Deeds. You must have them ready at all hours.
Everyman. How shall I get them hither?
Knowledge. You must call them all together,
    And they will hear you incontinent.[40]
Everyman. My friends, come hither and be present
    Discretion, Strength, my *Five-wits,* and *Beauty.*

---

[37] *behove*] advantage.
[38] *twain*] two.
[39] *hight*] are called, named.
[40] *incontinent*] immediately.

Beauty.   Here at your will we be all ready.
          What will ye that we should do?
Good-Deeds.   That ye would with *Everyman* go,
          And help him in his pilgrimage,
          Advise you, will ye with him or not in that voyage?
Strength.   We will bring him all thither,
          To his help and comfort, ye may believe me.
Discretion.   So will we go with him all together.
Everyman.   Almighty God, loved thou be,
          I give thee laud that I have hither brought
          Strength, Discretion, Beauty, and *Five-wits*; lack I nought;
          And my *Good-Deeds,* with *Knowledge* clear,
          All be in my company at my will here;
          I desire no more to my business.
Strength.   And I, *Strength,* will by you stand in distress,
          Though thou would in battle fight on the ground.
Five-wits.   And though it were through the world round,
          We will not depart for sweet nor sour.
Beauty.   No more will I unto death's hour,
          Whatsoever thereof befall.
Discretion.   *Everyman,* advise you first of all;
          Go with a good advisement and deliberation;
          We all give you virtuous monition[41]
          That all shall be well.
Everyman.   My friends, hearken what I will tell:
          I pray God reward you in his heavenly sphere.
          Now hearken, all that be here,
          For I will make my testament
          Here before you all present.
          In alms half my good I will give with my hands twain
          In the way of charity, with good intent,
          And the other half still shall remain
          In quiet to be returned there it ought to be.
          This I do in despite of the fiend of hell
          To go quite out of his peril
          Ever after and this day.
Knowledge.   *Everyman,* hearken what I say;
          Go to priesthood, I you advise,
          And receive of him in any wise

---

[41] *monition*] warning.

The holy sacrament and ointment together;
Then shortly see ye turn again hither;
We will all abide you here.

Five-Wits. Yea, *Everyman,* hie you that ye ready were,
There is no emperor, king, duke, ne baron,
That of God hath commission,
As hath the least priest in the world being;
For of the blessed sacraments pure and benign,
He beareth the keys and thereof hath the cure
For man's redemption, it is ever sure;
Which God for our soul's medicine
Gave us out of his heart with great pine;
Here in this transitory life, for thee and me
The blessed sacraments seven there be,
Baptism, confirmation, with priesthood good,
And the sacrament of God's precious flesh and blood,
Marriage, the holy extreme unction, and penance;
These seven be good to have in remembrance,
Gracious sacraments of high divinity.

Everyman. Fain would I receive that holy body
And meekly to my ghostly father I will go.

Five-wits. *Everyman,* that is the best that ye can do:
God will you to salvation bring,
For priesthood exceedeth all other thing;
To us Holy Scripture they do teach,
And converteth man from sin heaven to reach;
God hath to them more power given,
Than to any angel that is in heaven;
With five words he may consecrate
God's body in flesh and blood to make,
And handleth his maker between his hands;
The priest bindeth and unbindeth all bands,
Both in earth and in heaven;
Thou ministers all the sacraments seven;
Though we kissed thy feet thou were worthy;
Thou art surgeon that cureth sin deadly:
No remedy we find under God
But all only priesthood.
Everyman, God gave priests that dignity,
And setteth them in his stead among us to be;
Thus be they above angels in degree.

Knowledge.   If priests be good it is so surely;
    But when Jesus hanged on the cross with great smart
    There he gave, out of his blessed heart,
    The same sacrament in great torment:
    He sold them not to us, that Lord Omnipotent.
    Therefore Saint Peter the apostle doth say
    That Jesu's curse hath all they
    Which God their Saviour do buy or sell,
    Or they for any money do take or tell.
    Sinful priests giveth the sinners example bad;
    Their children sitteth by other men's fires, I have heard;
    And some haunteth women's company,
    With unclean life, as lusts of lechery:
    These be with sin made blind.
Five-wits.   I trust to God no such may we find;
    Therefore let us priesthood honour,
    And follow their doctrine for our souls' succour;
    We be their sheep, and they shepherds be
    By whom we all be kept in surety.
    Peace, for yonder I see *Everyman* come,
    Which hath made true satisfaction.
Good-Deeds.   Methinketh it is he indeed.
Everyman.   Now Jesu be our alder speed.[42]
    I have received the sacrament for my redemption,
    And then mine extreme unction:
    Blessed be all they that counselled me to take it!
    And now, friends, let us go without longer respite;
    I thank God that ye have tarried so long.
    Now set each of you on this rod your hand,
    And shortly follow me:
    I go before, there I would be; God be our guide.
Strength.   *Everyman*, we will not from you go,
    Till ye have gone this voyage long.
Discretion.   I, *Discretion*, will bide by you also.
Knowledge.   And though this pilgrimage be never so strong,
    I will never part you fro:
    Everyman, I will be as sure by thee
    As ever I did by Judas Maccabee.
Everyman.   Alas, I am so faint I may not stand,
    My limbs under me do fold;

---

[42] *Now . . . speed*.] May Jesus be the helper of all.

Friends, let us not turn again to this land,
Not for all the world's gold,
For into this cave must I creep
And turn to the earth and there to sleep.

Beauty. What, into this grave? alas!

Everyman. Yea, there shall you consume[43] more and less.

Beauty. And what, should I smother here?

Everyman. Yea, by my faith, and never more appear.
In this world live no more we shall,
But in heaven before the highest Lord of all.

Beauty. I cross out all this; adieu by Saint *John*;
I take my cap in my lap and am gone.

Everyman. What, *Beauty,* whither will ye?

Beauty. Peace, I am deaf; I look not behind me,
Not and thou would give me all the gold in thy chest.

Everyman. Alas, whereto may I trust?
Beauty goeth fast away hie;
She promised with me to live and die.

Strength. *Everyman,* I will thee also forsake and deny;
Thy game liketh me not at all.

Everyman. Why, then ye will forsake me all.
Sweet *Strength,* tarry a little space.

Strength. Nay, sir, by the rood[44] of grace
I will hie me from thee fast,
Though thou weep till thy heart brast.[45]

Everyman. Ye would ever bide by me, ye said.

Strength. Yea, I have you far enough conveyed;
Ye be old enough, I understand,
Your pilgrimage to take on hand;
I repent me that I hither came.

Everyman. *Strength,* you to displease I am to blame;
Will you break promise that is debt?

Strength. In faith, I care not;
Thou art but a fool to complain,
You spend your speech and waste your brain;
Go thrust thee into the ground.

Everyman. I had wend surer I should you have found.
He that trusteth in his *Strength*

---

[43] *consume*] decay.

[44] *rood*] cross.

[45] *brast*] break.

She him deceiveth at the length.
Both *Strength* and *Beauty* forsaketh me,
Yet they promised me fair and lovingly.
Discretion.   *Everyman,* I will after *Strength* be gone,
As for me I will leave you alone.
Everyman.   Why, *Discretion,* will ye forsake me?
Discretion.   Yea, in faith, I will go from thee,
For when *Strength* goeth before
I follow after evermore.
Everyman.   Yet, I pray thee, for the love of the Trinity,
Look in my grave once piteously.
Discretion.   Nay, so nigh will I not come.
Farewell, every one!
Everyman.   O all thing faileth, save God alone;
Beauty, Strength, and *Discretion;*
For when *Death* bloweth his blast,
They all run from me full fast.
Five-wits.   *Everyman,* my leave now of thee I take;
I will follow the other, for here I thee forsake.
Everyman.   Alas! then may I wail and weep,
For I took you for my best friend.
Five-wits.   I will no longer thee keep;
Now farewell, and there an end.
Everyman.   O Jesu, help, all hath forsaken me!
Good-Deeds.   Nay, *Everyman,* I will bide with thee,
I will not forsake thee indeed;
Thou shalt find me a good friend at need.
Everyman.   Gramercy, *Good-Deeds*; now may I true friends see;
They have forsaken me every one;
I loved them better than my *Good-Deeds* alone.
Knowledge, will ye forsake me also?
Knowledge.   Yea, *Everyman,* when ye to death do go:
But not yet for no manner of danger.
Everyman.   Gramercy, *Knowledge,* with all my heart.
Knowledge.   Nay, yet I will not from hence depart,
Till I see where ye shall be come.
Everyman.   Methinketh, alas, that I must be gone,
To make my reckoning and my debts pay,
For I see my time is nigh spent away.
Take example, all ye that this do hear or see,
How they that I loved best do forsake me,
Except my *Good-Deeds* that bideth truly.

Good-Deeds.   All earthly things is but vanity:
　　　Beauty, Strength, and *Discretion,* do man forsake,
　　　Foolish friends and kinsmen, that fair spake,
　　　All fleeth save *Good-Deeds,* and that am I.
Everyman.   Have mercy on me, God most mighty;
　　　And stand by me, thou Mother and Maid, holy *Mary.*
Good-Deeds.   Fear not, I will speak for thee.
Everyman.   Here I cry God mercy.
Good-Deeds.   Short our end, and minish[46] our pain;
　　　Let us go and never come again.
Everyman.   Into thy hands, Lord, my soul I commend;
　　　Receive it, Lord, that it be not lost;
　　　As thou me boughtest, so me defend,
　　　And save me from the fiend's boast,
　　　That I may appear with that blessed host
　　　That shall be saved at the day of doom.
　　　In manus tuas[47]—of might's most
　　　For ever—*commendo spiritum meum.*[48]
Knowledge.   Now hath he suffered that we all shall endure;
　　　The *Good-Deeds* shall make all sure.
　　　Now hath he made ending;
　　　Methinketh that I hear angels sing
　　　And make great joy and melody,
　　　Where *Everyman's* soul received shall be.
Angel.   Come, excellent elect spouse to Jesu:
　　　Hereabove thou shalt go
　　　Because of thy singular virtue:
　　　Now the soul is taken the body fro;
　　　Thy reckoning is crystal-clear.
　　　Now shalt thou into the heavenly sphere,
　　　Unto the which all ye shall come
　　　That liveth well before the day of doom.
Doctor.   This moral men may have in mind;
　　　Ye hearers, take it of worth, old and young,
　　　And forsake pride, for he deceiveth you in the end,
　　　And remember *Beauty, Five-wits, Strength,* and *Discretion,*
　　　They all at the last do *Everyman* forsake,
　　　Save his *Good-Deeds,* there doth he take.

---

[46] *minish*] diminish.
[47] *In manus tuas*] "Into thy hands."
[48] *commendo spiritum meum.*] I commend my spirit.

But beware, and they be small
Before God, he hath no help at all.
None excuse may be there for *Everyman*:
Alas, how shall he do then?
For after death amends may no man make,
For then mercy and pity do him forsake.
If his reckoning be not clear when he do come,
God will say—*ite maledicti in ignem æternum*.[49]
And he that hath his account whole and sound,
High in heaven he shall be crowned;
Unto which place God bring us all thither
That we may live body and soul together.
Thereto help the Trinity,
Amen, say ye, for saint *Charity*.

THUS ENDETH THIS MORALL PLAY OF EVERYMAN.

---

[49] *ite . . . æternum*] "Depart, ye cursed, into everlasting fire" (Matthew 25:41).